THE GREAT SWEEPSTAKES
OF 1877

*A True Story of Southern Grit, Gilded Age Tycoons,
and a Race That Galvanized the Nation*

MARK SHRAGER

Guilford, Connecticut

An imprint of Rowman & Littlefield

Distributed by NATIONAL BOOK NETWORK

British Library Cataloguing in Publication Information Available

Library of Congress Cataloging-in-Publication Data
ISBN 978-1-4930-1888-8 (hardcover)
ISBN 978-1-4930-1889-5 (e-book)

♾™ The paper used in this publication meets the minimum requirements of American National Standard for Information Sciences—Permanence of Paper for Printed Library Materials, ANSI/ NISO Z39.48-1992.

Contents

Preface

A Slow Day in Congress

October 24, 1877, was a day of minimal activity in the halls of Congress. The US Senate was not in session, having adjourned the previous day and calendared no activity until the twenty-fifth; the House of Representatives was largely empty, and in any event was scheduled to address only a few items, primarily a variety of petitions and claims remaining from the Civil War, which had concluded some twelve years earlier.

That small group of Congressmen—and they were all men; Congress had broken the color barrier in 1870 with the seating of Senator Hiram Rhodes Revels of Mississippi and House Member Joseph Rainey of South Carolina, but it would be nearly forty years before Montana's Jeannette Rankin would become the first female member of Congress—considered the petitions and motions dispiritedly. With so few members in attendance, Congress would accomplish nothing of note on October 24. One can readily imagine the few remaining legislators' voices echoing eerily in the cavernous, nearly empty halls of the House of Representatives.

The handful of legislators in Congress on October 24 was well aware of the reason so few were present for the day's session. Some may have glanced resentfully at the empty desks of their absent colleagues, but most participated resignedly, performing the work of the nation as they had been selected to do. Finally, at 3:25 p.m., the Honorable Fernando Wood, perhaps best known as the Civil War mayor of New York who had suggested that his city secede from the Union rather than sacrifice its profitable business relationship with the Confederacy, rose to move that the House adjourn. Upon passage of the motion, Congress called a merciful end to its unproductive day.

While October 24, 1877, represented something less than a shining example of the US Congress at its finest, the date nevertheless earned a unique place in history. It was on this date that the nation's senators and nearly all representatives abandoned the halls of Congress to attend an occasion of less repute but considerably more sporting interest— a specially arranged and long-anticipated horse race at nearby Pimlico Racetrack involving three of the nation's best-known thoroughbreds. It marked the first time in the nation's history that either house of America's most august legislative body had adjourned specifically so that its members could attend a horse race.

It was a race of enormous national interest, both to elected officials and to America's common folk. The race involved two high-profile "Eastern" thoroughbreds, Parole and Tom Ochiltree, one hailing from the New Jersey headquarters of one of the nation's preeminent sportsmen and industrialists, the other from the New York stable of his brother.

The third starter was Ten Broeck, an invader from the "West," in this case the state of Kentucky, whose unrivaled record on the turf had already made him legendary in his own time. The opportunity to partake of this East vs. West rivalry, and perhaps extract a profit through a few well-placed wagers, proved far more enticing to many of the legislators than the essential but less exciting business of Congress.

Although East and West were the compass points discussed in the day's newspapers, and in polite conversation in Congress and on the street, many would have recognized that the race also symbolized the North vs. South hostilities that had so recently and profoundly shaped the nation's racial relations, its family structures, its international relations, and its domestic politics. New York and New Jersey had, of course, been squarely pro-Union during the Civil War, even given the draft riots that had shattered the peace of the Empire State, even given the sentiments of Mayor Wood. Kentucky had been a slave state whose legislators had declared it a neutral party, doubtless in the hopes of doing business with both sides, Union and Rebel.

The Civil War had been the deadliest conflict in American history. It had long been estimated that the War Between the States cost the lives of at least 625,000 combatants—360,222 on the Union side and roughly 258,000 Confederates—but recent scholarly recounting of census records suggests that the toll may have been substantially higher—perhaps upwards of 850,000. More soldiers on both sides died of non-battle causes—primarily disease and hunger—than of gunshots, bayonet strikes, or other human violence. Multiples of these numbers were left permanently debilitated.

More than 150 years after the war's end, after two World Wars, after Korea and Vietnam, after two Gulf Wars and a protracted American presence in the Middle East, the Civil War remains the deadliest conflict in the history of a nation that has, by dint of its economic and military might, been among the combatants in many an armed struggle. Owing to the slow communications of the times, overt hostilities between North and South continued even after the war was diplomatically concluded; the final Confederate general to surrender was Cherokee leader Stand Watie, who conceded defeat at Doaksville in the Choctaw Nation (now Oklahoma) on June 23, 1865, some two and a half months after Lee laid down his sword.

The regional rivalries that had existed long before the Civil War had been nurtured in the years that followed the assassination of President Abraham Lincoln. The surrender of Robert E. Lee at Appomattox Court House had formally ended the war, but while most of the conflagration's nonfatal physical wounds were slowly healing, America's emotional scars remained and, in some cases, festered. The disputed presidential election of 1876, pitting Republican Rutherford B. Hayes against Democrat Samuel J. Tilden and decided by a single electoral vote after four states' electoral slates were claimed by both political parties, exacerbated tensions that were already near the breaking point.

It is no exaggeration to suggest that Hayes's hairsbreadth victory in the Electoral College, awarded to the Republican candidate despite Tilden's sizable margin in the popular vote, brought the nation to the brink of a second Civil War. When an election commission, established by Congress to sort out the votes in the four disputed states, awarded each of the states to Hayes by a strictly partisan eight-to-seven vote—the commission comprised eight Republicans and seven Democrats—Congressional Democrats threatened a filibuster to delay Hayes's inauguration. It is questionable whether an elected president could be denied his office because of a political maneuver in Congress, but the possibility was there. More ominously, one frustrated Democrat vowed that "a hundred thousand Kentuckians would see justice done to Tilden" and the Republicans reportedly considered using the army to enforce the election commission's rulings. Only when cooler heads prevailed, creating the "Compromise of 1877," was what historian James Truslow Adams described as "the filthy mess of 1876" brought to a conclusion.

A deeply divided nation was still seeking to implement—or subvert—the changes wrought by the deadly years of brother vs. brother hostility. The issues that created these lingering scars unquestionably played no small part in the desire of the elected representatives to participate, even if only by rooting for their particular regional favorite, in this East vs. West contest.

It was, however, not merely public officials who availed themselves of the opportunity to attend the Great Sweepstakes while shirking official duties. The October 25, 1877, edition of the *Chicago Tribune* noted that "the Stock Board early adjourned till to-morrow to allow the members to attend the race. At the Corn and Flower exchange very few members were present, and little business done." Businesses operated with skeleton crews that day; both managers and employees wanted to be nowhere but at Pimlico. This was an iconic, must-see occasion; if one's circumstances allowed it, he or she was going to the races.

And while Congress—and the Stock Board and the Corn and Flower Exchange and the rest of the nation—awaited the confrontation of the three great horses with fevered anticipation, discussed the horses' relative merits for weeks beforehand, argued the race's results heatedly for months afterward, and demanded a rematch in letters to the editors of hundreds of newspapers, it may well be that the horses were the least interesting of the cast of characters that came together on that cool October afternoon in Baltimore.

Certainly, the horse's owners were without peers as objects of public curiosity; the jockeys were men of accomplishment, each with a unique perspective on the race, on life; and the trainers ran the gamut from enormously successful and publicly revered to practically unknown. All of their stories will be told in these pages.

As our tale begins, the nation awaits the arrival from Nantura Stock Farm, in the heart of the Kentucky Bluegrass, of Ten Broeck, quite possibly America's greatest racehorse to that point in time.

The Champion

THE TOWN OF MIDWAY, KENTUCKY, CURRENT POPULATION 1,641, LIES equidistant between the state capital, Frankfort, and the city of Lexington, which describes itself as the "Horse Capital of the World." In many locales, of course, it would be rank hyperbole for a city of just over three hundred thousand to declare itself the world capital of anything, but one who travels beyond the environs of downtown Lexington in any direction and observes the vast and famous thoroughbred breeding and training establishments that dominate the area will quickly recognize that Lexington's self-proclaimed title is not an undeserved appellation. Midway was once a single farm belonging to one John Francisco. In 1835, however, Francisco sold out to the Lexington and Ohio Railroad Company for the then substantial sum of $6,491.25, and Midway became Kentucky's first railroad town. Long before this, the area had been the home of mound-building Indians. Two large Indian mounds remain, on farms within easy driving range of Midway.

Midway's primary claim to fame, however, is neither its Indian sites nor its railroads. Midway is a horse town. In fact, the area was once the home to not one, but two of the greatest thoroughbreds ever to compete on American soil, each of which was born (foaled, in the language of the breeding shed) on Nantura Stock Farm in Spring Station, within shouting distance of Midway. These two immortals of the track also summered and wintered there between racing campaigns, spent their breeding careers there, and died there. And both are buried there, beneath imposing monuments that were, when initially dedicated, within sight of the home of their long-ago owners.

One of these two immortals of the turf, a steed named Longfellow, was known throughout the nation as the King of the Turf. Foaled in 1867, he was famous for his imposing size, his speed, and his endurance. Newspapers throughout the nation carried the story when he suffered a crippling racetrack injury in 1872 that ended his career and left his devoted owner devastated; at that point, this prodigious animal had won thirteen of his sixteen races, although his headstone incorrectly claims another start, another victory. His plaque has long adorned a wall in the National Museum of Racing and Hall of Fame.

His stablemate, foaled in 1872, may have been even better. During his reign as equine superstar, Ten Broeck (the name is pronounced in the Dutch style: "10 Brook") shattered revered time records by impossible margins and routinely left challengers struggling in his dust. On one occasion, no owner could be found willing to send a runner against Ten Broeck, and he simply galloped around the track in regal solitude, the recipient of racing's greatest compliment: a walkover. Three other times, Ten Broeck was sent to the track not to win a race, but with the specific intention of destroying a world record.

On these occasions, pacesetters were dispatched ahead of the champion, running flat-out for a short distance in the hope that Ten Broeck would quicken his own pace, seeking to outrun the interlopers. When one pacesetter would tire, he or she would be eased to the outer rail, and a new target would charge onto the track. In these "races," one could wager either on Ten Broeck or the stopwatch, but the wise course was always to wager on the horse. All three times, Ten Broeck flew down the final straightaway and directly into the record books.

Ten Broeck's was a relatively brief racing career, consisting of just thirty races over three seasons, and he passed from among us at the fairly young equine age of fifteen. Even in death, Ten Broeck continued to fascinate the racing world; his Kentucky funeral was covered by the distant and serious-minded *New York Times*, not a publication that commonly reports on the last rites of equines.

Ten Broeck rests today, as he has since 1887, under the fertile soil of a Kentucky field, near his stablemate, Longfellow. Together, the two horses' headstones create a picturesque but curious Bluegrass tableau, an almost surreal echo of racing's distant past, surviving into the very real present.

The wording on Ten Broeck's imposing headstone might seem strange, perhaps even cold, to the casual observer, but then, this was the first headstone ever erected over the burial place of an American racehorse, and Ten Broeck's owner therefore had no models of appropriate tombstone verbiage from which to draw. The owner, Frank Harper, whose inheritance upon the death of his uncle had included this great horse, was a simple man, not given to flowery prose or rhetorical eloquence. His was the world of thoroughbreds, not that of belles lettres.

Decades later, the tombstone of the great horse Domino would gush, "Here lies the fleetest runner the American Turf has ever known, and one of the gamest and most generous of horses," but such bursts of prolixity were not for Harper. Ten Broeck's tombstone speaks of his great horse in facts and numbers, not in flowing emotions. The engraved eulogy, in fact, includes an egregious error, utilizing the word "folded" in place of the proper "foaled." In its entirety, the tombstone reads:

TEN BROECK
BAY HORSE
FOLDED [*sic*] ON NANTURA
STOCK FARM
WOODFORD COUNTY, KY.
JUNE 29, 1872
DIED JUNE 28, 1887

PERFORMANCES
1 MILE . . . 1:39¾
1⅝ . . . 2:49¼
2 . . . 3:27½
2⅝ . . . 4:58½
3 . . . 5:26½
4 . . . 7:15¾

The revered thoroughbred buried beneath this prosaic memorial was named for the legendary racing man and raconteur Richard Ten Broeck, who had imported Ten Broeck's sire, Phaeton, from England (see Appendix C for a more extensive biography of Richard Ten Broeck). While Phaeton was by no means a champion on the racetrack, his exotic blood coursing through the veins of Frank Harper's thoroughbred helped to create a superhorse.

Hewn from Italian marble, Ten Broeck's tomb was once a beautifully crafted monument, as was that of Longfellow. But while the two tombstones retain much of their grandeur, they are now somewhat in disrepair, their words and numbers becoming increasingly difficult to read. Nature's processes are inevitable, and the nature of the relatively soft Italian marble is taking its course.

For many years, the ground upon which the tombstones stand was grazed by cattle—an odd sight, to be sure, on land that had long felt the impatient hoofbeats of jostling thoroughbreds—and the corrosive bovine waste materials that once surrounded the marble tombstones have doubtless hastened the mineral's decomposition. The land's current owner honors it by continuing to call his farm "Nantura," and has built wooden borders around each of the headstones, separating them from the workaday world and from any cattle that might stray into their area. But the tombstones of Ten Broeck and Longfellow continue to deteriorate, slowly and gently, but inexorably.

Time has also taken its toll on Ten Broeck's place in racing's record books. *Spirit of the Times*, one of the nineteenth century's most popular sporting newspapers, had once declared that his achievements represented a "brighter and more brilliant record than any horse that ever appeared upon the American turf," but in the world of sport, nearly all records eventually are surpassed. Ten Broeck's proved to be no exception.

As inevitably as the slow deterioration of his headstone, Ten Broeck's record times for the mile, 1⅝ mile, 2 miles, 2⅝, 3, and 4 miles have been bettered by thoroughbreds both great and mediocre. His fastest time for most of the distances is many seconds slower than the records on the books today.

This does not, however, serve to denigrate Ten Broeck, which raced under the primitive conditions of the 1870s, when the era's simple dirt tracks became quagmires on rainy days and dust bowls when the Kentucky weather turned hot. Harper, defending his animal's legend, often maintained that the thoroughbred breed improved little from one generation to the next; that the faster times earned by the runners that followed Ten Broeck were the product of improved conditions, not greater horses.

And there was truth in Harper's contention. In racing, as in every other endeavor, eras change. Racetrack surfaces are modernized, and times improve. Equine nutritional practices are refined, and times improve. New veterinary medicines enhance the health of thoroughbreds, and times improve. New training and riding techniques are pioneered, and times improve. Knowledge of equine genetics progresses, and times improve.

And however insuperable they may have seemed at the time of their accomplishment, speed records fall. As did Ten Broeck's.

In appearance, Ten Broeck was usually described as "well-balanced" or "of faultless form," rather than as being in any way particularly striking. He was a blood bay—a reddish brown color, with black mane, tail, and legs—with no white markings other than small patches just above and at the rear of his hind hooves. A sketch of Ten Broeck "from life at Baltimore, Oct. 20, 1877," shows him with ribs clearly visible through his shiny coat, and with a tail that had been docked so that its end was parallel to the ground. He was 16.1 hands tall (a "hand" is four inches), taller than the average for the period without being either massive or gawky.

The Nantura colt had raced just once at age two, finishing third at Lexington on September 15, 1874, behind a runner that had not yet even been named, then was sent back to the farm to mature and prepare for his three-year-old season. This began at the Lexington Association course on May 10, 1875, when Ten Broeck earned an easy victory in the Phoenix Hotel Stakes. Among those chasing him home that day was a chestnut colt named Aristides, whose own career would be of near Hall of Fame caliber.

Ten Broeck lost his next start, the two-mile Citizens' Stakes, to Aristides's stablemate, Chesapeake, and three days later was shipped to Louisville for a new event on the racing calendar that had been named in honor of a race contested annually at England's Epsom Downs. In the first edition of the mile-and-a-half Kentucky Derby—the race would be shortened to its present mile-and-a-quarter distance in 1896—owner Hal Price McGrath had intended that the sluggish but distance-loving Chesapeake should win the race, with his speedy colt Aristides setting the pace.

Chesapeake, however, was not at his best that day, and when it became clear that his vaunted stretch run would not materialize—Chesapeake would finish eighth in the race—McGrath, standing at the finish line, implored jockey Oliver Lewis aboard Aristides to "Go on with him, Lewis!" Lewis went on with him, and Aristides and his African-American rider won in American record time. Ten Broeck, never a factor in the Derby, finished fifth and was dispatched to Nantura for the summer.

Ten Broeck returned on September 6, finishing fourth, at least five lengths in arrears, as a colt named Bob Wooley won by "two lengths well in hand," setting a record time of 1:54 for the 1⅛ miles. Possibly Harper had not prepared his colt for a top effort in his first start in nearly four months, but three days later Ten Broeck would avenge the loss to Bob Wooley, and in the process begin his own assault on racing's record book.

Ten Broeck earned his first record on September 9, 1875, at the Lexington Association track, traveling 1⅝ miles over a surface described as "deep with dust, precluding the possibility of a very extraordinary time being made," in a quite extraordinary 2 minutes, 49¼ seconds. The record had previously been attributed to the great colt Harry Bassett, winner of the 1871 Belmont Stakes in 2:56 and later the conqueror of Longfellow, although some claimed that Springbok had posted a faster time; thus, Ten Broeck may have lowered the existing record by a spectacular 6¾ seconds (if Harry Bassett were still considered the previous record holder), or merely a sensational 3¾ seconds (if one preferred Springbok).

No matter whose record Ten Broeck had destroyed, it was an impressive performance by a colt that had not, to this point, been particularly highly regarded. Bob Wooley had been the favorite in the race; Ten Broeck was grouped with other unlikely contenders in the wagering pools. It was the last time the bookies would treat him with such disdain.

Closing out his season with a second-place finish and three more wins, none of which eclipsed records, Ten Broeck was sent home to Nantura for the winter. But 1875 and the 1⅝-mile record would be mere prelude. The following year, Ten Broeck would rewrite important sections of the record book, and in the process become an equine megastar.

After winning four of his first five starts at age four—he pushed Aristides to a world-record time in his only loss—Ten Broeck appeared on September 16, 1876, at the Lexington Association track in an otherwise routine $600 race. Only one undistinguished opponent, a colt named Redding, had been entered, and Redding would not be a problem. "Running within himself from the start," Ten Broeck rendered the day memorable, winning "in a big canter" at the 2⅝-mile distance, and scoring "as he liked" by six lengths in 4:58½, which shattered the American record for the distance. With two records now to his credit, Ten Broeck was sent out for more.

He next went postward on September 23, in the three-mile Post Stakes at Churchill Downs, racing for a $700 purse and again challenged by just one overmatched opponent, a colt named Add. The two ran as a team for 1¾ miles, Add's jockey, a lad named Hargo, pushing hard to stay on even terms. Ten Broeck then began pulling away, and Hargo succumbed to the inevitable, allowing Add to settle into a comfortable stride while both observed Ten Broeck's stretch run from a respectful distance.

Ten Broeck continued extending his lead, reaching the finish in a magnificent 5:26½, which demolished Norfolk's record, set eleven years earlier to the day, by 1¼ seconds.

One racing publication took this occasion, the third record-setting effort by Ten Broeck in slightly over twelve months, to laud him as "doubt-less . . . the fastest four-year-old in the Western country." Ten Broeck, another claimed, might have run the distance even faster, had he not lost "fully a second or two in the last furlong by pulling up for he stopped just after going over the string."

Frank Harper's real aim that day had been the four-mile record, but he had signaled jockey William Walker to stop after the third circuit of the course "on account of the wet state of the track." It boggles the mind to consider how many more seconds Ten Broeck might have sheared from the record had he been ridden hard all the way over a fast surface.

But Harper's colt would soon own the coveted four-mile record. Ten Broeck stepped onto the track at Churchill Downs four days later, and 7 minutes, 15¾ seconds after the official timers first clicked their stop-watches, the name of Fellowcraft, who two years earlier had defeated by a quarter-second the 7:19¾ clocking established by the great Lexington in 1855, was erased from the record book. Lexington that day had "literally [run] out of his shoes; one of them, twisted, now hangs in the National Museum of Racing at Saratoga."

Fellowcraft's record run had been greeted at the time with what the *New York Times* had described as "the wildest excitement. . . . Men threw up their hats and jumped as if they were crazy. The ladies cheered and clapped their hands, and old turfmen who had witnessed Lexington's performance at New-Orleans stood in dumb amazement. The astonishment of every one was so great that people did not know what to say to each other, and did nothing but cheer and shake hands."

And now this. Add had been entered to ensure a fast pace for the record-setting effort, but with a mile still to go, Ten Broeck, carrying just 104 pounds and the willowy Walker, had left his pacesetter a hundred yards behind. Now Harper's speedy filly, Necy Hale, was sent out to keep Ten Broeck on task, and Harper "stood under the wire, and waved his hat to Walker to push ahead." Walker responded with hand, boot, and whip, and Necy Hale was quickly outrun. Ten Broeck, nearly drained from the effort, passed under the finish line, and the crowd waited impatiently as the judges compared stopwatches. Then the official time was posted.

Chaos ensued. *Spirit of the Times* described "a wild scene of enthusiasm, such as has not been seen for years in the good old State of Kentucky." The *New York Times*'s reporter, surrendering all pretense of journalistic restraint, described Ten Broeck's record-smashing run as "The Greatest Event in the History of the Turf," and well it may have been. Ten Broeck's margin over Fellowcraft's time was not a mere ¼ second, but 3¾ seconds, an eternity in horse-race clockings.

One sporting publication, *Turf, Field and Farm*, described Ten Broeck's feat as "the acme of equine power," and lauded Walker: "a bright-looking mulatto, aged eighteen . . . born a slave on the Harper estate in Woodford County. He now justly takes rank among the great jockeys of the country." The *Dallas Daily Herald* placed its coverage of Ten Broeck's astounding feat on its cover page, alongside stories of Tammany Hall leader Boss Tweed, the sudden death of Civil War general Braxton Bragg, and a dispute involving Serbia, Turkey, and Montenegro that threatened to erupt into war.

With nothing left to prove in 1876, having won seven of eight starts, destroyed three of racing's most revered records, and lost only once, to a record-shattering performance by the previous year's Kentucky Derby winner, Ten Broeck was sent back to Nantura for the winter. And as the runner now nicknamed "the Kentucky crack" went to the sidelines, both the sporting press and the common racing fan began speculating about what further prodigies Ten Broeck might accomplish in the coming year. The sport's bookmakers, conversely, were likely in a state of dread, awaiting the onslaught Ten Broeck's backers would surely unleash on their bankrolls when the new season commenced.

Ten Broeck's 1877 campaign began on May 16 in Lexington, in a common mile-and-a-half race, but when nobody could be found to oppose the Nantura colt he was allowed to walk over for a $350 purse. This was followed two days later by a ten-length victory at 2⅛ miles, Ten Broeck lugging ten pounds more than his outclassed rivals. And now, with all possible opponents cowering in their barns, Ten Broeck's assault on the record book was resumed in earnest, under the excited gaze of overflow crowds rarely seen at the nation's sporting venues.

He was first sent after the one-mile record. Quoting the *Turf, Field and Farm*'s report from Louisville, "The day was bright, clear and bracing, but cold, with strong wind, not favorable to fast time." The Churchill Downs crowd was a large one, primarily male, but liberally sprinkled with members of the fairer gender: "That portion set apart for the ladies was a living mass of beauty, decked in gorgeous apparel of the varied hues of the rainbow. It was brighter than a summer's morn, when all the heaven is streaked with dappled fires, and flecked with blushes like a maiden's cheek."

Despite the less than ideal weather, the five-year-old was favored by the crowd to break the record, and the Kentuckian succeeded in justifying the odds. Given a running start and the assistance of pacesetters Early Light and St. Louis, Ten Broeck scampered the distance in 1:39¾, feeling the sting of Walker's whip for a rare time as he tired nearing the finish. Ten Broeck's clocking lowered the previous standard for the oft-competed distance by two full seconds.

The racing world, which had never before seen a thoroughbred race a mile in fewer than a hundred ticks of the stopwatch, responded to Ten Broeck's feat with incredulity. One publication compared him first to a locomotive, and then to a lunar-bound missile:

> He made the mile in 1:39¾, that is, he ran at the rate of 36.042606 miles per hour. Dropping the decimals, and rating him, in round numbers, at thirty-six miles per hour, he would make 864 miles per day. He might run over the Short Line Railroad to Cincinnati in 3h. 3m. 19s. He might run over the Louisville and Great Southern Road to Nashville in 5h. 41m. 33s. He might give the through sleeping-car to New York several hours start and get in ahead of it. He might put a girdle round the earth at the equator in 27 days, 16 hours, and travel the average distance to the moon in 276 days and 8 minutes. . . . Ten Broeck could not hold out for very long at such a rate of speed, but for that matter neither can a locomotive be kept up to its highest rate of speed for any great distance. . . . When Ten Broeck goes home, if he goes

by rail, the fastest speed that the Lexington express will attain, even over the best mile of road, will not equal that at which he ran Thursday, and the mile stones will seem to pass him very slowly.

Less than a week later, again at Churchill Downs, Ten Broeck was sent after the two-mile mark, which had previously been True Blue's at 3:32½, but had been bettered just days earlier by McWhirter in 3:30½. Despite the defection of the injured Aristides, which had been expected to join in the quest for the record, an "immense," screaming throng followed Ten Broeck's progress with one eye, the ticking of their timepieces with the other. First St. Louis, and then Necy Hale provided moving targets for Walker and his flying mount, and Ten Broeck reached the finish in 3:27½, a full 3 seconds faster than the record. The ink commemorating McWhirter's historic run never even had time to dry on the record books.

At least one publication was ready at this point to declare Ten Broeck the "grandest horse that ever pressed the turf"; another insisted that he was "the wonder of the age," and pondered, "When shall we look upon his like again?" *Spirit of the Times* featured a reproduction of a Henry Stull portrait of Ten Broeck on its cover and declared him "the great conqueror." It was speculated that Harper would immediately retire Ten Broeck to stud duty, one publication insisting that the six-time record-setter would, in all probability, "never face a starter again."

Perhaps they should have checked this assumption with Harper. Ten Broeck, after summering at Nantura, reappeared on September 20, winning a $400 Lexington purse race "in a canter," then won a $500 race in which he was so obviously the best that he was barred from the wagering lest he bankrupt the bookmakers. He won again on October 1, and on October 4, a routine trouncing of two overmatched steeds named Tolona and Whisper marked Ten Broeck's fifteenth consecutive victory.

It had now been nearly seventeen months since the turf's reigning superhorse had last tasted defeat. Each of his wins had occurred within the boundaries of his native Kentucky, and it was conceded by all concerned that he was much the best horse in the Bluegrass State.

But outside Kentucky, there was doubt, and even a level of grumbling, about Ten Broeck's records. The belief outside the champion's home state was that his feats had been accomplished with the aid of "India-rubber courses and fast timers," and it was noted that his record-breaking dashes had employed pacemakers and running starts, and that he had carried light weights.

Frank Harper may have been a man of simple tastes, but he was anything but simpleminded. He must have felt concern, anger, perhaps even resentment as he read these critical assessments of his beloved thoroughbred—but he must also have recognized that they contained a germ of truth. Kentucky's thoroughbred industry had been ravaged during the war, and Nantura had felt the predations of both sides in the fiery conflict. Even twelve years later, and even given the growing prestige of the new Kentucky Derby, the Bluegrass State had yet to fully recover. Its reputation as a haven for great racing remained below that of such states as New York and Maryland.

Racing promoters elsewhere in the nation had long been clamoring for the champion to leave his Kentucky bastion, offering lavish inducements in the form of generous traveling money and enhanced purses to lure him north. And as the critiques of Ten Broeck continued, Harper began to consider them more seriously.

The most persistent challenge was emanating from the wealthy Lorillard brothers, who were loudly and publicly demanding that Ten Broeck journey north and take on their top thoroughbreds, Parole and Tom Ochiltree. With Ten Broeck having routinely run for purses that failed to reach four digits, Harper, much respected by his racetrack opponents but bearing "the reputation of being one of the stingiest horsemen in the country," could not help noting that the amounts being proffered by his Northern suitors were far greater than the Kentucky tracks were ever likely to offer.

The Lorillards had met with rebuff after rebuff from the cautious Kentuckian, but finally, in the aftermath of yet another round of offers and counteroffers, proposals and counterproposals, a telegram was received in the offices of *Spirit of the Times*:

Louisville, Oct. 10, 1877—Editor, Spirit of the Times: *Ten Broeck goes to Baltimore. Will reach there to-morrow.*

The battle, it seemed, was joined at last. The race was on.

CHAPTER 2

The Home Team

[Tom] Ochiltree is a horse of fine size and finish, with an excellent way of going. In him Ten Broeck will have an opponent worthy of his fame.
—LOUISVILLE COURIER-JOURNAL, OCTOBER 22, 1877

[Parole] had a very long light stride, and, like all long-striding horses, he was not a quick starter; his long stride made it difficult for him to force pace from the start. He won his races by lying away and coming with a burst of speed. . . . No horse of his time could live his pace in a finish.
—RACING IN AMERICA 1866–1921 BY W. S. VOSBURGH

A HORSE RACE IS BASICALLY A DIFFERENCE OF OPINION AMONG TWO OR more horsemen, a disagreement in which the opposing sides proclaim, "My horse is faster than your horse," and strive to prove their point. Ten Broeck's imminent arrival in the East created a frenzy of activity among owners and trainers anticipating that one of their thoroughbreds might settle the dispute by defeating Kentucky's champion. Foremost among them were the fabulously wealthy—and fanatically competitive—Lorillard brothers, whose tobacco company, founded by a great-grandfather but expanded a thousandfold by his heirs, was among the largest and most profitable in the nation.

The Lorillard brothers, Pierre and George, were gamblers of the first magnitude, always looking for a contest—a horse race, a yacht race, a shooting match, any competition would do—at which they might win some serious money. The brothers prided themselves on upholding the Lorillard name against nonfamily members, but each had equal enthusiasm for the prospect of competing against the other.

They were certainly not in the habit of issuing challenges that they might lose, and they had not enticed the great Ten Broeck into their territory merely to watch the Kentuckian append the names of Lorillard thoroughbreds to the long list of those he had already humiliated. It was the Lorillard brothers' belief that their thoroughbreds were more than capable of outracing even the great Ten Broeck, and given the accomplishments of their outstanding racers, it seemed difficult to dispute them.

From the Westbrook Stable of George Lorillard, located in Islip, New York, came the strapping Tom Ochiltree, which had originally been purchased by J. A. Chamberlain from the famed Woodburn Stud Farm as a yearling, for the bargain-basement price of $500. This was the farm where Tom Ochiltree's sire, the immortal Lexington, reigned as "The Blind Hero of Woodburn," a title he had earned by fathering—"siring," in the language of the breeding shed—more high-quality thoroughbreds, year in and year out, than any other stallion in the history of the sport.

It seems likely that the well-bred but overgrown youngster's low selling price resulted not from any injury or evident lack of quality, but because big, clumsy yearlings often spend their two-year-old seasons maturing on the farm rather than earning money on the track. There would be no quick return on investment from this colt.

Tom Ochiltree had been named for Colonel Thomas P. Ochiltree, a man whose attainments—or at least, his entertaining and perhaps occasionally accurate descriptions of them—had bestowed upon him near legendary status in the American Southwest. Also legendary were his Texas-sized appetites for good food, fine liquor, expansive conversation, and the opposite gender. A fuller biography of the human Tom Ochiltree is included in Appendix C.

Colonel Ochiltree's equine namesake grew into an imposing mass of horseflesh. To quote distinguished racing historian Walter S. Vosburgh, whose impact on the sport is reflected in the Grade 1 stakes race that continues to bear his name, "For size, bone, and coarseness, Tom Ochiltree surpassed all contemporaries. . . . He was always a monster of size."

A "life-like" portrait of Tom Ochiltree adorned the cover of the July 15, 1876, issue of *Spirit of the Times*, evidently from a Henry Stull portrait that George Lorillard may have commissioned. It depicts a large, heavily muscled animal in full flight, with bobbed tail, braided fore-lock and mane, and a large, wild eye ringed in white. He is a thoroughly impressive-looking beast.

His accomplishments on the racetrack were also impressive. Tom Ochiltree was victorious in his first career outing, then, in just his second start, won the Preakness. Following this auspicious beginning, however, the big colt went somewhat amiss, due, some said, to a change in train-ing regimen that stressed speed at the expense of Tom's natural strengths: power and endurance. He lost the Belmont Stakes to Calvin and Aris-tides, then the Jersey Derby to Calvin and Chesapeake. When he finished a disinterested last in the July 14 Ocean Hotel Stakes, Big Tom was sent back to the farm for the remainder of the summer.

When Tom Ochiltree returned to the races on October 2, he had a new trainer, Anthony Taylor, and a rekindled enthusiasm for racing. After tuning up with a fourth-place finish in the Jerome Stakes, behind Kentucky Derby winner Aristides and Belmont Stakes hero Calvin, the big horse began to regain form, winning by three lengths over Chesapeake in the Annual Stakes while held in so little esteem by the betting public that the bookies packaged him with other long shots as a single entry in the wager-ing field. He romped home again in Pimlico's Dixie Stakes, winning by two lengths at odds of at least 20-to-1, and then concluded his season with a third-place finish as the wagering favorite in the Breckenridge Stakes.

Sold to George Lorillard prior to the 1876 season for $5,000 plus 25 percent of the colt's winnings (he is thought to have netted Alexander $12,000, not a bad return on a $500 initial investment), Tom, now under the skilled handling of trainer R. Wyndham Walden, became arguably the best distance horse in the East, winning seven of nine starts, includ-ing the 2¼-mile Baltimore Cup, the 2-mile Jockey Club Handicap, the 2¾-mile Centennial Stakes, the 3-mile Capital Stakes, and the 2¼-mile Saratoga Cup, all before the end of July.

Thoroughbred racing in the 1870s was a far rougher enterprise than today's patrolled and policed version of the sport. Bookmakers proliferated on local tracks; drug testing beyond a visual inspection was the stuff of science fiction. Efforts both subtle and crude (e.g., shoving a sponge up the nostril of a racer to impair its ability to breathe; over-feeding or overwatering a thoroughbred during the hours before a race) were occasionally employed to secure victory or defeat. On one occasion, Tom Ochiltree, through the good fortune of the would-be fixers' incompetence, narrowly avoided being a poisoning victim, and, in the process, the vehicle for a betting coup.

The victim instead was his stablemate Leander, which received a dose of poison that nearly cost the colt his life. The *New York Times* provided the story:

> *It is known that an attempt was made to poison Tom Ochiltree while he was at Long Branch [New Jersey's Monmouth Park], but his stable companion, Leander, received the dose and has not yet recovered from its effects.*

Obviously, even the most benighted of would-be race-fixers—and this crew, unable to discern the hulking Tom Ochiltree from his smaller stablemate, would certainly qualify—would know enough not to poison a horse that isn't likely to win, anyway. Tom was good enough that "dosing" him could well promote the victory of a lesser runner, possibly at sizable odds. The unfortunate Leander, mistakenly fed the poison intended for Tom Ochiltree, was unable to race again in 1876.

Given the remainder of the summer off, Tom Ochiltree returned in the autumn to reel off the three-mile Maturity Stakes and the four-mile Centennial Cup before tossing in his only clunker of the season, a third-place finish to Add in a $700 race at two miles. Had there been Horse of the Year balloting in the nation's centennial year, Tom Ochiltree, with seven wins in nine starts, would have seriously challenged Ten Broeck for top honors.

At age five, in 1877, Tom Ochiltree was arguably even better. He won a second Baltimore Cup, the Westchester Cup, the Grand National Handicap, and the All-Aged Sweepstakes, plus a number of unnamed races designed to keep him fit for the season's important events. He was often required to carry top weight, not a problem for an animal of his musculature. In all, he raced fourteen times in 1877 and won nine, with four seconds and a third.

George Lorillard's impressive purchase had faced brother Pierre's gelding, Parole, on six occasions. Tom had run second to Parole in the 1876 All-Aged Sweepstakes while carrying 118 pounds to Parole's 99, and defeated Parole in the Saratoga Cup, hauling 21 pounds more than his rival. In 1877, Tom had finished ahead of Parole three times in four confrontations, each time carrying more weight than his opponent, in accordance with the period's scale of weights for five-year-old horses and four-year-old geldings. Overall, Big Tom had twenty-one wins from thirty-two starts, and was regarded as unquestionably one of the best horses in America. The big son of Lexington was, by any measure, a formidable opponent for Ten Broeck as the "Kentucky crack" arrived at Pimlico.

Pierre's four-year-old gelding, Parole, was smaller and plainer than Ten Broeck and Tom Ochiltree, and was decidedly less favored by both the sporting press and the wagering public. Despite the media's lukewarm reviews, however, he was a solid horse that had earned his way into whatever race Frank Harper might choose for Ten Broeck.

Lorillard had purchased Parole at a yearling sale for $780, a figure that, even based on 1874 exchange rates, was unimpressive. But the gelding blossomed under the conditioning of trainer William Brown, and was deemed ready for his initial start early in his two-year-old season. Parole was an impressive winner of Monmouth Park's July Stakes, and a month later defeated Shirley, which would win the following year's Belmont Stakes.

Lorillard and Brown were firm believers in keeping all bases covered, and while Parole was winning four of six starts and earning accolades as the season's best juvenile, Pierre's Faithless was laying waste to the East Coast two-year-old filly division. The pair would almost certainly have earned their respective juvenile championships, had such awards existed in 1875.

Parole would not, however, win any awards as a show horse. Vosburgh described the gelding as "lengthy and narrow . . . 15.3 [hands, not very tall], with a lean, 'varminty' head, light neck." The *New York Times* also professed to be unimpressed with Pierre's plain brown gelding: "a stranger looking at Parole for the first time, would not exclaim in admiration for him." Years after the Great Sweepstakes, covering the ten-year-old Parole's amazing career, the publication the *New York Sportsman* displayed on its cover a drawing of Parole, clearly showing his solid color and plain head, the ribs showing through his coat. He looked exactly as Vosburgh had described him.

Vosburgh was far more impressed with Parole as a racehorse, however: "He had a very long light stride. . . . He won his races by lying away and coming with a burst of speed. . . . No horse of his time could live his pace in a finish."

To begin his three-year-old season, Parole had been shipped to Louisville for the second running of the Kentucky Derby, at the time offering a purse of $3,150. He did not respond well to the change of food, water, and surroundings, and finished fourth, as Vagrant took home the winner's share. Sent to the farm to recuperate, he reappeared two months later at Saratoga in the All-Ages Stakes, in which he defeated Tom Ochiltree for the first time. This was to be the high point of Parole's season, however, as he proved anything but a champion at age three, winning just three times in an abbreviated seven-start campaign.

At four, however, Parole regained his form. He began his season with a second-place finish in a six-furlong prep race, then won the 2½-mile Woodburn Stakes. Returning a month later, he finished third as the fine colt Vera Cruz defeated Tom Ochiltree in the 1¼-mile All-Aged Stakes, then reversed the order of finish in the 2½-mile Saratoga Cup, leaving Tom and Vera Cruz behind. Parole then won his next three starts, including a 2½-mile walkover at Saratoga, then lost twice to Tom Ochiltree, by four lengths on October 2 in the 2¼-mile Grand National Handicap, then by two on October 13 in a 1½-mile stakes for runners of all ages.

And now came word that Frank Harper had accepted the Lorillards' challenge, and that the legendary Ten Broeck would at last be journeying east.

As this electrifying announcement made the rounds of the racing world, Parole's record stood at thirteen wins in twenty-three lifetime starts, with a number of the losses occurring against such good ones as Virgil, Vera Cruz, and Tom Ochiltree. He had won seven of eleven as a four-year-old, rebounding from his mediocre three-year-old campaign, and while there might be some doubt as to whether he was quite as good as the talented Tom Ochiltree, few could question that his accomplishments at least placed him in the conversation. On his best day, he could provide a sterling challenge to any thoroughbred that might be entered against him, up to and including Ten Broeck.

CHAPTER 3

The Harpers

*Mr. [Frank] Harper is a heavily built, white bearded old gentleman,
of the utmost simplicity of manners and life. He knows few greater
pleasures than to sit on the front porch of the little one and a half story
cottage, part log and part brick, of five or six rooms, which constitutes
his home, and to talk with deep feeling of his noble animals, whom he
has loved with an affection rarely given by man to man, and almost
unheard of between man and beast.*
—NANTURA 1795–1905 BY JONELLE FISHER

THE HISTORY OF THE HARPER FAMILY IN THE UNITED STATES BEGINS
long before Ten Broeck and the Great Sweepstakes at Pimlico. Emigrating from Germany, a young couple, Jacob Harper and his wife, Mary, arrived in Virginia in 1795, following an earlier migration of family members during the 1740s. Family legend claims that there were Harpers assisting George Washington and his troops during America's struggle for independence. If so, the Harper family shares with the Lorillard family stories involving both acquaintances with America's first president and participation in the Revolutionary War.

In 1795, for the sum of "nine hundred and ten pounds, lawful money," Jacob Harper purchased from the heirs of General Hugh Mercer, who had been granted the land in appreciation for his service during the Revolution, approximately fifteen hundred acres of fine Kentucky land in Woodford County, within a few miles of the town of Midway. The Harpers would eventually own more than two thousand acres in the lush Kentucky Bluegrass.

An industrious family, the Harpers went about building on their land, creating two modest houses—one log, the other brick—and added facilities for raising farm animals. The Harpers spun their own clothing, raised much of their own food, and bred and raised horses, although not racehorses, for Jacob was "not of the turfman type." It would be future generations of Harpers that would breed and raise some of the most noteworthy thoroughbreds to tread the Bluegrass.

Jacob and Mary produced ten children: George, Jacob, Adam, Nicholas, John, William, Henry, Barbara, Elizabeth, and Mary. After their parents died, most of the children moved on, many settling in other states and other areas of the country. It was a grandson, John Harper, very much "of the turfman type," who would eventually inherit the farm, name it Nantura (the name of the broodmare who produced the great racehorse Longfellow), and use it as a headquarters for raising thoroughbreds. John's siblings, brothers Jacob and Adam and sister Betsy, also lived at Nantura, Jacob overseeing the farm's operations while Betsy cooked, weaved, and sewed. Adam, the money man, handled the family's finances.

When war broke out between the North and South, Kentucky was something of an anomaly, a slave state that had not seceded from the Union. Neutrality may have afforded the state a modicum of protection from the harshness of the period's economic realities, but no mere political designation could shelter it from the war: more than 100,000 Kentuckians fought, approximately 64,000 on the Union side, between 30,000 and 40,000 for the Confederacy, and 13,000 as State Guards. President Lincoln, a Kentucky native, saw Kentucky's neutrality as essential to the prosecution of the war, declaring that while he hoped to have God on the Union's side, "I must have Kentucky."

As a buffer between North and South, the Bluegrass State became fair game for the depredations of both sides, and Nantura, with its livestock and its location in the midst of the area's breeding farms, was sometimes visited by bands of armed raiders in search of food, valuables, and, most important, fast horses. Some of these were marauding Confederates, some Union, and some were unattached or unidentifiable armed bandits.

At times, it became necessary for Nantura's residents to protect their farm, their horses, and their family. On one such occasion, old John

Harper, his long gray hair flowing as he confronted a group, succeeded in driving them off by proclaiming that he intended to protect the farm with his life if necessary.

In 1864, however, a less easily persuaded gang of raiders approached the farm, and when Adam Harper confronted them, possibly firing off his pistol in the effort to send them fleeing, they fired back, and Adam fell, mortally wounded. The guilty soldiers—it proved to be a gang of Union troops—were identified, ordered by their commander to dig their own graves, and executed.

Mercifully, the armistice at Appomattox Court House brought the war to a close, and with the conclusion of hostilities Kentucky, and the Harpers, was able to return in peace to their favored economic and sporting pursuits: breeding and racing fine horseflesh.

The unpretentious John Harper, "clad in faded homespun and leaning upon a stout stick," had long been a familiar figure on the Kentucky thoroughbred circuit. He sent postward under his orange racing silks a steady stream of competitive colts and fillies, and was known as a no-nonsense owner who insisted that his racing stock make the maximum effort in every race they contested. They were not to be held back, never to be used in the race-fixing schemes that were endemic to the period, never to be worked into shape in races that they were not intended to win. Harper's horses would, in his quaint phraseology, battle "from eend to eend" every time they took to the track.

It is a long-held maxim of thoroughbred breeding that one should "breed the best to the best, and hope for the best," and perhaps this was the philosophy that guided Old John when he decided to send one of the farm's best broodmares, Nantura, to the court of the stallion Leamington. Whatever may have been his philosophy, the result was a colt that would be named Longfellow, and would prove to be a very special thoroughbred indeed.

Longfellow was an exceptionally large animal, standing 17 hands high, and Harper probably recognized at the colt's birth that he would be a long-term project. When the formidable animal was finally deemed raceworthy, it was as a three-year-old in 1870. Entered in a race at one-mile heats, he promptly lost the first to Enquirer, finishing third. He failed to reach the distance flag in the second.

Enquirer would remain undefeated throughout the 1870 season, so perhaps Longfellow's debut was not as inauspicious as it may have seemed. The big colt was returned to the farm for the summer, and upon his reintroduction to racing went about making amends, defeating all opposition in his remaining four races at age three. Local owners and trainers began to realize that Longfellow might become a difficult adversary when racing resumed the following spring.

Harper returned his colt to the races at age four, in a $400 race at one-mile heats, but when nothing was entered to oppose the big son of Leamington he was allowed to walk over. Following two consecutive authoritative victories, Longfellow's opposition again remained in the barn, and he was conceded a second uncontested victory. And then, shockingly, he lost a four-mile race in the Saratoga mud to a horse he'd beaten earlier in the year, the slop-loving Helmbold. Longfellow, it seemed, was not fond of getting mud in his eyes.

It had been Old John who had named the colt, and it was naturally assumed that the moniker was intended to honor Henry Wadsworth Longfellow, the poet who had given the world such beloved volumes as *The Courtship of Miles Standish*, *Tales of a Wayside Inn*, and *Household Poems*.

Longfellow, in fact, wrote to Harper to express his appreciation for the honor, which thoroughly befuddled the grizzled horseman. There are innumerable versions of Harper's reaction to Longfellow's letter, but they generally agree that when the poet's missive was brought to Harper's attention, his response was something akin to, "Never heard much of that feller, but that colt of mine's got the longest legs of any feller I ever seen." Longfellow's final race of 1871 was scheduled for September 12 over the Lexington Association course, at two-mile heats against a colt named Pilgrim. The race itself, however, paled in comparison with the tragic events surrounding it, which would haunt John Harper for the remainder of his long life.

Harper, as was his custom during the days when runners could be "got at" by race-fixers, had elected to sleep in Longfellow's barn during the prerace hoopla. This time, however, Harper was summoned back to Nantura, and upon arriving at the farm learned that his brother Jacob, seventy-five, and his sister, Miss Betsy, seventy-three, had been savagely attacked with a hatchet while they slept on the night of September 11, 1871.

It was the family's servants, some of them former slaves who had stayed with the family following emancipation, who discovered the carnage. When Jacob and Miss Betsy failed to respond to the early-morning knocks on their bedroom doors signaling breakfast, the servants broke into their rooms, then recoiled in horror.

Jacob was dead at the scene, his face obliterated by hatchet wounds, blood covering his bed linens, his pillow, even the canopy under which he had been sleeping. Miss Betsy, whom a bout with tuberculosis had left as weak and feeble as a child, was clinging to life, her skull fractured in three places by hatchet blows. She would hang on for a few days in pain and delirium, but would regain consciousness only intermittently before dying of her wounds without identifying the killer.

John Harper may have narrowly avoided becoming a third victim. Around midnight, he had been awakened by knocking on the barn door. He wasn't opening up, not to anyone, not with his most prized possession sleeping nearby.

"Who's there?" he called to the intruder.

The response: "I want to see Longfellow."

John wasn't having it. He shouted, "You can't come in. Go away."

The door rattled ominously; then John heard retreating footsteps, followed by the sound of a horse galloping off, possibly toward Nantura and a deadly confrontation with Jacob and Miss Betsy. It was the next morning that news of the vicious attacks reached John. In his haste to return to Nantura and learn the fate of his brother and sister, Harper apparently neglected to withdraw Longfellow from the race, and the Lexington Association's $400 Jockey Club Purse, at two-mile heats, went forward as planned, with Harper's absence the only unusual factor. Longfellow easily defeated Pilgrim in both heats, with the odd result that in some newspapers, coverage of the grisly murders and Longfellow's victory ran side by side. The murder weapon, a small hatchet with a short, eight-inch handle, had been hurriedly discarded in a rose bush as the killer made his escape, and was quickly located. Fresh horse tracks were discovered that may have been left by the murderer—or perhaps not, because hoofprints are not, after all, uncommon around horse farms.

As local residents pondered the events of the terrible night and discussed the few available clues, frustration grew. John Harper hired a private detective to assist with the investigation, and Clint Butts of Covington, Kentucky, would come to be well known in his own right through his commentary in the daily newspaper coverage of the murder. The *Lexington Observer and Reporter* had only one succinct wish for whoever was proved to be the killer: "a long rope and a short shrift."

To some, it appeared that the case should be an easy one. The *Daily Press*, for one, expressed confidence that "[the investigators] will succeed in a day or two in solving the problem of who committed the murder." But this scenario proved too optimistic. By the thirteenth—approximately thirty-six hours after the homicide—many of the Harpers' servants had been arrested and hauled off to the Midway jail, pending an "examining trial" before Judge W. W. George that would determine whether sufficient evidence could be found to implicate any of the accused. By this time, Detective Butts, who had been investigating clues in cooperation with local police, was describing the case as "one of the most difficult with which he has had to deal for many years." The paucity of relevant evidence led him to request a postponement of the examining trial until Friday, September 15, and despite the detective's lack of any legal standing to extend the detention of the prisoners, Judge George granted his request.

In the meantime, as they will in unsolved homicides, theories began to evolve. One concerned an argument that had ensued a few days earlier between "Uncle Jake" and one of the stable's jockeys, Will Prior. During the altercation, it was alleged, Harper had struck the African-American rider with his cane, and Prior had kicked the older man and threatened to kill him. When this information reached the police, who knew that Prior had been present when the victims were discovered, they promptly arrested the jockey. Evidently, cane attacks upon employees were considered acceptable in those post–Civil War days, for the *Daily Press* concluded that, "This brutal act [Prior's alleged kicking of Uncle Jake] is the more unaccountable as both Jake and his sister, Miss Betsy, were extremely kind to their colored servants."

One major stumbling block for the investigators was motive. Why were Uncle Jake and Miss Betsy attacked? It was known on the farm that the frugal Harpers kept very little money in their home, but four drawers in John Harper's room had been opened. All of those being held were employees who would have known that the house had little worth stealing. Perhaps this was something other than an inside job.

Upon interviewing the Nantura servants, a reporter reconstructed the conversation that had occurred between young Will Prior and his mother at 5:00 a.m., as the body of Uncle Jake and the severely battered Miss Betsy were discovered:

Mrs. Prior (hearing a groan, apparently from Miss Betsy): "Will, let me in!"

(Will opens the door).

Mrs. Prior (shrieks): "Will! Miss Betsy is all beat to pieces!"

Will: "Oh, I reckon not."

Mrs. Prior (rushing now to Uncle Jake's room and finding him dead): "Will!"

(Will comes running).

Mrs. Prior (in what are described as "terrified accents"): "Uncle Jake is dead!"

Will (in same tone as before): "Oh, I reckon not."

The correspondent learned that the intruder had not merely bludgeoned Miss Betsy, but had also choked her, noting that "her neck was blackened and bears finger marks upon it . . . there are prints of fingers also behind the ear." In contradiction to the search for the family's nonexistent cash, the effort to strangle Miss Betsy suggested that the attacker may well have been an insider, one who had been "aware of the feeble hold which she retained on life on account of her consumptive condition." The more clues that were discovered, it seemed, the more contradictory the evidence became.

By the close of September 13, there were five people in custody: Will Prior; another stable jockey named Will Scott, who had been arrested in

Lexington; Prior's father, Sam, who had been mysteriously missing the morning after the attacks; a stable boy named Henry; and Tom Parker, described only as "a negro man once owned by the Harpers."

Clues continued to turn up, serving primarily to muddle the case further. On Thursday evening, Will Prior's mother—one of the rare black employees who had not been imprisoned—brought to John Harper a pocketbook that she claimed to have found near the family's cabin. The local constabulary, noting that the pocketbook was inexplicably dry despite recent rains, promptly dispatched Mrs. Prior to the jailhouse.

The once-delayed examining trial took place on September 15, and found insufficient evidence to hold any of the prisoners except Will Prior, who would also be released shortly. Detective Butts was now becoming frustrated. After three days on the case, the circumstances surrounding "the perpetration of the fiendish murder" remained "very mysterious, baffling the best detective's sagacity." Now, an advertisement appeared in newspapers in and around Lexington:

Reward of $5,000
I will give five thousand dollars for the arrest of the murderer or murderers of Jacob and Elizabeth Harper, or either who were killed in Woodford county on 10th of September. The money payable on the conviction of the murderer or murderers of either.
John Harper

Further arrests were made. Two white men named Kirk and Bolan, and a black woman who was with Bolan at the time of his arrest, were jailed after an overheard conversation in which one of the male arrestees allegedly asked the other why the latter "had killed the old woman, she couldn't have told anything anyhow." It came to nothing. After a few more days, with Butts remarking enigmatically that "time would unravel the mystery, with the aid of men and money," the good detective returned to Covington.

And now questions began to be raised regarding the younger Harpers, who would inherit the ranch and its valuable livestock upon the deaths of their unmarried aunt and uncles. Suspicion focused gradually on a nephew, Adam Harper, who was badly in need of money and had been heard to brag that he would be "expecting some relief soon."

At least one family member, a vocal cousin named Wallace Harper, formally accused Adam of the crime, and was sufficiently convincing that a grand jury was convened. The grand jury, however, found insufficient evidence to indict Adam, who in turn filed a $500,000 slander suit against Wallace. After a jury found in favor of Wallace, Adam was questioned a second time by the grand jury, but again escaped indictment.

And here the murder case foundered. The killer was never identified, the $5,000 reward went unclaimed (there were rumors, never authenticated, that Butts submitted a claim for the money), and, in a gesture that would have profound implications for both the Harper family and the Sport of Kings, Frank Harper, who shared John's love for fast and beautiful thoroughbreds, moved to Nantura to provide companionship and assistance to his grief-stricken uncle.

Frank, who would one day inherit the farm from Old John, would wait until his own death to offer an opinion as to the killer, when his will, which would become the subject of a bitter court dispute, pointedly excluded Adam Harper and his offspring from acquiring any portion of Nantura. This, however, was decades in the future.

With his brother and sister buried and nephew Frank assisting with stable management duties, Uncle John Harper rededicated himself to racing, and particularly to Longfellow, as he awaited the following spring's new challenges. The huge five-year-old began his season with an eight-length thrashing of two outclassed runners at the Lexington course, then took on the four-year-old Harry Bassett, winner of the previous year's Belmont Stakes and Travers, in the $1,500 Monmouth Cup. Harry Bassett, himself regarded as a superstar, was sent postward as the odds-on 1-to-2 favorite.

Harry Bassett would conclude his career with twenty-three wins in thirty-six starts, and in 2010 would be belatedly inducted into racing's Hall of Fame. On July 2, 1872, however, before an overflow crowd estimated at thirty thousand, he was raced into discouragement by his outsized rival, refusing to exert himself following a rousing head-and-head battle over the race's first mile and a half. Once Bassett had capitulated,

Longfellow "cantered home nearly two hundred yards ahead." Old John, described in one publication as "the proudest man in America this afternoon," celebrated the victory with typical frugality, enjoying a dinner of "bacon and corn bread, drinking his coffee out of a tin cup."

Two days later, Longfellow returned at Long Branch in the Jersey Jockey Club Stakes, a race that required the winner to take three of five one-mile heat races. Longfellow was so obviously superior to the other three entrants that no wagering was permitted on him, and he delivered on this expectation, winning three consecutive heats with the jockey pulling double on the reins, to restrain his mount from expending more energy than necessary. Next on Longfellow's schedule was the July 16 Saratoga Stakes at 2¼ miles, and a much-demanded rematch with Harry Bassett. This time, however, the fates would conspire against John Harper, nearly taking from him his beloved horse.

In a race that the *New York Times* would hail the following day as "The Greatest Contest in American Turf History," the two outstanding thoroughbreds once again dueled on almost even terms from the start. Harry Bassett briefly gained a slight advantage, then Longfellow battled back to even terms as the crowd roared. As the two neared the midway point, victory teetered in the balance.

It was at about that point that one of Longfellow's front shoes broke. No one will ever know whether it had been applied improperly or had simply given way under the pounding of the big animal's massive hooves, but the steel shoe twisted upward, puncturing the soft, sensitive underside of Longfellow's heel and driving into the tendons. The pain must have been hideous, but Longfellow battled on against his rival, causing more damage with every stride. Gradually, Harry Bassett edged ahead, arriving at the finish in 3 minutes and 59 seconds, by a decisive 2½ seconds the fastest time ever recorded for the distance. Longfellow, defeated by three-quarters of a length, nonetheless became the second horse ever to run the distance in less than four minutes.

At first, all that was readily apparent was that Harry Bassett had won, and his backers were jubilant. As the racing writer for the *New York Times*, in the decidedly non-P.C. style of the day, reported:

The scene which followed is incredible. The colored jockeys and train-
ers yelled like maniacs, tumbled over one another, and fought to get to
the judges' stand first. Hats and sticks literally darkened the air, and
I am not sure that many a colored stable-boy was not tossed aloft for
joy. In the grand stand men shouted and almost embraced one another;
ladies, though half alarmed at the torrent of excitement, waved their
handkerchiefs and parasols.

But Harper knew. He watched jockey John Sample's hasty dismount, saw Longfellow struggling on three legs, and realized that disaster had befallen his colt. Later that day, a reporter visited Harper in the stable area, and reported that "Uncle Harper is completely overcome and walks about with sorrowful looks." The next day, the veterinarian confirmed that Longfellow's tendons were shredded and that, in the pained words of the colt's trainer, "he'll never more than walk—run he couldn't."

As rains drenched Saratoga the next day, a *Times* reporter, his interview with the devastated Harper completed, waxed poetic, citing Lord Byron in bidding farewell to one of the great horses of the era: "Even the elements weep at thy departure." Uncle John was more prosaic: "Well, the shoe broke and then he broke. It's dogon bad luck."

For Old John, it was the end. "The pet and pride of his heart was a cripple, and he dared not hope to own another such horse. The last leaf in the turf romance was turned, and it was blotted with tears." Longfellow concluded his short but brilliant career with thirteen wins in sixteen races. His induction into thoroughbred racing's Hall of Fame at Saratoga Springs, New York, in 1971 occurred well in advance of those of Ten Broeck and Parole.

Returned to Nantura, Longfellow was saved for stud duty, and proved a highly successful stallion, producing, among a host of fine racers, two Kentucky Derby winners, Leonatus (1883) and Riley (1890). Old John didn't live to see either of them; he passed away in August of 1874 at what was described as the "ripe old age" of seventy-eight. He certainly seemed older. By the end he was being described as "alone—desolate," "worn, weary, and hermitlike," his farm a "sad and silent homestead."

He was lowered into his final resting place surrounded by family and the members of the racing community against whom he had competed for decades. Many of those in attendance would still remember the brother and sister who had been taken from the old horseman four years earlier. And all would recognize this as the closing of an era; Old John was the last surviving member of his generation of the Harper family.

Chapter 4

The Lorillards (Part 1)

[Pierre] Lorillard had a tendency to do things in the grand manner. Having entered racing, he thought he really ought to have a training center. He picked out 400 acres near Jobstown, N.J. and named it Rancocas Farm after a stream which ran through it. He immediately set 200 men to work fixing up the place. Ditches were dug all over the farm for an elaborate water system, barns rose, plank fences formed paddocks, and a six-furlong training track suddenly appeared.

He bought an enormous iron gate from the old Bowery Bank of New York (complete with winged Mercury at the top) for his carriage way and did some work on the Victorian manor, adding a dozen or so rooms, not the least of which was a gaming hall with roulette wheel. . . .

So you can see Pierre Lorillard was a sportsman of some style. He was 40 and his brother George was 30 when they entered racing in 1873. They maintained separate stables and they split up all the big pots in the game.

—KENT HOLLINGSWORTH IN *THE GREAT ONES*, 1970

THE LORILLARDS WHO PLAY SUCH A VITAL ROLE IN THE STORY OF THE Great Sweepstakes are Pierre Lorillard IV and his younger brother, George. As was the case with Frank Harper, any biography of the Lorillard brothers must begin with progenitors who arrived in America during the previous century. And, as with the Harpers, any biography of the Lorillards must include discussion of a controversial last will and testament that was challenged in the courts by disgruntled members of the departed's family, in this case nearly a quarter-century after the Great Sweepstakes had passed into history.

The essential Lorillard progenitor was a tobacconist named Pierre Lorillard (sometimes anglicized as Peter Lorillard or Pierre Lorillard I), who in 1760 founded an entity that he named "Lorillard's Snuff and Tobacco." It would one day grow a billionfold, but in Pierre I's time it was something very small, a fledgling business that is sometimes considered to be America's first tobacco firm. At the least, it was the first to make snuff.

The first Pierre Lorillard, whose name was probably a corruption of l'Oreillard or l'Aureillard, began his business in Lower Manhattan with facilities that might generously be described as meager. His "factory" was a converted house, and the snuff he produced was packaged in the dried bladders of slaughtered animals, which, while the notion may not seem appealing, were lightweight and waterproof, two essential qualities for snuff packing. Generations later, in one of many innovations pioneered by the company, Lorillard cigarettes were the first to be packaged in a new invention: cellophane.

Much of the tobacco converted to snuff by the first Pierre Lorillard was grown in Virginia, and one corporate legend contends that some of it was purchased from the farm of George Washington, a factoid repeated in print nearly two centuries later in the company's promotional materials. A surviving recipe for Pierre I's basic black snuff confirms that production even in those early days was a process far more complex than merely cutting and mixing together random tobaccos:

> *Take a good strong virgin tobacco without stems. Cut this in pieces and make it wet in a barrel [the moistening ingredient was more likely to be rum than water]. Set it in sweet [sweat] room at 100 degrees for 12 days. Make into powder, letting stand three to four months, adding 1½ pounds salmoniac, 2 pounds tamarind, 2 oz. vanilla bean, 1 oz. tonka bean, 1 oz. chamomile flowers.*

Achieving the beginnings of success with recipes such as this, Lorillard married at the age of twenty-one, in August of 1763. His marriage eventually produced five children, the eldest of whom, born in 1764, was christened Pierre II; his next child was born in 1766 and called George. Pierre I's last-born child, Jacob, entered the banking profession, and "rose from being an obscure tobacconist's apprentice" to become wealthy.

The first Pierre Lorillard may have met a tragic end, although the circumstances of his death, as depicted in corporate publications, may be as much the stuff of legend as reality.

Three made-for-the-public P. Lorillard Company publications describe Pierre Abraham Lorillard's arrival in America, his career as a young, ambitious tobacconist, and his death, but they differ dramatically in their accounts of how and when the first Pierre Lorillard met his end. The first, published in 1947, detailed Lorillard's efforts to grow his company, and its bequest to his sons when they became of age. The tobacconist's later years are described as follows:

> For the first 20 years, Pierre made slow, steady progress with his new business. At times it was touch and go; but young Lorillard had picked a winner: a promising new line of business in a vigorous, thriving new colony—now the most prosperous nation in the world. During those two decades, the up-and-coming tobacco trade and Pierre's own little business had to weather the Revolution. Naturally, the war threw everything out of gear as far as business was concerned, but somehow the new Lorillard Company came through it all, not much the worse for wear. By 1780, Pierre's two sons, Peter and George, were old enough to join their father in his business venture and learn the trade. Twelve years later they were his partners in the firm.

By 1951, the section regarding "slow, steady progress" had disappeared from the corporate newsletter; in fact, Pierre I's role in founding and nurturing the fledgling company was drastically shortened. The remaining section reads simply:

> In 1780 Pierre had taken his two sons, Pierre and George into the business and a few years later admitted them to the firm as partners.

It was not until nine years later, when the P. Lorillard Corporation celebrated its bicentennial with a document titled *Lorillard and Tobacco: 200th Anniversary, P. Lorillard Company, 1760–1960,* that the corporate founder, who "came through [the Revolutionary War] not much the worse for wear" in the 1947 document, was depicted as a fatality of that same war. In the wake of Pierre I's newly disclosed tragic end, his widow became very much a corporate heroine, although the bicentennial document neglected to mention that the given name of the company's alleged savior was Catherine:

> *Pierre's expanding business activities were hampered as waves of revolutionary events washed through New York. He had to grit his teeth when Hessian soldiers took up quarters in his parents' home outside of town, to which the patriotic Pierre had fled from the Tory occupied city. Perhaps he showed his resentment. In any case there was an explosion of violence—and Hessian soldiers killed Pierre Lorillard, the Huguenot who had come to the New World to find freedom and opportunity. Pierre's widow dried her tears and struggled heroically— and successfully—to hold the business together until her two small sons would be old enough to take over. The two very young men graduated as fast as they could from running errands to becoming enterprising businessmen.*
>
> *Presently P. Lorillard Company was more prosperous than ever.*

Whatever may have been the reality of the first P. Lorillard's passing, by 1792 the tobacconist's two eldest sons had fully taken charge, the business was flourishing, and the brothers had purchased a grist mill and dam on the Bronx River in what was then Westchester County. Around 1840, the original wooden mill was torn down and replaced by one of solid granite, with stables for blooded horses nearby—the first entry of the Lorillard family into the realm of pedigreed horses, although on a far more modest scale than would be the case just two generations hence. The Lorillards grew a flower garden, nicknamed the "Acre of Roses," which was more than merely ornamental; the petals were used to perfume the snuff produced at the mill.

The brothers went about applying principles of mass production in the newly purchased Bronx River mill, and the business continued to grow. By 1793, the new factory was operating at full capacity, and the younger Lorillards had added a warehouse. Shortly thereafter, homes were being built for the factory's workers and their families.

The company had also begun advertising its products, seeking broader distribution. On May 27, 1789, the House of Lorillard ran its first newspaper advertisement, describing a variety of products and offering one of the first unconditional money-back guarantees in the history of American advertising:

> *The above Tobacco and Snuff will be sold reasonable, and warranted as good as any on the continent. If not found to prove good, any part of it may be returned, if not damaged.*

Here, again, we encounter what may be Lorillard family legend, although one that again calls into question the dramatic death portrayed in the bicentennial document for Pierre I. The 1951 corporate publication presents an amusing vignette involving the corporate founder's two sons and their retired but still active father in which the company's tradition-bound founder, bridling at what he considered the presumptuous idea of advertising, would sometimes hire groups of men to follow his sons' workers and tear down their freshly posted advertising handbills. Obviously, this would have been quite a feat if the father had been killed by Hessians during the War of Independence.

Pierre II, like his father, sired five children, the third of whom, born in 1796, would be his only son, the appropriately named Pierre III. The second Pierre lived into his late seventies, dying in 1843, and at his death inspired both fond memories and gentle sarcasm on the part of Philip Hone, who had served as mayor of New York during a portion of Pierre II's management of the company. On May 22 of that year, Hone wrote in his diary:

> *Died this morning at his seat in Westchester County, Mr. Pierre Lorillard . . . in the 80th year of his age. . . . He was a tobacconist, and his memory will be preserved in the annals of New York by the celebrity of*

"Lorillard's Snuff and Tobacco." He led people by the nose for the best part of a century and made his enormous fortune by giving them to chew that which they could not swallow.

One reads in materials related to the Lorillard family that the word "millionaire" was coined in 1837 by an obituary writer seeking an as yet uninvented term to describe Pierre II's wealth, but in fact *The Oxford English Dictionary* attributes the term to an 1826 writing of British Prime Minister Benjamin Disraeli. What is noteworthy, however, is that by the time of Pierre II's passing, the company was producing enough wealth that a term such as "millionaire" could reasonably be applied to the corporate leader.

The third Pierre, through a combination of inheritance, purchase, and, so another family legend claims, a victory over family members at the poker table, found himself the owner of more than six hundred thousand acres of undeveloped New York land, located approximately a one-hour train ride from the city. This would eventually become Tuxedo Park (from the local Native Americans' word for the area, "Ptuck-sepo"), but this would be the work of the next Pierre Lorillard.

When Pierre III died in 1867 at the age of seventy-one, he was notable for having managed a quantum growth in the fortunes of his family business, for retaining within the family the Tuxedo land, and, presumably, for his otherworldly skills at the poker table. At the time of his death, it was estimated that he was the sixth wealthiest man in New York—and another Lorillard was the wife of the seventh wealthiest:

Millionaires

A writer in the Galaxy *gives the names of the following ten men as the owners of one-tenth part of the taxable property of New York:*

William B. Astor	$16,114,000
Wm. C. Rhinelander	7,745,000
Alex T. Stewart	6,091,000
Peter and George Goelet	4,417,000

James Lenox	4,260,000
Peter Lorillard	4,245,000
James D. Wolfe	3,997,000
M.M. Hendricks	1,690,000
Rufus L. Lord	1,500,000
C.V.S. Roosevelt	1,346,000
Total	$51,405,000

Astor inherited his property, as did Rhinelander; the Goelets made their fortune, partly by selling iron, and partly by buying a lot to pasture a cow, on which have since been built Fifth, Lexington, and Fourth Avenues; Lenox inherited his riches, and each year gives away nearly his whole income; Lorillard, now dead, made his fortune by selling tobacco; Wolfe inherited a fortune, and married a Lorillard; Hendricks inherited part, and added to it by selling copper; Roosevelt inherited some, and has increased it by the advance of real estate; Lord and Stewart began poor, but got righ [sic] by selling dry goods.

Pierre III's most important role, however, may have been that of father, for it was his eldest son, Pierre Lorillard IV, who would, in addition to his dynamic furtherance of the family business, create from Pierre III's six hundred thousand acres an elaborate playground for the rich and famous of the era. Pierre IV would also achieve unprecedented success in the sporting world, pushed to the pinnacle of accomplishment by another of Pierre III's sons, George Lyndes Lorillard.

Born into exceptional affluence on October 13, 1833, in Westchester, New York, the fourth Pierre Lorillard received as his birthright $1 million and a joint interest in the family business that the first three American generations of his family had nurtured, as well as his fair share of the Tuxedo property. He also inherited the business acumen that had enabled his family to create a corporate giant from a company that began its existence with practically no assets. Having bought out control of the family business from his brothers, Pierre IV proceeded to grow the company even larger.

He was very much a man of his era, and his era was that of the robber barons. It was a time of huge, often monopolistic business empires, the age of what economist Thorstein Veblen labeled "conspicuous consumption." The newly rich classes (as well as those who, like the Lorillards, could claim multiple generations of wealth) chose not merely to enjoy their fortunes, but created purposefully ostentatious lifestyles that included, among other highly visible symbols of wealth, the requisite baronial estates.

Pierre Lorillard seemed to come by this lifestyle almost instinctually, doing nothing on a small scale if it could be done extravagantly. And it was in the area of sports, a pursuit with almost infinite potential for ostentation and lavish consumption, that he became not merely a historic figure, but a singular one.

Lorillard's first sporting love was yachting, although unlike his brother George, whose competitive fires demanded that he participate physically, Pierre's contributions to the sport were less those of the competitor, more those of the innovator and benefactor. As the purchaser of ever more luxurious seacraft that reflected his wealth, his taste, and his ability to spend fortunes to maximize his creature comforts and those of his privileged acquaintances, Pierre earned the title of "yachtsman" while remaining at a safe distance from any dangers his vessels might encounter.

Among the most famous of his competitive yachting expeditions was the participation of his schooner, the *Vesta*, in an 1867 transatlantic race that was beset by a fearsome storm at sea. The frightened crew was in near mutiny, demanding that the endangered vessel return to port, but Lorillard's commander, a loyal salt named Captain Low, refused to turn back, and despite losing two of its spars, the yacht managed to limp to the finish after thirty-two harrowing days at sea.

Lorillard, while much concerned during the course of the schooner's travails, was elsewhere occupied throughout the *Vesta*'s perilous journey.

It was Pierre Lorillard who first recognized the potential of Newport, Rhode Island, as a haven for yacht racing, and who commissioned trophies for races there. To position himself for this purpose, he built a mansion at Newport that was, true to the Lorillard style, among the grandest houses in an area replete with grand houses. Eventually, when Lorillard had begun exploring other forms of sporting ostentation, he would sell his estate to multimillionaire Cornelius Vanderbilt.

Lorillard's yachts tended to be costly affairs, ostensibly intended for speed but with a strong emphasis on comfort, and it was therefore logical that he should next embrace the emerging field of houseboating. As with all interests, Pierre entered this new endeavor with an open wallet, and a $100,000 floating palace called the *Caiman* was soon navigating the southern rivers. The expensive houseboat exemplified perfectly the Lorillardian philosophy of spending: one spent for comfort, to be seen, and to be envied, particularly by the wealthy.

From 1891 until 1900, the *Caiman* served as a sort of second winter home for Lorillard, "meandering along the Florida coasts and rivers, from one hunting or fishing district to another . . . always accompanied by a flotilla of other boats, used as servants' quarters, kennels, storehouses, &c." When the first *Caiman* burned in 1900, Pierre replaced it with "a houseboat even larger and more costly, the new vessel being fitted with . . . every convenience that comfort possibly could require."

Lorillard also dabbled in other sporting fields, breeding coaching horses, Shetland ponies, hunting dogs, and gamebirds. Any area of sporting endeavor that might bespeak the financial resources necessary to participate in well-publicized luxury was potentially an area of ardent interest for Pierre Lorillard.

But it was Lorillard's thoroughbreds, their conspicuous display and their well-publicized exploits, that provided the grandest, most public stage for the tobacco magnate, and it was their successes that would earn him enduring fame as a sportsman. Veblen, the economic theorist of conspicuous consumption, had much to say about racehorses and the rich: "It gratifies the owner's sense of aggression and dominance to have his own horse outstrip his neighbor's. . . . Beyond this, the race-horse has also . . . use as a gambling instrument." Lorillard would explore and master both aspects of matters thoroughbred.

Lorillard had eschewed the sport's traditional breeding grounds in the Southern states, observing that successful racing men such as Francis Morris in Westchester, New York, and Aristides Welch near Philadelphia had remained in close proximity to their horses and the racecourses over which they competed. How, after all, could an owner enjoy owning and racing horses that he could rarely see? Lorillard stepped from a train one day in early 1872 in the New Jersey community of Jobstown, a mere forty miles from the family's snuff factory and within reasonable distance of some of America's most opulent racing facilities, and determined that here would be an acceptable locus for his breeding and racing empire.

Lorillard purchased fifteen hundred acres of what had previously been known as the Dr. Conover Farm, bestowing on his new facility the name Rancocas, after a creek that flowed through the property. And shortly thereafter, in what would be a dress rehearsal for his rapid-fire creation fifteen years later of Tuxedo Park, armies of laborers descended upon the New Jersey countryside, joined by multitudes of artisans and architects. A mansion arose, fashionably decorated in Victorian splendor, one huge room dedicated to games of chance imported from Monte Carlo. This was not intended as a solitary retreat; it was to be a splendiferous showplace, with plentiful rooms for invited guests.

Huge barns and miles of wooden fencing seemed to appear overnight. An intricate watering system was hand-dug by cadres of workmen. A three-quarter-mile racetrack was laid out and leveled by hand, a task requiring two hundred men, followed by an indoor, all-weather training track. Barns arose, one intended as a "playhouse" for Rancocas weanlings and yearlings, boasting a rotunda nearly as large as that of the US Capitol, its floor covered by fine sand and straw. The stallion barn was constructed of the finest brick. In a wooded area nearby, Lorillard created a game reserve, and an elaborate swimming pool.

As Lorillard began acquiring and breeding horses and visitors became ever more plentiful, the need for additional access became evident. A spur line was added to the existing railway system, and soon Lorillard cars were unloading Lorillard visitors and livestock at a Lorillard platform. A reporter, visiting Rancocas during its glory days, would write, "I will only just say that in extent and perfection of detail Rancocas stands alone in this country, and there is probably nothing as complete on the globe."

But for all its glamour and luxury, for all the long Rancocas weekends that became, for the day's social set, *de rigueur*, it is neither for its architecture nor its showplace beauty that Rancocas is remembered today. Rancocas is remembered for its horses.

Pierre's first thoroughbred, an otherwise undistinguished steed called Free Lance, served as his entrée to the races in 1873, but it was during the following season that Saxon, purchased in England the previous year but now carrying Rancocas silks (cherry, with black whips and cap and gold tassel) properly introduced Lorillard to the racing world, winning the eighth edition of the Belmont Stakes at fashionable Jerome Park. Pierre would shortly have his second classic win, when the upper-crust crowd at Saratoga watched his Attila, another recent purchase, dead-heat with Acrobat, earning a share of the "Midsummer Derby," the Travers Stakes.

Over the next quarter-century, thoroughbreds topped by jockeys wearing those prestigious cherry and black silks would dominate racing on the East Coast. Lorillard would never win what is today America's most famous race, the Kentucky Derby, but this was because the Derby was contested so far from his operating base that only one Rancocas runner, the little gelding Parole, ever competed in the newly minted race. And though Parole finished fourth behind Vagrant, Creedmore, and Harry Hill, the Lorillard entrant, unlike his three Derby Day conquerors, had a dazzling future ahead, a future that would on more than one occasion place his high-visibility owner exactly where he desired to be: in the nation's spotlight.

As Lorillard's thoroughbreds were winning many of the East Coast's great races, amassing for their owner a monumental trophy collection and earning the proceeds of his famously enormous wagers, the tobacco magnate was simultaneously collecting one of the finest groups of breeding stock anywhere on the North American continent. Since 1871, he had been purchasing highly regarded stallions and broodmares in England, spending, as was his wont, as much as necessary to bring to Rancocas the best horses he could import. As one close observer noted, "While Mr. Lorillard was always a liberal purchaser [of racehorses], he considered it a greater honor to win with horses of his own breeding." If Pierre Lorillard couldn't outrun you with his homebred horse, however, he would sometimes pay a premium price to obtain the horse that had just beaten him.

During much of Rancocas's reign as the largest and most successful thoroughbred establishment on the East Coast, Pierre's staunchest competitor was his brother George, who established a stable that occasionally displaced Pierre's from the leading position on the seasonal earnings lists. George Lorillard was what we would call today a renaissance man, an achiever whose successes seem too numerous, too extreme, to have been accomplished by a single individual, a single mortal.

Born in New York in March 1843, George Lorillard rapidly established himself as an individual of exceptional intelligence and drive. He breezed through school, emerging from the Yale Scientific School in 1862 as a nineteen-year-old physician, and continued his medical training at New York's Bellevue Hospital. A distinguished medical career was well within the grasp of the younger Lorillard brother.

After a short time, however, George concluded that business held more interest for him than medicine, and he resigned to join with Pierre in creating the P. & G. Lorillard firm. George and Pierre maintained their partnership for four years, at which point George retired to devote his time to managing his brother's many sporting activities.

George Lorillard was a big, physical man, reaching six feet three inches and two hundred pounds at maturity, and unlike his brother was an excellent athlete. Described as "a model sportsman," he excelled as a marksman, winning the Grand Prix of Monaco over many of the finest shots in Europe; was an expert fisherman; and was—ignoring the occasional shipwreck—a world-class yachtsman. In 1866, after building and selling the sloop *Eva*, he sailed Pierre's yacht *Vesta* in a great transoceanic race on Pierre's behalf, and the following spring purchased a yacht called the *Magic*, with which he won the prestigious New York Yacht Club regatta. George was less fortunate with his next yacht, the *Challenge*, which was lost in a gale near the Bahamas.

He had a 130-foot schooner, christened the *Meteor*, constructed for him at a cost of $50,000, and saw it launched on April 6, 1869. The well-named vessel, built purely for speed, "probably contained more timber than any yacht of her size . . . that has ever been constructed in these waters." Aboard it, George cruised the Mediterranean; then, on August 20, 1869, he began an around-the-world journey that was intended to consume a leisurely three years, and to include stops in numerous ports.

Late in the year, however, disturbing reports began flowing to Pierre. Having made port in Bermuda and Great Britain, the *Meteor* was reported wrecked near Tunis, with all aboard—Lorillard, sailing master George Howe, ten men before the mast, a mate, a boatswain, two cooks, two stewards, and two quartermasters, plus three guests—safe. While this was somewhat reassuring, there were no specifics as to the actual location of the group. Where were they? For nearly a month, the question remained unanswered.

It was not until January 21, 1870, that Pierre Lorillard received a telegram stating that the travelers were safe in Naples, and at this point it was learned that the twenty-three had not merely undergone the trauma of a shipwreck, but in its aftermath had been taken hostage by Arab tribesmen intent on ransom. They may have been at significant risk for assassination until the arrival of the American consul with $15,000 in cash, at which point the kidnappers finally were persuaded to release their hostages.

Upon George's return, he commissioned the construction of a new vessel, the *Enchantress*, which was "launched, and made the trip in which the *Meteor* had failed." Having achieved this closure, George sold the *Enchantress* to another enthusiast, and is not known subsequently to have taken an active role in competitive yachting.

Instead, George found himself drawn, probably with Pierre's relieved blessing, toward the world of thoroughbred racing, a sport his brother was already seeking to dominate. Recognizing that a second-rate effort would not merely fail to overcome Pierre's head start, but would lose his older brother's respect, George entered the sport with all the energy—and, of course, all the money—a Lorillard could muster.

Learning the game, he briefly entered into a partnership with noted owner J. G. K. Lawrence, and the two won the 1874 Champagne Stakes with Hyder Ali. After leaving the partnership in 1875, George began accumulating good runners at a remarkable rate. He brought Hall of Famer Duke of Magenta, Sensation, and Spinaway to the races, and for five consecutive years, 1878 through 1882, his orange and blue silks were atop the Preakness winners. He acquired Tom Ochiltree as a four-year-old after the imposing son of Lexington had won the 1875 Preakness.

His Westbrook Stable covered more than a thousand acres, and while it may not have rivaled Pierre's Rancocas in opulence, it nonetheless was considered "a princely racing establishment . . . one of the most magnificently-appointed establishments in America." As would befit a Lorillard, George seemed to have spared "no pains or expense."

And with Hall of Fame trainer Wyndham Walden at the helm, Westbrook sent winners to the races, important winners. In addition to its record five consecutive Preaknesses, Westbrook won four consecutive Hopeful Stakes and three consecutive Dixie Stakes. It won five editions (nonconsecutive) of the Vernal Stakes and four Juvenile Stakes. Duke of Magenta alone earned George the trophies for the Preakness, Travers, Sequel, Kenner, and Harding Stakes; the Withers, Belmont, Jerome, and Annual Stakes; the Dixie; and the Breckenridge—all in 1878, when he won eleven of twelve starts. It was a season the National Museum of Racing and Hall of Fame, many decades later, would laud as "one of the most prolific 3-year-old campaigns in the history of the American turf."

Competitive, wealthy, willing to commit to the highest level of excellence in the creation of an outstanding thoroughbred stable, George Lorillard possessed every quality needed to challenge his brother for decades, with one tragic exception. It was George's health, in the form of a painful rheumatic condition already affecting the younger Lorillard, which would one day cut short the sibling rivalry that drove both brothers to greatness on the turf.

CHAPTER 5

Working Men

William Walker . . . a son of slaves . . . was born in 1860 in Woodford County, Kentucky, the records disagreeing on whether it was at John Harper's Nantura Stud or on Abe Buford's Bosque Bonita Farm. Billy was already riding at Jerome Park by the time he was eleven . . . and he claimed a stakes victory at thirteen.
  —THE GREAT BLACK JOCKEYS BY EDWARD HOTALING

WHILE THE LORILLARDS, FRANK HARPER, AND THEIR MAGNIFICENT thoroughbreds were the unquestioned stars of the Great Sweepstakes, victory would ultimately depend upon others. Thoroughbreds, after all, do not prepare themselves for a race, cannot care for the injuries they sustain, do not ride themselves, and are incapable of plotting their own strategies for victory. These functions are performed by specialists. By working men.

Some of the most capable trainers and jockeys of the era worked on a daily basis with the three equine superstars that would duel for supremacy in the Great Sweepstakes. Others, while garnering fewer headlines, were every bit as important as their better-known allies and competitors.

THE TRAINERS

R. Wyndham Walden

The conditioner of huge Tom Ochiltree for George Lorillard, Robert Wyndham Walden was among the most successful thoroughbred trainers of the nineteenth century.

Though Walden was but thirty-four years of age at the time of the Great Sweepstakes, he had already trained Tom Ochiltree to victory in the Preakness. In a career that was to last thirty-one years, his trainees would win the Maryland classic a total of seven times, more than any other conditioner in the race's 139-year history. Five of his Preakness victories, all with runners owned by George Lorillard, were consecutive. He would also win four Belmont Stakes and two editions of the Travers, among 101 credited stakes victories, this in a time when the racing season was far less extensive than today's, and travel between race meetings far more difficult.

Walden was portrayed in a *Turf, Field and Farm* cover photo as a bald-headed but elegant-looking older gentleman with deep-set eyes, a white walrus mustache, and a diamond horseshoe-shaped tie pin. He was born in 1843 into a racing family; his father was a trainer, and Jeter Walden, one of his brothers, conditioned 1877 Preakness winner Cloverbrook, the first Maryland-bred to win the state's premier race. Walden's son, Rob, sent out three Preakness starters, and served for years as a high-ranking administrator for the Maryland Jockey Club.

Walden began as an exercise rider for his father's stable and then, following an apprenticeship period, was promoted to journeyman jockey. As with so many in his profession during this era, he turned to training when weight gain terminated his riding career. Walden evolved the use of interval training—the use of leisurely gallops, interspersed with brisk walks and short, speedy sprints—to keep a runner prepared.

It was during the prerace tumult at Pimlico that Walden noticed a persistent cough emanating from Tom Ochiltree's stall, a circumstance he duly reported to his employer, George Lorillard. Today, a horse as valuable as Tom Ochiltree would be instantly withdrawn from the race, prescribed antibiotics, and sent to the sidelines, but "Prince George" insisted that his big colt remain in the race. The conversation would one day become known to the public, and would provoke controversy in the days following the Great Sweepstakes.

Harry Colston

A younger, less experienced, less publicized trainer at the time of the Great Sweepstakes, Colston conditioned Ten Broeck, the best-known thoroughbred in America, under the close scrutiny of an owner whose ideas regarding the appropriate regimen for the Kentucky crack may have differed substantially from those of the horse's official trainer.

Colston might have been among the more intriguing personalities involved in the Great Sweepstakes, but he worked during an era when trainers, with the exception of a handful of high-profile conditioners such as Walden, were practically unknown by the press, their names not even included in the official race charts. Rather than seek out Colston for their pre- and postrace interviews, reporters flocked to the side of the great horse's owner, the hard-bitten, cantankerous Frank Harper, and his rider, the quotable William Walker. Colston's fascinating story seldom appears in the press; his likeness, unlike those of competing trainers Walden and William Brown, is not seen in the newspapers.

For a young African American such as Colston to be the trainer of the great Ten Broeck might have implied a connection to the Harper family, and one newspaper account claimed that a slave named Charles Colston, possibly Harry's uncle, had long used a large sycamore tree as his "place of refuge" at Nantura. This is, however, not the only possible explanation for Colston's occupying so important a place in Ten Broeck's entourage at so young an age. Harper was well known for his tight-fisted approach to every penny, and it is equally possible that Colston was simply willing to work cheap and follow orders.

While Colston was nominally the trainer of Ten Broeck, however, it was Frank Harper, who preferred that his great horse be worked out sparingly before a race, who may have controlled the training regimen for the son of Phaeton. This would have been decidedly in opposition to the strenuous work that was routine for Ten Broeck's Great Sweepstakes adversaries under trainers William Brown and R. Wyndham Walden. This did not escape the notice of the racing press.

After Ten Broeck's retirement, it was noted that the great thoroughbred had often raced "high in flesh"—the word in common usage today might be "flabby"—because of undertraining, and, oddly, the individual most often assigned the responsibility for Ten Broeck's conditioning issues was not his trainer, Colston, but Harper. Even the *Kentucky Live Stock Record*, generally supportive of Harper and Ten Broeck, admitted after Ten Broeck's death that his seven defeats "were owing to a want of condition."

This would have substantial implications for Ten Broeck's chances in the Great Sweepstakes, and a catastrophic impact on those who wagered on the entrant from the Bluegrass. As we approach Ten Broeck's performance on October 24, 1877, we should bear in mind as one of the important factors affecting the race's outcome that as Tom Ochiltree and Parole were receiving rigorous workouts in preparation for the contest, Ten Broeck's possibly overconfident owner was insisting on a less intensive training approach as the likeliest path to victory.

William Brown

A Canadian by birth, the trainer for Pierre Lorillard at the time of the Great Sweepstakes, William Brown, was responsible for the conditioning of Lorillard's four-year-old gelding, Parole.

Unlike so many of the trainers in this saga, Brown did not begin his career as a jockey. He entered the racing game instead by finding his way into the employ of legendary racing man Richard Ten Broeck, serving as his agent, stable foreman, and trainer.

This created a unique opportunity for Brown, who learned the fine points of racing over a stretch of seventeen years from one of the game's true insiders. Unfortunately, employment by Ten Broeck also included a downside: Brown's employer was an unrepentant gambler who would occasionally hand his trainer an IOU rather than a paycheck. And thus it was that on December 9, 1864, as Brown prepared to depart for new opportunities in America, Richard Ten Broeck could reimburse only a small fraction of the sum still owed his trainer, who was asked to trust that the note on an outstanding balance that was both substantial and by no means guaranteed would eventually be paid:

> Brown, I owe you over $6,000 and here is $500 on account; now if you keep still about it I will some day pay you the balance.

Rather amazingly, Brown would one day receive a draft for the outstanding amount. By this time, however, his reputation had landed him employment with the Morris family, which was soon to become a major force in the sport. Brown would spend ten years with the Morrises, conditioning a string of successful runners.

It was in 1875 that Brown left the Morrises to train the Rancocas Stable of Pierre Lorillard. Brown placed a condition on joining Rancocas, however; he would accept Lorillard's "princely offer" only if the tobacco magnate obtained some of the better Morris horses. Lorillard proceeded to purchase the Morris two-year-olds, procuring the services of a trainer who believed in the value of regular, daily work, regardless of weather. The Lorillard horses thrived under his regimen.

Pictures of Brown depict a decidedly good-looking and well-dressed man, with a wide mustache, muttonchop whiskers and a goatee, deep-set eyes, and a serious demeanor. Brown was noted for his direct, bluff manner, as reflected in a conversation that took place after Lorillard's filly, Faithless, won the 1875 Juvenile Stakes. Seeking out Brown, the owner bragged that he had won $17,000 wagering on the former Morris runner. Brown, who had been less than certain that the filly was ready for a top effort, replied, "You were darned lucky."

Nor was Brown above turning his bluntness on himself. When Parole unexpectedly lost the Westchester Cup, Lorillard, who as usual had wagered on the gelding, rushed to his trainer, demanding, "Brown, what was the matter with Parole? Somebody must have got at him last night and poisoned him!" Brown accepted full responsibility for the loss, citing an overly aggressive prerace workout: "Poison be damned; that two miles in the mud the other morning in 3:47 is what poisoned him."

Brown was reputed to be a sagacious wagerer, which could be useful to those able to pry information from the tight-lipped conditioner. At Saratoga in 1869, a down-on-his-luck old-timer asked one of the Morrises about the chances of the filly Remorseless in the Flash Stakes. "A good chance," was the reply. "Brown is going to bet $50 on her." A bet of this magnitude by Brown was treated as practically a guarantee of victory, and the gentleman wagered with confidence. Remorseless scampered home in front.

It was Brown who had said "yes" when street urchin William Barrett turned up at Rancocas one day looking for work. The trainer soon had

Barrett on horseback, and barely three years after Brown hired the skinny teenager as a stable lad, Barrett was aboard Parole as Pierre Lorillard's entrant went postward for the Great Sweepstakes.

Jacob Pincus

One of the advantages of being a wealthy, high-profile thoroughbred owner in the mold of a Pierre Lorillard is the ability to hire the best trainers in the business to supervise your livestock. One of those he deemed worthy of conditioning his runners was Jacob Pincus.

Born in Baltimore in 1833 (or perhaps it was 1838), Pincus was riding successfully at Charleston and New Orleans by the time was fourteen, and soon thereafter was booting home winners for the rich and famous at Saratoga. From there, Pincus's story becomes a familiar one: He soon outgrew his first profession, and as his mounts and riding fees diminished, he transitioned to the ranks of trainers.

Pincus found his opportunity in the stable of August Belmont, whose three-year-old colt Fenian would win the third edition of the race named for his owner in 1869, and in the process place the name "Pincus" among the sport's leading trainers (it is Fenian's likeness that stands atop the modern-day Belmont Stakes trophy). Training a Belmont Stakes winner, even in those long-ago days—Fenian earned $3,850 for his victory—was not an altogether negative start to a training career, and Jacob Pincus went on from there.

Pincus would not join the Lorillard stable until 1880, however, and thus had none but a rooting interest in the Great Sweepstakes. But his association with Pierre Lorillard would bring international racing immortality to both men.

Matthew Byrnes

Another late arrival to the burgeoning Rancocas operation, the Irish-born Matthew Byrnes was yet another who began as a jockey and outgrew the profession. He was good enough to have ridden such top thoroughbreds as Glenelg and Kingfisher before weight gain took its inevitable toll. Byrnes trained Parole during the gelding's later years, but was employed elsewhere when the Lorillard star matched strides with Ten Broeck and

Tom Ochiltree. Before his training career ended, he would condition some of the most revered thoroughbreds ever to compete in America.

THE JOCKEYS

George Barbee

Born in the early 1850s in Norwich, England, by 1865 George Barbee was a stable boy for trainer Tom Jennings Sr. One can imagine that the typical teenage lad apprenticed to racing trainers in 1865 spent considerable portions of his day shoveling equine excrement, but Jennings must have observed something special in Barbee, for by 1866 the youngster was exercising the great Gladiateur, which a year earlier had won the 2,000 Guineas, Epsom Derby, and St. Leger Stakes, sweeping the English Triple Crown. By 1872, Barbee was one of the top jockeys in England.

Barbee was described by one observer of the 1870s turf scene as "one of the most muscular and powerful jockeys that ever wore silk. He is built like a gladiator." This author went on to note that:

> *The size and power of his bicep muscle is tremendous; as a consequence his whipping is very severe. In 1874 Springbok became so savage that no one could ride him until Barbee was put up, and one stroke of the whip was such the horse never forgot. His potent whip was the only means of conquering the savage [horse] Uncas.*

The whip rider has always been a lamented but tolerated part of the racing game. During the 1890s, newspapers described the unstinting battering the great sprinter Domino received during his races from jockey Fred Taral, and of Domino's resultant hatred for his rider. Citing William Robertson in *The History of Thoroughbred Racing in America*:

> *[Young jockey Foxhall Keene] once volunteered to ride Domino because regular jockey Fred Taral had whipped the colt so unmercifully that Domino hated the sight of him, and a blanket had to be thrown over Domino's head before Taral could mount.*

But Barbee was known for more than merely pummeling his mounts. He was considered a fine judge of pace and an unequaled finisher, particularly on late-charging older horses such as his mount in the Great Sweepstakes, Tom Ochiltree.

Barbee had initially journeyed to America in 1872, riding for J. F. Chamberlain, who would shortly purchase the yearling Tom Ochiltree from the Woodburn Stable. While the young jockey did not meet with immediate success, he scored some notable victories the following year, including the first Preakness, aboard Chamberlain's colt Survivor. Barbee's 10-length margin of victory in that first Preakness stood as the race's greatest for 132 years, until Smarty Jones won by 11½ lengths in 2004. His three Preakness victories were not surpassed until 1951, when Eddie Arcaro won his fourth aboard Bold.

By 1874, Pierre Lorillard had purchased his services, possibly after the inimitable Fred Archer elected to remain in England rather than join the Rancocas contingent. It was Barbee in the saddle when Lorillard's Saxon won the 1874 Belmont Stakes, Barbee who pushed Attila to Lorillard's first Travers victory.

He continued as a leading rider in 1875, winning another Travers aboard D'Artagnan, although not for Lorillard, and in 1876 accepted the position of lead rider in the stable of Pierre's brother George, who also permitted him to ride for other owners. Barbee crisscrossed the country to accept stakes engagements as far away as California, winning twenty-eight of his ninety-five starts in 1877—an outstanding 29.5 percent.

Near the end of the 1877 season, however, Barbee was involved in a racing scandal that would lead to his suspension from the sport.

The race in question occurred nearly two weeks prior to the Great Sweepstakes, on October 13, 1877. Barbee was aboard a runner named Piper Hiedsieck that had previously been known as Auburn. Piper's ownership was problematic: In the season's early days he had been known as "Crouse's Auburn," then on August 29 became "Barbee's Auburn," a designation that remained in effect until October 5, when the three-year-old became "Drennan's Piper Hiedsieck." The horse was notably unsuccessful under the latter name, finishing ninth under another rider in a minor race at Jerome Park, then fourth at the same venue, this time with Barbee in the saddle.

On October 13, just hours after Tom Ochiltree defeated Parole and six others in Jerome Park's All-Aged Stakes, the thoroughbred now known as Piper Hiedsieck, still listed as belonging to Drennan, and an otherwise nondescript steed known as Longstaff's W.I. Higgins came onto the track for a one-mile match race. The on-track bookmakers favored W.I. Higgins at $100 to $60, and he delivered, outfinishing Piper Hiedsieck by a head. But now trouble began for nearly everyone involved.

Even the *New York Times*, not usually attuned to the minutiae of stable whisperings, caught wind of the stench emanating from this race, noting on October 16 that "there appears to be some scandal attached to the match race between Higgins and Piper Hiedsieck which was run at Jerome Park on Saturday last. Piper Hiedsieck was the favorite in the poolrooms at $100 to $25, and the slow time of the race opened the eyes of turfmen to the fact that something was wrong. It seems to be a case worthy of investigation."

Indeed. The radical difference between the "poolroom" odds heavily favoring Hiedsieck and the on-track odds favoring Higgins suggested that some form of odds manipulation was taking place, and the race's pathetically slow time of 1:56¾, on a day when conditions were "weather fine, track good," would have added to suspicions that the race might not be on the up-and-up. Lady Salyers, a decent but not star-quality mare, had raced a mile at Jerome Park earlier that day in 1:47; the stakes horse Barricade had run the distance in 1:54—but carrying 159½ pounds, nearly 50 more than Hiedsieck.

An investigation was practically mandatory under these circumstances, and one was conducted. The results were reflected in a revision to the race's official chart, which now read: "Nearly a month after the race, it was investigated by the Executive Committee of the American Jockey Club, when Longstaff, Drennon, and Barbee were expelled."

Barbee's suspension was a harsh one—his name appears nowhere in the racing records for 1878 and is absent for much of 1879. But although the Piper Hiedsieck Affair, as it came to be called, occurred prior to the

Great Sweepstakes, its suspensions would not apply to the race. Barbee would retain the mount on Tom Ochiltree.

On October 24, 1877, then, Barbee was in his prime and unquestionably one of the most successful jockeys in the nation. During discussions of Tom Ochiltree's chances against Ten Broeck and Parole in the Great Sweepstakes, it is likely that the phrase, "and he'll have Barbee in the saddle," would have arisen frequently, as a positive inducement to wager on the big son of Lexington and his powerful jockey.

William Barrett

Born in 1859 in Kinsale, County Cork, Ireland, William Barrett overcame a rough-and-tumble childhood to find himself aboard Parole in one of the most talked-about races of the era.

The son of a buyer for a large dry-goods establishment, Barrett's early childhood was a comfortable, middle-class existence. With his father's unexpected death, however, came poverty, and with the Barrett family's dissolution, young William was soon homeless and in desperate circumstances. Somehow finding the money for passage across the cold Atlantic Ocean, Barrett "knocked about New York for some time in a very humble capacity till the late Mr. William Brown, trainer for Mr. P. Lorillard's horses, took him under his protection."

This was to prove a stroke of amazing good fortune for the youngster, who in 1874 began employment as a fifteen-year-old stable lad at Pierre Lorillard's sprawling Rancocas Stud. Brown's gruff but patient style apparently worked wonders for the teenager, whose determined attitude appealed to the trainer. Even more important, Brown quickly observed that Barrett possessed "considerable aptitude in riding and handling horses."

Barrett's untutored skill on horseback must have been immense, for the youngster rapidly graduated from the stall-mucking and hot-walking pursuits of most stablehands, and was soon riding in races for Rancocas. He made his first appearance under silks at Saratoga on July 31, 1875, and won his first stakes race later that year, defeating, among others, a Pierre Lorillard runner named Parole. Barrett, still just sixteen years of age, could ride at seventy-five pounds, ensuring that he would receive many riding opportunities, aboard Rancocas runners and others.

One source close to the Rancocas operation described Barrett's riding skills:

> *For so youthful a jockey he had great patience, and could ride a waiting race to perfection. . . . His 'set-to' in a finish was not especially vigorous, but his overhand whipping, for one so apparently delicate, was very effective.*

By 1876, Barrett was Lorillard's number-two rider behind Dan Sparling, and with second choice of the Rancocas horses (and the occasional mount on other stables' runners), he closed the year with a record of five wins from thirty-two starters. It was a fine apprentice year for a seventeen-year-old who two years earlier might have harbored doubts as to which end of a horse bit and which end kicked. Barrett accompanied the Lorillard string to Kentucky in spring of 1876, but was on the sidelines observing Sparling when an unacclimated Parole ran fourth in the Derby.

By 1877, riding for both Lorillard brothers, Barrett had supplanted Sparling as lead jockey and was winning substantial numbers of races for Pierre and Brown, including the prestigious Withers Stakes aboard Bombast, the Juvenile Stakes on Perfection, and the Woodburn Stakes aboard Parole. Barrett's masterful victory aboard the filly Zoo-Zoo in the West End Hotel Stakes, accomplished in a driving thunderstorm, gained him substantial praise. So popular a rider was Barrett that one source suggested he "could have had a mount in almost every race for which he could ride the weights."

But here was the problem: weight. The muscular Barbee had reached the 110 pounds at which he would ride for the rest of his career, and the waifish William Walker would never struggle to make weight. But Barrett harbored a secret that would profoundly affect the remainder of his career: He was still growing, gaining weight at a worrisome rate. And while this would not affect the rider's performance in the Great Sweepstakes, it would have a profound impact on what remained of his life.

William Walker

Born the son of slaves as the bitterly divided nation contemplated war in 1860, Walker probably came into the world at Nantura, but may have been born at Abe Buford's nearby Bosque Bonita Farm. He was a top rider while still in his teens, leading the Churchill Downs meeting in the autumn of 1875 and the spring campaigns at the Kentucky track between 1876 and 1878. As he climbed aboard the great Ten Broeck at Pimlico, lining up alongside the older George Barbee and William Barrett, Walker was a youthful but accomplished rider of great promise, with a Kentucky Derby victory already to his credit.

Walker's 1877 Derby win had been earned aboard Baden-Baden, a long shot trained by Hall of Famer Ed Brown, also an African American, who was known by the nickname Brown Dick. The trainer had advised Walker that Baden-Baden was overmatched against the other top runners in the field, most notably the highly regarded Vera Cruz, future two-mile record holder McWhirter, and Frank Harper's promising Early Light. It must have seemed daunting to a youngster who was probably still just sixteen.

But the diminutive black jockey allowed his mount to pursue race favorite Leonard, then charged furiously past the leader to capture the trophy, with Leonard second, King William third, and Vera Cruz, which had broken behind the field, fourth under famed African-American jockey Isaac Murphy. Following the race, Walker was presented a purse as the "best behaved jockey on the track," which today seems an odd tribute for a young man who has just ridden a Derby winner. As we will shortly see, however, jockey fees in those days were decidedly penurious. Even a slightly insulting bonus for "good behavior" would have been welcome.

Walker's life as a horseman had begun "as soon as he could walk." He doubtless spent his early years performing the menial but necessary tasks that even today consume a significant portion of the lives of those who tend to horses. He would have acquired an intimate knowledge of the use of pitchforks and shovels, of the odor of equine excrement.

But at some point in his childhood, Walker must have snuck onto the bare back of a Nantura thoroughbred, and thrilled to the power of the half-ton beast beneath him. The rest, as they say, is history. Walker demonstrated qualities that made him special among those toiling at Nantura: He was bright; he was strong; he followed instructions; and he had an unmistakable talent as a rider. Soon, Walker was riding professionally, winning for the first time as an eleven-year-old at the Lexington Association track. At age thirteen, in 1873, he won his first stakes races.

Riding fees for beginning jockeys in the 1870s were determined by the owners for whom they rode. Walker's earliest victories probably earned him little more than room and board; his Derby victory aboard Baden-Baden brought him only $50 of the $3,300 winning purse. Even as a journeyman, Walker received a monthly retainer of just $15, close to the maximum that could be expected by a top jockey, from owner Dan Swigert. Even for Walker's most lucrative victory, aboard Ten Broeck in his 1878 race with the California mare Mollie McCarthy, Frank Harper elected to pay Walker only the customary riding fee, keeping for himself nearly the entire $10,000 winner's purse.

By the time Walker led Ten Broeck onto the track for the Great Sweepstakes, he was something of a wunderkind. As turf historian Betty Borries wrote, "Until Isaac Murphy's rise to fame, [Walker] was the leading American rider." For the penurious Frank Harper, the idea of having a jockey of this quality whose salary was entirely at the Kentuckian's option must have appealed mightily.

There was one potential concern regarding Walker, however. No one denied that he was a talented horseman, but compared to Barbee and Barrett he was decidedly lacking in experience. Walker simply had not ridden in as many races as his opponents, and as the jockey for Ten Broeck, who sometimes raced against the stopwatch rather than against other horses, some of Walker's rides would have required simply that he urge his mount along at a brisk pace, and hang on as the champion rampaged around the course.

Krik's Guide to the Turf, the most authoritative and comprehensive source of racing information during this period, can be used to re-create the level of riding experience for the three Great Sweepstakes jockeys. During the 1877 calendar year, there are 96 races in which the name "Barbee" is among the competing riders; 114 in which "Barrett" is a participant.

The corresponding number for "Walker" is 31.

One sees no discussion of Walker's comparative inexperience in the newspaper accounts leading up to the Great Sweepstakes, no concern expressed about his age. Walker's ability to compete against Barbee and Barrett is treated as a given; there is no apparent concern that a young-ster, even one of Walker's talent, might be manipulated into defeat by the more seasoned jockeys who would be piloting Ten Broeck's rivals.

Perhaps, given what was to follow, there should have been.

Chapter 6

The Buildup

Ten Broeck, Kentucky's mighty representative, is at Baltimore, taking daily gallops. Tom Ochiltree and Parole are also there.
—THE TURF, FIELD AND FARM, OCTOBER 19, 1877

THE BUILDUP TO THE TEN BROECK–TOM OCHILTREE–PAROLE CONfrontation was a lengthy one.

On October 18, 1876, more than a year before 1877's Great Sweepstakes, the *New York Times* had reported a telegraphic exchange between George Lorillard and General James F. Robinson, president of the Kentucky Association, representing "the friends of Ten Broeck" (i.e., representing Frank Harper) that read as follows:

Lexington, Ky.
To George Lorillard, New York:
The friends of Ten Broeck seeing by the Associated Press dispatches that you desire to match Tom Ochiltree against Ten Broeck in a four-mile dash, to be run in the Spring of 1877, have authorized me to say that such a match can be made if you will run over the Kentucky Association Course, for $10,000 or more, the parties here to allow you $1,000 to cover traveling expenses. The Kentucky Association will add one-half of the gate receipts of that day to the winning horse, and will extend to you a hearty welcome.
J.F. ROBINSON

Lorillard's response could not have been less encouraging. Tom Ochiltree was not coming to Kentucky. If a Ten Broeck–Tom Ochiltree race were to occur, Harper would need to bring his horse north:

New York
To Gen. James F. Robinson, President:
I have received your telegram. The Associated Press have mistaken my proposition. I offered, and still offer to match Tom Ochiltree the last day of the Baltimore Races, or the extra day of the Jerome Park Races in November, against Ten Broeck a four-mile dash for $10,000. American Jockey Club rules and new weights.
Yours truly, G.L. LORILLARD
Please answer by telegraph.

A northern journey, however, was not in Harper's plans:

Lexington, Ky.
To George Lorillard:
The race proposed by you is impossible. Ten Broeck is not in training. Should you desire to accept my proposition, or alter its terms to run over the Kentucky Association Course I shall be pleased to hear from you.
J.F. ROBINSON

General Robinson's response was notable primarily for its obvious disingenuousness. Ten Broeck out of training? He had shattered Fellowhood's four-mile record just three weeks earlier, on September 27. Even if Ten Broeck was not currently in training, why would this affect his condition for a race the following spring? If Ten Broeck's condition was at issue, why had Robinson offered the match? And why would it matter whether Lorillard would be willing "to run over the Kentucky Association Course"?

What is clear from the general's telegram is that Harper had not the slightest interest in confronting a runner of Tom Ochiltree's caliber at the big horse's preferred venue, Jerome Park, or on any terms dictated by

George Lorillard. This issue—whether Ten Broeck would travel north or one or more northern-based runners should journey south—would continue to delay any summit meeting of America's most illustrious thoroughbreds for another year.

The venue for such a race was not an insignificant issue. Rail travel in the 1870s could be grueling, and the horse(s) that undertook the seven-hundred-mile journey between New York and Lexington, or even the more than five hundred miles between Lexington and Baltimore—in either direction—would be at a substantial training disadvantage. They would be leaving behind familiar surroundings, familiar food and water, and contact with familiar humans.

There were also social and financial implications that would not have been lost on any of the negotiators, including the untutored but country wise Frank Harper. Eastern racing had been left unscathed by the Civil War's depredations, and tracks such as Jerome Park were thriving, attracting wealthy owners such as the Lorillards and their conspicuously consuming ilk of the East. Pimlico, located in Maryland, which did not secede despite its citizens' generally anti-Union sentiments, had survived the Civil War, had been remodeled as a luxurious home for racing, and was rapidly achieving the same patina of desirability. The nation's greatest newspapers were centered in the East, assuring maximum nationwide publicity for the race.

Kentucky racing, and, indeed, racing below the Mason-Dixon Line, retained its rich history, but some of its best horses and much of its splendor had been lost during the war. A race involving Tom Ochiltree and Parole, arguably the North's ranking thoroughbreds, and the already legendary Ten Broeck, staged in the Bluegrass, might accelerate the area's rebirth as a racing venue. For the Lorillards to bring their top thoroughbreds south, accompanied, of course, by their wealthy friends and fellow travelers, would provide a much-needed boost to the area's prestige, as well as its economy.

All of this, however, was rapidly becoming moot as 1876 neared its end and the telegraphic challenges continued to fly. With Frank Harper refusing to ship his champion north and the Lorillards equally insistent that Big Tom and little Parole would not travel south, there would be no confrontation during the remaining days of the centennial year.

With negotiations at a standstill over the winter and early spring, the *New York Times*, in its preview of the 1877 eastern spring/summer racing season, could only note that "[t]here is no four-year-old of recent years that has gone through a campaign with more brilliancy than Tom Ochiltree," and that among Tom's challengers would be "such good ones as . . . Parole." There was nary a mention of the possibility that the spring racing season might be highlighted by a challenge from Ten Broeck.

The *Times*'s exclusion of the Kentucky crack proved to be prescient. The powerful Tom Ochiltree swept before him the best of the eastern thoroughbreds, while Parole was clearly the second best of the easterners and Ten Broeck remained unconquerable racing over Kentucky soil. And as summer turned into autumn, and the Lorillards again turned up the pressure on Harper, speculation arose anew that the Kentuckian might finally send Ten Broeck north. As rumors flew, the *Times* proclaimed that "[t]he meeting of Ten Broeck, Whisper, Tom Ochiltree, and Parole in the Bowie Stakes, four-mile heats, would be the sensation of the year."

Was Harper going to relent? *Spirit of the Times* confirmed the following day that he had decided to bring Ten Broeck north—but confirmed it in a manner that was as confusing as it was hopeful. *Spirit* suggested to its readers, in the flowery prose typical of the era's sports pages, that Ten Broeck would shortly be on his way to Baltimore:

> *Despatches and letters from Kentucky assert that [Ten Broeck] will cross the mountains for the first time, and pick up the long cast gauntlet of the East, and measure lances with the long distance and fleetest flyers in this section. . . . Baltimore is to be congratulated.*

And in the same issue, it informed its readers that those wishing to attend Ten Broeck's next appearance should begin planning their journey—to Tennessee:

> *[T]he great Ten Broeck . . . will claim the Merchants' Stakes, two-mile heats, as his own. Mr. Harper must not flatter himself, however, that he can claim this prize without a stout fight, for Longbow, McWhirter, Joe Rhodes [sic], Courier, Bill Dillon, Largenteen [sic],*

and other good ones are in, and will not yield the palm of victory
without a struggle.

The Merchants' Stakes would be contested on October 16 in Nashville. L'Argenteen—*Spirit* neglected to include the apostrophe, also adding an "h" to Joe Rodes's name—would win the race's two-mile heats, each by a half-length, with Courier second in both heats, Lizzie Whipps third, and Longbow fourth in the first heat and distanced in the second.

By the date of the Merchants' Stakes, Ten Broeck, which during his lifetime would never set down a hoof in Tennessee, had been in Baltimore for days. On October 10, the *New York Times* reported that "Ten Broeck, Vera Cruz and King Faro left Louisville last night for Baltimore, where they are to appear in the coming meeting at that place." And by October 13, *Spirit of the Times* could inform its readers that Ten Broeck would shortly "be comfortably located at Pimlico."

To this point, discussion of Ten Broeck's engagements at the Maryland racetrack had centered around the Bowie Stakes at four-mile heats, in which he was formally entered by Harper before his train left Kentucky. The racing world anticipated that the Bowie would provide the stage for the long-awaited confrontation between Tom Ochiltree, Parole, and the brilliant Kentucky crack, with perhaps some of the East's other top thoroughbreds also in the mix.

Meeting Ten Broeck in the Bowie Stakes, however, was not what the Lorillard brothers had intended when they enticed Harper north. Any horseflesh other than Ten Broeck and their own thoroughbreds, they had decided, should be superfluous, and this should be assured through the scheduling of a unique race. Additional negotiations between the Lorillards, representatives of Harper, and the Pimlico brass were scheduled, an agreement to add a special event was reached, and with the next day's headline, the Bowie Stakes was rendered little more than an afterthought:

Extra Race at Baltimore

An extra race, a sweepstakes of two miles and a half, to be run on the
first day of the coming meeting, at Baltimore, has been opened, and
will close Oct. 20, at noon. The entrance fee is $500, p.p. [pay or play],

*and the added money will be $1,000, if Ten Broeck and either Tom
Ochiltree or Parole shall start, all three of whom are entered.*

Press coverage now began in earnest, and it was made instantly clear
which of the three entrants was the featured attraction, which were the
second bananas: "Ten Broeck, Kentucky's mighty representative, is at Baltimore, taking daily gallops. Tom Ochiltree and Parole are also there."

While Ten Broeck was the unquestioned star of the occasion, it was
generally conceded that Tom Ochiltree might be a worthy challenger
. . . and that Parole might not embarrass himself too badly: "Ochiltree
is a horse of fine size and finish, with an excellent way of going. In him
Ten Broeck will have an opponent worthy of his fame. . . . Parole . . . is
not believed to have been really fit at Jerome [a reference to his October 2 defeat by Ochiltree in Jerome Park's Grand National Stakes], and
it may be that he will be a much better horse at Baltimore. Time will
tell."

Waxing poetic, as was so often its wont, the *Turf, Farm and Field*
noted a stipulation that would become crucial as the Great Sweepstakes
approached:

*Fine weather and good track have been stipulated for by the gentlemen
controlling the horses. . . . October is commonly the finest month of the
year in and about [Baltimore], and nothing can excel the drive to the
course at Pimlico, through beautiful Druid Hill Park, with its rustling
leaves, chirping birds, and flitting sunshine and shadow.*

Ironically, it was a Kentucky-based publication, the *Kentucky Live Stock
Register*, that sounded the first ominous note regarding Ten Broeck—or
was it merely attempting to improve the odds on their choice, which had
opened at levels so low that early-arriving Kentuckians were expressing
outrage? Certainly, the *Register* appeared concerned: "If Ten Broeck is in
condition he will forever set at rest his superiority as a racehorse, but at
Louisville [he had won easily on October 1 and again three days later]
we did not like his condition he was coughing [*sic*] and to our eye looked
too low in flesh."

A cautionary note? Perhaps. *Spirit of the Times*, however, insisted that the Kentucky champion was

very fine, and showing his managers all they desire of him, a state of things hardly credible under all the circumstances. He must be a wonderful horse, if, so soon after his long journey, he is able to jump out and show his usual speed in his exercise.

The entry deadline was 12:00 noon on October 20, three days prior to the race's scheduled date, and no one was surprised to learn that the requisite forms, accompanied by drafts for $500, had been filed for Ten Broeck, Tom Ochiltree, and Parole. The Maryland Jockey Club would add $1,000 of its own, creating a total purse of $2,500. And the *New York Times* informed its readers that:

All three . . . are certain to start, if no accident happens. . . . The track is in splendid condition, and the attendance promises to be the largest ever witnessed on an American course.

But while the fevered anticipation of the October 23 race built, Kentuckians continued to express frustration regarding the odds offered on Ten Broeck. It would be unthinkable to travel hundreds of miles to wager on a horse race and then put one's wallet away, but while the visitors were vocal in agreeing that the race would be "certainly . . . the most important that has ever happened," they also seemed dismayed at their treatment by the Baltimore bookmakers:

The backers of Ten Broeck . . . are not taking him so heavily as has been supposed, the reason being that the odds asked on him are too heavy. Plenty of turfites make it a practice just now of remarking, "I guess I won't buy Ten Broeck in the pools—because if I win I won't get legal interest." . . . Perhaps when the day comes around they will change their minds.

That day would not, however, be October 23. The evening before the race's scheduled date, rains began soaking the track. The owners had specified that the Maryland Jockey Club's Executive Committee would determine whether the track qualified as "good," and on the morning of the twenty-third the members of that august body, after examining the track surface, declared that "although the disappointment [would be] very generally and keenly felt . . . the track as influenced by the rains . . . did not fill the requirements of the match," which was duly postponed until the twenty-fourth.

Or so went the official announcement. An important meeting between the owners, however, had preceded the Jockey Club's visit to trackside, and a separate agreement had been made. And as a result, the Executive Committee's decision would be based on more than merely an objective examination of moisture on the track surface. As the *Baltimore Sun* reported:

> *Sunday night's heavy rain left the course rather wet on Monday morning, but the strong wind prevailing all day and the bright sunshine quickly restored it. Mr. P[ierre] Lorillard . . . asked for a postponement of the race until to-morrow. . . . This was objected to by Mr. J.T. Williams, who was also on the ground representing Mr. F.B. Harper, owner of Ten Broeck. . . . Mr. Lorillard then offered Mr. Williams $500 to postpone the race, in order to secure his object. Mr. Williams agreed to the offer, and the matter was referred to the executive committee of the Maryland Jockey Club. Their decision was that the track was . . . in every respect such a course as had been stipulated in the original terms . . . but as Mr. Lorillard had put his request so forcibly, and was suggested [sic] by the true instincts of a sportsman, they would consent to the postponement, which was ordered.*

And thus it was that on a day described in the official charts as "[w]eather clear and cold, track stiff and heavy," on which the Executive Committee of the Maryland Jockey Club had determined that the track conditions were in keeping with the owners' agreement, the race anticipated as "[one of] the greatest events that have come off on the American

turf during the past decade" was postponed on the basis of a $500 pay-
ment from one of the nation's wealthiest businessmen to the man representing his entrant's most dangerous opponent.

For Lorillard, the postponement was a strategic masterstroke. A race
contested over a "stiff and heavy" surface would have forced his entrant,
the late-running Parole, to pursue his rivals through an avalanche of flying mud, while the slop-loving Ten Broeck would have a favorably muddy
surface to navigate. Pierre's $500 had purchased for Parole the possibility
that twenty-four hours of sun and breeze might help dry out a sloppy
track surface that would, on October 23, have seriously compromised the
gelding's chances.

And this is precisely what happened. The conditions on October 24
would be "weather fine, track fair, not good"—but "fair, not good" would
be less troubling for Parole than "stiff and heavy." The racing world already
knew from long experience how loudly money could speak, but Lorillard's
purchase of an improved track surface for the modest sum of $500 repre-
sented a new and improved version of the Power of the Purse. Pierre had
also demonstrated how persuasive the entreaties of an older brother could
be. "The owners of Ten Broeck and Ochiltree were willing to run," but
Pierre, with his powerful checkbook and his ability to invoke his younger
brother's family loyalty, found the means to gain that all-important extra
day.

A postponement was certainly not what racing-mad Baltimore had
had in mind. As the *Louisville Courier-Journal* would pun in its commentary, "Unfortunately, some of the interest in to-morrow's sport, [was]
somewhat dampened by the postponement." Perhaps the odds on Ten
Broeck fell even farther, in recognition of his prowess on muddy tracks; by
October 23 the wagering pools reflected Ten Broeck at $50, Tom Ochil-
tree at $25, and Parole at $15, which would provide to Ten Broeck's backers, if he won, a return of less than $2 for each dollar wagered. Even given
Ten Broeck's assumed superiority as a racer, this was hardly an attractive
wagering proposition for a horse that just two weeks earlier had undergone a bumpy five-hundred-mile rail journey.

Despite the postponement, Pimlico presented racing on October 23,
and it was the Kentucky contingent that scored first blood, with a victory

in the Dixie Stakes by King Faro that sent his jubilant backers swarming toward the "corsairs"—the bookmakers—in their enclosure. The next race featured George Lorillard's two-year-old Duke of Magenta, who earned an easy victory in the $2,300 Central Stakes with William Barrett in the irons. Now it was the locals who stampeded toward the bookmakers.

The final event of the day, a $700 contest at two-mile heats, included Pierre's Barricade and George's Ambush. Both were well regarded by the bettors, but it would be the 1876 Belmont Stakes winner, Algerine, who posed in the winner's enclosure. Algerine was owned by Major Thomas W. Doswell, who, following his service in the Confederate Army, had rushed back to his Bullfield Farm in Virginia to return to the breeding of fast horses. Prior to the war, Doswell had raced a number of sterling thorough-breds, including Planet, likely the best thoroughbred of the pre–Civil War era.

With their bets cashed and the abbreviated racing day completed, many in the crowd likely glanced skyward as they exited Pimlico's con-fines. Would the clear weather of October 23 continue through the next day, enabling Ten Broeck to match strides with the stars of the two Loril-lard stables, or would the rains return, again washing out the long-awaited equine showdown? Perhaps, before leaving Pimlico, some might also have observed the *New York Times*'s reporter peering closely at the track and jotting in his notebook the words that the nation would read the next day: "The track . . . dried very rapidly under a bright sun and gentle breeze from the south-west."

The track would continue to dry, and the Maryland Jockey Club, the following day, would make a positive certification. Pierre Lorillard would be writing no more drafts to Frank Harper. Under partly cloudy skies on October 24, before an overflow crowd that would include much of the Congress of the United States of America, Ten Broeck, Tom Ochiltree, and Parole would contest the Great Sweepstakes of 1877.

CHAPTER 7

The Great Sweepstakes

The third race was the greatest event that has ever been seen on the American turf. . . . It is beyond the descriptive powers of the most facile pen to present any idea of the scene that ensued.
—BALTIMORE AMERICAN AND COMMERCIAL ADVERTISER,
OCTOBER 25, 1877

AND SO THE TWENTY-FOURTH OF OCTOBER DAWNED, AND ONE CAN imagine each of the individuals involved in the Great Sweepstakes—the Lorillard brothers and their entourages, Frank Harper and his friends and representatives, the trainers, the jockeys, the Maryland Jockey Club members, the bookmakers, the senators and congressmen, the hangers-on, and those who merely wanted to see a great horse race—awakening and peering hopefully out their windows. We can picture them all, observing with a relieved sense of anticipation that the morning sun shone clearly through a few scattered clouds. We can feel their realization that today, at last, they would be witnessing the legendary Ten Broeck defending his own honor and that of his owner, his state, and his region, against the best runners in the North.

As the *New York Times* proclaimed, "A more beautiful day for the races at Pimlico could not have been desired." And as the sun began its slow journey across the sky, a trickle of vehicles could already be seen streaming toward Pimlico, striving, with a determination that persists in the American consciousness some fourteen decades later, to beat the traffic.

Those who arrived early were well served. Baltimore's hotels and boardinghouses, bursting at the seams with travelers from every point on the compass, had begun disgorging racegoers shortly after dawn. Pimlico's attendance for the day would never be officially announced, but veteran racegoers estimated that it surely exceeded twenty thousand.

Those fortunate enough to be at Pimlico for Great Sweepstakes Day were a combination of the common and the elite, with the latter especially well represented, helping to comprise:

> *the grandest gathering of notable people seen on an American race-course for many a year. There must have been a thousand in the New York delegation alone, and Kentucky, Ohio, Virginia, Louisiana, Tennessee and other States sent full complements of their sport-loving sons. . . . Grave Senators and dignified representatives of foreign governments went arm in arm along the quarter-stretch, while thousands of beautiful ladies graced the balconies of the club-house.*

The first field of horses stepped onto the track at 1:00 p.m., and the response was a deafening roar, reflecting both the heightened interest in the day's festivities and the hopeful optimism implicit in having one's own money riding on the outcome. This first event, however, was not the Great Sweepstakes. Racetrack operators had known for decades that, for reasons both artistic and financial, the most prestigious race on any day should be run near the conclusion of the program, never at its beginning, when anticipation is still on the rise, when late-comers are still arriving, and when the amount available to be wagered is therefore not yet at its maximum. There would be four races on the October 24 program. The Great Sweepstakes would be the third.

Many in the crowd had already wagered on the featured race, in pool halls and "commission houses" (bookie joints), and with private book-makers and with one another, but those who had not yet done so could now brave the enormous crowd's jostling and bumping, dodging pick-pockets and touts and, in some anxious cases, constituents, on their scur-rying way into Pimlico's betting areas. The bookmakers were organizing the wagering into betting pools, in accordance with complex mathematical formulas that guaranteed to them a predetermined percentage of each dollar wagered.

History has long forgotten the results of those first two races, and for good reason; they were unimportant contests involving horses of little interest whose primary claim to fame was their participation on the program highlighted by Ten Broeck and his rivals. It is worth noting, however, that both were won by runners among the wagering favorites, which created even more back-and-forth struggles for racegoers seeking to collect their winnings and wager additional funds on the Great Sweepstakes.

In the uncomplicated format of the era's sporting newspapers, the complete results of the preliminary races were as follows:

SECOND DAY, OCT. 24—Weather fine, track fair, not good. Purse $300, for all ages: to carry 105 lbs; winners after September 29, 1877, extra; one mile; $250, $50.

G.L. Lorillard's. . . Idalia, 3 yrs, 102 lbs . . . . Costello 1

Medinger's . . . . First Chance, 6 yrs, 102 lbs . . Richardson 2

Smythe's . . . . Madge, 6 yrs, 102 lbs . . . . Sparling 3

Kennon's . . . . Waco, 4 yrs, 102 lbs. . . . . McLaughlin . . . 0

Smythe's . . . . Explosion, 4 yrs, 101 lbs. . . . . Spillman. 0

Bell's . . . . Fugitive, 4 yrs, 102 lbs. . . . . . Evans. 0

Gillespie's. . . . . Patriot, 4 yrs, 102 lbs . . . . Miller. 0

Ayers'. . . . . Frederickstown, 4 yrs,
103 3¾ lbs
(including 3¾ lbs over). . . . . . Booth 0

Longstaff's. . . . . . . Yorkshire Lass, 4 yrs, 102 lbs .Hughes 0

Harbeck, Jr.'s . . . . . Bertram, 4 yrs, 105 lbs. . . . . . Donohue. 0

Doswell's. . . . . King Bolt, 6 yrs, 105 lbs. . . . . Fisher 0

Time: 1:45¾
Bertram the favorite, Idalia second choice. The latter won by two lengths, King Bolt and Bertram failing to get away at the start.

Same Day—Purse and Stake: a handicap for all ages; mile and three-quarters; $475, $50.

Carr & Co.'s . . . . . Viceroy, 4 yrs, 109 lbs . . . . Hughes 1
Bowie's . . . . Mary, 4 yrs, 98 lbs . . . . Barrett 2
Davis & Co.'s . . . Kenney, 4 yrs, 104 lbs . . . . . . Spillman 3
McDaniel's . . . . . . Lady Salyers, 3 yrs, 96 lbs . . . Donohue 0
Doswell's . . . . King Bolt, 6 yrs, 105 lbs . . . . . Fisher 0

Time: 3:11
Viceroy the choice and winner by a length.

There was a decided oddity in these two races, as King Bolt started poorly and finished last in the first race, then returned to finish last again in the second. After having failed to break with his field the first time, perhaps King Bolt had been pulled up by jockey Fisher, then deemed sufficiently rested an hour later to race again.

It was shortly before three o'clock that the sound of a bell echoed through the Pimlico grounds, followed almost instantly by an immense roar from the grandstand as Parole, led by jockey William Barrett in the Rancocas Stable's familiar cherry and black silks, pranced nervously onto the track. Barrett, perhaps startled by the wall of sound emanating from the grandstand, stared momentarily into the huge crowd, then mounted and galloped the restive Parole away from the din, onto the less clangorous backstretch.

A few moments later Tom Ochiltree, accompanied by jockey George Barbee in the orange and blue silks of owner George Lorillard, "danced into the middle of the track and cut up all sorts of didos while the people fairly howled." The cheer from Parole's backers had been loud, but more money had been wagered on Big Tom, and the sound that greeted him was at a level seldom heard at Pimlico. Barbee recognized that the best place for Ochiltree would be on the backstretch, and Big Tom joined Parole there for his prerace warmup.

And now, to the loudest explosion of noise yet, a blast of sound that included a profusion of war whoops from the Kentuckians, Ten Broeck emerged from near the clubhouse and stepped onto the track, riderless but wearing a blanket over his withers. Jockey William Walker, clad in Nantura's orange silks and red cap, accompanied his mount, with trainer

Harry Colston holding Ten Broeck's reins and leading the Kentucky champion.

The Ten Broeck contingent sauntered past the frenzied crowd, which by now was approaching delirium. Walker and Colston casually acknowledged the cheers with waves and a tip of Walker's cap, Ten Broeck a half-ton bundle of pent-up energy prancing behind them, as "[f]air women waved their handkerchiefs and fairly threw kisses to the gallant son of imported Phaeton. Men shouted themselves hoarse and brandished hats and canes until the grouped mass of humanity wore the semblance of a troubled sea lashed to wild commotion."

Here, finally, was the first opportunity for Eastern racegoers to view the much-publicized Kentucky crack. The Northeast had read about his successes for years, marveled at the impossible times he had posted almost routinely, and now the oversized crowd curiously measured Ten Broeck against the smallish Parole and the enormous Tom Ochiltree. For those whose wagers had remained uncertain until they could visually assess the challenger from the South, now was the time to make a belated dash to the betting areas. They struggled against a human torrent returning from the bookmakers' enclosure.

Colston relieved his charge of the blanket and nodded to Walker, who mounted Ten Broeck and made a regal circuit of the course. Pimlico's track, then as now, measured 1 mile in circumference, and the 2½-mile race would therefore begin midway down the backstretch, directly opposite the grandstand. Ten Broeck's prerace warmup concluded, the Nantura superstar was jogged toward the starting point as the fans, horses, jockeys, and owners awaited the start of what the *Baltimore American and Commercial Advertiser* would the next day describe as "the greatest event that has ever been seen on the American turf."

Commander William Conner, who would, eight and a half years later, be an invited guest at the funeral of George Lorillard, had been retained by the Maryland Jockey Club to start the race, and he went about the task of lining up the three horses. The owners had drawn for post position the previous day, and in accordance with the results of the draw, Tom Ochiltree, carrying 114 pounds, was placed closest to the rail; the smaller Parole, shouldering 105, was next in line. Ten Broeck, under his 114-pound impost, was maneuvered to the outside.

These were professional racehorses, each a veteran of more than twenty races, and all three knew what the next moment would bring. As Conner looked them over before the start, "the horses were almost on their haunches . . . their strength gathered for a mighty spring." Conner raised his flag, hesitated, and then, at 3:25 p.m., dropped it with a flourish and shouted, "Go!"

The outspoken William Walker, aboard Ten Broeck, had been overheard boasting on the twenty-third, "I'll show these boys how a race should be won this time," and he immediately sent his mount to the lead, closely attended by Tom Ochiltree, with the stretch-running Parole, under restraint by the slender Barrett, dropping behind as the field turned into the stretch for the first time.

As the field approached Pimlico's overpacked grandstand, Ten Broeck had opened a lead of about a length while Walker, as front-running jockeys have attempted to do from the beginnings of the sport, eased back on the reins, slowing the pace in an effort to conserve his mount's energy, with Barbee aboard Tom Ochiltree content to track him in second. The field now passed the grandstand, throughout which "the most intense excitement prevailed," and the Kentuckian dropped to the rail and extended his lead almost effortlessly to two lengths, while Barbee waited with Tom Ochiltree, and Parole, seemingly traveling in reverse, continued losing ground. The more knowledgeable racegoers may have begun to feel concern: would the local runners offer any resistance at all, or would Ten Broeck be permitted to win on an uncontested lead?

This question was answered as the field made the turn into the backstretch and Barbee began pushing Tom Ochiltree. Tom responded with a burst: "Up went his tail. That's Tom's signal for speed," and the big stallion moved to Ten Broeck's tail, then his flank, then his neck, and then past the Kentucky champion altogether, into a lead that he extended to fully two lengths as the field completed the first mile. "Walker began to realize that this was no walk-over for him."

Walker was riding with one eye on trainer Harry Colston in the infield, awaiting a pre-arranged gesture, and now Colston signaled him to ask Ten Broeck for more. Kentucky's representative let out a notch, and as the field passed the grandstand for the second time, with a mile remaining to be covered, he began closing in on the straining Tom Ochiltree, with Parole continuing to trail, but now lengthening stride under Barrett's gentle urging.

Around the turn and down the backstretch again, Ten Broeck's surge was eating into Tom Ochiltree's lead, and Parole, while still far behind, was showing decidedly more enthusiasm for the task. Some had conjectured that Parole was in the race only because the powerful Pierre had demanded it, but . . . was he closing in on the leaders?

And now, turning into the stretch for the final time, Walker used the whip freely to communicate the urgency of the moment to Ten Broeck, and the Kentuckian accelerated past Tom Ochiltree and into the lead . . . but only for a moment. As Ten Broeck briefly inhaled the clean, clear air breathed only by the leader, the Kentuckians in the crowd set up another din, which died quickly as Parole, sprinting through along the rail under Barrett's perfectly timed ride, exploded past the tiring front-runners.

Walker swung his whip once more and dug his spurs into Ten Broeck's sides, but with an eighth of a mile to go the outcome was decided. Parole now rapidly increased his advantage, widening the lead to two lengths, then three, then four. The overflow crowd watched in disbelief as Pierre Lorillard's disregarded gelding, with a grinning Barrett now standing tall in the stirrups, swept past the judges' stand five lengths ahead of Ten Broeck, with Tom Ochiltree a distant third.

Parole's backers responded with something approaching insanity. Legions of them stormed the track to celebrate with the winning horse and rider, while from the rest of the immense throng issued

long and prolonged shouts, hats were thrown in the air, and the jockeys, forgetful of their dignity and usual composure, turned somersaults like men of elderpith loaded with mercury. The fence that forms the barrier between the stretch and grand stand afforded no obstacle to the crowd who surrounded the winner, and it was only with great difficulty that Barrett, the winning jockey, got into the scale room to weigh out. When he did come out the crowd seized upon him and holding him high upon its shoulders, cheered until it seemed as if pandemonium prevailed and silence could never come to heal the blows of sound. Barrett's . . . natty colors were torn, his cap carried off in pieces as a trophy, and he himself buffeted on the shoulders of the crowd, borne to the fence and hoisted on the upper rail, where he was cheered and cheered again. Surely no jockey ever received such an ovation, and when finally the brave little fellow was let down, he limped off, probably much more sore from his greeting than from the ride. . . .It seemed as if nine out of every ten had suddenly become mad.

History does not record where the three owners spent their post-Sweepstakes moments, but one can certainly proffer an educated guess. Winning owner Pierre Lorillard had bet heavily on Parole, and for Lorillard, who enjoyed risking as much as $20,000 on a single bet, the returns must have been enormous, particularly in the deflated, depression-era currency of 1877. It surely dwarfed by a factor of dozens the check for $2,500 he received from the Maryland Jockey Club for Parole's victory.

The most favored of Lorillard's exultant friends would have been invited to join the winning owner at his private clubhouse table, overflowing with fine foods and beverages, alcoholic and otherwise, and it is easy to picture the rotund but beaming Lorillard, surrounded by backslapping well-wishers, toasting his winning steed with round after round of the finest champagne.

The teetotaling, roughly dressed Frank Harper would have had little interest in experiencing the celebrations inside the clubhouse. His most likely postrace venue would have been the stable area, to which he would have retreated to confirm that Ten Broeck had emerged from the race without injury. He would also have had a second purpose for repairing to the barn, and one prefers not to imagine the tongue-lashings Colston and Walker must have received from the losing favorite's defeated and humiliated owner. All would have felt responsibility for the losses of the many Kentuckians who had traveled to Maryland to revel in the inevitable Ten Broeck victory, recognizing that some had been almost ruined by the champion's defeat. One reporter wrote that the Kentuckians would be obliged to walk home for want of funds to pay their fare, so completely did the result clean them out.

George Lorillard, whose Tom Ochiltree had helped to ensure Ten Broeck's defeat with his early pace-pressing tactics, would also have missed his brother's clubhouse celebration. Bearing the physical pain of his crippling affliction, he almost certainly watched the race from the solitude and quiet of his carriage, parked in a preferred spot in the infield. Because neither he nor older brother Pierre had any interest in the day's final race, a one-mile hurdle event, George would have departed Pimlico immediately upon receiving trainer Wyndham Walden's messengered confirmation that Tom Ochiltree had suffered no injury during the race.

Practically every newspaper in the nation carried the news of Parole's astounding victory, Ten Broeck's shocking defeat. It made the front page—not of the sports section but *the* front page—of the *Bismarck Tri-Weekly Tribune* in the Dakota Territory, and the *Daily Intelligencer* in Wheeling, West Virginia. It was a cover story in the *Memphis Daily Appeal* and the *Dallas Daily Herald*. It was reported on the front page of the *Register* of Iola, Kansas, and that of Washington, DC's *National Republican*. It was above the fold in the *People's Vindicator* of Natchitoches, Louisiana, directly below that august publication's proud self-designation as the "Official Organ of the White Citizens of Red River, Sabine, Winn and Natchitoches Parishes."

Momentous events in the 1870s often inspired poetry, some of it good, some not. The following offering, "Parole, Ten Broeck and Tom Ochiltree," memorialized without attribution in W. S. Vosburgh's book *Cherry and Black: Career of Pierre Lorillard on the Turf*, probably falls somewhere in between:

> At Baltimore 't was, in the autumn late,
> "Parole and Ten Broeck" were on every lip,
> When the East and the West their issues joined
> In the final race for the championship
>
> 'T was Ten Broeck led, three lengths ahead;
> With Ochiltree second, they swept past the stand;
> For two miles they speed, Ten Broeck in the lead,
> Parole in the rear, but running in hand.

The pace becomes fast, Tom Ochiltree's last;
They straighten for home at the three-quarter pole,
As the stand fairly shook with "Come on, Ten Broeck!"
Then we heard a shrill cry of "Look at Parole!"

There rises a cheer as he steals from the rear.
Now he's closing the gap, as the cheering proceeds,
"Now he's at Ten Broeck's side"—they race stride for stride
"Now he's gaining"—"he's closing"—"by heaven, he leads!"

From the head of the stretch, to the field, to the stand,
'Mid tossing of hats, roll the deafening cheers;
"Ten Broeck's beaten," they cry, as up goes Walker's whip—
Parole gallops home gaily pricking his ears.

Oh, wasn't he "cockey," that Lorillard jockey,
As he rode back to scale, to the judge raised his whip.
"Weight's correct," said the clerk. "All right," from the stewards.
Parole wins the race for the championship.

CHAPTER 8

The Aftermath

Alas for race-course wisdom and prophecies!
—*BALTIMORE AMERICAN AND COMMERCIAL ADVERTISER,*
OCTOBER 25, 1877

LOSING HORSEPLAYERS ARE NOT NOTEWORTHY FOR THEIR GRACEFUL concessions of racetrack defeat; owners whose prized runners fail to run to form are traditionally magnanimous in public, less so behind closed doors. And if the outcome of an important race is truly unexpected, everyone involved, from the wealthiest owner to the meanest two-dollar bettor, can be depended upon to raise the question, "How did this happen?"

And so it was in the aftermath of the Great Sweepstakes. While Pierre Lorillard continued to receive accolades in the wake of Parole's decisive but shocking victory, the rest of the racing world began dissecting the race in detail, seeking to comprehend Ten Broeck's failure to defend the honor of the "West" and Tom Ochiltree's disappointing performance.

The initial response was pure incredulity. If the mighty Ten Broeck were to fall, surely it would be to George Lorillard's big, talented five-year-old, Tom Ochiltree, rather than to brother Pierre's "varminty" little four-year-old gelding. Parole had been a fine two-year-old, to be sure, and he was unquestionably a quality thoroughbred. But in this company he was regarded as distinctly third-best.

The *Baltimore American and Commercial Advertiser,* for one, was aggressively forthright regarding its opinion of the race's results, harrumphing in its postrace coverage, "Parole, indeed! Nobody would name Parole in the same conversation with Big Tom and the Kentucky pride."

A few paragraphs later, the newspaper further demeaned the conqueror of the mighty Ten Broeck, labeling him "poor little Parole."

Nearly three weeks later, *Spirit of the Times* was still incredulous, punctuating its disbelief with an exclamation point: "Parole!"

The surprisingly slow time of the race became an immediate *cause célèbre*. Racing pundits everywhere dissected the fractional times of the race, seeking with slide rules, abacuses, and pencil and paper to analyze the jockeys' pace strategies. At Pimlico, the first ¼ mile had been completed in 30½ seconds; the ½ mile in 59½; the ¾ mile in 1:28½; the mile in 1:55½; the 1¼ mile in 2:20¼; the 1½ mile in 2:47¾; the 1¾ mile in 3:15; the 2 miles in 3:42; the 2¼ miles in 4:09½; and the 2½ miles in 4:37¾.

The analysts compared these times with Ten Broeck's clockings in previous races and shook their heads in puzzlement. The Kentuckian had plodded through the first Pimlico mile in a time nearly 16 seconds slower than his record 1:39¾ clocking. Just 3½ weeks prior to the Great Sweepstakes he had easily defeated Courier at 1¼ miles in 2:11¼, nine seconds faster than his Pimlico time; if Courier had offered resistance, Ten Broeck would have run faster. Ten Broeck had once run 2 miles in 3:38, four seconds faster than the fractional time at Pimlico—in the second heat of a two-heat race.

Ten Broeck's best time for the 2½-mile distance was 4:35¾, established at Louisville on May 20 of the previous year, and he had finished the 20-furlong distance "in a canter," 2 full seconds faster than Parole's clocking for the Great Sweepstakes. As one publication noted, "Ten Broeck's three-mile race at Louisville was run in 5:26¼. Had he run at the same rate [in the Great Sweepstakes], the two and a half miles would have been made in 4:32, or 5¾ seconds faster than Parole's record."

The fractional times of the Great Sweepstakes become more comprehensible when viewed in tabular form:

Distance	Time (cumulative)	Time (fractional)	Speed (in mph)
¼ Mi.	:30½	:30½	29.5
½ Mi.	:59½	:29	31

Distance	Time (cumulative)	Time (fractional)	Speed (in mph)
¾ Mi.	1:28½	:29	31
1 Mi.	1:55½	:27	33.3
1¼ Mi.	2:20¼	:24¾	36.4
1½ Mi.	2:47¾	:27½	32.7
1¾ Mi.	3:15	:27¼	33
2 Mi.	3:42	:27	33.3
2¼ Mi.	4:09½	:27½	32.7
2½ Mi.	4:37¾	:28¼	31.9

Based on this depiction, the early portion of the race becomes something of a cat-and-mouse game, with jockey William Walker aboard Ten Broeck initially being conceded the lead by George Barbee aboard Tom Ochiltree, then slowing the son of Phaeton to a near crawl through the first mile, as both he and Big Tom relax on a pace that either could maintain for many circuits of the track. The most likely victim of this early strategy, had it continued much longer, would have been Parole, asked to rally from many lengths behind talented horses that had barely exerted themselves.

But after the first mile, Barbee, following the dictates of the clock that every good jockey carries in his head, determined that the time had come to force Ten Broeck out of his tortuous pace. Moving his hands and chirruping to his mount, Barbee asked Tom Ochiltree for more speed approaching the conclusion of the first mile, and from this point the pace increased from languorous 29-second quarter-miles to a quarter in the 27-second range. Now Tom Ochiltree increased the pressure on Ten Broeck sharply, with a sprightly quarter-mile in 24¾ seconds, and blew past the Kentucky superhorse, forcing him to consume reserves of energy that Walker had hoped to save for the stretch drive.

It was too early a move for Tom Ochiltree, which would wilt in the final half-mile, but the brazen sixth quarter also took a toll on Ten Broeck, and both of the leaders began to weary, with moderate quarter-miles in the 27- to 28-second range. It was then that Parole, which had been dawdling behind his rivals' unhurried early fractions, showed what appeared to be a burst of speed, but actually wasn't. Parole was simply moving at more or less the same pace he had maintained throughout, as his two tired opponents slowed abruptly. It was enough to allow Parole to leave the competition behind.

The *Louisville Courier-Journal* quickly recognized what any knowledgeable racing fan might have understood: that the Lorillard brothers, their prized thoroughbreds confronting in Ten Broeck a seemingly overwhelming force, may have conspiratorially undertaken two-on-one tactics to keep the victory in the family.

It is a strategy as old as racing itself: When facing a superior thoroughbred whose favored running style is to lead from start to finish, a stable might enter two runners—a speedster (or "rabbit," as the sport long ago labeled such sacrificial entrants) to force the targeted runner to maximize its early efforts, and a stretch-runner to sweep by the leaders when the tiring victim begins to feel the effects of the strategy.

The Lorillards had no intention of losing to Ten Broeck, and they and their trainers, both of whom could boast vastly more experience than Harry Colston, may well have concocted a cooperative approach to maximize the likelihood of a Lorillard victory. If Walker unexpectedly conceded the early lead to Tom Ochiltree, George's big horse would be free to lope through 2½ easy miles; if Walker was more aggressive aboard Ten Broeck, Tom Ochiltree could press the Kentucky superstar, maximizing the impact of a late charge by Parole. It was the latter scenario that unfolded before the Lorillards' eyes.

The brothers had made everything happen. They had formulated the challenge and coaxed Harper and his champion north. They had invested $500 apiece to create a special race that would exclude any runner except their own horses and Ten Broeck. The Maryland Jockey Club had been persuaded to add $1,000, creating a purse that Harper might find irresistible, and to lengthen the Pimlico meeting by one day so that Harper would enter the Lorillards' race rather than waiting for the Bowie Stakes. They had paid a portion of Harper's traveling expenses, and had gambled $500 to delay the race for twenty-four hours in the hope that a drying-out surface might minimize Ten Broeck's advantage.

They had imagined every possible contingency, and seized those that could be turned in their favor. This is the way successful businessmen attack issues.

The *Courier-Journal,* perceiving that the Lorillard brothers' horses had combined to steal the race from the pride of the Bluegrass, expressed something close to outrage at the conspiracy perpetrated against those who, believing that Ten Broeck's opponents were competing as individuals rather than as a tag-team, had wagered on the Kentucky crack. Now, too late, they recognized the implications of Walker's relative inexperience:

> *The purpose of the Lorillard entries seemed to be to have Ochiltree worry Ten Broeck. . . . It was evidently the purpose of the Lorillards to run the race exactly as it took place, and they succeeded admirably in fooling the fool on Ten Broeck. There is much soreness and considerable comment over the result.*

Nor was the *Courier-Journal* alone in this assessment. According to the *Baltimore Sun*, the Great Sweepstakes was a simple case of

> *two against one. . . . Ochiltree took the first turn, and pressed "the king of the turf" all he could. After it was all over many said it was Parole who carried off the money, but Ochiltree won the race for him.*

The brothers' alleged collusion, however, was far from the only excuse offered for Ten Broeck. Some cited an array of factors that, in combination, may have led to Ten Broeck's downfall. After journeying from Kentucky, went this theory, and then being fed local food and water to which his system was unaccustomed, and subjected to attention that might be lavished upon a visiting potentate, Ten Broeck had simply lost the razor-sharp edge needed to compete in elite company. Borrowing the slang of an upstart sport that was rapidly gaining in popularity, one reporter suggested that "in base ball parlance, it was an off day with him."

Or perhaps Ten Broeck, though the superior horse, had not been properly prepared for the race. As the *Turf, Field and Farm* posited, "The opinion gains ground here, in the country where Ten Broeck was bred, reared and ran his best races, that he . . . lost the race through lack of condition. . . . He was low in flesh . . . there was but little luster in his coat. . . . Parole appeared to have been timed to the hour. His coat shone like polished ebony." The *Kentucky Live Stock Record* expressed its agreement: "Ten Broeck was sadly amiss. . . . Ten Broeck's condition beat him."

In some quarters, it was alleged that Ten Broeck, despite the prerace insistence of his owner that the horse was "as well as he ever had been in his life," had been observed "scouring" (a racetrack term of the day describing the effects of a diarrhea attack) during the race's final stages, and may not have been fit to run at all. The *Kentucky Live Stock Record* stated directly that Ten Broeck's "action was labored, and . . . when the rider struck him with the spur he purged and scoured freely, which continued throughout the remainder of the race." Obviously, a severe attack of diarrhea would compromise the winning chances of even the greatest thoroughbred.

And, inevitably, some theorized more insidious reasons for Ten Broeck's unexpected defeat and possible illness. As the *Kentucky Live Stock Record* noted, "Some assert their belief that Ten Broeck was got at, and many clever gentlemen believe there was some foundation for the report, from the way the horse ran and his violent purging during the progress of the race."

The Eastern press, however, begged to differ. In their view, Ten Broeck was not a victim of race-fixing, or illness, or poor conditioning. He was simply overrated, his greatness now disproven, his records and victories the result of the conditions under which he had raced. The *New York Times*, for one, sought to distance itself from any suggestion that Ten Broeck might have been a superhorse:

> [R]aces against time under light weight . . . is the favorite method of Kentuckians, and the result of the contest yesterday is but another link in the chain of evidence to prove that the only true test of a racer's merits is in a contest with other horses. This is not said in a spirit derogatory to the fame or reputation of Ten Broeck, who has shown himself to be a wonderful horse, but . . . his competitors were held too cheaply by the Western men and they have paid dearly for it.

Spirit of the Times, also New York-based, derided Kentuckians for extolling fast times that were created by "slow watches and India rubber tracks."

But Ten Broeck was not the only thoroughbred whose reputation suffered in the Great Sweepstakes, nor was Frank Harper the only horseman to suffer a loss of credibility. Before long, the omnipresent *Turf, Field and Farm* reported that Tom Ochiltree had been in less than perfect health when Commander Conner dropped the flag, informing its readers that he "was coughing the morning of the race."

Two insiders, however, had been well aware of Ochiltree's persistent cough. Trainer Wyndham Walden had sent news of Tom's illness to owner George Lorillard, who had directed his conditioner "to start Tom Ochiltree and not spoil the race, and put $500 on Parole." George's telegram was not received by Walden until after the race, costing George the substantial amount his $500 wager might have yielded. Some expressed dismay that the information of Big Tom's illness had been withheld until after the race, by which time the public had wagered thousands on the runner they had so often seen posing in the winner's enclosure.

Forgotten in the controversy swirling around the aftermath of the Great Sweepstakes was that the Bowie Stakes, at four-mile heats, was scheduled for the twenty-sixth, just two days later. Parole, Ten Broeck, and Tom Ochiltree had initially been entered in the Bowie, but Pierre Lorillard would certainly allow Parole to rest on his laurels for awhile, and Big Tom, recuperating from his cough, would remain in the barn.

But Harper had not withdrawn Ten Broeck, and thus it was that a mere forty-eight hours following his Great Sweepstakes debacle, amid rumors that he was sick or overrated or poisoned or perhaps just flabby, Ten Broeck returned to Pimlico on a chilly, drizzly day and obliterated his competition in the Bowie Stakes.

Before a crowd that, despite the inclement weather, was "larger than on any previous day except [Great Sweepstakes Day]", the Kentuckian, carrying 114 pounds to imposts of 105 to 108 for his rivals, faced Algerine, Pierre Lorillard's Barricade, and George Lorillard's Ambush, an overmatched speedster entered to set a sprightly pace to prevent Ten Broeck from simply running off with the first heat.

There had been controversy from the moment Ten Broeck was confirmed as a starter in the Bowie. *Spirit of the Times* predicted that the Kentuckian would surely meet with a second ignominious defeat: "Western turfmen condemned in strong terms the naming of Ten Broeck. They regarded his chances for the race, even against the three named, as very slim, and declared that they expected to see him beaten." Based on Ten Broeck's prerace appearance, his chances for victory must have seemed remote indeed:

> *He moved as timidly and slovenly as a sick man. He had no spirit, no vim. . . . [T]here was none of the fire of other years in his expressive countenance.*

The wagering pools established for the Bowie's first heat, however, made the Kentucky invader the overwhelming favorite. Some sold at $100 for Ten Broeck to $25 for Algerine, $15 for Barricade, and $10 for Ambush, suggesting that of every three dollars wagered, the bookmakers anticipated that two would be wagered on Ten Broeck. This time, the bookmakers got it right.

Ambush shot away to the expected early lead, extending it to nearly twenty lengths while Ten Broeck, "under a heavy pull," was satisfied to volley for second with Barricade, and Algerine lagged behind. After three miles at a suicidal pace, the leg-weary Ambush began losing ground to the field, and Barricade drew a roar from the crowd when he was first to overtake the tiring front-runner. But he was no match for Ten Broeck when the Kentuckian challenged at the start of the final quarter-mile. Ten Broeck eased past the Lorillard representative as the pair reached the top of the stretch, and "had no difficulty in stalling off Barricade's final effort, two lengths separating them at the wire."

The final time of 7:42½ was nearly a half-minute slower than Ten Broeck's four-mile record of 7:15¾, but against Barricade and company Ten Broeck had not had the benefit of a running start. Walker and Harper were not dissatisfied.

Wagering on the second heat was even more lopsided than on the first. The visiting Kentuckians, seeking to recoup another fraction of their disastrous Great Sweepstakes losses, accepted odds as low as 1 to 5 against Ten Broeck; there was not much wagering interest in Barricade at any odds.

The second heat, started forty minutes after the first, proved even an easier victory for the Kentucky crack, who allowed Barricade an eight-length lead through the early stages, then began reeling in his rival as the second and third miles progressed. Barricade was still three lengths ahead after the third mile, but at that point Walker lightened his pull on the reins, and as the frenzied shouts of delighted Kentuckians echoed through the grandstand, Ten Broeck closed the gap, then opened up on his lone rival.

With a half-mile to go, Ten Broeck was pulling away at will. When his lead reached ten lengths at midstretch, Walker allowed Ten Broeck to practically walk to the finish, his victory margin three lengths, achieved "in a canter." Whatever malady, whether microbial or chemical, had seized Ten Broeck on Great Sweepstakes Day, he had recuperated at an amazing pace. He ran the second four-mile heat 2½ seconds faster than the first, a rarity in the sport.

But even the Kentucky journals were left unimpressed. As the *Kentucky Live Stock Record* grudgingly admitted: "True he won the race, but beat nothing."

Everyone, then, was left dissatisfied. Harper had been devastated by Ten Broeck's loss (one publication's subheadline had read, "Harper in Sorrow"), and remained convinced that his was the best thoroughbred on the continent. The press was continuing to claim, variously, that his great horse had been sent to the post suffering from dysentery, drugged by race-fixers, undertrained, or overrated. Harper would have seen all of these opinions as deeply insulting. His was the tradition of the South, which prided itself on "being born and bred to work with Thoroughbreds."

George Lorillard, who had knowingly allowed an unfit horse to race against Ten Broeck, and was now reading that he and trainer Wyndham Walden were responsible for the loss of thousands of dollars wagered by Tom Ochiltree's backers, continued to believe in Tom Ochiltree. Allowed a second opportunity, he was certain that his big horse, which had rarely run as poorly as he did on Great Sweepstakes Day, could redeem himself by administering a beating to Ten Broeck.

Even Pierre Lorillard, his wagers cashed and Parole's trophy now decorating his already bulging trophy case, must have been profoundly frustrated as he read excuse after excuse for the runners his thoroughbred had defeated. He surely noticed that in the tumult surrounding the race result and the search for ever more explanations of Parole's shocking victory, the Pimlico race was no longer being hailed as "the greatest event that has ever been seen on the American turf."

It was not long before challenges began to fly again. Typically, Pierre's proposal was the most audacious: a four-race series in which he would match one of his two-year-olds against any juvenile in the West at ¾ mile or a flat mile, one of his three-year-olds against any sophomore at 1½ miles, would race any four-year-old at 2½ miles, and would challenge any older horse at 3 miles, each for $2,500 a side with a $5,000 bonus to whichever horseman's runner won the majority of the races—all of this in addition to a Parole–Ten Broeck rematch. All the races, Pierre emphasized, were to be run either at Pimlico or at a New York venue, either Saratoga or Jerome Park.

Kentucky-based horsemen, finding no compelling reason to contest all four races in their rival's backyard, promptly dismissed Lorillard's proposal:

> *Why not allow us to select the place where two of the events shall transpire, and Mr. Lorillard select for the other two? If he has a preference about the different events then let us cast lots for choice, and abide the result. The four matches can be made on these terms.*

But Lorillard did not want to send his horses south. And even *Spirit of the Times*, normally squarely in Lorillard's camp, struggled to support his reasoning:

> *I cannot see the force of his objection. . . . This is not right. It is as far from Kentucky to New York as it is from New York to Kentucky; it is as expensive for [southern stables] to go to New York as it is for*

*[northern ones] to go to Kentucky. The lines of travel are the same,
the accommodations the same, the tracks West and South are quite as
good as they are here, no man who has carried horses there from the
North and East has ever complained of the treatment he received at
[southern] hands. . . . [I]s there any earthly reason for Mr. Lorillard's
claim to fix the place where all four of the races shall be run? . . . [I]f he
will run two of the races at Louisville or Lexington, he may select the
points where the other two shall be run, and we will agree as to everything else, and . . . he shall have all the money bet that he may wish.*

With winter approaching, it seemed certain that if Lorillard's four
races, or any sort of challenge, were ever to occur, it would assuredly not
take place during the remainder of 1877.

But now, something almost miraculous happened. In the midst of a
last-minute flurry of negotiations, with no headway having been accomplished for days, one of the many challenges somehow took root. An
arrangement was hammered out; a handshake occurred. And the racing
world was reenergized:

Parole and Ten Broeck to Meet Again

*Parole and Ten Broeck will come together again at Jerome Park, New
York, on Saturday next, November 3, the distance and weights to be
the same as in the great two and a half mile race on Wednesday last at
Pimlico. Ochiltree, however, will not be in. The American Jockey Club
will add $2,000 to the sweepstake of $100 each, and an outside bet of
$5,000 a side between the respective owners is pending the result. . . .
The horses will remain at Pimlico until Tuesday."*

Newspapers throughout the nation headlined the forthcoming event.
A Ten Broeck–Parole rematch would bring clarity to a racing world still
confounded by the results of their first confrontation, and might resur-
rect Ten Broeck's tarnished image—or forever disprove Harper's claims
regarding his horse's greatness. All could now look forward to November
3. The rematch was on.

Or was it?

CHAPTER 9

The Rematch

Mr. Pierre Lorillard seems to be disposed to settle the question of supremacy between Ten Broeck and Parole, by proposing to go to Louisville, in May next, and run the brown gelding against the Kentucky crack, for $20,000 a side. This is the proper spirit, and leaves but one road out for Mr. Harper, and that is to accept the challenge.
—*SPIRIT OF THE TIMES*, NOVEMBER 10, 1877

THE STRUCTURE OF THOROUGHBRED RACING NO LONGER ALLOWS FOR extra days, created on a moment's notice, to accommodate a particular owner or to allow for the last-moment scheduling of a special race. Racing in the modern world is, sadly, not merely a sport, perhaps not even primarily a sport. It is as much an economic entity, one that generates a revenue stream to the public coffers, creates a profit margin for the track's owners, provides jobs to racetrack employees and private contractors (such as jockeys and trainers), and supports the owners whose thoroughbreds create the sport.

These economic functions necessitate that the racing year be arranged in advance, and this is achieved primarily by politically appointed functionaries who seek to maximize funding by ensuring that one race meeting begins as quickly as practicable after the previous nearby meeting has concluded. Sometimes racing moves *en masse* to the next track literally the day after the preceding venue has closed.

Such scheduling precludes the possibility of extra days. The economics of the sport simply do not allow for them.

This was decidedly not so in 1877. We have already seen an extra day inserted into that year's Pimlico meeting to provide a respite for Ten Broeck, Tom Ochiltree, and Parole between their Great Sweepstakes confrontation and their anticipated participation in the Bowie Stakes. In November, learning that representatives of Ten Broeck and Parole had agreed to a rematch, the New York Jockey Club announced that an extra day would be inserted into the schedule at sumptuous Jerome Park, which, with its upper-class flavor, was considered, with Pimlico, one of the "twin queen[s] of the American racing club."

Preparations began at once to accommodate an onslaught of humanity that could strain the facilities to near bursting. Admission for the featured race, the Jockey Club announced, would be just fifty cents; entry to the track at any other point in the program would be free. The two sides again set the distance at 2½ miles, and stipulated—probably at Lorillard's insistence—a "good and dry course" for the event. Three other races were scheduled for the day: a 1¼-mile race for a purse of $500, a $600 event at 1½ miles and, to close the day, a steeplechase. Kentucky's King Faro was promptly entered in the 1¼-mile race, and the 1½-mile contest drew an outstanding field that included Vera Cruz, as well as Ten Broeck's Bowie Stakes rival, Barricade, and Viceroy, St. James, and Tom Ochiltree.

Tom Ochiltree? Rather than being offered a place in the rematch, the Great Sweepstakes' last-place finisher was demoted to the undercard. Perhaps disdaining so reduced a role, George Lorillard elected to keep his big horse in the barn.

Publicity for the Parole–Ten Broeck rematch began ramping relentlessly upward. This time, it was promised, Ten Broeck was truly at the peak of condition, and would be fully prepared to gain his revenge. Nor was the East vs. West theme abandoned:

> On occasions like this, sectional feeling runs high, and there is necessarily a vast amount of interest centered in the coming struggle.

As had happened eleven days earlier in Maryland, an autumn deluge drenched the track, and the originally scheduled date was declared "not propitious" for a race of this magnitude. The rescheduling of the event from November 3 to 6, however, would be far from the most damaging event to befall the rematch.

On November 5, Ten Broeck was sent to the track for what was intended to be a workout at near racing speed, but Harper and Colston were appalled at his lack of anything approaching racing condition. Perhaps, assuming no race would be possible prior to winter, the Ten Broeck camp had elected not to send their horse to the track after his resounding Bowie Stakes victory. Whatever the case, Harper elected to pay the forfeit fee rather than subject his horse to another humiliating loss. And the next day's headlines blared:

Ten Broeck Withdrawn

The American Jockey Club has truly been unfortunate in getting up the extra meeting. The members went to great expense, and sent a committee to Baltimore to induce the "cracks" to run at Jerome Park, but it has all gone for nothing. Circumstances over which they had no control thwarted the club's efforts to give New-Yorkers an opportunity of witnessing a contest between Ten Broeck and Parole. It was to have taken place last Saturday, but the track not being good, it was postponed until to-day. During the interim, it is said, Ten Broeck has got badly out of condition, and last night he was withdrawn from the race. . . . [T]he horse was coughing badly and also had a swelled ankle. An effort was then made to match Vera Cruz against Parole. . . . Mr. Lorillard refused to accede to the proposition of Vera Cruz's owner, and the consequence will be that Parole will to-day gallop over the course for the money, no matter what the condition of the track may be. Should it be pleasant, the other three races announced will come off.

The official chart of the race, in the emotionless shorthand of the era, barely hints at the disappointment inflicted on the racing world by Harper's withdrawal of Ten Broeck:

Summary

Same Day—*Purse $2,000 for Ten Broeck and Parole at $100 each, h. ft.; two mile and a half.*

P. Lorillard's br g Parole, 4 yrs, by Leamington–Maiden, 105 lbs
. . . Barrett w o
F.B. Harper's b h Ten Broeck, 5 yrs, by Phaeton–Fanny Holton,
114 lbs . . . pd ft

In the abbreviations of the day, "h. ft." meant that a runner not able to race would be subject to a half-forfeit payment of $50. Parole's "w o" indicated that he walked over for the victory, and Ten Broeck's "pd ft" meant that Harper paid the forfeit price to withdraw his horse.

It was an especially bitter moment for Harper, who had been "more than mortified, he was grieved, sorely grieved, at the unexpected result" of the Great Sweepstakes, and had fought a "fearful struggle between pride and prudence" before succumbing to the temptation to again send Ten Broeck postward against his conqueror. The notion that Ten Broeck was "coughing badly" and had a "swollen ankle" can be dismissed as face saving; Harper and Colston would never have worked out a horse suffering from either ailment.

Following the injury- or illness-related scratch of a horse as valuable as Ten Broeck, his owner and trainer would have been expected to arrange for a veterinarian to initiate treatment of the horse's upper respiratory ills, and begin a regimen to address the swelling in his ankle. Once Ten Broeck's health had been stabilized, Harper would likely have had the animal placed, as quickly and unobtrusively as possible given the disappointment his withdrawal had engendered, aboard the first available train heading in the general direction of Nantura.

But no. Rather than seek veterinary treatment and plan a surreptitious southerly retreat, Harper elected to display Ten Broeck before the throng that had, anticipating another epic racetrack struggle, arrived at Jerome Park *en masse*, only to learn that Ten Broeck's late withdrawal had necessitated the race's cancellation.

Parole, of course, had to be there. To claim his victory, the gelding would be required to meet the requirements of the race: to complete two and a half circuits of the course and cross the finish line. This he did. With Barrett in the saddle, the gelding jogged the first 2¼ miles to polite applause, then was allowed to run a bit down the stretch to give the overflow crowd a thrill.

But prior to Parole's gallop, a "weak and lifeless" Ten Broeck, displaying "none of that springy, easy motion that he ever shows when at himself," was led down the stretch "by a colored attendant," probably Colston. As the erstwhile Kentucky crack slowly paraded past the grandstand, hundreds of angry racegoers voiced their opinions regarding the cancellation, some with more than a hint of real venom: "Some one in the crowd shouted, 'Parole's his boss!' and 'Why don't you run him?'" It was, in the understated words of *Spirit of the Times*, "a very unpleasant situation." "[T]he disappointment and chagrin were great."

And this was thoroughly understandable, given that many of those at trackside had lost their "play or pay" wagers when the runner now plodding forlornly before them was withdrawn, costing them even the possibility of winning their bets in a fair race.

Once again, the Kentuckians had suffered the greatest losses. King Faro had precipitated yet another hemorrhage of Kentucky cash when he lost the opening race to August Belmont's filly Susquehanna, and although Vera Cruz captured the second, his victory at minuscule odds replaced little of the lost cash of previous days. And now, with the Kentucky horses preparing to ship home, the visitors from the Bluegrass would have no further wagering opportunities.

Harper now came under public opprobrium for his decision making throughout Ten Broeck's Eastern debacle, particularly in the newsprint of *Spirit of the Times*, which asserted that Harper's most reasonable course would have been to retire Ten Broeck. But instead, the horseman had been illogically "seized with a strange infatuation to see his great horse once more upon the turf, measuring strides with the cracks of the country." The result? "He came, but not to conquer. The race is not always to the swift, and so it proved in this case."

With Ten Broeck finally returned to Nantura, *Spirit* learned of a casual conversation in which Pierre Lorillard had discussed the possibilities for yet another rematch. *Spirit* reported it hopefully—if inaccurately—to its readership:

Rumors were now in order. They were thick, and took as many shapes as can be conceived. . . . Mr. P. Lorillard had declared his willingness *to go to Louisville in the spring, and run Parole against Ten Broeck a dash of one, two, three, or four miles, for $20,000 a side . . . but nothing definite was settled.*

The Kentuckians cannot fail to respond to this. They must fight or back down, for Mr. Lorillard, if he made such a proposition, means business, and will do just what he says. Mr. Harper is in no condition to pass such a challenge by unnoticed. He has too often declared that he would match any horse that would come to Kentucky. Besides, his horse is under a cloud, and he must remove it, or he will stand far below the estimation placed upon him by the public up to the time he arrived at Pimlico.

By November 16, however, both Parole and Ten Broeck had been retired to their stables to enjoy a few months' well-earned repose. Ten Broeck, in particular, was reported by a visiting journalist to be badly in need of recuperation: "a mere wreck of the grand horse he was last Spring. He looks weak and dull out of the flesh. . . . [I]t will take him some months to get back in form for a spring campaign."

Harper had apparently not been informed at this point of Lorillard's alleged willingness to challenge Ten Broeck in Louisville, though the tobacco magnate's statement had reportedly been made to Kentucky horseman H. P. McGrath, a close acquaintance of Harper's. As the first to inform the master of Nantura that his rival might be considering a southerly journey, the reporter now became the first to inform the racing world that Ten Broeck's owner was

perfectly willing to make the match and [put up] a portion of the stake, $20,000, and let his friends take the remainder. . . . It was his intention to make a season [at stud] with Ten Broeck next Spring, and then train him for a Fall campaign, but, in view of his recent defeat the plan has been changed, and he will be trained in the Spring with the opening of the season.

Lorillard was chagrined to learn that a casual conversation regarding a theoretical rematch had been communicated to Harper as a serious proposal. The tobacco man still had no interest in sending the Great Sweepstakes winner to Kentucky to challenge Ten Broeck over the latter's favored racetracks. He communicated this in no uncertain terms to one of the premier racing newspapers, also reiterating his proposal for a series of match races, none of which would, under Lorillard's terms, be contested in Kentucky:

> *Jersey City, Nov. 13, 1877*
> *Editors* Turf, Field and Farm.—*I have not challenged Ten Broeck, but I am willing to run Parole against him for $25,000 a side, $10,000 forfeit, two miles and a half, western weights and dry track. The race to be run at Saratoga, and I will allow Ten Broeck $5,000 for expenses if it comes off.*
>
> *I will also run from my Rancocus [sic] stable—*
> *A two-year-old at three-quarters of a mile,*
> *A three-year-old at one mile and three-quarters,*
> *A four-year-old at two miles and a quarter,*
> *A five-year-old at three miles, against Western horses of same ages. . . . The four races to be run at Jerome Park or Saratoga, for $2,500 a side each race, $1,000 forfeit. To be named at the post. The four races to be accepted, or none.*
>
> *This offer means that I am willing to run my stable against the pick of the entire West.*
>
> *Yours, respectfully, P. Lorillard*

The *Turf, Field and Farm*, its editorial offices located on New York's Park Row, Lorillard territory, responded to this already public proposal by bestowing praise upon Lorillard, describing his offer as "manly, straightforward, and sportsmanlike . . . liberal," opining that "Mr. Harper is compelled to accept it." Surely, the newspaper speculated, Ten Broeck must defend his reputation by again journeying north early the following year. Or, in the more poetic journalistic argot of the time, "when the feathered songsters of the grove are warbling the praises of Spring."

From Harper, Lorillard's alleged proposal received a definite maybe. He replied that "Ten Broeck had done so badly since he went North, that he would prefer waiting several weeks before definitely accepting the offer, and there was plenty of time, as it would remain open until the first of January, 1878. He promised to visit Lexington next week, or the week after, and put the matter into a definite shape." The master of Nantura would propose no specific date for a rematch, or even for discussion of a rematch. All the world could truly know at this point was that he would be disinclined to race in the North, where Ten Broeck had fared so badly.

And for once, even the curmudgeonly *Spirit of the Times*, usually une-namored of both Ten Broeck and Harper, implied that Harper should be accommodated; that compromise might be necessary if these races were to occur. After applauding Lorillard's suggestion as "liberal and plucky," *Spirit* found itself compelled to admit, concurring with its journalistic rival, the *Kentucky Live Stock Record*, that "it gives Mr. Lorillard a great advantage in compelling Southern and Western horses to travel East to meet him. We have never seen any kind of horses—saddle, harness, coach, trotter, or thoroughbred—taken East that did not have to undergo accli-mation . . . from three days to two weeks after their arrival."

There were simply no issues affecting the Lorillards, were they to travel south, that would not equally affect Frank Harper, were he to again bring Ten Broeck north. Pierre would protest, for example, that bringing Parole to Kentucky would be impossible because he had but one trainer and many racing commitments, and could not divide his stable. But this was equally true of Harper, whose sole trainer was Harry Colston, and who had split his stable during Ten Broeck's northern foray. Surely, Loril-lard's estimable trainer, William Brown, with Lorillard's bankroll to back him, could persuade a competent trainer to care for the Rancocas horses during the limited duration of a southerly visit with Parole.

An argument was made that because Lorillard had invested more money in his stable than did Southern racing concerns, he was at greater risk transporting strings of thoroughbreds south than a Southerner would face in bringing horses north. This, too, was easily dismissed: Lorillard was far wealthier than any of his southern or western counterparts, some of whom had "all their earthly goods and possessions invested in the turf and the thoroughbred." Proportionately, Lorillard was at less risk travel-ing with Parole than Harper had been in transporting Ten Broeck.

A trip south would also be far less taxing on Parole physically than was the case for Ten Broeck shipping north. Lorillard had had a special railroad car created for Parole, certainly not something Harper had ever considered for Ten Broeck, and the Rancocas thoroughbred could therefore ride more comfortably than his rival. Indeed, for a time it was believed that even if a match race could be arranged in Kentucky, Parole's car might not fit through some of the tunnels between New York and Lexington. This was duly researched, however, and a workable route was mapped. Lorillard's team needed merely to lead Parole into his car, attach it to a locomotive, and point the locomotive south.

There was also a historical argument favoring a southern venue for the rematch. As southern newspapers were at pains to point out, good southern-based thoroughbreds of the past had generally been forced to ship away from their familiar climes to challenge their northern-based counterparts, with results that were, for the most part, predictably favorable for the northerners.

The first of the great North-South contests had been won in 1823 by the New York–based American Eclipse, which took two of three four-mile heats at New York's Union Course from Virginia's Sir Henry, with sixty thousand in attendance. The brilliant but evil-tempered Boston, whose sale had once been rejected by a potential buyer who suggested that the vicious animal be "either castrated or shot—preferably the latter," had traveled from Virginia twice to face New Jersey's great filly Fashion—in 1841 across the river from Philadelphia, where racing was illegal, and in 1842 over New York's Union Course. Fashion had won both times, the second by an estimated sixty yards.

Major Doswell's colt Planet had proven unbeatable racing over southern courses at Petersburg, Richmond, Savannah, Charleston, New Orleans, Mobile, Ashland, and Augusta, and was sent to Long Island to prove his greatness, both as a runner and as a trotter (Planet, a rare "binary," could do both). He reversed the trend, distancing the only runner that dared take the track with him.

Nantura's Longfellow, of course, had in recent years made the South-to-North journey with disastrous results, a factor still weighing heavily on Harper.

But none of this was of the slightest consequence to Pierre Lorillard, a hard-headed businessman who existed in the present-day world of 1877, not the dim history of American Eclipse and Fashion.

As the days of November passed without resolution and the weather turned ever colder, both in Frank Harper's Kentucky and in Pierre Lorillard's New Jersey, the war of nerves continued between the Kentucky hardboot and the New Jersey tycoon. And now, with the public clamoring for a Ten Broeck–Parole summit meeting, a third party unexpectedly reentered the fray through a telegram transmitted to the ever-alert racing press:

> *Editors* Turf, Field and Farm.—*On Mr. Jerome's return from Baltimore after the Parole–Ten Broeck–Ochiltree race, I authorized him to match Tom Ochiltree against Ten Broeck, any distance from two miles to four, for five thousand dollars, half forfeit, the race to be run next Spring at Jerome Park, and I to allow one thousand dollars for expenses. The challenge was sent to Mr. Harper by Mr. Jerome, and he received no reply.*
>
> *Very Truly yours, George L. Lorillard*
> *5 West Twenty-first Street, Tuesday evening, Nov. 21.*

For Harper, the most relevant phrase in George Lorillard's telegram would certainly have been "at Jerome Park," a suggestion the Kentuckian would have viewed as merely a new helping of Lorillard bombast. Harper's not even bothering to reply was effectively a reply in itself, a southern-accented snort of derision. Was Lorillard seriously proposing that Harper ship his champion north for a second time, to engage a challenger he had already defeated?

With all possible contestants retired to their respective farms for the long, cold winter, the debate now centered on the following year. One newspaper asked, "Will there be a match race next Spring between Ten Broeck and Parole?" and flung the gauntlet directly at the feet of Pierre Lorillard:

> *The question is, will Mahomet go to the mountain, now that it is known the mountain will not come to Mohamet? In other words,*

will Mr. Lorillard go to Louisville with Parole the moment it becomes
settled that Mr. Harper will not come to Saratoga with Ten Broeck?

Spirit of the Times added, "Let's have a little reciprocity in racing as
well as in trade."

But by this time, "reciprocity" would have been viewed by both sides
as synonymous with "surrender." In truth, there was but one issue preventing a spring rematch of Ten Broeck and Parole, but it was a huge
issue, one that would require insight on the part of Frank Harper and
Pierre Lorillard that neither seemed to possess.

The issue was the egos of two enormously successful and stubborn
men.

Pierre Lorillard was a person who got what he wanted. Everything
he cared about—his business, his horses, his farm, his society—was in
the North. And what did Pierre have to gain by journeying south with
Parole? His gallant little gelding had already defeated Ten Broeck, and
would gain no additional repute by winning a rematch, regardless of the
venue. If Parole should lose, it would benefit Harper and Ten Broeck
while largely invalidating the results of the first race.

Perhaps most important, agreeing to face Ten Broeck on Harper's
terms would seem a sign of personal weakness. Pierre, whose formidable
testosterone level was now surging, was most assuredly not about to yield
to Frank Harper.

Harper, who had already performed his reciprocal gesture, was a
man long accustomed to deference, to whom employees hastened to
respond, "Yes, sir." He was arguably the greatest racing man in Kentucky, accorded this position by the towering superiority of the thoroughbred he had nurtured. Would Harper be bullied into another
disastrous northern invasion by the recalcitrant Lorillard, who insulted
not only Harper but his entire culture when he refused even to entertain
the notion of sending his thoroughbred to the Bluegrass? The master of
Nantura was not about to concede this point, not to Pierre Lorillard,
not a second time.

All that remained was for one of the two sides to issue a succinct and
unambiguous statement, and Pierre took the initiative. His response to

Harper was delivered via telegram to the editors of *Turf, Field and Farm,* and it was unequivocal:

> *Jersey City, N.J., Dec. 6, 1877.*
> *Editors* Turf, Field and Farm.—*I do not propose to send Parole or any other horse to Louisville to run next Spring. I have a large number of horses in training, and but one trainer, and it will be impossible for me to separate my stable.*
> *Yours respectfully,*
> *P. Lorillard*

Even in the face of Pierre's clear declaration, the racing press attempted to intercede. On December 7, the *Turf, Field and Farm* editorialized a challenge, seeking intervention from Kentuckians still proclaiming Ten Broeck's superiority: "What do the friends of Ten Broeck and Harper propose to do about it? We should like to hear from *them.*" The friends of the aged horseman and his great horse were, by this time, surely as frustrated as the rest of America, but this was Harper's battle, not theirs. If there was ever a reply to this challenge, it did nothing to bring about the needed compromise.

A week later, *Spirit of the Times,* evidently deciding that if Pierre Lorillard could not be persuaded south, perhaps George could, published a letter to the editor that demeaned Parole as having "accidentally" won a "spurt race," and declared that Tom Ochiltree—"the *only* horse who has ever won *all* the great cup events" [italics those of the letter-writer] and the victor over Parole four times in seven tries—was clearly the better thoroughbred." Tom Ochiltree and Ten Broeck were, the letter-writer opined, "the best matched in America."

But it was all to no avail. Pierre Lorillard's efforts to induce Harper north came to nothing; George Lorillard's proposal for a Ten Broeck–Tom Ochiltree match was never taken seriously. Frank Harper, secure in Ten Broeck's ownership of vast stretches of the racing record book and perhaps viewing with disdain his opponents' affluent, high-profile lifestyles, so different from his own, would offer no concession. Merely accepting the Lorillards' terms might have subjected him to additional ridicule.

With no one willing to concede, Ten Broeck, Parole, and Tom Ochiltree went separate ways. The clamor for a rematch was loud and ongoing, and each of the owners had the money and the human resources and, many would argue, the need to confirm or refute the results of the Great Sweepstakes.

But given the owners' refusal to make concessions, given the intransigence, born of wealth, success, and position, that both sides brought in such profusion to the negotiation, the rematch remained forever a nonstarter. Pierre Lorillard's multi-race proposal was never implemented, Ten Broeck was never again sent north to compete, Tom Ochiltree and Parole never journeyed south. And Frank Harper and Pierre Lorillard, whose compromise might have created a second Great Sweepstakes, whether in Kentucky or New York or on neutral turf elsewhere, never permitted such a race to occur.

CHAPTER 10

The Lorillards (Part 2)

"It is hardly dignified to speak of Mrs. Allien in association with the affairs of the family of Mr. Lorillard. There is no mystery about her, and has not been for the past twelve years. All the world knew that she was a Miss Barnes, and for convenience sake was married to Lewis Allien, who was a sort of farm hand at Rancocas, and who dropped out of sight years ago."

—*NEW YORK TIMES*, JULY 14, 1901

DESPITE THE GRANDEUR OF RANCOCAS AND THE EVER MORE IMPRES-sive stock of stallions and broodmares in residence there, it was a pur-chased racehorse that brought Pierre Lorillard his greatest sporting success, when in 1881 Iroquois became the first American-owned horse to defeat the haughty British and win the historic Epsom Derby. Iro-quois's victory bestowed upon Lorillard the title "most famous turfman of his time."

His acquisition of the colt had begun with the purchase of a batch of yearlings, followed by a horse trade involving his brother that would, in the course of events, provide George a handful of the top racehorses of their generation—and Pierre the thoroughbred that would shake the sport to its tradition-bound roots.

The proposition had been a simple one. Both Pierre and George were fond of the offspring of the imported English stallion Leamington, who had sired, among others, John Harper's gallant Longfellow, Pierre's own Parole, and Aristides, the first Kentucky Derby winner. Breeder Aristides

Welch owned Leamington, and had on his hands an enviable collection of the stallion's young foals. Pierre and George inquired as to their availability, a deal was negotiated, and the brothers bought them all.

They proved to be an exceptional group. George received one of the Leamington fillies, named Spinaway, which proved so outstanding that a race in her name is now well into its second century as an integral part of the Saratoga season. George also laid claim to a colt that he called Saunterer, which in 1881 would win the stable's fourth consecutive Preakness, and, for good measure, the Belmont Stakes.

One of Pierre's colts, from the mare Maggie B.B., was a full brother to George's 1879 Preakness winner, Harold, but seemed a bit underdeveloped to Pierre, and he offered the colt to George for $3,000. George, however, waited too long to say yes, and the offer was rescinded. Reconsidering, George next offered $5,000, but Pierre, noting his sibling's heightened interest in the colt, countered at $7,000, which George rejected; and the youngster, given the name Iroquois, was returned to Rancocas to mature.

It may have been the yearling's disposition that had led George to reject Pierre's offers. According to the groom who had handled the Leamington foals, "Iroquois was the most arrogant youngster we ever had. His brother Harold was bad enough, but . . . Iroquois was a real devil."

Fast forward to 1881, and Pierre Lorillard's so-called "real devil" would become the most important thoroughbred on the planet. And the *New York Sportsman*, whose editor, Charles J. Foster, had all but begged George Lorillard "to secure the brother to Harold at any price," would shortly be declaring in print, "We are glad now that Mr. George Lorillard did not succeed in his endeavors to get this colt from his brother."

Pierre Lorillard had made his first assault upon the British turf in 1879, seeking to challenge what was then considered common knowledge: that British runners were vastly superior to America's overhyped and underbred racing stock. With Parole's triumph over the great English racehorse Isonomy, followed by several other prestigious victories (Parole's exploits are discussed in more detail in the Epilogue), Pierre had already begun undermining the Brits' claim to unassailable superiority. But Pierre wished to fire a stronger salvo at the stubbornly skeptical British.

Shipped to Great Britain prior to the 1880 season, Pierre's under-whelming colt from the Leamington haul was subjected by trainer William Brown to an extraordinarily arduous two-year-old campaign, racing twelve times, including twice in a single day, and winning four races. While some saw him as a possible threat for the following year's British classic races, others noted that Iroquois had tailed off toward the end of the year, and questioned whether a runner worked so hard as a two-year-old could recuperate to contend in the Triple Crown events—the 2,000 Guineas, Epsom Derby, and St. Leger.

Iroquois thrived over the winter, and on May 4, 1881, was sent post-ward for his three-year-old debut in the 2,000 Guineas, contested at one mile plus a few steps. Asking a colt to contest the season's first classic event without a prep race was equivalent to asking a modern-day American three-year-old to begin its season in the Kentucky Derby, and not surprisingly, Iroquois was dismissed by the bookmakers at 50-to-1 odds. But the colt raced well, earning a second-place finish for Lorillard and his new trainer, Jacob Pincus.

Recognizing that he had a legitimate classics contender in his stable, Lorillard extracted his bankroll and set about improving Iroquois's chances, engaging jockey Fred Archer to ride his colt four weeks later in the Epsom Derby. Archer's seemingly diabolical talent over the Epsom course had earned him the sobriquet "The Demon Jockey," and the book-makers, noting Iroquois's sparkling 2,000 Guineas performance and the presence of a stronger rider, lowered the American colt's odds to 7-to-1. When a race day rumor that Archer had switched mounts temporarily swept the crowd, the bookies promptly doubled the odds to 14-to-1 until the rumor was disproven, and the colt's odds were returned to their previous level. Iroquois looked impressive enough during his prerace stroll around the saddling paddock that some lowered his odds to 11-to-2.

In London on June 1, Derby Day, "the sky was cloudless, the sun bright, the air sultry, and the dust stifling." The crowd was enormous—nineteen thousand had traveled to Epsom Downs from Victoria Station alone. In attendance were the Prince and Princess of Wales, the Duke and Duchess of Connaught, Princess Louise, the Marchioness of Lorne, the Duke of Cambridge, and Prince Edward of Saxe-Weimar. From their premium boxes they would have an unimpeded view of a race that would produce what one observer described as "the wildest hilarity"—on the other side of the Atlantic:

America Wins the Derby
A Grand Triumph Achieved by Iroquois
Mr. Lorillard's Colt Beats the English Favorite by Half a Length—
Heavy Betting at Large Odds Against the Winner—An Immense Crowd
Witnesses America's Victory—The Story of the Race

London, June 1.—For the first time since the Derby Stakes have been run for, they have been carried away by an American horse, and the whole world of London is asking itself to-night what it all means. At the meeting on Epsom Downs this afternoon, Mr. Pierre Lorillard's b.c. [bay colt] Iroquois snatched the victory from 14 competitors, among which were some of the most famous horses on the English turf, covering the mile and a half of the course in 2:50, and winning by a good half-length over the favorite, Peregrine, owned by Capt. R.W. Grosvenor. Many thousands of pounds were staked on the English horse, and those who had the courage or the sagacity to back Mr. Lorillard's stable have taken fortunes from the pockets of the English turf-men. . . . [I]t can be easily seen that a vast amount of money must have been transferred to the pockets of the fortunate backers of the winner.

In a contest described in the sporting press as "splendid and exciting," Iroquois, with Archer at his diabolical best, had run a waiting race, relaxing near the back of the pack until nearly the final turn, when "Peregrine cannoned against Geologist at the corner, and nearly capsized him." At this point, approaching the stretch run, Peregrine opened a sizable lead, but now "Archer's colors were seen pressing forward on the stand side."

The *New York Sportsman* had warned its readers during the pre-Derby buildup to wager cautiously, observing that to win the race, "the horse must be trained to perfection. . . . His jockey must be a master of the art; bold as a lion, wise as a serpent, quick as lightning to seize the right instant to make play." At the top of the long Epsom Downs stretch, Archer went about proving that he was that jockey.

Under his strong handling, Iroquois overcame Peregrine's lead and gradually begin to edge away from the stubborn English colt, opening a lead that would grow to a half-length at the finish. The victory was a near thing, but Archer, who would be lauded in the *Sportsman* as "the greatest living master of the art of race riding horsemanship," claimed afterward that he "could easily have won the race by three lengths if it had been required." At such a moment, no one could be found so uncouth as to ask the obvious: If you could easily have won by three lengths, why did you cut it so close?

Iroquois's victory produced mass hysteria in America. Trading on the New York Stock Exchange became chaotic as the news reached the traders, and for a time activity was suspended. Hotel bars and local taverns suddenly filled with customers eager to revel in America's victory with anyone of a sporting persuasion. Gents at the city's elite sporting clubs spoke of little else, and washed down extra doses of bubbly to celebrate the occasion. *Spirit of the Times*, recognizing that some Americans might never actually have heard the Indian nation's name pronounced, added an educational bent to its Epsom Derby issue, headlining its feature article "IROQUOIS! (Pronounced ĬR-O-KWOY')."

June 1 was also race day at Jerome Park, and one of the finish line judges found himself too excited at the day's events to perform his job. He raced from stable to stable, shouting, "Iroquois has won the Derby! Iroquois has won the Derby!" The official starter decorated his flag with the word "Iroquois" and a rough drawing of a tomahawk. At the theaters that evening, actors made hasty revisions to their lines, inserting the word "Iroquois" wherever minimally appropriate as a surefire means of drawing applause.

In Albany, the news caused a rare interruption to the contentious political bickering of the day, and legislators immersed themselves in seeking more information about the nation's triumph overseas. Newspapers had special editions on the streets as quickly as the type could be set, and "newsboys reaped small fortunes by the sale of extra editions of the evening papers." In New Jersey, flags were raised in triumph at the Lorillard factory, and the mayor of Jersey City, provided an office in the politically astute Pierre's facility, received updates on his private ticker.

Surprisingly, Pierre had not journeyed to England for the race, and learning of this, reporters "besieged Mr. Lorillard's residence for an interview, but he eluded them," traveling to Jerome Park, his carriage draped in bunting for the occasion. Along the way, the easily recognizable public figure was stopped numerous times by jubilant well-wishers.

Telegrams offering congratulations, including one from the Duke of Manchester, poured into the factory, the Lorillard mansion, Jerome Park, and the many clubs of which Lorillard was a member. Perhaps the most amazing moment of a decidedly amazing day occurred when Pierre, now safely ensconced in Jerome Park's Turf Club and surrounded by beaming backslappers, opened a telegram sent by his wife, who was in London with friends. Mrs. Lorillard, the tobacco magnate explained to his rollicking table mates, had been persuaded to attended the Epsom races, a shocking occurrence, given that his wife had "never taken much interest in his horses, and frequently has not even known his colors when they came in ahead."

Most British bookmakers had continued to offer 7-to-1 odds on Iroquois until the end of wagering, believing that the Lorillard colt had "no chance of winning" but British punters had wagered primarily on local horses, and the "corsairs" had taken in enough pounds on the remainder of the field that they had earned their usual winning percentage on the race.

In America, however, Lorillard's three Derby entrants had drawn a flood of wagering money, and bookmakers on this side of the Atlantic, attributing the wagers to chauvinism, had accepted all action on Iroquois at generous 5-to-1 odds. They should have lowered the odds further.

One doesn't generally anticipate finding detailed bookmaking results in the portentous print of the *New York Times*, but on this occasion the newspaper had its reporters in neighborhood barrooms, back-room bookie joints, and pool halls. Comparing notes, the reporters concluded that:

all of [the bookmakers] lost heavily on the race. . . . At Lovell's pool-rooms, the cashier said that $11,000 had been lost by that establishment alone. At Hackett & DeLacey's, Mr. Hackett declined to make

known the amount of his loss, but admitted that it was consider-
able. . . . [A]t the exchange of Kelly & Bliss, in West Twenty-eighth-
street, the cashier informed a reporter that the establishment had lost a
scant $10,000 on the Derby. . . . At the "commission house" of Cridge
& Co. the cashier said that they had done a business of about $40,000
on the race, but he declined to make known the amount the house had
lost. In addition to the money invested with the book-makers many
thousands of dollars were invested in outside bets, and in these the odds
given were generally larger than in the pool-rooms. It was estimated
at Lovell's exchange that at least $250,000 will change hands on the
result of the race. At other sporting resorts nobody would hazard an
estimate.

Lorillard himself, usually the most enthusiastic of bettors, had, rather
shockingly, invested only minimally on the Derby, and had actually lost
money. This claim was disputed in at least one publication, which headlined that Lorillard had won "Two Millions in Bets," but Pierre was not
one to wager quietly, and the likelihood is that his version of the day's
financial outcome is the correct one.

Quizzed by the press about his unusually small investment in his
colt's Derby chances, Lorillard responded, "I did not think he could stay
the course, so I put the bulk of the money on Barrett and Passaic believing
that either could beat Iroquois." The withdrawal of Barrett, practically on
the eve of the Derby, was said to have made his backers "very wroth," as
losing bettors have been known to be.

Lorillard paid Archer a £1,000 bonus for his winning ride, and
divided another £1,000 among the trainers and stable boys. The amount
paid to Pincus was not stated, but the trainer had followed to the letter
Lorillard's instructions, which had been to give his three potential Derby
entrants "such a preparation that they would break down or go to the post
the best prepared horses that ever faced the starter for the Derby." The
result of this order was that Passaic suffered an injury, and Barrett was
found unequal to the task. Lorillard was not heard to complain, although
there must have been a level of regret that Pincus had not given Iroquois
a prep race prior to the 2,000 Guineas. Perhaps, with just that minimal

additional preparation, Lorillard's colt might now be a challenger for the greatest of all racing prizes: the British Triple Crown.

While all involved understood that June 1, 1881, was a historic day for American thoroughbred racing, no one could have realized at the time just how unique it would prove to be. The *New York Herald* had suggested editorially that the city "reproduce Iroquois in bronze, to occupy some well chosen point in Central Park," a suggestion rejected by the *Turf, Field and Farm* "for the reason that the commissioners may be called upon hereafter to appropriate space in other 'chosen points' for future winners of the Derby."

For the next seventy-three years, however, or until 1954, when Never Say Die became the second American horse to triumph over the British on Derby Day, a statue honoring Iroquois would have basked in splendid isolation. Lorillard was forty-seven years of age on the day Iroquois passed the finish marker first at Epsom Downs, and for the remainder of his life he would be introduced as the only American in history to have defeated the British at their own game. It must have been heady stuff for the descendant of an immigrant tobacconist.

The Derby was not, however, the only race on Iroquois's calendar, and Pincus now set the colt to work solidifying his achievement. Iroquois won the Prince of Wales Stakes under 131 pounds, four more than any previous winner had carried to victory, and two days later won the St. James's Palace Stakes. Even for a trainer as demanding as Pincus, a winning streak of this magnitude must have seemed deserving of a break as the hot, humid summer approached. Iroquois was not, however, permitted to lose form, undergoing rigorous training for the English Triple Crown's final jewel, Doncaster's demanding 1¾-mile St. Leger.

After Iroquois's extraordinary spring and summer campaign, it became impossible to find satisfactory odds on the Lorillard colt on either side of the Atlantic for the St. Leger. Iroquois opened as the wagering favorite in the United States at odds of 7-to-2 and in England at 100-to-30, odds that drifted downward to 2-to-1 on race day. But as the field neared the finish of its daunting journey, it became clear that the favorite's plummeting odds were going to be no more than a minor detail of this St. Leger Day:

Iroquois!
America Captures the St. Leger

Doncaster, September 14—The St. Leger of 1881 has passed into his-
tory, and Iroquois is the winner. The victories of the fabulous American
colt at Epsom and Ascot, are supplemented by a still greater triumph to
day. All the spleen and opposition displayed against the fleetfooted rep-
resentative of America, have vanished in the splendor of his achieve-
ment this afternoon.

On a day described as "cloudy and cheerless," but with no rain, a massive crowd, anticipating the scheduled 3:30 start of the third race of the
British Triple Crown, began invading Doncaster shortly after 6:00 a.m.,
when the first of many trains arrived. Local storekeepers, catering to the
whims of the day, were open early, selling banners in the colors carried by
the various crowd favorites. Pictures of Archer in the Lorillard cherry and
black were in almost every store window.

There were other races on the day's card, but "little interest was taken
in the interlude, as one might term the races preceding the St. Leger,
the book-makers having their time fully occupied with business on the
important race." Finally, with the preliminaries completed, the St. Leger
starters paraded onto the track.

The day had begun with the disturbing rumor that an inmate had
escaped from an insane asylum, with the intention of invading the Doncaster stables and "nobbling" Iroquois, but the Lorillard runner was the
picture of equine health as he stepped onto the track. With few preliminaries—a warm-up gallop around the track, a parade to the starting
point—the starter dropped his flag and sent the field of fifteen on its
journey.

Archer again played a waiting game, easing Iroquois to the rear of
the pack and allowing other runners to perform pace-setting duties. One
of the crowd favorites, Ishmael, earned a roar from the crowd when he
opened a daylight lead with a half-mile to go, but as the field turned into
the stretch, "Iroquois came on in full running, winning easily by a length."
He was only the third American-bred runner ever to compete in the St.
Leger, which had been inaugurated in 1778, and was the first to win the

race. As with the Derby, he would hold this distinction until Never Say Die won his St. Leger in 1954.

Iroquois certainly had nothing more to prove in 1881, and he was retired for the season, with the intention that he would be returned to racing the following year in the United States. He was welcomed home by enthusiastic crowds and a storm of ticker tape at the loading dock; Pierre was lauded in the press as "a pillar of American courage and rewarding success." But Iroquois suffered a burst blood vessel in training, and would not be seen on the track for over a year. He would return to the races in 1883, a mere shadow of the thoroughbred that had defeated the British. And Pierre Lorillard would never again achieve racetrack glory of the sort he had seen in 1881.

Which is not to say that the Lorillard racing empire abruptly crumbled. Rancocas continued to turn out winners, and Lorillard continued stocking his showplace with fashionable stallions, including the enormous Mortemer, "probably the best race-horse that was ever imported into America," winner of the Ascot Gold Cup and considered "by 7 pounds the best horse in Europe." Mortemer's offspring, which included the outstanding filly Wanda, kept Rancocas perpetually among the nation's leading stables, both as owner and breeder.

But Pierre Lorillard was now turning his fertile mind in another direction. The eldest son of Pierre III had long ago bought out his siblings' shares of the undeveloped Tuxedo property, and now he began building "one of the most famous communities on the American social scene" upon the land that his father had won in the legendary family poker game.

It was in October 1885 that Tuxedo Park, through Pierre Lorillard IV's energetic oversight and the labor of some 1,800 Italian and Slovak workmen, practically sprung from the soil. "Eventually two separate villages were created . . . as well as a train station, stores and other houses. . . . By June 1, 1886, when the Tuxedo Club opened with 200 members, a massive Gate and Keep, a large shingle-style Clubhouse resembling a seaside hotel, 13 cottages, 18 miles of carriage roads, an ice house, a fish hatchery, stables, an 8-foot-high barbed wire fence surrounding some 3,000 acres and the first water sewage treatment and telephone systems outside a major city had been constructed."

Lorillard had the land stocked with deer that were intended as hunting targets, but the putative trophies soon became "so tame that they ate out of people's hands." Shortly after the seven brief months Pierre permitted for the first round of building, "specially chartered trains brought 700 of Lorillard's guests to the formal opening of the Tuxedo Park Club. He invited his friends to buy the existing cottages and build more, and Tuxedo Park grew to be "a pleasure ground for the Astors, Iselins, Millses, Havermayers, and Venderbilts."

But Pierre was just getting started. The number of houses and the amenities of the community grew rapidly. A boathouse, racetrack, lawn tennis courts, a court tennis and racquet facility, one of the nation's first golf courses, a swimming pool, a toboggan run, and miles of bridle trails were built for the members' recreational use. There were fifty-four stables along thirty miles of carriage roads. By 1900, Tuxedo Park had become synonymous with luxurious living in a forested setting.

Among its other distinctions, Tuxedo Park added a new word to the American fashion lexicon. "At the first Autumn Ball held at the Tuxedo Club, in 1886, the founder's son, Griswold Lorillard, appeared not in white tie and tails like the other men but in a short jacket with black tie, a fashion he had observed being worn by the Prince of Wales in England that year at the Cowes Regatta. The new fashion for informal evening wear immediately caught on, and, ever since, most Americans have called it a tuxedo."

The new garment was not an instant success with all segments of the fashion world. One critic suggested that Griswold Lorillard looked "for all the world like a royal footman. There were several others of the abbreviated coats worn, which suggested to the onlookers that the boys ought to have been put in straitjackets long ago."

Which is an amusing story and a funny line, but Pierre IV's youngest son, Nathaniel Griswold Lorillard—he preferred to be addressed as "Griswold"—would meet a tragic end. Contracting consumption—in the modern era, we know the disease as tuberculosis—a year or so after he and his acquaintences debuted Tuxedo's namesake garment, the young man died at Rancocas in October, 1888, at the age of twenty-four.

After graduating from college, Griswold had been given his introduction to the family business by Pierre, who created a partnership within the company that included himself and his two sons, but, "[Griswold's] tastes not being in that direction, he retired from the partnership, his father making him a regular allowance. His time after this, up to his sickness, was spent either at the clubs and in society, or with his gun and dog at his father's place"

Griswold's obituaries were notable for their brevity, and for their references to his lack of what might be defined as people skills. One described him as possessing a "reserved and quiet disposition, and thought to be cold and indifferent by his slight acquaintences"; another deemed him "rather serious in his manner." The *New York Times* declared that he "was reserved and did not care to make friends readily." While the author makes no claims to mental health expertise, one wonders whether such a person today, with the Lorillard resources and the advantage of over a century of progress in matters psychological, might find improved life skills through some combination of counseling and medication.

There was no cure at the time for the disease that ended Griswold Lorillard's life; while a few successful cures had been effectuated through the use of pneumothorax—collapsing the affected lung to "rest" the diseased organ—a generally available medicinal cure for tuberculosis and a vaccine to prevent the disease were not available until well into the twentieth century.

It was said that Pierre exerted his will over every possible aspect of Tuxedo life, "as the czar rules Russia." Tuxedo's bylaws were stringent, and invitations to the Lorillards' lavish balls were strictly in accordance with the tobacco magnate's wishes. Rumor had it that when a male member with a theatrical background was invited to instruct a female member in dramatic arts in the privacy of the woman's cottage, Lorillard was so incensed at this breach of protocol that he challenged the male malfeasor to a duel, "but nothing came of it." Lorillard managed to exercise control over Tuxedo Park even after his death; his will directed his executors to "sustain any and all provisions of the by-laws."

But this desire to control, to have decision-making power over all things within his physical or intellectual reach, was a central element of Pierre Lorillard's psyche. Even at the helm of the family's enormous tobacco company, the bigger-than-life Lorillard would occasionally be found at the factory, inspecting facilities and products and chatting with the workers over a cigarette.

Lorillard was a man of varied curiosities, a man with a seemingly constant need to explore new areas of interest, to participate, to accomplish. He was anything but a member of the idle rich. As Lorillard Tobacco Company was in the process of being merged into a corporation, he was offered the presidency of the combined entity. He declined the offer, insisting that he was "too busy" to attend to the duties of the office. One publication declared that he "worked like a Trojan though rich by inheritance,"and the *New York Times* concurred, noting that, "although he was above the necessity of working for his living," Mr. Lorillard, who had been described as "the most 'expensive' man in New York," was "too active-minded a man to be a mere man of pleasure."

At one point, fossil woolly mammoth bones were discovered on Lorillard land in Orange County, New York, and Pierre developed an interest in things ancient. Never one to take a half-hearted approach to a new interest, Lorillard learned of a planned expedition into Mexico and Central America by the French archaeologist Désiré Charnay. Pierre contacted the French Republic and offered to share the expedition's expenses, and upon the conclusion of the exploration was granted one of the highest honors awarded by the French government, the Chevalier of the Legion of Honor.

As Tuxedo Park became a success, Pierre found himself shaken by a series of events that caused him to question his desire to remain active in horse racing. In 1886, the tobacco magnate had become enmeshed in a controversy regarding the prices of horses in selling races, an important source of new blood for Rancocas. In the 1880s, selling races involved a postrace auction, at which any horse entered could be purchased upon reaching its reserve price. Lorillard bid above the reserve when a horse particularly appealed to him, and was frustrated when auctions were halted when the minimum was reached. He concluded that the racetracks conducting the auctions were conspiring to prevent him from acquiring the horses he wanted.

And by 1884, George's health was clearly in decline, the result of the inflammatory rheumatism that had afflicted him for much of his life.

George was, by this time, "little more than an invalid . . . assisted by crutches, or sitting in his carriage, swathed in heavy wraps." Reluctantly conceding that his pain was increasingly preventing him from enjoying his sport, he sold off the farm and most of his horses, essentially retiring as an owner.

Throughout the ordeal of his illness, George, who seems to have been a genuinely kindly man, had taken pains to provide caring treatment for his employees:

> *The stable arrangements are superb. There is room for thirty-nine horses, besides apartments for the boys, saddle room, feed room and a commodious school room for Winter instruction of the lads, so that they may not only become proficient in the saddle, but may also have a fair share of culture upon quitting their present employment, to enable them to start forward in the battle of life, if they so will. The generous care of the proprietor not only provides for their welfare as far as comfortable quarters, warm clothing and wholesome food go to make up the pleasant part of the lives of the lads in his stable, but by the distribution of presents—watches, sets of books and other suitable prizes for the boys—to be won by good conduct and advancement in study. He has opened stakes for these youngsters in a generous strife, likely to prove advantageous to them in all after life. There is no great congregation of stalls, or clutter of numerous buildings, or grand barn-like structure with an immense roof, to exclude sunlight and air necessary for the health of the occupants; on the contrary, the arrangements are of as simple a nature as it is possible to imagine.*

Then, at the end of 1886, George Lorillard died at age forty-two. His death did not come as a shock to family or to the thoroughbred industry; as one obituary noted, "His death had been expected for years, and many times all hope had been abandoned."

Pierre, deeply involved in building the community at Tuxedo Park, increasingly disillusioned with racing, and now facing the loss of his brother and chief competitor, decided to give it up. As a shocked racing world considered the implications of losing two of its most committed supporters, the elder Lorillard announced that Rancocas would sell all of its horses during 1886.

Pierre's racing stock went first. On February 27, 1886, in the famed Glass Barn at Rancocas, twenty-seven horses in training, of which twenty-one were either two- or three-year-olds, sold for $149,050, establishing a record per-head average of $5,520. Pierre, on vacation in Florida, awaited the results, which were wired to him via telegraph.

In a separate sale later that year, thirty-four Rancocas yearlings went for $23,685, and on October 15, eighty-three head of breeding stock, including Iroquois, sold for $142,895. Those on hand prior to the sale were greeted by Lorillard himself, who was said to have escorted potential buyers around Rancocas in a "measured and icily regular manner," as though not wanting to betray his feelings. Later, he sold twenty mares to William K. Vanderbilt for a reported $50,000, providing the stock that would form the basis for Vanderbilt's breeding empire in France.

Pierre's retirement from the game didn't last long. He craved the glamour and the limelight and the horse-trading, and missed the opportunities to indulge his own vast ability to conspicuously consume. Knowing the world was watching, he casually tossed off $30,000, at the time one of the largest prices ever, to purchase Lamplighter in 1891. In a high-priced, well-publicized effort to improve American bloodlines (and in the process, he hoped, win a few classic races), he bought the stallion Simon Magus, the only son of the phenomenal English stallion St. Simon to be imported to the United States.

As in the olden days, when Lorillard and Rancocas were the biggest names in the sport, the familiar cherry and black silks were flying down homestretches and returning to winners' enclosures. Vans carrying valuable Lorillard bloodstock were plying the roads of Jobstown, on their way to the sheds and paddocks of Rancocas.

And now Lorillard had new roles to play. The corporate titan, who had built Tuxedo Park and whose family had introduced to the world such precedent-setting innovations as product advertising, unconditional guarantees, cellophane-wrapped cigarette packages, and rose-scented snuff, applied his genius to the sport, becoming one of racing's most creative owners and executives.

He pioneered the use of aluminum horseshoes, which one day would replace the speed-retarding steel then in common usage. Aluminum in the nineteenth century was a rarity, so Pierre's horses were shod in precious metal obtained from one of the few suppliers able to gain access to such a commodity. Each of the shoes on Rancocas runners bore the logo of Tiffany & Company.

Pierre replaced his brother George as president of Monmouth Park, and challenged the power of the bookmakers, who he believed had rewritten the regulations of racing to the detriment of the sport. He applied his knowledge and his intelligence and his hard-won experience to improving the game, seeking to standardize the rules and level the playing field for all participants.

He sought centralized control over the racing dates of individual tracks, which "before the Gay Nineties . . . operated under [their] own individual rules," attempting to create cooperative relationships through which nearby tracks would coordinate racing dates, increasing attendance at both. He challenged the forfeit rule, under which an owner might withdraw his horse at the last moment without forfeiting even a portion of the entry fee. In some cases, a large number of late scratches would render a supposedly important event almost valueless to the winner.

He publicized the need to control the naming of thoroughbreds. During the 1870s, horses could be raced with no name at all, names could be changed in midcareer, and the same name could be given to multiple horses. Racing historian John Hervey is said to have counted 102 different "Fannys" and 139 "Johns" in the first two volumes of the *American Stud Book*. Confusion about names could lead to manipulation of horses, generating betting coups for unscrupulous gamblers and damaging the sport's credibility.

There were already many local jockey clubs exercising various levels of control in individual areas, but Lorillard believed that an organization with national reach, similar to the English Jockey Club, was required to address these and other concerns. At a dinner organized for discussion of racing issues chaired by James R. Keene, he proposed the creation of such a group. The short-term result was the Board of Control, founded on February 16, 1881. On February 9, 1894, following demands by the

New York State Legislature for reforms beyond even those pioneered by the Board of Control, the Jockey Club was formally chartered. Once established, the American Jockey Club became the sport's accepted rule-making body, a position it has held for generations.

In 1893, Lorillard's doctors informed him that his health was in decline and suggested that he retire from racing, and live out his years in the quietude of Rancocas. But this was not the life Pierre craved, and he soon proclaimed that fresh air and sunshine were more likely to produce a healthy life than enforced retirement. He announced plans to travel with a string of his top thoroughbreds to England.

Pierre had made many friends across the sea, and the cherry and black silks were warmly welcomed back. His best runner this time was another son of Leamington, David Garrick, but this was no Parole, no Iroquois. The Lorillard string won some races and Pierre was observed to have retained his plunger's enthusiasm, "[wagering] large sums if he thinks his horse is in winning form." As the world awaited the turn of the new century, however, Lorillard, his health deteriorating ever more rapidly, must have been anticipating the end.

It had been Pierre's hope to see David Garrick win the Epsom Gold Cup, but he was too ill to attend the races, and even had he been there, David Garrick's second-place finish would have been a disappointment. Eden II won the 1901 Exeter Stakes, Lorillard's final victory over the British, while the tobacco magnate remained in his country estate, awaiting news of the race. A few days later, the filly Cornette became the last thoroughbred to race in Pierre Lorillard's name during his lifetime. "And thus," as one racing historian noted, "the career of the 'cherry and black,' which had begun at Long Branch in 1873, ended at Epsom in June, 1901."

Lorillard's doctors were now insistent: If he wished to see his family again, he must sail for home now. This he did, with a staff of medical personnel, but his doctor warned Lorillard that he did not expect his patient to survive the journey. Even here, Pierre sought to exercise his will: "You don't, eh?" he asked the doctor. "Well, I do. I'll live to get in." And he did.

Even with death approaching, Lorillard's final return to American soil was accomplished with panache. The tobacco magnate had been hastily transported from his English lodge, and delivered pierside to the

Hamburg-American Line's ship the *Deutschland*, which for good reason had been nicknamed the "Millionaire's Ship." On board with Lorillard was essentially a who's who of wealth, science, and power: industrialist J. Pierpont Morgan, astronomer W. L. Elkin, sportsman and philanthropist Harry Payne Whitney, shipping magnates Clement A. Griscomb and Bernard A. Baker, sugar tycoon Claus A. Spreckels, entrepreneur/ sportsman P. A. B. Widener, Mr. and Mrs. W. K. Vanderbilt, and New York Lieutenant Governor Timothy L. Woodruff. Lorillard was unable to partake of such distinguished company; he was confined to his cabin, desperately ill. He was, however, not without companionship aboard the *Deutschland*, although this would not become a matter of public knowledge until later.

Lorillard was greeted upon arrival in New York by an ambulance that rushed the tobacco magnate to the Fifth Avenue Hotel, where a suite of rooms had been reserved and a medical team assembled. Present at his arrival were two doctors, two trained nurses, and Lorillard's valet. His son, Pierre Lorillard Jr., and other family members had been called to his bedside. All had been told to expect the worst.

Lorillard had long been a robust man, who had lived a life so full as to border on the hyperactive. But he was also a large man of substantial appetites, who had partaken generously of the richest food and drink the era could offer. He had undergone decades of stress as a corporate leader, and as the scion of a tobacco mogul, he had been introduced early to the noxious one-two punch of nicotine and cigarette smoke.

He was now reaping the consequences of his lifestyle. Pierre Lorillard was sixty-seven years of age, but it was an old sixty-seven. He had suffered for over a decade with gradually increasing symptoms of kidney disease, and his renal system was now failing altogether under the assault of uraemia and Bright's disease. The oxygen being administered by his doctors might be assisting his labored breathing, but would not contribute toward solidifying his dwindling grasp on life.

Uraemia, sometimes described as "uremic syndrome," is defined as "a serious condition of chronic kidney disease and acute renal failure. It occurs when urea and other waste products build up in the body because the kidneys are unable to eliminate them. These substances can become poisonous (toxic) if they reach high levels." "Severe complications of untreated uraemia can include seizure, coma, cardiac arrest and death." Nowadays, dialysis may be prescribed to relieve the buildup of waste materials; in Lorillard's day, nothing like dialysis existed.

"Bright's disease" is a diagnosis seldom used in modern times; the medical world prefers the more descriptive terms acute nephritis or glomerulonephritis. An individual diagnosed with this nasty malady will experience severe back pain, vomiting, fever, and dropsy, another medical term that passed its shelf life long before the modern day, describing a swelling of soft tissue, or edema, from accumulation of fluids. Pierre Lorillard's would not be an ending "prolonged in comparative comfort." He had been severely ill for weeks, and the medications available to control his pain would be of limited effectiveness.

Upon Lorillard's arrival, on Independence Day, July 4, 1901, his doctors issued a release to the press stating that he was "resting easily . . . perfectly conscious and rational." None of this was true. Lorillard was passing in and out of consciousness and was in agonizing pain. It was later reported that he had for some time been in a semi-comatose condition.

Lorillard was receiving stimulants and what medications were available, but the doctors' primary goals by this time were to relieve his convulsions and moderate his pain level. Lorillard's family remained with him until the end—with the exception of his wife, whose absence would be reported with increasing frequency in the days ahead.

His death, at 2:10 p.m. on Saturday, July 7, 1901, at age sixty-seven, of kidney failure secondary to his Bright's disease, occasioned nationwide headlines and, within weeks, a vortex of scandal and recrimination. Pierre Lorillard's will, which all had anticipated would distribute his vast fortune among the extensive Lorillard clan, would include one bequest that would prove shocking, not only to his family, but to society, the sporting world, the business world, and the throngs of readers who purchased the nation's daily newspapers. It would affect the Sport of Kings for generations.

Lorillard's obituaries touched on his many accomplishments and talents: his business acumen; his success as a sportsman; his contribution to archaeology; his foresight in buying out the majority share in his family's tobacco company; his ownership and eventual sale to Cornelius

Vanderbilt of Ochre Point at Newport, Rhode Island. He was remembered in London's *Telegraph* as "the man who dealt a death blow to those narrow-minded insular persons who resented the intrusion of the Star-spangled Banner among the silks and satins of the British race course."

He was particularly singled out for his brilliant stewardship of the property at Tuxedo Park:

> *No one but a genius in divination and a Napoleon in execution would have even thought of turning this waste land into a garden. But there were beautiful lakes on the property, the wildness of the woods and hills was fascinating, the climate exhilarating.*
>
> *It was in 1884–85, when every one supposed that Mr. Lorillard was engrossed in business, that he was going over the plans for founding Tuxedo, for establishing a great game and fishing preserve there, for building a great club house, and for selling off building plots to those who would become members of the organization and subscribe to its laws. . . . The original outlay in building roads, laying water and gas pipes, and hauling material over miles of mountainous roads was tremendous, but he refused to be discouraged and lived to see his greatest hopes realized.*

But behind Lorillard's accomplishments was a secret, and Lorillard's survivors, wife Emily, son Pierre Jr., and two daughters, were shortly to become featured players in a drama that would be discussed nationwide, by both the loftiest elements of high society and the commonest of street people. As they prepared to bury their unquestioned patriarch, however, the Lorillards mercifully did not yet suspect the trauma Pierre's will would soon inflict upon them. For now, all effort was consumed in providing an appropriate sendoff for the recently departed.

By July 13, however, with Lorillard's funeral and burial at Greenwood Cemetery in Brooklyn, the extended laudation of the tobacco man had gradually receded. The family now awaited the next chapter in the drama that accompanies the passing of any multimillionaire: the reading of the deceased's will. And as this duty was fulfilled, the reporters invited to attend the reading with the family suddenly recognized that this was anything but a commonplace allocation of resources to a cadre of already wealthy relatives. The reporters had, in fact, stumbled onto front-page news:

How Mr. Lorillard Divided His Estate
Bequest of Rancocas to a Woman Arouses His Family

Many of the elements of Lorillard's will were as routine as could be anticipated from the final testament of a multimillionaire with extensive personal belongings, vast real estate holdings, stocks, bonds, and a world-wide racing empire. The estate would be placed in a trust of "the most rigid and binding character," befitting the nature of one with so control-ling a nature, and this was particularly true of the Tuxedo property, which was left "so tied up that until the death of his three children . . . nothing can be disposed of." The proceeds of sales at Tuxedo were to be reinvested in the trust fund.

No members of Lorillard's immediate family would be left in any-thing approaching compromised circumstances, but the amount to be divided was less than might have been anticipated. It had been publicly estimated as long ago as 1884 that the value of his estate was from $15 to $20 million but when the accountants had completed the com-plex calculation of Lorillard's wealth, the amount at the bottom of their spreadsheets was a mere $1,797,925.23 (the *New York Times* placed the value closer to $4 million). Of course, these were 1901 dollars; even the lower estimate would be equivalent to nearly $50 million in modern funds.

Some family members might have recalled one of Lorillard's recent interviews, during which he had remarked that "I have a couple of mil-lions to play with, and I think that will last me to enjoy myself for the rest of my life." Lorillard, it was now opined, "was evidently set upon making the best of his time, rather than making money, and that accounts for the comparatively small amount of the personalty he left behind him."

Most of the so-called "small amount" was left to family members. His widow, the former Emily Taylor, was granted a $50,000 life annuity, in addition to "all my household goods, useful and ornamental, bric-a-brac, articles of vertu, jewels, silverware, paintings, pictures, and other personal property belonging to me and now in her possession or use, or in her possession or use at the time of my decease, as and for her absolute property." A $1 million trust fund initiated by Pierre III was to be shared equally by Pierre's two daughters. Much of the estate would be consolidated, divided into three equal parts, and set aside in trust for Lorillard's children.

To some, a mere $50,000 annuity for Lorillard's widow may have seemed a trivial sum, but family spokespersons were quick to emphasize that Mrs. Lorillard had "much property in her own right," and that the Lorillards had been separated since the early 1890s. Neither had made any effort, even as Pierre lay on his deathbed, to bring about a reconciliation. Reporters were assured that Mrs. Lorillard would not contest probate of her husband's will, nor would she be discovered living on the street owing to her husband's lack of deathbed largesse.

Mrs. Lorillard was succinct on this point: "I am not worrying. . . . I am content. The portion [of the will] he settled on me when we separated is ample for my needs and for the small charities, including the little east side crèche I am interested in."

But an important piece of the Lorillard bequest was not left to family, and with the reading of the section of the will covering Rancocas and the tobacco magnate's racing and breeding empire, the bombshell fell:

I give and bequeath to Lily A. Barnes, known also as Lily Barnes Allien, now or late of the City, County, and State of New York, all farming implements, utensils, wagons, carriages, and all other vehicles belonging to, in use, or connected with my farm known as Rancocas Farm, situated partly in the township of Springfield and partly in the township of Pemberton in the County of Burlington and State of New Jersey, at the time of my decease; also all live and dead stock on, belonging to, or connected with said farm, and all household effects, useful and ornamental, including books, pictures, paintings, silverware, bric-a-brac, articles of vertu, consumable stores and all other goods and chattels or personal property of whatever kind or description, directly or indirectly in use on or connected with said farm or any part thereof, its building, appurtenances, at the time of my decease;

also all horses, mares, and geldings in England, the United States, or elsewhere, in training or otherwise, as and for her absolute property.

A remembrance to a friend or acquaintance would certainly not be unusual in the will of a wealthy man, but the property that Lorillard had built from nothing, that was "the apple of [Lorillard's] eye," on which he had reportedly lavished a million dollars in upgrades, the historic farm that had nurtured Iroquois during his early days? Lorillard's English horses were valued at $55,840 ($1.5 million in modern dollars); his American stables at $69,775 (nearly $2 million).

And just why had Mrs. Allien been left Rancocas? An unnamed family member dismissed out of hand the notion that she might have reasonable claim to so sizable a portion of the Lorillard estate:

> *In regard to Mrs. Allien, she gets Rancocas—if she gets it. All that I care to say of her is that she is a plain, every-day, money-making person. I don't say that there will be a contest, but this is substantial property, real estate, not money, and all the world knows that when it comes to a will it is a very difficult thing for a man to will away real estate from his wife and family. It is hardly dignified to speak of Mrs. Allien in association with the affairs of the family of Mr. Lorillard. There is no mystery about her, and has not been for the past twelve years. All the world knew that she was a Miss Barnes, and for convenience sake was married to Lewis Allien, who was a sort of farm hand at Rancocas, and who dropped out of sight years ago.*

Legalese is a language that changes only moderately over time, and modern day readers will encounter little difficulty in deciphering the above commentary. "I don't say that there will be a contest, but . . .," of course, translates readily to "there will most assuredly be a contest," and the reference to Mrs. Allien as "a plain, every-day, money-making person" is clearly the first projectile in a fusillade of words intended to demean Mrs. Allien as inhabiting a lower class stratum than the upper-crust Lorillards and, incidentally, a reprehensible gold-digger.

Surely, no one of the Lorillard family's societal standing would find it comprehensible that a so important, and valuable, a portion of their patriarch's estate should fall into the hands of the wife of "a sort of farm hand" receiving a wage in return for laboring at the family's famous farm.

All of which was nonsense, anyway, for the woman known as Mrs. Allien was herself not without social standing. She had been born Lily A. Barnes, the niece of Alfred S. Barnes, who for a time was "the biggest publisher in New York," and her cousin, Alfred C. Barnes, had ascended to the rank of army colonel, then served as president of the American Book Company. The Barnes family might not have boasted the wealth of the Lorillards, but they were people of prominence and learning. And they perceived the married Pierre Lorillard's pursuit of their daughter as a scandalous act, magnified by the tobacco magnate's bequest to her of Rancocas.

There had been between Lorillard and Mrs. Allien what was described as a "mutual sympathy . . . for they were close companions until the entrepreneur's death. They were abroad together, and in East Thirty-first street [*sic*] a house was magnificently furnished and bestowed upon Mrs. Allien. There the woman and her father and brother lived, and [were] still living, upon the proceeds of wealth bestowed . . . by the millionaire."

And there was more than just the house: It was "claimed that he had provided for her very liberally during the years they were together, presenting her with whole blocks of stocks and bonds. Her jewels are among the finest in New York . . . many of the handsomest gems ever seen."

Lorillard and Mrs. Allien had engaged in an elaborate subterfuge, which appears to have thoroughly flummoxed the Lorillard family, and which had but one intent: to keep the two in close proximity. There was even a sham marriage to a mysterious Mr. Allien that would become the basis for sensational headlines and salacious rumor when the facts of the situation became known to the press:

It was said that Mr. Allien had come over from England to become the husband of Miss Barnes; that he had received $10,000 after marrying her to conveniently disappear. He was reported to have died, to have gone to Africa or Asia or Greece, to have been swallowed up by *an earthquake or a cyclone. He had disappeared and every one was trying to explain how.*

At last came the real explanation, which for once outdid fiction:

Mrs. Allien had married a woman—the wife of one of Mr. Lorillard's employees on the Jersey estate. . . . $10,000 . . . this woman had received . . . to discard male clothing immediately after the marriage ceremony and to reappear in a woman's gown.

News writers could not have asked for more. "Mrs. Allien Married a Woman, Friend Says," blared the headline on one major daily.

Nor had Mrs. Allien been merely Lorillard's fellow passenger aboard the *Deutschland*. It had, indeed, been Mrs. Allien who, as the ship pulled into harbor and Lorillard was being prepared for transfer to the ambulance, "stroked his face tenderly and said: 'You're home now, dearie.'"

Mrs. Allien had been at the English lodge with Lorillard when his final illness had befallen him, and it had been Mrs. Allien accompanying Lorillard during the ambulance ride to the Fifth Avenue Hotel. She had been in the hotel room as doctors struggled to maintain some semblance of comfort for the dying tobacco magnate, and had remained by his side until the end.

Curiously, as Lorillard's heirs considered their options in the effort to recover from this interloper the remnants of their patriarch's racing legacy, a controversy erupted in the press as to which woman, Mrs. Lorillard or Mrs. Allien, was physically the more attractive. One source described Mrs. Allien as the "beautiful woman who estranged him from his wife." Another, while not disputing that Lorillard had developed an "infatuation" for Mrs. Allien, found Mrs. Lorillard more appealing:

[Lorillard] married a beautiful woman. That was thirty years ago, and she is a beautiful woman yet, although she is a grandmother. . . . And the other woman? She is handsome, but possesses none of the regal beauty and the queenly dignity of the wife.

But still others disputed the description of Mrs. Allien as merely "handsome." She was "a beautiful woman. She is tall, with a charming figure. She has long wavy brown hair and great brown eyes. As a girl she had many admirers. Her parents were in moderate circumstances, but her suitors were mostly the sons of wealthy men, and it is said that she had in her train not a few bachelor and middle-aged beaux." Additionally, Mrs. Allien was "witty, clever, and at [Lorillard's] board easily held her own with the bon vivants whom Mr. Lorillard gathered around him."

Notwithstanding the eternally debatable question of which woman might possess greater feminine wiles, there could be little question that at the end, Mrs. Allien cared more deeply for Lorillard. "[Mrs. Allien] was at the bedside of the millionaire when he died; the wife was at Southampton. . . . [S]he wears deepest mourning now; the wife's dress has no somber note."

While the widowed Mrs. Lorillard continued expressing her contentment with her husband's bequest, however, this was not necessarily the case for the spouse of one of Lorillard's children. The husband of one of Lorillard's daughters, Maude Louise, a man named T. Suffern Tailer, had been "desirous of possessing the Lorillard stables, as he is as enthusiastic a horseman as was his father-in-law." But "Lorillard had no love for his daughter's husband"; in fact, the master of Rancocas had expressed his dislike openly on many occasions. At one point, Tailer may have made too public his hopes for obtaining the Lorillard horseflesh, and found it necessary (or been directed by the family's attorneys) to retract his words via telegram:

> *I have never made, and do not now authorize statements attributed to me. Alleged interview never took place. —T. Suffern Tailer.*

Mr. Tailer's comments aside, the Lorillard family now closed ranks and began utilizing its attorneys to savage Mrs. Allien in the press, anonymously disparaging her claim to either Rancocas or the Lorillard heritage. On July 16, an unnamed Lorillard family spokesperson declared that "we are not disposed to discuss the half dozen rumors published today concerning the will of Mr. Pierre Lorillard," while another—or perhaps the same spokesperson; one suspects that it may have been a member of Messrs. Brinkerhoff & Fielder, the attorneys handling the probate—proceeded to discuss those very intentions. In the process, the second spokesperson strove not merely to supersede Mrs. Allien's right to pursue her inheritance, but her ability to dispose of Rancocas if the legal system should determine her to be the proper owner:

> *Mrs. Lillian B. Allien is not going to take possession of Rancocas or anything that does not belong to her. Nor is she going to take the initiative in any contest that may occur. She will be on the defensive but she will surely defend her rights. As to that she has as yet retained no lawyer, so that she has no legal advice on this point. She needs none at present. . . . I can say that if Rancocas comes to her by the will she will not sell it. I do not care to say if her means would permit her to keep the property in good condition for her own use. She will, however, retain Rancocas if the law says it is hers. What she will do with it in view of her resolve not to sell is another matter.*

After a few days of this, Mrs. Allien fought back, with a maneuver that deftly deflated the Lorillard family's offensive strategy.

It was a two-part sortie that began with a commentary on the Lorillard heirs' efforts to overturn Pierre's will, and in the process sully her good name. "I have kept silence," she stated, "during the vilest calumny, but now I shall speak for the first and last time. During my acquaintance with Mr. Lorillard I acted as his secretary. He treated me more as a man friend than as a woman. It was pure comradeship."

And with her pithy but articulate commentary now on the public record as a counterpoint to the Lorillard family's legal and publicity output, Mrs. Allien undertook the second component of her Rancocas strategy. She took possession of the farm and barred the gates:

> *The gates at Rancocas are closed, and no one can obtain access to the grounds or the house who is not known, nor can anyone see or talk to Mrs. Allien.*

Lorillard had taken pains to ensure that challenges to his will would have dire consequences, stipulating that family members undertaking a legal contest would find their inheritances paid instead to St. Mary's Church at Tuxedo. This point became almost entirely moot when it was determined that every Lorillard named in the will, with the exception of the deceased's two daughters, Emily Kent and Maude Tailer, had joined in the probate application and had thereby waived their standing to contest it. Mrs. Kent, while not an applicant in the probate action, had separately waived her right. This left Mrs. Tailer as the sole family member still legally able to contest the will—and possibly fulfill her husband's dreams by regaining Pierre Lorillard's thoroughbred empire.

But the Tailers would never own Rancocas. There were occasional leaks to the press suggesting that a cash settlement might be offered to Mrs. Allien, and at one point there was a report that she had actually sold out to the Lorillards, but this proved to be magical thinking on the part of the family. Mrs. Allien would, in the end, inherit the showplace farm and its contents, Lorillard's numerous horses in training, his six stallions, seventy mares, forty-five foals, and forty-two yearlings. If it walked on four legs or was physically connected to Rancocas, it would remain the property of Mrs. Allien.

Having validated her claim to the Rancocas horses, Mrs. Allien promptly went about selling them. Perhaps there was a hint of revenge to this action, given that the Lorillard family had outraced her to the offices of the local Jockey Club, and with a $75 payment purchased lifetime rights to Rancocas's renowned cherry and black colors. Though the Lorillard family might no longer own even a single racehorse, it would prevent Mrs. Allien's runners from competing in the colors that had for so long adorned her benefactor's thoroughbreds.

Mrs. Allien sold her yearlings on September 12, 1901, as Pierre Lorillard Jr., sat "in the front row of chairs . . . and, leaning down upon his cane, watched with evident interest, and perhaps some regret, the sale of . . . yearlings . . . that had been bred and trained [*sic*—Pierre Lorillard would never have dirtied his hands as a trainer; he left this task to employees] by his father." The *New York Evening World* declared that the sale portended nothing less than "the end of the historic stud, as prized by the millionaire and his family." While this drastic conclusion was an overstatement—Mrs. Allien could breed a new collection of foals the following spring—there would assuredly be no Rancocas thoroughbreds in 1902's important juvenile races, nor in the following season's three-year-old classics: the Kentucky Derby, the Preakness, the Belmont Stakes, the Travers.

Much of the English racing stock went next. On October 3 at Newmarket, sixteen of the new owner's horses sold for a total of 9,081 guineas, or about $45,405. The American-based racing stock, disparaged as not "remarkable for speed, and it is not believed that any will emulate the performance of Iroquois" (as though breeding farms routinely turned out runners capable of carrying off the English classic races), were next to go, and now it was official: Mrs. Allien, whose Rancocas Farm had produced the winner in the Great Sweepstakes, the first American-owned English Derby champion, and the winners of numerous other major races, was out of the horse racing business.

Mrs. Allien had, over just a few months, not merely demonstrated that she controlled Rancocas, its operations, and its emphases, but in the process, despite being no more than the former wife of "a sort of farm hand," had moved to cut costs decisively while retaining her benefactor's property. She was, perhaps to the shock and dismay of many, demonstrating the ability to manage of one of America's renowned breeding facilities.

In November 1901, Mrs. Allien leased Rancocas to William C. Whitney, one of the era's most notable breeders and the scion of a family devoted to racing at the highest level. Speculation swirled that Rancocas would soon be sold outright to the Whitney family, but Mrs. Allien would not sell the farm. It was, in fact, another sound business decision, one that guaranteed Mrs. Allien significant income for the length of the lease, while Whitney, who had desired closer access to the New York racing scene, now had his entrée into the area. As win-win propositions go, this one was top-grade.

As a woman of considerable wealth and even greater notoriety, Mrs. Allien was forever the subject of rumors, some of which predicted imminent marriage. In December of 1901, the *New York Evening World* believed it had scooped the industry with news of possible engagement plans involving Mrs. Allien and George Livingston, a Tammany Hall veteran and former New York director of Public Works. The *World* managed to wangle an interview with "one of the Negro servants at Rancocas, who has a position of some authority," and in order, one supposes, to provide its readers as realistic a glimpse as possible into the exchange, quoted the servant not merely at length, but in dialect:

> *I have heard as how Mistah Livingston ast her to hab him, but from what I kin learn she gib him no civilized answer. I know she calls him "George," and he has a powerful lot to say about dis place—more than Mistah Pierre Lorillard had.*

Despite the rumors, however, and despite implications gleaned from interviews with staff, Mrs. Allien would not marry—at least, not in 1901.

By 1903, Pierre Lorillard Jr. was not merely attending sales of Rancocas yearlings, but was actively buying there; by one sale's end, he had purchased four youngsters for a total of $925. Mrs. Allien could now claim more than mere title to Rancocas; with Pierre Jr. as a client, she was now operating with the explicit approval of her late companion's family.

Mrs. Allien was wed—for real this time—in 1906, quietly marrying the man who had long been her rumored suitor, George Livingston. Their relationship had crossed the threshold into intimacy purely by accident, when Mrs. Allien asked him for financial advice and, on an overnight visit to Rancocas, Livingston slipped in the bathtub and fractured an ankle. Love bloomed when Mrs. Allien nursed him back to health amid the comfort of her farm.

Married life proved largely uneventful for the new Mrs. Livingston, although there was one decidedly nasty occurrence, when a lamp stationed near the owner's chair at Rancocas exploded, showering her with flaming gas and igniting her clothing. The Livingstons employed a staff of servants at the mansion, and this proved fortuitous, for it was a servant who heard Mrs. Livingston's screams and rushed to extinguish the flames, saving the life of the woman who had inherited the Lorillard showplace.

The Livingstons would remain at Rancocas until 1919, living in semi-retired comfort, breeding a few horses, occasionally sampling the New Jersey and New York social scenes, and traveling south from time to time to hunt, fish, or attend horse-related events. Mrs. Livingston was fifty-four years of age—her husband George was eight years her senior—when she decided to sell Rancocas and depart for Canada, ending a tumultuous period of nearly two decades during which she resided near the top of any listing of America's most reviled individuals.

For the Lorillards, life, generally a quite privileged life, went on, but theirs was not always an existence to be envied. Most of Pierre and Emily Lorillard's offspring had long since drifted out of the public limelight, earning headlines only when they married, gave birth, or died. Pierre IV's eldest son, Pierre Jr.—never called Pierre V—found his way into the news with some frequency, however, in ways that ranged from the felicitous to the unfortunate, to the downright tragic.

In May of 1903, Pierre Jr. and his wife of twenty-two years, the former Caroline Hamilton (their 1881 wedding, to which over two thousand were invited, had been labeled "the social event of the season"), were robbed while staying at London's Berkeley Hotel. The loss was extreme: more than $50,000 in jewelry, as well as a letter of credit and other items. The thieves had apparently followed the couple from Monte Carlo, then "waited for a favorable opportunity, and . . . gone off with the valuables." Assuming the estimated value of the stolen property was close to accurate—and it was speculated that the amount reported may have been conservative—this was a staggering loss (the modern day equivalent would exceed $1.3 million) even to a family as wealthy as the Lorillards, and the thieves got away clean. It must have both horrified and, one imagines, titillated the followers of society.

Pierre Jr. had inherited the family's sporting genes, but was a sportsman more in the mold of his athletic Uncle George, who vigorously competed in sporting events, than his ponderous father Pierre, whose participation was usually limited to well-publicized sponsorships and pricey purchases. Pierre Jr. was, at the very least, a versatile athlete on the club level. He participated frequently in Tuxedo Park tennis and golf tournaments, winning more than his fair share, and occasionally tried his hand at other sports.

On April 10, 1906, for example, Pierre Jr. reached the finals of the Gold Racquet court tennis tournament on his home Tuxedo Park court.

He found himself, unfortunately, paired against a truly outstanding player, amateur champion of the world Jay Gould. The results were described as "too one-sided to be interesting," the invincible Gould utilizing his "rail-road serve" to treat the fashionable gathering in attendance to a 6-0, 6-1, 6-0 shellacking of the local favorite.

But one-sided losses were far from the norm for Pierre Jr., who in June 1907 won the Tuxedo Golf Club's trophy as the golfer with the lowest combined score during the month of May, and on December 29 scored an easy victory in the Tuxedo Tennis and Racquet Club's court tennis club championship. It was the second time Lorillard had won the event.

Pierre's sporting pursuits, however, were set forcibly in perspective when on March 26, 1909, the world awakened to a shocking headline:

Mrs. Lorillard a Suicide
Kills Herself with Gas Following Washington Society Dinner

Pierre Lorillard Jr. and his forty-nine-year-old wife had been attending a dinner honoring Lady Paget, an author and former lady-in-waiting to Queen Victoria. Mrs. Lorillard had participated fully in the festivities, and was later described by an attendee as having been "in fine spirits"; another reported that she had "appeared to be having the best time of any one present."

Returning to the couple's residence on DuPont Circle, however, Caroline Lorillard apparently experienced a bout of profound depression. She turned on the gaslights in her room, blew out the flames, closed the door, and "began to prepare for her death." When Mrs. Lorillard was not present for breakfast the following morning, a servant notified Pierre Jr., and he and the servant went to her room, where they noted a strong odor of gas. Breaking down the door, the two discovered Mrs. Lorillard on the floor, "clad in a silk petticoat and chemisette," having removed one stocking. Still in her hair was the circlet of diamonds she had worn the previous evening.

The servant was dispatched for a physician, while Lorillard attempted artificial respiration. When family physician Dr. M. F. Cuthbert and another doctor arrived, both resorted to every method within their power to revive Mrs. Lorillard. After an hour's effort, the group gave up in despair.

His efforts at saving his patient having failed, Dr. Cuthbert now set about protecting the family's image, pleading with Coroner J. Ramsey Nevitt to list long-standing heart disease, rather than suicide, as the official cause of death. Nevitt was duty-bound, however, to perform a full autopsy, and upon its completion concluded that gas poisoning was the cause of death. He directed that this be inscribed on the death certificate.

With this, the quest began to determine a reason for Mrs. Lorillard's tragic action. It was hypothesized that "from her debutante days," the young Caroline Hamilton had been particularly fond of society and its trappings, and that her marriage to Lorillard had, if anything, "brought much greater liberty than she had before." After years of dinners, balls, and other social functions, however, "this sort of life . . . began to tell on her constitution, which was gradually undermined."

Mrs. Lorillard had recently grown increasingly concerned regarding her health, and had been directed by her physicians to consult with a heart specialist. Traveling to Paris for this purpose, she was informed that there was, indeed, a serious heart problem, and that "if she wanted to live another year she would have to go into retirement entirely, and give up any thought of society." This she attempted for a time, "but she craved excitement, and finally decided that if she could not have it she would die of ennui."

Sadly, the diagnosis proved accurate. Mrs. Lorillard's heart disease continued to progress, and she developed a severe melancholia, living in fear that she might die at any moment. Adding to her misery was insomnia, which she combated until the end by "taking a sedative each night to bring on the desired sleep and rest."

Two sealed notes, one in Mrs. Lorillard's handwriting and bearing the words, "Bury this with me—unopened," were discovered not far from the diamond collar she had worn to the previous evening's dinner. It was the coroner's duty as part of his investigation to read the notes regardless of the written instruction, and he took them into custody, pledging to Pierre Jr. that their contents would never be made public.

It was a pledge on which the coroner might have been forced to renege, had the police investigated the death, but the quick ruling of suicide snatched jurisdiction from them even before their arrival at the scene. Neither Nevitt nor Pierre Lorillard Jr. ever divulged the contents of the notes, which were buried with Mrs. Lorillard along with a few favored pieces of jewelry—the press always described them as "trinkets"—in an envelope "placed in the bosom of Mrs. Lorillard's grave clothes."

One might have hoped that Mrs. Lorillard's funeral and burial, following so tragic an end, might be serene and peaceful, but it was not to be. The funeral, conducted at the couple's home, brought friends and family together to remember Mrs. Lorillard in a quiet and dignified ceremony. Her burial in Tarrytown, New York's Sleepy Hollow Cemetery, however, would be quite another thing. It would be covered in the *New York Times*—in part, on the editorial page.

Mrs. Lorillard's body had been transported to Tarrytown via a special three-car train, necessitated when the Lorillards were unable to make arrangements on short notice for a funeral car. Somehow, it became necessary to pass Mrs. Lorillard's coffin through a car window upon arrival at the cemetery, an awkward task that was captured on film by a persistent and most unwelcome newspaper photographer, who would be excoriated in the press over the next several days as "The Vulgar Snapshot Man."

This predecessor of the modern-day paparazzi had hired a carriage to drive him at breakneck speed to the cemetery, reaching the graveside ahead of the burial party. He set up his camera there, and upon the arrival of the mourners began photographing them, unmoved by their objections, and unintimidated by the presence of the local sheriff and armed guards from Tuxedo Park, one of whom attempted unsuccessfully to grab and smash the camera.

Following a family conference, the funeral attendees formed a human shield between the photographer and the burial chamber, precluding any further photography, and after considerable delay Mrs. Lorillard's black-draped coffin was placed in the family vault. Detectives remained on duty in the cemetery for a time to guard the crypt and prevent efforts to retrieve the mysterious notes. To the best of anyone's knowledge, Mrs. Lorillard's hermetically sealed tomb remained undisturbed, the notes unread.

Just a few months later, Louis Lorillard, brother of Pierre IV and uncle of Pierre Jr., passed away in Paris after a long illness. A prominent sportsman, as was *de rigueur* for that generation of Lorillard men, Louis Lorillard and his wife had traveled abroad the previous spring for his health, but to no avail. Louis Lorillard left behind three sons, one of whom, Beeckman Lorillard, was soon to experience yet another family tragedy.

The appropriate mourning period for his wife having passed, Pierre Lorillard Jr. had returned to the courts and links. On December 11, 1910, playing before "galleries crowded with a fashionable audience," he battled gallantly before losing to C. S. Lee in the Tuxedo Tennis and Racquet Club's first-class court championship, 3-6, 7-5, 6-4, then, less than a month later, wore down a stubborn H. O. Brokaw to win Tuxedo Park's second-class racquet handicap. Here, Lorillard demonstrated a sportsmanlike generosity, agreeing to postpone the match for a week rather than accept a forfeit when Brokaw's travel requirements conflicted with the date of the final match.

And then, just fourteen months later, on Sunday, March 16, 1912, another Lorillard family member ended her own life.

The twenty-eight-year-old wife of Beeckman Lorillard, the former Kathleen Doyle of Asheville, North Carolina, had celebrated what was described as a joyful reunion with her husband in New York's Holland House Hotel following his return from an around-the-world sea cruise that Mrs. Lorillard had been forced to miss. Just two days after his arrival, Mrs. Lorillard tied one end of a canvas strap around a shower fixture in her hotel room, the other end around her own neck, and stepped off the edge of the tub. Discovered by her distraught husband, Mrs. Lorillard died almost instantly.

The couple's travel plans had been derailed by a series of mishaps affecting both, including Mrs. Lorillard's illness and surgery shortly before the planned departure, her husband's illness, which had prevented their reunion in Australia, and a serious accident in which Mrs. Lorillard was thrown from a horse-drawn buggy. When the two reunited at the hotel, they had been apart for a year.

In the aftermath of the tragedy there was intense speculation as to why a wealthy, attractive, twenty-eight-year-old woman who had just rejoined her husband after a year apart might have wished to harm herself. Beeckman Lorillard insisted that he had no explanation other than his wife's high-strung nature: "My wife had been extremely nervous for a long time. We had had no quarrel."

The physicians involved offered explanations for the unexplainable that the modern reader will find surprisingly unscientific. Coroner Israel L. Feinberg explained her action as "the sudden impulse of a neurotic woman," while Dr. A. A. Moore, who had been among the first at the scene and had attempted to resuscitate the dying woman, speculated that she may have fallen victim to "a fit of sudden insanity."

It was Mrs. Lorillard herself, however, in a hastily scrawled and crumpled note found at the scene by a hotel maid, who suggested the most probable explanation for her tragic action. The note stated that only Mrs. Lorillard should be held responsible for the suicide. She was simply "tired of it all."

On July 13, 1912, Pierre Jr. undertook a new sporting challenge, entering the world of standardbred racing—as a driver. The event was a day of racing at the village of Goshen, New York, and Pierre piloted two winners, while a blue-blooded competitor, Averill Harriman, took home a ribbon. Here was an athletic feat to which neither Pierre Jr.'s all-conquering father nor his athletic Uncle George could lay claim; neither had ever piloted one of his own steeds to victory. Pierre Jr. repeated the feat at Goshen the following year, driving his mare Notice B. to a victory over Amasis, driven by County Judge A.H.P. Seeger, before 2,500 spectators.

All families have foibles; most families suffer theirs privately. If you happened to be named Lorillard, however, your dirty laundry was likely to be aired in public, sometimes embarrassingly so. Such was the case on November 8, 1914, when the *New York Times* detailed the story of Irving Lorillard, jailed for refusal to pay alimony to his wife, Lenora, claiming that he could not afford the cost.

A poverty-stricken Lorillard? Here was grist for any slow news day. Irving Lorillard claimed to be living as a near-hermit in a "small cottage, poorly furnished, near the mansions of the millionaire colony in Scarsdale [presumably a reference to Tuxedo Park, some twenty-five miles from Scarsdale]." Separated from his wife, Lenora, since 1901, Irving Lorillard had paid no alimony for thirteen years, and claimed to have no objection to a jail term, but no funds with which he could possibly pay alimony.

Lenora Lorillard's legal representative countered his claim of poverty and questioned his alleged hermit's existence, noting that Irving attended church regularly, was popular among his neighbors, owned a telephone, and lived in relative comfort in what was described as a "hermitage de luxe." Somehow, a settlement was reached and the case vanished from the media, perhaps with the assistance of one or more Lorillard family members willing to part with a small fraction of the family fortune to avoid further embarrassing headlines.

The sixty-seven-year-old Lorillard Mansion, built in 1856 just above the Bronx River, burned on March 31, 1923. Property of the City of New York since 1915, the building's roof, attic, and upper stories were extensively damaged, but the underlying floors remained sound, and city personnel urgently searched the budget, seeking funds to repair the damage before the unpredictable spring weather could further compromise the structure.

And here is one instance—modern-day taxpayers may experience difficulty in recalling others like it—in which governmental bodies successfully cooperated to accomplish an urgent task. The mayor became involved, the Board of Finance discovered the needed funding, and repairs were made. The fine architectural touches of this unique home remain in place more than ninety years later. In its modern usage, the mansion serves as the Bronx Society of Arts and Sciences, incorporating in its 250 acres not merely the historic home, but also the winding pathways to the former Lorillard stables, an old-fashioned flower garden where once Lorillard's famous "Acre of Roses" bloomed, and what is reputedly the most splendid hemlock forest anywhere.

Mrs. Pierre Lorillard, the former Miss Emily Taylor, whose husband had bequeathed Rancocas Stud to his female companion, breathed her last in 1925, at her family home in Monroe, New York. As was so often the case for women in those unliberated days, many of the published obituaries devoted as much ink to the accomplishments of her late husband as to her own, dwelling at length upon his triumphs in business and on the turf. Mrs. Lorillard might have found her *New York Times* obituary, which recalled her husband's relationship with Mrs. Allien, particularly offensive.

Since his father's death, Pierre Jr. had become increasingly the head of the family, in business as well as in the continuation of his late father's sporting tradition. It had been Pierre Jr. who had taken command of the family's tobacco business when his father's sporting interests had again sent him across the ocean, and it was Pierre Jr. who negotiated the merger of the company with six other corporate entities, creating the giant Continental Tobacco Company. Pierre Jr. even attempted to extend his family's influence with an unsuccessful run for a State Assembly seat.

An extraordinarily eligible bachelor since his wife's much-publicized suicide in March 1909, Pierre Jr. waited nearly twenty-two years to remarry, wedding Ruth Hill Beard, the widowed daughter of one of the founders of the Great Northern Railroad, in 1931. Lorillard and Beard were married in a quiet ceremony at the bride's home, certainly the antithesis of the groom's "social event of the year" first marriage. The couple honeymooned in Palm Beach.

As newspapers would continue to do for the rest of his life and, indeed, in his own obituary, much of the news coverage of Pierre Jr.'s pending marriage mentioned prominently the near-mythical exploits of his father, dead now for thirty years. Pierre Jr. was an impressive figure in his own right, but it must have been clear to all by this time that no one named Lorillard could escape the all-consuming shadow of the extraordinary Pierre IV. By now, it was almost entirely in Lorillard-related news items that one ever read of the old Fifth Avenue Hotel, where Pierre IV died in 1901, and which itself was demolished in April of 1908.

And now Pierre Jr. himself was growing older. Born in 1860, he was seventy-five years old when he succeeded Alfred B. Maclay as president of the American Horse Show Association in January of 1936. At the time, only Maclay and Reginald Vanderbilt had served as president of the association. Of the nine organization founders, only Maclay and Lorillard remained among the living.

Pierre Jr. would not have an extensive term as the organization's leader. He had served on the US Olympic Committee during the turbulent run-up to the 1936 Olympic Games in Berlin, which served as both a showplace for Adolf Hitler and a phenomenal stage for the athletic talents of Jesse Owens. Perhaps it was too much for a seventy-six-year-old man—even a seventy-six-year-old Lorillard.

Almost one year to the day after announcing Lorillard's appointment to the position, the assistant secretary of the AHSA announced that Pierre Jr.—now known as "Colonel Lorillard" for his efforts on behalf of the US Remount Association and his service at Fort Riley, Kansas— would not seek a second one-year term.

Pierre Lorillard Jr. succumbed quietly in his sleep in his beloved Tuxedo Park on August 6, 1940, following a lifetime devoted to the family business, to continuing the Lorillard sporting legacy, and to traveling, socializing, and living a good life. Death at age eighty spared Pierre Jr. one of the worst possible events that can befall a parent: his son, Griswold Lorillard, died a year and a half after his father, stricken at the age of fifty-six.

The second Mrs. Lorillard Jr. did not wait long to remarry. On October 8, 1941, Ruth Hill Beard Lorillard was married in a simple ceremony in Tuxedo Park that came as "a surprise to society." The groom was Emile Heidsieck, a cousin of the fabulously wealthy champagne entrepreneur, who had spent much of his life in France and Belgium.

Chapter 11

The End of Rancocas

Dear Sir—At a meeting of the stewards of the summer meeting of the Saratoga Racing Association, the following resolution was adopted:

In the case of the Rancocas Stables' filly Ladana, entered for the Burnt Hills Handicap, August 13, but scratched by the stewards owing to her condition, the stewards find the filly was admittedly poisoned, and take occasion to condemn the management of the stable for not having taken measures to prevent the same. They consider the incident as scandalous, and calculated to impair confidence in racing; therefore, it is ordered that no further entries by the Rancocas Stable to overnight events be accepted during the meeting.

—Communication from Saratoga Race Course stewards George D. Widener, Walter M. Jeffords, and W. S. Vosburgh to Frank Taylor, trainer for Rancocas Stable, following the poisoning of the filly Ladana in the Saratoga paddock, August 13, 1931

When Lily Allien took possession of Rancocas on August 5, 1901, the Lorillard family had responded with shock, concern, and speculation. Why, exactly, had the widow of "a sort of farm hand" occupied Rancocas? Was she there to oversee the government's inspection process, which, assuming she could wrest legal control of the property from the Lorillard heirs, would result in taxes at 5 percent of Rancocas's assessed value? Was she seeking to liberate valuables from the house before being evicted?

These questions became moot when the courts awarded Rancocas to Mrs. Allien, but she and her husband did remove a number of mementos before selling the property to oilman Harry Sinclair in 1919. These included two massive cast-iron lyres that had previously resided atop one of the Rancocas entrance gates, and a set of baroque stained-glass windows so heavy that two boats were required to ferry them across the Delaware River. And then the Livingstons took their leave of the property, in favor of a simpler, less tumultuous, less public existence.

Sinclair began his occupancy of Rancocas with enormous plans, a huge bankroll, and the intention that the farm would again rise to the top of the thoroughbred industry. And, most important, he began by taking on an accomplished and knowledgeable trainer and farm manager, Sam Hildreth, as his business partner. It would be Hildreth who would shepherd Rancocas through a succession of successful seasons, and in the process would add to a resume that was already of Hall of Fame caliber.

By the time Sinclair learned that Rancocas was on the market, he had already earned a reputation for relying on his instincts, for sinking his own cash into successful, high-risk, high-reward ventures. His first oil fortune had been earned from a piece of Oklahoma land that had been purchased in the as yet unproven expectation that there might be oil beneath the surface. He persuaded a bank to loan him money for drilling equipment and hired a crew, knowing that a dry hole would mean bankruptcy. The well came up a gusher, on which he built one of the nation's largest oil fortunes.

As Sinclair and Mrs. Livingston completed negotiations for Rancocas, the Sinclair Consolidated Oil Corporation already exceeded an estimated $100 million in value. By 1949, when Sinclair retired from the industry, its assets would top a billion.

A story is told, perhaps apocryphal, of Hildreth's first meeting with Sinclair, who was attending the races at Belmont Park with racetrack concessionaire Harry Stevens. Sinclair was already considering purchasing some racehorses, but the oil magnate knew almost nothing about the entrants at Belmont that day. Introduced to Hildreth by Stevens, Sinclair asked the trainer which horses he fancied, and Hildreth marked his program. By the end of the day, a procession of Hildreth's choices had posed in the winner's circle.

And thus began an association that seemed predestined to succeed—Sinclair, the man with riches and ambition; Hildreth, the man who knew horses. Hildreth had already led the nation's trainers in earnings on five occasions—in 1909, 1910, 1911, 1916, and 1917—and had topped the owner standings in 1909, 1910, and 1911.

With money not an object and one of history's great horsemen as his business partner, it was Sinclair's intention to emulate Pierre Lorillard's hands-on approach as an owner and breeder of thoroughbreds. He would begin with the purchase and complete renovation of Rancocas, a decision that he unfortunately had not made sufficiently clear to his partner. Hildreth, though reasonably well-to-do, could not imagine where he might find his share of the cost:

> *"I think we ought to buy the Rancocas Farm," was the sudden way [Sinclair] put it to me one day when the breeding germ had taken such a grip on his system that there was no cure. And I'll admit I was staggered. Rancocas! The great establishment which Pierre Lorillard had developed at Jobstown, New Jersey, a half-century before when I was a kid . . . a great estate of 1244 acres . . . and its stables for every breeding purpose and its broad paddocks, some of them covering 100 acres. And its fifty acres of deer park and its swimming pools and the training track . . .*
>
> *"I'll tell the world you're no piker," I managed to observe after a spell of thinking. But Mr. Sinclair paid no attention.*
>
> *"And I think we can do a lot to improve it. I've already been down there to look it over and it needs plenty of fixing up. But that's easy; all you need is a crew of carpenters and plasterers and plumbers and an architect and an engineer or two. And I think a few more buildings are needed . . ."*
>
> *"What's all this going to stand us?" I finally blurted out. But Mr. Sinclair went right on, ignoring my practical question.*
>
> *"And then in a couple of years we'll have our own horses to send to the post, the horses we raised on our own farm."*
>
> *"What's the bill going to be?" I broke in.*

"I think we'd better call ourselves the Rancocas Stable; that will be an appropriate name for a stable racing the horses bred at Rancocas Farm."

"How much?"

"I've always had a leaning toward white and green. We'll have to have white and green in our racing colors."

"Name the cost; you know what I mean, say something about what I'll have to chip in to do all this. Slip it to me in dollars and cents, if you know what I mean." This in a feeble voice from me.

Sinclair earmarked a fortune for repairs and maintenance, still more for improvements and additions, all while a shocked Hildreth watched the expenses mount and his bankroll dwindle alarmingly. There seemed no expense Sinclair did not find acceptable, including retaining Earl Sande and Lavern Fator, two of the nation's best—and highest paid—jockeys, to pilot the Rancocas horses.

Finally, a beleaguered Hildreth all but begged his partner to buy him out, agreeing to train the Rancocas thoroughbreds and manage the farm. Hildreth received the title of general manager of all operations at Rancocas. And Sinclair returned to the task of reinventing the farm as a modern showplace.

Even with the full-time demand of an oil company and the diversion of rebuilding one of America's most historic thoroughbred operations from the bottom up, Sinclair, owner of an active mind in the Lorillard mold, also sought riches in other ventures. In 1920, sensing potential profit in the monopolistic approach of the National and American Baseball Leagues toward providing adequate pay to their top athletes, Sinclair created the Federal Baseball League, offering exorbitant salaries to star players willing to jump from their current teams. The existing major leagues fought back in the locker rooms and the courts, and Sinclair eventually took a $500,000 loss on the venture.

For Sinclair, this was tipping money. Shrugging off the loss, the new master of Rancocas rededicated himself to thoroughbred racing and breeding, with success that soon became unprecedented in the industry.

None of it would have been possible without Hildreth. Born in 1866, the Rancocas general manager had, like so many of the era's trainers, begun his racing career as a jockey, riding for his father, a small-time tobacco planter whose true passion was the breeding and racing of quarter horses. The racecourses were improvised, hardscrabble quarter-mile straightaways that had been hacked out of the fields, and with his father seeking any advantage he could find in these catch-as-catch-can races, Hildreth went almost directly from cradle to saddle. Once he could hang on to a straining racehorse for a full quarter-mile, his feathery light weight proved a huge advantage.

Hildreth was not, however, the only underaged, lightweight jockey to achieve national prominence after scrambling on horseback over those scrubland trails. One who competed against him was a lad named Charles Curtis, who would express fond memories of Hildreth decades later, when Curtis was serving under Herbert Hoover as vice president of the United States.

Hildreth grew and gained weight, and by age sixteen had been forced to transition from jockey to horse shoer. From there, he advanced to training horses for others, and then to owning a few of his own. Along the way, he also learned the craft of the handicapper, essential at a time when skillful wagering could mean the difference between a stable's remaining viable and its being sold off for meal money. For years, Hildreth's life emulated that of his father. He trained his stable and traveled from racetrack to racetrack, wagering and swapping horses.

Hildreth was training for multimillionaire Charles Kohler in 1911 when a fanatically anti-gambling New York state legislature passed the Hart-Agnew Act, shutting down wagering at the state's racetracks. Rather than padlock his racing operation, Kohler decided to move his entire stable, horses and humans alike, to France.

This was not a trivial decision, particularly given that many French races were limited to animals bred in France. An exception was the International Week meeting at Maisons-Lafitte, which lasted only five days.

Tragedy struck the Kohler stable when the owner died suddenly less than a week after arriving in Paris, leaving the trainer with sole responsibility for the stable. Hildreth solved the problem by shipping most of the Kohler runners to the sales yards of Deauville, and shortly thereafter the trainer crossed paths with another American expatriate, August Belmont. The Hart-Agnew Act had been repealed, and Belmont was looking to restore his operation to its previous prominence. Would Hildreth consider returning home?

"The stay in Paris had been fine, and we had our share of success with the Kohler horses," Hildreth recalled, "but after all there's no place like home. I was anxious to see the old familiar faces again in the paddock. I was itching for someone to come along and give me a hard slap on the back and shoot a few American cuss words in my direction."

Those were good years for Hildreth. He would resume in New York almost as though he had never been away, leading all conditioners in earnings in 1916 and 1917, and challenging H. G. Bedwell for the top spot in 1918 and 1919, when Triple Crown winner Sir Barton pushed Bedwell to the head of the list. Nobody was going to top Louis Feustel among the nation's conditioners in 1920, when $166,140 of his $206,728 in earnings were banked by Man o' War, which won all ten of his starts.

In 1921, for the first time since the Lorillard era, Rancocas led the nation's stables in earnings. Sinclair and Hildreth repeated the following year, and topped the list for a third consecutive season in 1923, setting a record for purse money, with earnings of $438,849, that would stand until 1941, when Triple Crown winner Whirlaway, earning $272,386 by himself, pushed the Calumet Stable to record earnings of $475,091. Rancocas's peak season would be 1923, with its enormously popular three-year-old, Zev, described by one racing historian as "pre-eminently the horse of the year 1923," winning the Kentucky Derby and Belmont Stakes, then defeating the Epsom Derby winner, Papyrus, in a $100,000 match race at Belmont Park.

But not all of Rancocas's headlines during those years were positive. Among the most annoying of the negatives proved to be the stable's highly publicized purchase of the great Man o' War's younger brother, a horse that had been named Playfellow.

Given Playfellow's pedigree, it was inevitable that his availability for sale would cause the lords of Rancocas to salivate. A son of Fair Play and the mare Mahubah, Playfellow's siblings included not only Man o' War, but also an older sister named Masda, which had briefly been trained by Hildreth. Masda had won some races for other trainers, but what Hildreth recalled was her ability to flat-out motor. "Several times when I had held the stop-watch on Masda," he recalled, "she had run so fast that I thought there must be some mistake."

Playfellow was the property of veteran horseman James F. Johnson, who had purchased Man o' War's sibling as part of a group of yearlings for his Quincy Stable, paying an average of $2,000 per head, then watched delightedly as his new purchase's brilliant brother rewrote racing's record book.

It was Johnson's belief that he could realize a six-digit windfall profit on Playfellow, and he had already turned down several offers of $100,000. Hildreth had reportedly offered as much as $115,000 in the spring of 1921 (Johnson later admitted that Hildreth's offer had been only $100,000), but Johnson wanted more. It was his belief that the colt would earn at least $75,000 during the following racing season, more in future years, and princely amounts in stud fees upon retirement. He could, Johnson claimed, "do anything Man o' War ever did, and I know he can beat any other three-year-old in America."

No one, unfortunately, had explained this to Playfellow. Man o' War had won nine of ten as a two-year-old, and earned $83,325; his brother concluded his juvenile campaign winless, with just $800 in earnings. Johnson hastened to remind potential buyers, however, that Man o' War had been unbeaten as a three-year-old. Just one more winter's maturation, it was hinted, should surely vault Playfellow into the leadership of his generation of thoroughbreds.

When Playfellow won his first two outings at age three, Sinclair and Hildreth resurfaced the $100,000 deal that Johnson had turned down previously, and this time the offer was accepted. The colt's much-anticipated debut for Rancocas occurred on June 18, 1921, in Belmont Park's Carlton Stakes, but another new Sinclair purchase, Knobbie, earned the victory. Knobbie could not, however, pilfer the headlines from his exorbitantly priced stablemate ("Playfellow, Under Wraps, Runs Second to Knobbie in Carlton Stakes").

This could only have been viewed as a promising first effort for the expensive new Rancocas purchase, and Playfellow was quickly returned to the races, heading postward in the June 22 Fair Play Handicap, a race named for his sire. Playfellow ran third this time, earning another paycheck, but enthusiasm for his effort was decidedly muted, given that the Fair Play had drawn only three starters.

This time, in fact, the headlines focused less on Playfellow's potential and pedigree, more on his cost and what was increasingly appearing to be his lack of ability. "Playfellow Finishes Last in Field of Three in Fair Play Handicap at the Aqueduct Track: Fair Gain Beats $115,000 Colt in Race at Mile," headlined one newspaper. "Playfellow, $115,000 Horse, Last in Fairplay [*sic*] Handicap . . . Brother of Man o' War Gives Talent Hard Jolt," trumpeted another.

Worse yet, some in the press were beginning to treat the high-priced Rancocas purchase as something of a joke. In the *Washington Herald*, columnist Ed Curley, whose creatively prosaic approach to the sport occasionally conjured forth colorful, if apocryphal, Yiddish-accented racetrack denizens, "quoted" one derisively: "Sammy Hildreth paid $115,000 for that skate? Would that he'd do business in my line with me. . . . Sammy must be meshuggah." The Rancocas duo must have been simmering at such coverage. The most successful pair in American racing, they were being ridiculed in the nation's sports pages.

Some in the media, however, had excuses for Playfellow. Aqueduct racing secretary Walter S. Vosburgh was cited for the "enormous weight concessions" he had asked of the colt, which had carried 114 pounds in the Fair Play, to 102 for the victorious Fair Game and 106 for Thunderstorm. During the previous season, readers were reminded, Fair Game had been "one of the most consistent three-year-olds among the handicap brigade." Thunderstorm was "considered one of the best milers in the country."

There were those who assigned the blame to Hildreth personally, citing his decision to disregard the advice he received from Playfellow's former trainer, "Sunny Jim" Fitzsimmons, not to use blinkers on the colt. Fitzsimmons informed the *Evening World*'s reporter that he had "tried

Playfellow in blinkers in private last season, and the big son of Fair Play showed that he would be better off with a free eye by his failure to run with his workmates whenever they attempted to pass him." Fitzsimmons diplomatically avoided comment on the possibility that Playfellow may simply have lacked the velocity to match paces with his workmates.

Entered in a June 27 race, Playfellow was abruptly withdrawn by Hildreth after demonstrating "an amazing lack of speed" in a workout, plodding a half-mile in fifty-two seconds. That was the end for Hildreth. Summoning the media, he alleged that while he and Sinclair had bought Playfellow in good faith, "with the understanding that he was perfectly sound . . . now I find that he is not sound," that they had "bought a gold brick in Playfellow." Sinclair and Hildreth demanded the return of their money from Johnson, and when the Quincy Stable's owner refused to undo the horse trade that had, after all, been initiated by Hildreth, the Rancocas duo contacted their attorneys.

Legal maneuvering began almost at once. On June 28, Johnson trotted out "one of the highest authorities on thoroughbred health in this country," veterinarian R. W. McCully, who insisted that two days before the transfer of Playfellow to Rancocas, he had "examined and passed upon Playfellow as a worthy risk for two insurance companies." As a result, "the Hartford Insurance Company had written a policy on Playfellow for $47,200, and Lloyds of London had written another on the colt for 14,000 pounds sterling." With McCully's testimony likely to garner substantial respect in the forthcoming legal battle, there were claims that "betting on the outcome has already been engaged in, with the Quincy Stable favorite."

Hildreth countered by announcing that Playfellow would not race again in 1921, and probably not ever again for Rancocas, alleging that the colt was fundamentally unsound due to a pair of stable vices known as "cribbing" and "windsucking," either of which would constitute a *prima facie* case for unsoundness in any horse expected to earn its keep through speed and stamina.

In cribbing, a horse "will place his upper front teeth on a stall door, rail, or post, then tense his neck muscles and gulp air, emitting a grunting sound." One source suggested that an afflicted horse might crib more than three thousand times per day. Cribbers were considered more susceptible than those without the habit to potentially fatal attacks of colic.

A windsucker (the malady is technically known as aerophagia) will suck down air for extended periods of time. This is not normal breathing; windsucking places a physical demand on the animal, which can also develop stomach and intestinal issues. It is widely believed that other horses will readily emulate the behavior of a single cribber or windsucker, until potentially an entire stable of horses can acquire the maladies.

The habit that seemed most to concern Hildreth and Sinclair, however, was Playfellow's habit of running too slowly to defeat other horses. With an expensive thoroughbred in their barn that appeared incapable of earning back more than a tiny fraction of its cost, added the possibility of spreading a nasty psychological issue through the stable, and accomplished all of this to the accompaniment of reams of negative press coverage, Hildreth and Sinclair would look to the courts to rescue them from their unfortunate purchase.

There were three Playfellow trials, and in some ways they were unlike any ever seen in the New York courts. The first took place in December of 1921, in the Brooklyn courtroom of Supreme Court Justice Frank B. Gannon Jr. A jury of twelve businessmen was convened—women would not win the right to serve on New York juries until 1937—with one primary attribute: They were required to have no firsthand knowledge of thoroughbred racing.

As the first trial began, Johnson insisted that Playfellow was sound. The stable's assistant trainer, however, contradicted the owner, testifying that he had used a specially designed windsucking bit on Playfellow— but "merely as a precautionary measure." This comment, which could have been devastating to the Quincy Stable case, was followed by testimony from common stablehands, blue-blooded owners, veteran trainers, respected veterinarians, and others brought forward to strengthen the case of one side or the other. The jurists, bombarded by divergent opinions, unfamiliar racing jargon, and abstruse veterinary terminology, rapidly became overwhelmed.

The resulting deadlock was probably inevitable. The vote was reportedly ten to two, with both sides claiming the majority, and this became

Wyndham Walden trained Tom Ochiltree for the Great Sweepstakes.

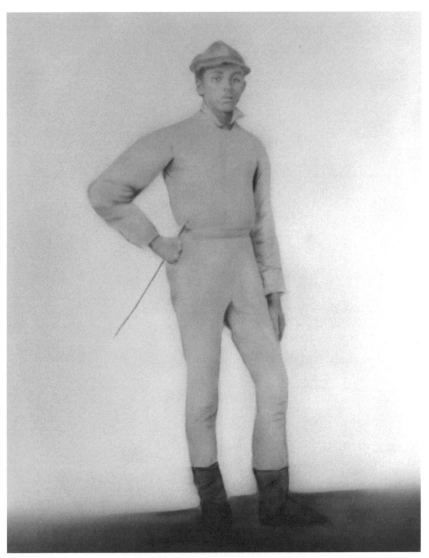

Billy Walker piloted Ten Broeck in the Great Sweepstakes.

Blunt-spoken William Brown trained Parole and Iroquois for Pierre
Lorillard.

William Barrett, rider of Parole, died tragically in 1883 at age twenty-four. KEENELAND LIBRARY

Big Tom Ochiltree was considered Ten Broeck's chief competition.
KEENELAND LIBRARY

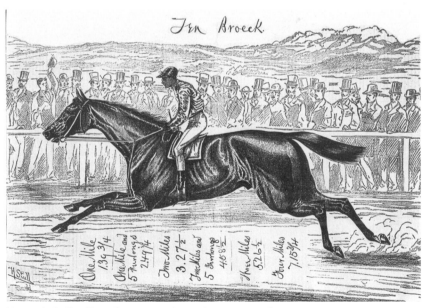

Kentucky's Ten Broeck set records at almost every distance.
KEENELAND LIBRARY

Ten Broeck's was the first equine tombstone in America. MARLIN MITCHELL

Hall of Famer Sam Hildreth helped return Rancocas to prominence.
KEENELAND-COOK

Pierre Lorillard's English Derby victory demonstrated that American thoroughbreds could compete on the international scene. KEENELAND LIBRARY

Pierre IV's eldest son, Pierre Lorillard Jr., was a sportsman in his own right.

Lily Livingston's inheritance of Rancocas from Pierre Lorillard was considered scandalous. KEENELAND-COOK

Lexington, sire of Tom Ochiltree, was known as "The Blind Hero of Woodburn."
KEENELAND LIBRARY

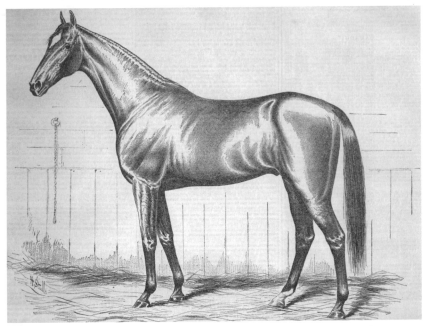

The great stallion Leamington fathered Parole and numerous other top horses.
KEENELAND LIBRARY

Longfellow (with owner John Harper) was the first great Nantura runner.
KEENELAND LIBRARY

Harry Sinclair (right, shown with racetrack concessionaire Harry Stevens) purchased Rancocas Farm from Lillian Livingston and later became a central figure in the Teapot Dome Scandal.   KEENELAND-COOK

Hall of Famer Jacob Pincus trained Iroquois for the
English Derby.

George Barbee, rider of Tom
Ochiltree, was known for
his powerful riding style.
KEENELAND LIBRARY

Fred Archer won the
English Derby aboard
Pierre Lorillard's
Iroquois.
KEENELAND LIBRARY

Frank Harper was a hands-on owner who helped train Ten Broeck. KEENELAND LIBRARY

After winning the Great Sweepstakes, Parole became a favorite in England.
KEENELAND LIBRARY

Iroquois won the English Derby for Pierre Lorillard.   KEENELAND LIBRARY

the official result when the court clerk dismissed the jurors before deliberations were concluded. Denied his victory, Sinclair's counsel notified the court that he would refile the case.

Playfellow II convened in March of 1922, this time in the Brooklyn courtroom of Supreme Court Justice James Church Cropsey. The issue, Judge Cropsey made clear, was a simple one: whether or not Johnson had issued either a verbal or written guarantee as to Playfellow's soundness at the time of the sale to Sinclair.

And so, once again, twelve male businessmen not involved in the sport were impaneled, once again a procession of horsemen offered testimony that was often contradictory and confusing to the jurors. Deliberation was brief, barely three hours, and when Justice Cropsey called for the verdict, the jury foreman announced that the twelve men had awarded the full amount of $100,000 to Rancocas. The court added $2,000 in accrued interest, and gave Johnson fifteen days to either remit the funds or file an appeal. Johnson's attorney, Henry F. Cochrane, assured the court that the filing would occur "right away."

Throughout this trial, a Runyanesque group of spectators, including jockeys, trainers, gamblers, grooms, touts, and, inevitably, bookmakers, inhabited the jury gallery, creating a lively wagering market on the trial's outcome. With the announcement of the verdict, money changed hands in the gallery, and there was celebrating in Brooklyn that evening; the in-court odds against the Rancocas side had gone as high as 10-to-1.

As the racing world awaited a third Playfellow trial, Johnson presented new recommendations for Sinclair and Hildreth's consideration. The first of these was that Playfellow be allowed to race once again for the Quincy Stable, which would assume responsibility for all of the four-year-old's entry fees and expenses, with Playfellow's earnings "either held in escrow or turned over to any charitable institution which Messrs. Sinclair and Hildreth may name." This proposal, which could have enabled Johnson to demonstrate Playfellow's soundness, was dead on arrival when posed to canny negotiators Hildreth and Sinclair.

A second Johnson suggestion would have allowed Rancocas to race Playfellow under court supervision. Man o' War's brother would be limited to races that included no other Rancocas runners, thereby precluding any effort by the stable to sacrifice him as front-running cannon fodder to assist the stretch-running exploits of Grey Lag, Mad Hatter, Thunderclap, or other Rancocas runners. Playfellow would be accorded every opportunity to win, again enabling Johnson to demonstrate the colt's soundness, while reducing his usefulness to Rancocas.

There have probably never been two racetrack professionals less likely than Sinclair and Hildreth to indulge such propositions. The Rancocas owner and manager would not allow Johnson to dictate the race schedule of any horse bearing their stable's green and white silks. Johnson's proposals were rejected out of hand.

Johnson's appeal was filed on March 22, and as Playfellow languished in his stall at Rancocas, blissfully unaware of the chaos his equine bad habits had created in the sporting and legal worlds, the third Playfellow trial opened on June 13. Johnson continued to insist that he had made no false representation to Hildreth, and that the Rancocas team itself had damaged Playfellow's reputation to the point that the colt was no longer worth the $100,000 that had been paid for him.

"We could not sell him now after all this talk if we took him to the boneyard," claimed Johnson's attorneys. The court, unmoved, announced that it would reserve judgment.

It was about two weeks later that the odd case took yet another bizarre turn, as Johnson returned to Hildreth and Sinclair Playfellow's $100,000 purchase price plus $2,000 in interest, apparently abandoning his appeal. He accepted delivery of Playfellow, which was duly shipped to Saratoga to resume his long-interrupted racing career. The lengthy proceedings over his disputed soundness appeared, at last, to be resolved.

But no. Two weeks later, Johnson denied that his payment to Sinclair constituted an admission of wrongdoing in the initial negotiation for Playfellow. Instead, it represented something of a legal guerrilla action, allowing Johnson to regain custody of the horse so that the owner might demonstrate over a sufficient period of observation that Playfellow was neither a cribber nor a windsucker.

Perhaps someone on the Quincy Stable legal team had suggested that this legal stratagem might finally enable their client to demonstrate the validity of his arguments. This time, however, Johnson and his legal team had strategized themselves into defeat.

In the history of jurisprudence, could there have been a more open-and-shut case, a case in which both parties to the disagreement had apparently achieved their stated ends? Johnson had evinced a desire to regain Playfellow, and had repaid Sinclair's $100,000—plus interest—for this purpose. Sinclair had wished only to return Playfellow to Johnson in exchange for his purchase price. This was done. What more was there to say? Reopening the case on November 28, 1922, the court determined that the agreement, though perhaps inadvertent, would not be overturned. The judge banged down his gavel, Johnson's last appeal was formally denied, and, finally and forever, the Playfellow legal saga was over.

With Playfellow out of their lives and $102,000 returned to the stable's accounts, Sinclair and Hildreth might now have anticipated a stretch of pure sport, a reintroduction of positive headlines, and an end to the adverse publicity that had been their lot for far too long. This, sadly, would not be the case.

It was less than six months later, on April 13, 1923, that a devastating fire struck Rancocas, causing an estimated $1 million in damages and killing sixty horses, including the promising stallion Inchcape, recently purchased for $115,000. Based on the initial investigation, the blaze, which had so obliterated the half-block-long broodmare barn that it would be a day before a comprehensive listing of the dead mares and foals could even be compiled, was deemed to have been of suspicious, "incendiary" origin.

A bereft Sinclair insisted that the fire could only have been caused by an electrical problem, originating where wires entered a stable building. The fire had clearly been in progress for some time, burning through dry straw used as bedding for horses before its discovery by farm personnel, and due to the isolation of Jobstown, valuable time was lost before fire trucks from other communities could reach the farm. The investigation never did implicate a human cause for the disastrous conflagration.

Sinclair was dramatically depressed as he discussed with the press the impact of the fire on his efforts to improve the thoroughbred breed, suggesting that "my breeding work at Rancocas has been set back at least five years. The stock destroyed represented most of the best breeding

combinations on the farm and was the pride of my breeding operations. . . . You can't go to another owner and ask him to sell you his brood
mares and colts any more than you would go to a man and ask him to sell
you his wife and children."

But there was an even darker cloud on the horizon for Sinclair and
for Rancocas, an issue that even Sam Hildreth could never have anticipated, and that Harry Sinclair certainly couldn't fix. Sinclair had been
implicated in a growing scandal that would assume national proportions,
one that would eventually send him to prison. He was to be one of the
central characters in the oil scandal that would bear the name Teapot
Dome.

Teapot Dome was the name of a Wyoming oil field, one of a number of such fields that in 1912 had been incorporated by President Taft
among the federal government's oil reserve lands. These lands remained
under government control until 1920, when a group that included Interior Secretary Albert Fall recommended to President Harding that the
Department of the Interior be assigned responsibility for their administration, which might include the leasing of oil lands to private commercial developers. Harding signed the executive order on May 31, 1921,
creating concern among conservationists and setting off a feeding frenzy
among attentive oilmen.

It also created opportunity for Fall, whose personal finances had
become badly overextended through his ownership of a New Mexico
ranch known as Three Rivers, which was simply larger than Fall's pay
grade could support. Described as "a big, bluff Westerner with a round
face and sizable nose . . . who if a reporter or citizen glimpsed him strid-
ing down a street, or, more likely, clambering into a limousine, would have
impressed the observer with his importance," Fall perceived the newly
signed presidential order as a solution to his financial woes.

He went about leasing the oil lands to rich men who had befriended
him and who, made aware of his precarious finances, would be willing to
make what Fall would later insist were "loans." These included $100,000
from "elderly, grandfatherly" Edward L. Doheny of Pan American Petroleum, an acquaintance of Fall's since the pair's prospecting and poker-
playing days in the New Mexico Territory during the mid-1880s, and

$304,000 in cash and bonds from Harry Sinclair, whose "stocky figure was offset by a hard face, especially the straight mouth, which presumably had been shaped by years of calculating oil deals." In exchange, the oilmen were spared the tedious formality attached to most governmental oil leases: There would be no competitive bidding process for these lands.

Senator Thomas Walsh of Montana, who would investigate Fall and the accelerated leases provided his oil friends, would later be told by Doheny that $100,000 was "not much money at all. It was a 'bagatelle,' no more than $25 or $50 to the ordinary individual." He had lent the money, he said, because he had been "'greatly affected' by the extreme pecuniary circumstances that had resulted from Fall's lifetime of futile efforts. He did it for a friend." In response, Senator Walsh observed, "I can appreciate that on your side, but looking at it from Senator Fall's side it was quite a loan." Doheny conceded the truth of this statement. Fall's standard of living had, in fact, improved substantially following these increases to his assets.

By July of 1924, both Doheny and Sinclair had been indicted on charges of defrauding the US government, and the Supreme Court had vacated the contracts between the Department of the Interior and the oil companies. All that now remained was the investigation of how the oilmen had obtained the land, how Fall had become so suddenly and conspicuously wealthy.

For Doheny, the Congressional hearings, civil suits, and trials were an ongoing inconvenience from which he would escape without prison time when the jury dismissed all charges after only an hour's deliberation. His legal team's brilliant defense reportedly earned them a million-dollar bonus from the oilman. But the stress of his lengthy involvement had left Doheny in an exhausted state, from which he never fully recovered. He died five years after his acquittal, on September 8, 1935. For three of those years, he had been bedridden.

In 1929, sixty-eight-year-old Albert Fall, wheelchair-bound and spitting up blood as the result of pneumonia, was convicted of receiving a bribe from Doheny (who had been acquitted of offering the bribe), fined $100,000, and sentenced to a year in prison, thereby becoming the first cabinet member ever imprisoned as a result of illegal acts while in

THE GREAT SWEEPSTAKES OF 1877

office. Fall's lawyer (the cost of his defense had been borne by his friend Doheny) moved to have his client imprisoned in New Mexico's warm climes until his health returned, but Presiding Judge William Hitz was unsympathetic, instructing the jury, "You have nothing whatsoever to do with the sunshine of New Mexico. . . . You are here to decide the case on the evidence and nothing else."

Sinclair, too, managed to escape conviction for the conspiracy charge, eliciting howls of protest from the political world. "Disgusting and discouraging," exclaimed North Dakota Senator Gerald Nye, chairman of the Senate Public Lands Committee, whose work in uncovering the misdeeds of Fall, Sinclair, and others had earned him the nickname "Gerald the Giant-Killer." Nebraska's Senator George Norris, who would one day be lauded by President Franklin Roosevelt as "the very perfect knight of American progressive ideals," had perhaps the most perceptive comment regarding Sinclair's acquittal: "He has too much money to be convicted."

But Sinclair didn't get away clean. Accused of employing a private detective to shadow the jurists considering his conviction, he earned a contempt of court citation, as well as a contempt of Congress charge resulting from his refusal to respond to questions posed by a congressional committee. When the US Supreme Court refused to vacate the contempt of Congress charge, the oilman was sentenced to 6½ months in prison. He began serving his jail term in May 1929.

Prisoner 10520's incarceration involved something less than hard labor. Delivered to the Washington, DC, prison in his chauffeur-driven limousine, Sinclair arrived bearing two suitcases of clothing, which he would don daily in preference to the standard prison garb. Included were several sets of silk pajamas, a sartorial touch seldom encountered within prison walls.

Nor would the oilman be assigned to such mundane pursuits as laundry duty or the license plate press. Sinclair, who had helped run his father's Independence, Kansas, drugstore some thirty-five years earlier, was assigned to the prison pharmacist's office as a physician's assistant, occasionally traveling beyond the prison walls to attend to convicts who had been injured or fallen ill in work details.

One perquisite of working in the pharmacy was Sinclair's stewardship of the prison's medicinal liquor supply, of which Sinclair may occasionally have partaken. In 1930, following Sinclair's release, the *Pittsburgh Gazette* obtained access to a fellow inmate at the Washington, DC, prison, and published a series of articles about life in the facility that had so memorably housed Sinclair. According to this prisoner, Sinclair had been treated almost as a guest, receiving meals of roast squab on toast, berries with fresh cream, and sumptuous salads. His meals, prepared by his private chef, were served in his cell by "The Salad Man," a prisoner who had previously been employed as a railroad dining club waiter.

The unnamed "Fellow Prisoner," as he signed the article, compared such elegant repasts with the more typical inmate's daily fare:

> *For breakfast we would get baked potatoes and gravy, bread and coffee; or some cereal—oatmeal on some days, cornflakes on another and so on—bread and coffee. The milk on the cereal, by the way, was always of the "substitute" variety.*
>
> *For dinner there would be lima beans, bacon, bread and water; or kidney beans, bread and water; or navy beans, bread and water; or kidney stew, bread and water; or turnips, bread and water. I don't mean we have our choice of these dishes. It would be one thing one day, another the next.*
>
> *For supper there would be, probably dried peaches or apples or prunes, and bread and tea.*

Shipments of outside food to other prisoners were promptly returned to sender. "If such food is sent," the Fellow Prisoner noted, "it is refused at the jail office." Sinclair was sent boxes of delicacies on a weekly basis, and, it was alleged, paid prison staff for the privilege of receiving fresh fruit and Cuban cigars. These special privileges did not increase Sinclair's popularity among the members of the general prison population, who would speculate over their dismal meals, "I wonder how Sinclair would like this!"

Harry Sinclair emerged from his prison experience at 12:07 a.m. on November 20, 1929, wearing a pinstriped suit, shiny brown shoes, and a new hat, to the clicks of shutters and the whir of movie cameras. He proclaimed that he had been "railroaded" into prison and informed the press that he intended to stay overnight in a Washington hotel, then depart for Rancocas the next morning. In a statement released to the press, the oil magnate, who had allegedly bribed a national official and retained private detectives to tail the jurors trying his case, then been accorded the royal treatment while serving a federal prison sentence, requested that he be accorded the respect "to which I am entitled as a man of honor and integrity."

But the Rancocas to which the newly freed oilman would return was profoundly changed from the powerful operation he had headed just six months earlier, for on September 24, 1929, during Sinclair's prison stay, his brilliant general manager, Sam Hildreth, had died at age sixty-three following abdominal surgery (see Epilogue).

At the time of Hildreth's passing, Rancocas had remained competitive among the leading stables, but now, with the late trainer's wise counsel no longer available, the racetrack earnings of the historic stable fell into a decline from which it would never recover.

Annual Earnings and Ranking: Rancocas Stable

Year	Earnings	Rank
1923	$438,849	1st
1924	$228,563	2nd
1925	$175,840	2nd
1926	$111,840	11th
1927	$161,569	8th
1928	$84,442	19th
1929	$190,680	3rd
1930	$137,705	8th
1931	$72,970	20th

And with the 1931 season, another scandal would envelop Rancocas, this time directly involving its racing operations.

It became known as the Ladana scandal, after the name of the Ranco-cas filly that was observed on August 13 frothing at the mouth as she was being saddled for Saratoga's Burnt Hills Handicap. A closer inspection determined that the filly's mouth was blistered where a corrosive material had burnt delicate skin, confirming the diagnosis of racetrack veterinar-ians: Ladana had been poisoned with a chemical known as chloral.

Ladana, a multiple stakes winner, would have been among the favor-ites for the race, having finished second, within a half-length of the well-regarded filly Buckup, in her previous start. In the Burnt Hills, however, the wagering heavily favored a runner named Happy Scot, who had no wins in six 1931 outings. When the Saratoga stewards, a formidable contingent composed of longtime racing men George D. Widener, Walter M. Jeffords, and W. S. Vosburgh, ordered Ladana withdrawn, the odds on Happy Scot plummeted to 1-to-2. The favorite won the race by a head.

The next day, Harry Sinclair's trainer, Frank Taylor, received a blister-ing communication from the Saratoga stewards via the assistant secre-tary of the Jockey Club, a gent with the memorable name of Algernon Dangerfield:

Dear Sir—At a meeting of the stewards of the summer meeting of the Saratoga Racing Association, the following resolution was adopted:

In the case of the Rancocas Stables' filly Ladana, entered for the Burnt Hills Handicap, August 13, but scratched by the stewards owing to her condition, the stewards find the filly was admittedly poisoned, and take occasion to condemn the management of the stable for not having taken measures to prevent the same. They consider the incident as scandalous, and calculated to impair confidence in racing; therefore, it is ordered that no further entries by the Rancocas Stable to overnight events be accepted during the meeting.

The resulting rush to judgment was less than universal. While the *Thoroughbred Record*, one of the sport's leading publications, described the stewards' ruling as "a pretty harsh judgment," noting that Taylor had acted promptly to determine the guilty party and fire "the recreant groom who had been a party to the skullduggery," the *Blood-Horse*, then and now the ranking publication of the thoroughbred breeding industry, defended the stewards, insisting, "it is up to the trainer to so surround himself with proper employees that such things as poisoning, sponging, stuffing and doping horses cannot be done."

The most important result of the ruling, however, was announced in the following issue of the *Blood-Horse*:

To Sell Rancocas Horses

As a sequel to the poisoning of Ladana and the barring of entries from Rancocas Stable to the overnight events at Saratoga, Harry F. Sinclair has arranged with C.J. Fitz Gerald to sell the entire string of 25 horses, including Ladana, in the paddock at Saratoga Race Course on Thursday next, September 3.

The reason given for Sinclair's sudden decision to sell his racing stock—in fact, to commence a series of well-publicized and heavily attended sales in which he sold nearly every horse Rancocas owned—was the crush of his oil business. But many believed it was a direct response to the Ladana affair.

More likely it was a combination of factors: increasing concerns about the profitability of his racing empire as the Great Depression intensified; the crush of his oil business, staggering under the same economic pressures; the death of his resident racing genius; and his apparent disapprobation by the sport in the wake of Teapot Dome and the Ladana affair. What can be stated without question, however, is that despite the *Thoroughbred Record*'s contention that Sinclair would return the following season "with another strong stable," it is beginning in 1932 that the oilman and the historic name of Rancocas disappear permanently from the list of leading thoroughbred owners.

A week later, the *Blood-Horse* suggested (while avoiding the obvious step of actually interviewing Rancocas's owner) that "Sinclair had been waiting, since the death of Samuel C. Hildreth, to sell his breeding stock and racing stable to his satisfaction and he was finding it too great a tax on his time and a draft on his business. It, then, would seem that the incident at Saratoga merely created a welcome opportunity, and that Mr. Sinclair very likely is truly thankful to those stewards for their action."

Well, hardly.

Even the *Blood-Horse* eventually admitted that "only a dope" would have driven so committed a patron as Sinclair out of the game, conceding, long after the fact, that racing had "lost a good man in Sinclair." The petroleum multimillionaire's final act as owner of Rancocas was to lease it, with option to buy, to another oilman, William G. Helis, whose own biography would be worthy of a separate volume.

A native of the tiny Greek village of Tropea (by 1991, its population had grown to 5,637), Helis emigrated to the United States at age seventeen, a penniless wanderer. His initial employment in his new country was as a dishwasher, but he managed to save enough to wend his way to California, intrigued by its booming oilfields. He found work there as a laborer, then invested his savings in oil leases and briefly struck it rich. Helis made and lost several oil fortunes over the course of a long and colorful career, but ultimately, the money stayed with the Greek immigrant.

Upon acquiring the historic Rancocas property from Harry Sinclair in July 1944, Helis vaulted quickly into the ranks of leading owners. He won a Travers with Adonis; a Coaching Club American Oaks with Elpis; a Louisiana Derby and a Saratoga Handicap with Olympic Zenith; an Arlington Futurity, Cowdin Stakes, Discovery Handicap, and Lawrence Realization with Cosmic Bomb; an Acorn Stakes with Earshot; a Santa Anita Derby with Salmagundi. His Rippey won the Derby Trial, the Carter, the Bay Shore, the Fall Highweight, the Count Fleet, the Roseben, and two editions of the Toboggan.

Not everything Helis touched turned to gold; his bid of $66,000 in 1943 for a yearling that he called Pericles would earn headlines only because of the colt's utter failure to earn back more than a fraction of his purchase price: In his one season as a racer, the expensive purchase earned only $5,200. Generally, though, the more the "Golden Greek" became involved in the sport, the more success he had.

But by this time, the legendary Rancocas, Pierre Lorillard's pride and joy in the nineteenth century and Harry Sinclair's Roaring Twenties gold mine, was no more. The land was now something called "The Helis Stock Farm," and was no longer identified as Rancocas. It seems fitting, then, that with the death of William Helis in 1950, the story of Rancocas can be said, nearly eighty years after a young Pierre Lorillard stepped from that train in Jobstown, New Jersey, to have reached its conclusion.

EPILOGUE

Ol' Man Harper has gone to rest
Sleepin' whar the bluegrass blows,
On the verdant Uplands crest
Where the merry daisy grows.

Ten Broeck's slab of marble white,
Glistens 'neath the golden sun.
By the paddock whar the might
And glory of his fame begun.

Love that race horse? Time o' day
Harper loved him like a child,
And the first quick tremblin' neigh
Ringin' from the woodland wild,

It fell upon old Harper's ear
Like a strain of music sweet.
Weren't no music he could hear
Like the tread of race hoss feet.

—JAMES TANDY HARRIS

AND, AS IS ALWAYS THE CASE IN MATTERS BOTH HUMAN AND EQUINE, the passing of time brought closure to many aspects of the Great Sweepstakes. The adulation subsided and much of the controversy faded away, sometimes to be replaced by satisfaction, sometimes by dissatisfaction, sometimes by newer controversies. Disputes were settled or remained disputed, agreements remained agreements or transformed into disagreements. Truths remained true, or morphed into untruths. Lies generally remained lies.

Time and other presidential elections gradually clouded memories of the taint of controversy surrounding Rutherford B. Hayes's election and four tumultuous years in the White House. The end of Reconstruction affected relations between Americans in the still seething land for decades, bringing with it an inexcusable delay to the civil and moral rights owed to a deserving but long-suffering people.

In 2000, some six score and four years after the Hayes-Tilden battle, another hairsbreadth election occasioned the Supreme Court's involvement in determining the winner of a presidential vote, and the din of anger on the part of those who lost, the loudly disputed claims of "mandate" by the winners, again echoed throughout the land. It may well be another 124 years before a presidential election is close enough to require the attention of America's highest court, but one would certainly prefer that the nation be spared forever this particular version of electoral insanity.

Not surprisingly, thoroughbred racing, which annually produces a new generation of equine athletes, moved readily beyond the events of October 24, 1877. Other racehorses—many not as good as Parole, Ten Broeck, and Tom Ochiltree, but some that would be considered even better—populated the racetracks, the breeding sheds, the stables, and the imaginations of those whose heartbeats quicken to the sound of hooves pounding over a racecourse. There were Hindoo, Domino, Sysonby, and Exterminator; Man o' War, Zev, Gallant Fox, and War Admiral; Whirlaway, Count Fleet, Citation, and Coaltown; Native Dancer, Swaps, and Nashua; Kelso, Buckpasser, Dr. Fager, and Damascus; Secretariat, Seattle Slew, Affirmed, and Alydar; Spectacular Bid, Sunday Silence, and Easy Goer; Personal Ensign, Curlin, and Zenyatta; American Pharoah . . .

And Parole, Ten Broeck, and Tom Ochiltree gradually faded into the ever more distant and forgettable past.

And yet . . . for each of the individuals in this volume, life and, in some cases, glory continued after the Great Sweepstakes of 1877. Some experienced happy endings, some were afflicted by sad ones; some reached new heights of fame, some disappeared into obscurity. It would represent nothing short of a failure to leave the reader uncertain as to these outcomes.

It is in this concluding chapter, then, that we will seek to answer the inevitable question: "What finally became of . . .?"

Those Who Would Be President

Rutherford B. Hayes

The nineteenth president of the United States, who even before his four contentious White House years had determined not to seek a second term, appears never for a moment to have regretted or reconsidered his decision.

As "Rutherfraud" ("His Fraudulency" was another derisive nickname) wrote to a close friend after three long years at the nation's helm, "I am now in my last year of the Presidency and look forward to its close as a schoolboy longs for the coming vacation." While denying any role in the political machinations that had handed him the nation's highest office, Hayes expressed no lamentations regarding his decision to step aside for the ill-fated twentieth president, James A. Garfield.

Hayes's diary presents a vivid picture of his dismay and barely suppressed anger at the assassination of his successor on July 2, 1881, at the hands of Charles J. Guiteau, an attorney who had sought unsuccessfully from Garfield a consular posting. Hayes also decried "the folly, the wickedness, and the danger of the extreme and bitter partisanship which so largely prevails in our country." It is a lesson that has yet to be learned, more than 130 years later, in our own highly politicized era.

Though Hayes willingly stepped down from the presidency, he had no intention of dropping out of the political process, or of abdicating his position as president emeritus. He continued to play a role in public affairs, particularly in the areas of education and civil rights, what was then known as "the negro question." In Hayes's view, education was the point from which all progress began:

> *Reading all that I can get hold of on the negro question. I find nothing which overthrows or even tends to overthrow the position that education will help him wherever he needs help, will strengthen [him] where he is weak. . . . The question then is how best to educate him.*
>
> *We must educate the people. Find a higher level. . . . Education—discussion, general and intelligent, is the conserving force and at the*

same time the progressive force. . . . A frivolous people will have a frivolous pilot—a feeble government.

Hayes served as trustee for the Peabody Fund for the education of black children in the South, and on the Board of Trustees of Ohio State University, the school that, as governor, he had helped to found. He attended conferences on the subjects that most interested him. But while his role as adviser to presidents and force for education distinguished his post–White House years, Hayes remained somewhat in the background, content to live quietly with his wife, the former Lucy Ware Webb, who owns the distinction of having been the first college graduate to serve as first lady.

Despite Hayes's questionable victory and the outrage of the defeated Democrats, the nineteenth president's family won the affection of the American people. "Because of her refusal to serve wine at the White House, society might nickname Mrs. Hayes 'Lemonade Lucy,' but she won the hearts of the ordinary people, who were interested in the doings of the Hayes children and the unaffected hospitality to old friends with whom the White House was often overflowing."

The former president's life was changed drastically when Lucy, his wife of thirty-seven years, suffered a stroke on June 22, 1889, and passed away three days later. While attended by friends and family, the grieving Hayes wrote movingly about his wife, as her last moments approached in their Spiegel Grove, Ohio, home:

And Lucy herself is so sweet and lovely, as she lays unconsciously breathing away her precious life, that I feel a strange gratitude and happiness as I meditate on all the circumstances of this solemn transition we are waiting for. Would I change it? Oh, yes, how gladly would we all welcome the least indication of the restoration of the darling head of the home circle. But we cannot, we must not repine. Lucy Hayes is approaching the beautiful and happy ending of a beautiful, honored, and happy life. She has been wonderfully fortunate and wonderfully honored. Without pain, without the usual suffering, she has been permitted to come to the gates of the great change which leads to the life where pain and suffering are unknown. . . . If ever a man or woman found exquisite happiness in imparting happiness to others, the dear companion of my life, my Lucy, is that woman.

Three and a half years later, on January 17, 1893, Hayes suffered a massive heart attack. His last words were, "I know that I am going where Lucy is."

Samuel J. Tilden

Defeated for the presidency in 1876 despite earning an absolute majority of the popular vote, Samuel Tilden never again ran for public office. Never a robust individual, the Democratic candidate's health was affected severely by the stress of his campaign for the presidency. The emotional intensity of the election continued for him even after the results were official, when his backers were accused of having sent coded telegrams offering bribes to the returning boards that were to decide the electoral votes in the disputed states. These were the so-called "Cipher Dispatches."

Tilden vigorously denied any involvement with such doings, though it was later claimed that his supporters had, in fact, discussed possible bribery scenarios with him, which he had emphatically vetoed. Called before a House committee in February 1879 investigating alleged fraud in the vote counts for Florida and Louisiana, Tilden

seemed to have aged considerably, and . . . looked quite old and feeble. . . . [I]t was a painful spectacle to see the slow, halting lame walk with which he passed the table and reached his seat. His figure was stiffly drawn up and seemed incapable of bending, as though from a paralytic contraction of the limbs.

Tilden was briefly considered for the 1880 Democratic nomination, but reluctantly declined, offering "unfeigned thanks for the honors bestowed upon me," and admitting that the task of the presidency was "now, I fear, beyond my strength." He was mentioned again as a possible candidate for the 1884 nomination, but by this time, all such possibilities were well behind him. He died on August 4, 1886, at the age of seventy-two.

Tilden is buried at Cemetery of the Evergreens in his boyhood home of New Lebanon, New York, under a tombstone that proclaims, "I Still Trust in The People." John Greenleaf Whittier penned a final tribute to the fallen leader:

> Once more, O all-adjusting Death!
> The Nation's Pantheon opens wide;
> Once more a common sorrow saith
> A strong, wise man has died.

> Ambitious, cautious, yet the man
> To strike down a fraud with resolute hand;
> A patriot, if a partisan,
> He loved his native land.

Tilden died a very wealthy man, and a substantial portion of his estate—"rumored to be as much as the then-astronomical sum of 10 million dollars, though it was actually a few million short of that"—was bequeathed "to establish and maintain a free library and reading room in the City of New York," which today remains part of the New York Public Library.

THE HORSES IN THE GREAT SWEEPSTAKES

Parole

The Great Sweepstakes marked the four-year-old Parole's twenty-fifth appearance under silks, and he would eventually race through age twelve, competing 113 more times. At his retirement, Parole had matched strides with the best thoroughbreds in America, crossed the ocean to engage with—and, more than occasionally, defeat—the best in England, and then recrossed the Atlantic to conclude his career with still more American triumphs.

With Ten Broeck remaining in Kentucky and Tom Ochiltree on the farm and soon to be retired to stud, Parole, a gelding who would be servicing no broodmares, was left without serious competition on the Eastern circuit. He responded as a true champion should, with eight wins in ten starts, annexing the Baltimore, Monmouth, and Saratoga Cups while defeating weak runners that history has long since forgotten: Tom Bacon, Hattie F., Danicheff, Joe. His one poor effort was a fifth-place finish to George Lorillard's Loulanier in Jerome Park's Grand National Handicap; he returned two days later to win his eighth race of the season.

What happened next in the Parole saga remains slightly mind-boggling. Perhaps multimillionaires like Pierre Lorillard see things differently from others; perhaps trainer William Brown was more of a yes man than his straight-talking reputation would suggest. Lorillard's star racer having just completed a sparkling eight-for-ten season, and barely a year removed from his victory over the seemingly insuperable Ten Broeck, the tobacco magnate somehow persuaded himself that the five-year-old Parole was now "past his prime." And Brown, somehow, agreed with him.

Pierre was preparing to ship future Hall of Famer Duke of Magenta, recently purchased from brother George, to England to challenge the British for world-wide leadership in the sport, and he and Brown decided that Parole, though no longer likely to shine as a racer, should nonetheless be sent there as well, to serve as Duke of Magenta's training partner. Pierre, seeking as always to conduct a top-class (and high-profile) racing operation, also persuaded Brown to accompany the horses to the British Isles, and, sparing absolutely no expense, also sent along three of his top jockeys.

Occasionally, terrible decisions have wonderful outcomes. Duke of Magenta, upon arriving in Britain, fell ill with a severe influenza that developed into pneumonia. The newly turned four-year-old, just weeks earlier being prepared to take on the elite of the British turf, was now seriously ill, his lungs ravaged, his racing career over. In his stead Parole, derisively labeled "the Yankee Mule" in the British sporting press, was sent postward. Even Lorillard professed to have "no great expectations" for the little gelding, but Brown was quietly confident: "I know he's not the showy kind they like," he predicted, "but wait till they see him extended."

Parole proved to be a sensation. His first assignment was the Newmarket Handicap, in which he would take on the powerful Isonomy, one of the finest English thoroughbreds of the era. As had been his habit in America, Parole allowed others to make the early pace, then surged to the lead nearing the finish. Pursuing his American opponent from three lengths behind as the leaders approached "the rails," Isonomy made a determined charge, but ran out of ground before overhauling the Lorillard gelding.

A suddenly subdued crowd reacted with disbelief bordering on horror. Parole, dismissed in the wagering at 100-to-15 odds, was a length and a half clear, with Isonomy second and the rest of the field "in a cluster a hundred yards off." In America, one publication likened Parole's unexpected victory to "a bolt of lightning from an undimmed sky." Another suggested that Parole's victory might finally demonstrate to the British that "we breed something else than weeds in America." Even an English sporting newspaper, the *Sporting Life*, admitted that Pierre Lorillard and his diminutive gelding could "claim to have taken the shine out of this 'effete old country.'"

Seeking to redeem his colt's reputation, and perhaps enhance his bankroll in the process, Isonomy's owner, Frederick Gretton, challenged Parole to a match race over the Newmarket course. Lorillard, however, always sensitive to the nuances of a gamble, recognized that the conditions suggested by Gretton would bring the two runners together at weights favorable to Isonomy, over the course on which the British horse had won the previous year's Cambridgeshire Handicap. (Gretton had, in fact, won £40,000 wagering on the Cambridgeshire.) Lorillard managed to extricate himself gracefully from Gretton's challenge, citing Parole's "long list of engagements extending into the autumn."

Six days later, Parole stunned the British again, sauntering home ahead of seventeen other runners in Epsom's City and Suburban Handicap. A pessimistic Lorillard had bet cautiously on the Newmarket, but now the owner's wagers reflected his full confidence in his gelding's abilities, against even the British. He reportedly profited on Parole in the City and Suburban to the tune of £20,000.

Parole had always been considered a less than hardy thoroughbred, "somewhat difficult to train, and two or three races in quick succession generally [unfit] him for some days." Brown, however, believed firmly in staying with a hot hand, and Parole was on the track again for the following day's 2¼-mile Great Metropolitan Stakes. By this time, British trainers were less inclined to doubt the American, and Parole was a heavy favorite, opposed by only one challenger, the hapless Castlereagh.

It was no contest. Parole allowed his opponent to steal away for the first two miles, then coasted almost nonchalantly past him to win by a reserved three-quarters of a length. The *Spirit of the Times*, by this time perhaps slightly giddy at the American's unprecedented success, noted that Parole was the only horse in history to win the Newmarket, City and Suburban, and Great Metropolitan Stakes in succession, and dubbed the Lorillard gelding "a second William the Conqueror."

But there was still more to come. On May 7, Parole brought home the trophy for the Great Cheshire Stakes while lugging 134 pounds, and on May 30 he won England's most prestigious event for older runners, the Epsom Gold Cup, "cleverly by half a length" over Alchemist, with Primrose "a bad third."

It was just as it appeared that Parole might destroy all notions of the innate superiority of the British thoroughbred, and that Lorillard might personally bankrupt the nation's bookmaking industry, that Parole proceeded to lose the remainder of his engagements for the season, including a rematch with Isonomy in the Goodwood Cup. Still, Lorillard had made his point: A good American horse could compete with the best of the heretofore unassailable British. It wasn't a bad showing for a runner that just months earlier had been dismissed as little more than a stablemate's workout partner.

Parole wintered in England in anticipation of the coming season, but 1880 would not be another triumphant cavalcade for the now seven-year-old. If the British horses couldn't fell the American, the British handicappers would have a go, hoisting 130 pounds or more onto the gelding's back almost every time he stepped onto a racecourse.

He finished first under top weight of 131 in the season-opening 1¼-mile Liverpool Sprint, but was disqualified to second for crossing in front of another horse. The bookmakers had considered it a near enough thing to have offered 4-to-1 odds that the American's victory would be upheld by the stewards' review. Parole would then fail in his nine subsequent starts, carrying as much as 144 pounds and conceding as much as 53 to the competition. Following runner-up efforts in the Epsom Gold Cup and the Lennox Stakes, Lorillard decided to return Parole to America. Back at home, he was assigned lighter weights and promptly won four consecutive starts.

At age eight, Parole seemed to return to form, winning the Manhattan Handicap and, in what would be his final stakes victory, the Westchester Cup. By now, his lifetime earnings of nearly $70,000 placed him atop the all-time thoroughbred rankings. He was deposed, however, when Hindoo, the previous year's Kentucky Derby and Travers winner, defeated him in the Champion Stakes, raising the mark to $71,875. Parole won a minor race two weeks later and regained the lead.

Ultimately, the earnings race between Parole and Hindoo would become an issue of longevity. Hindoo, who had won eighteen consecutive races in 1881, damaged a tendon and was retired during the 1882 season, but Parole continued on, winning races, raising the standard. At the end, his career log showed 138 starts, 59 victories, 28 seconds, and 17 thirds. His earnings of $82,816 topped all of history's runners.

And now, at the end of his career, Parole had fans. "[T]he impulse Parole's success gave to racing was enormous. People that had never attended races became interested, the attendance at the races increased, new racing clubs were formed. . . . Social clubs were named for Parole, there were Parole poolrooms, Parole saloons, Parole billiard parlors, and Parole baseball clubs. . . . The entire country from Maine to California, thence to the Gulf, rang with praises of the old gelding."

The early days of Parole's retirement were active ones. The gelding was so friendly that he could be led by a child with a string, and would respond to familiar faces by prancing to the paddock fence to accept an apple or a bunch of carrots. He was occasionally brought back to the track, and fans would shout, "Here he comes!" when the aging champion led a parade of racers postward. "[T]he cheers [would roll] from the field stand, and taken up by the lawn, [swell] to an ovation."

Parole had been entered in the 1885 National Horse Show, but was withdrawn when he became ill prior to the event, and it was decided that he should no longer be subjected to stressful public situations. Turned out in a tree-bedecked paddock, he lived out his remaining years in the sort of comfort reserved for retired thoroughbreds of rare quality, with all the good food and veterinary care money could provide. He lived a very long life, succumbing at Tuxedo Park on New Year's Day, 1903, at the extraordinary equine age of thirty. Pierre Lorillard's great gelding, whose style on the track had been to lay back early, then outfinish his opponents, outlasted even Lorillard himself by two years.

The thoroughbred who had opened the British turf to American challengers by conquering the mighty Isonomy was inducted into the National Museum of Racing and Hall of Fame at Saratoga Springs, New York, in 1984, two years after Ten Broeck, whose measure he had taken so decisively in the Great Sweepstakes.

Ten Broeck

The loss to Parole marked Ten Broeck's twenty-seventh lifetime appearance under silks. The record credits Ten Broeck with nine wins in ten 1877 starts, but only six actually involved defeating another horse; he raced twice against the stopwatch and earned a walkover in yet another race. It was only Parole's Great Sweepstakes victory, in which illness may have compromised Ten Broeck's performance, that marred a rare perfect season.

Returned to Nantura in late 1877 amid rumors that he would race no more, Ten Broeck was prepared for the 1878 season, with Harper perhaps preserving a forlorn hope that one or both Lorillard brothers might relent and agree to a Kentucky race. Instead, a unique opportunity presented itself when a promoter negotiated a match race between Ten Broeck and Theodore Winters's undefeated mare Mollie McCarthy (often spelled McCarty), at four-mile heats. Mollie's perfect thirteen-for-thirteen record created a mystique nearly as compelling for Kentuckians as Ten Broeck's multiple time records had been for Northern racegoers nine months earlier. Winters and Harper agreed upon a $5,000-per-side buy-in, creating a $10,000 purse that would be by far the richest of Ten Broeck's storybook career.

First, however, the six-year-old was asked to take on some good ones in his seasonal debut. On May 13, 1878, following six months away from the races, he was entered at Lexington in a 1½-mile race that also drew the likes of Leonard, the prior year's Kentucky Derby runner-up, Vera Cruz, one of the previous season's top three-year-olds, and 1875 Derby winner Aristides, considered by some to be Ten Broeck's superior. A fifth starter, something called Bill Bass, was entered as a pacesetter.

On the day Mollie McCarthy left California for the Bluegrass, Ten Broeck managed to outfinish Leonard to win his seasonal debut. The victory was less than impressive, however, tainted by the glacial final time of 2:48¼ and by the breakdown of Aristides, which would never race again. Harper and Colston were relieved to return a healthy and victorious Ten Broeck to Nantura, recognizing that a great deal of preparation would be required before he could contend with a runner of the reputation of a Mollie McCarthy.

Publicity for the match race was extraordinary. The press was on hand to cover Mollie's departure from San Francisco, and her arrival at Omaha on May 18, and reported that with the seven hundred miles between Omaha and Louisville still to be covered, the mare remained "in excellent condition." (No one seems to have questioned how the mare's fitness could be gauged in the midst of a three-thousand-mile railway journey.) She reached Louisville on schedule, and on June 21 it was reported that "Mollie McCarthy takes her training kindly on Kentucky soil. . . . Ten Broeck is also doing well. His trainer is well satisfied with his form." Ten Broeck was favored in the early wagering, but "the residents of other States manifest[ed] an eagerness to back the mare."

On June 22, the *Kentucky Live Stock Record* reported that Ten Broeck was "as fine as he can be, and his trainer, Colston, and jockey, Walker, never liked him better," comments that would pique interest following the race. Mollie McCarthy's trainer described her as "never better in her life," a characterization that would also echo strangely following her Independence Day performance.

But now the publicity machinery made a curious detour—and an ominous one. While continuing to trumpet the upcoming event as likely "the grandest race ever witnessed in America," newspapers began offering vague references to chicanery, hippodroming (the practice of prearranging a result through collusion between managers and contestants), even race-fixing. One publication reported that "every precaution has been taken to secure a fair race, and our readers may be sure that the public will be protected and Kentucky's honor saved from any stain." Another asserted that "it would not be safe, in the presence of a great roaring crowd, gathered from the four quarters of the continent, to attempt anything that would smack of legerdemain."

A fair race? Kentucky's honor saved? Legerdemain? Hippodroming? With less than a week remaining before the race, readers across the nation must have shaken their heads in wonderment. Just what was going on in old Kentucky?

As Independence Day approached, a swarm of thunderstorms bucketed the Louisville area, but "the glorious fourth of July broke with a cloudless sky, the sun beaming down with the greatest intensity." "Greatest intensity" was an understatement; the temperature on race day would peak at a humid ninety-two degrees. Racegoers began arriving early at the Louisville course, and by eleven o'clock—still four hours before the feature race—"every available space was filled with people. They went in all manner and sorts of ways, on foot, in carts, omnibuses, stage, wagon, carriage, horseback, rail and street car."

The day's first race was won by a horse named Dan K.; the second, a sprint for nondescript two-year-olds, by Goodnight. The third was a walkover for Joe Rodes, which earned a $350 purse for his non-effort. None of these races is even minimally important historically, but each group of struggling thoroughbreds further muddled a track surface that needed no further muddling.

Track condition for the match race would take on ever more significance, given that the track superintendent had misconstrued his instructions to prepare Churchill Downs's main course, and instead concentrated his crew's attentions on the inside driving track, where no July 4 races would be contested. Recognizing its error, the maintenance crew had labored in the broiling sun with sponges prior to the first race, clearing most of the standing water from the main course, but by the time of the featured contest the track remained sloppy with sticky mud.

Joe Rodes had scarcely completed his one-mile stroll when the bell rang to summon the Kentucky crack and his California challenger. To a prolonged ovation, Ten Broeck was first to answer the call, led onto the track by trainer Harry Colston, with jockey William Walker walking alongside and owner Frank Harper bringing up the rear, the entire contingent "surrounded by an escort of mounted stewards, police and stable-men."

Mollie McCarthy, to her own chorus of cheers and accompanied by an entourage that included jockey George Howson, imported from California for the event, stepped onto the track a few moments later. Both horses were restive in the steamy, raucous environment, and both jockeys had been instructed to wait as long as possible before mounting. Following a slow jog around the course, the two runners were led to the starting point in front of the grandstand. A tap of the starter's drum, and the pair "went by the string like twin bullets."

For the first half-mile, Ten Broeck and Mollie raced in lockstep, but then the mare's nose showed in front, and a loud cheer arose from the grandstand. The California invader, known for her easy, fluid stride, was setting a furious pace, seeking to drain her opponent with a blistering opening mile, while Walker was pushing Ten Broeck hard merely to stay close. Walker was also struggling to prevent the wily Howson from herding Ten Broeck against the rail and unseating him. Finally, Walker retaliated:

> *I just got tired of his fouling, and I ran into the mare and knocked her out of the way.*

Initially, Walker had wanted no part of the race. "The colored boy who rode Ten Broeck" had told Colston that he had "no confidence in the horse from the first, and . . . that if the mare did not go lame, he would [rather] be 100 miles from Louisville" than ride him. Walker, indeed, may have ridden the race in fear for his life. "Everybody expected [Ten Broeck] to win," he said later, "and if he lost the people would hang the rider and the trainer, because they would not believe but that the race was thrown."

Walker's fear increased when he was approached by Louisville Jockey Club president Colonel M. Lewis Clark, who had heard rumors that a fix might be in the works. "I hear you are going to throw the race," Clark reportedly told the eighteen-year-old. "You will be watched the whole way, and if you do not ride to win, a rope will be put about your neck, and you will be hung from that tree yonder. And I will help to do it."

In Walker's opinion, neither Ten Broeck nor Mollie was in condition for the race, and he had been told that Mollie's trainer knew "she could never go four miles, but he hoped to wabble through with Ten Broeck in some shape." After one mile, Mollie was continuing to set a torrid pace, but it seemed impossible that the mare could maintain such an effort for four intense miles in Louisville's heat and humidity. Could Mollie possibly be that good? The crowd strained forward to await the answer.

Under a fierce drive, gaining an inch at a time, Ten Broeck pulled even with his rival during the second mile, and "a Kentucky yell, such as was heard for miles, rent the air." But the Kentuckians' joy was short-lived, for Mollie surged again, opening a half-length lead as the pair turned for the second time into the long stretch. Ten Broeck, carrying six pounds more than the mare, was nearing the end of his endurance, when suddenly, Mollie let up. Ten Broeck stampeded past as Walker, attempting to gauge the situation, glanced back over his shoulder.

As the president of Churchill Downs, Colonel Matt J. Winn, described it, Mollie McCarthy was game to the end:

> *Howson drew the whip, and for the first time in her career, Mollie felt the sting of the lash. She leaped forward, apparently amazed by this strange new pain. She charged forward, trying to get away from it. For an eighth of a mile—perhaps a little farther—she gave all she had left in her sleek and beautiful body. And then she could give no more. Every last ounce of energy was gone from her, and she slowed down, and she staggered from side to side, and many in the stands felt she might collapse, and fall dead on the track.*

Cries of "The mare's broke down!" were heard from the crowd, but no, after racing 2½ miles at top speed on a blisteringly hot day over a poorly prepared track, with one of the era's great racehorses at her throatlatch, Mollie had simply reached the bottom of her physical strength. Walker pushed Ten Broeck to run a bit farther while Mollie was managing no more than "a mere hand gallop," and then, recognizing that the mare was done, the rider allowed the champion to simply jog much of the final lap. The pair reached the finish in 8:19¾, more than a minute slower than Ten Broeck's American record for the distance. Mollie McCarthy having failed to reach the distance flag, there would be no second heat: Ten Broeck, staggering with fatigue, was the winner.

Howson, fearing Mollie McCarthy might collapse beneath him, scrambled off her back without the formality of obtaining the judges' permission, and led his mare off the track; it would be a half hour before the jockey returned to be weighed out. This violation of the rules might have drawn a suspension under other circumstances, but given Mollie McCarthy's obvious distress, the stewards would take no action.

By unanimous decision of the press, the long-awaited and highly publicized Ten Broeck–Mollie McCarthy encounter would be perceived as a dismal failure. The *Pulaski (Tennessee) Citizen* dismissed it in three withering phrases: "The Race Disappointing, the Time Wretched, and the Victor Shorn of Glory." The *Daily Los Angeles Herald*, scrambling for excuses for Mollie McCarthy in the sultry Kentucky heat and the muddy track, proclaimed it "The Great Fiasco." The *Louisiana Democrat* labeled it a "Frightful Fraud." *Spirit of the Times* headlined its coverage, "The Great Turf Farce."

And now, almost every aspect of the race drew criticism. It was disclosed that John W. Conley, the entrepreneur who had brought Ten Broeck and Mollie McCarthy together on the Louisville racecourse, had actually leased Ten Broeck for the occasion from Frank Harper, paying a minimal fee for the champion's services. It was hinted that Harper might somehow have been intimidated into this arrangement. Conley had also leased Churchill Downs for the day, and following the debacle, Colonel Clark wrote that he would not "lease the track again for $50,000."

Conley was demeaned in the press as incompetent to have brokered so important a race, "a man who never owned a racehorse in his life, a speculator." His lack of experience, it was suggested, had led directly to the lack of preparation of the two horses, the shoddy track maintenance. Colonel Clark, who had "pledged his word to protect the public; declared that he would throw the mantle of the Jockey Club over both horses, and that it should be a fair race; that the public should not be swindled," was also roundly criticized.

Inevitably, there was speculation that Ten Broeck or Mollie—perhaps both—might have been drugged.

Most of these claims concerned trainer Harry Colston, who was accused in the press of having accepted $1,500 to drug Ten Broeck, practically under Harper's nose. Harper, informed the day before the race of Colston's possible complicity in the scheme, had refused to believe the charges, continuing to allow Colston full access to the horse. But Harper had every reason to dismiss such a notion. Unknown to the press, he had offered Colston one of Nantura's top colts, worth well in excess of $1,500, if the trainer could bring Ten Broeck to the race in winning condition.

Despite Colston's apparent noninvolvement, there was compelling evidence that Ten Broeck may have been dosed. One source reported that "Ten Broeck cramped and showed a state of congestion after the heat that looked very much like the horse had a dose of morphine. The symptoms were very characteristic of the drug, and he would have been totally unable to have run another heat."

This allegation was supported by a "distinguished physician and professor of anatomy in one of the Louisville medical colleges" (later identified as a Professor Keller of the Louisville Medical College), who came forward, claiming to have "examined Ten Broeck after the heat . . . [and] stated that the horse was laboring under the effects of a powerful opiate. His eyes were injected [*sic*], the pupils contracted, the brain and lungs congested, the muscular strength greatly diminished, and there was a feeling of great langour [*sic*] and drowsiness, and it was necessary to fan, whip, and keep the horse moving to prevent him from lying down and going to sleep." How certain was the professor that Ten Broeck had been drugged? "He offered to bet $1,000 to $10 on it."

And the good professor wasn't done. "[O]ne could smell the drug six feet from the horse," he claimed. "It is a great pity for the truth of the matter, that the horse's discharges from bowels and bladder were not preserved and analyzed, which would have settled the fact of the dosing beyond question." Harper disputed all of this, insisting that no doctor had examined his horse, and asserting that he would never have allowed such an individual near Ten Broeck before or after the race.

Spirit of the Times, in the race's aftermath, would hold Harper in contempt for allowing his horse to be used in such a way: "In regard to Mr. Harper, it is a shame upon all decency that such a man should be the owner of the best horse on the American continent." Even the *Kentucky Live Stock Record*, based in the Bluegrass and usually supportive of the old horseman and his thoroughbred superstar, admitted that Harper and his trainer might have been over their heads dealing with the slick Conley and his ilk: "Ten Broeck is owned by a plain farmer, a man with no experience either in training or managing of horses. . . . The horse was entrusted to a young colored man, Harry Colston, who has never trained or prepared horses before, and of course with his inexperience cannot tell when a horse is fit to race."

With accusations continuing to fly and theories regarding the unsatisfying result proffered in the press long after, the lives of the participants moved forward. Harper would shortly announce Ten Broeck's retirement from racing. This time, the champion would stay retired.

Mollie McCarthy's life took a more circuitous path. Sold for $7,500 to a shadowy figure named Budd Doble, whose train car had transported the Californian to the race and whose money had helped finance it, Mollie's new owner stated his intention to "patch the mare up and run her at Baltimore this Fall." Mollie was sent to the sidelines for two months, but when she returned it was in the colors of the legendary California horseman E. J. "Lucky" Baldwin in the 2¼-mile Minneapolis Cup, which, as one might imagine, was conducted some distance from Baltimore.

Mollie, perhaps in the throes of an equine version of post-traumatic stress disorder, finished last of the field of five, and was given the autumn and winter to recuperate. She would return in excellent form the following spring, winning both of her starts for Baldwin before being added to the Californian's broodmare band.

In the end, it was *Spirit of the Times* that provided the ideal coda for the Ten Broeck–Mollie McCarthy fiasco, suggesting that the public "let it rest, disturb it no more, for its blushes are the ever present witnesses of its own shame and disgrace." Even the most successful of sporting events seldom inspire artistry, except, ideally, of the athletic variety, and the Ten Broeck–Mollie McCarthy match race qualified in no way as either successful or artistic. It did, however, unaccountably provoke a spate of what may loosely be described as "poetry" and/or "music," some of which became quite popular, particularly in Kentucky, where wagers on Ten Broeck had provided a measure of financial relief for the region's long-suffering horseplayers.

One example of this follows. Poetic license runs wilder in these lines than even the thoroughbreds whose race it celebrates, and the reader is forewarned that for the unknown author, factuality placed a distant fourth in importance to rhythm, meter, and the picturesque dialect of the narrator.

And thus we note for the record that Ten Broeck was bred by John Harper and was never bought or sold, certainly not for "10 bushels of corn." Mollie McCarthy was a bay rather than a sorrel, and nobody in Ten Broeck's retinue ever labored under the nickname "Tusslin' John." Further, "Old Mastah"—this can only be a reference to Frank Harper—was never observed to wager even a dollar upon his horses, let alone "hundreds." He would often recall promising to his mother that he would never bet on a race, and insisted with pride that "I have never forgotten nor violated that promise." Harper was a lifelong bachelor, so "Old Missus" was nothing more than a literary device. And there is no known record of anyone ever referring to William Walker as "Jedge."

> Down in Kentucky where Ten Broeck was born,
> Dey swore by his runnin', he came in a storm.
> But Ten Broeck was bought for 10 bushels of corn;
> He drank in de ditches and grazed on de lawn.
> Oh, Ten Broeck's a bay horse, long and fast,
> Wid a ring around his forehead, just like a giraffe.
> One day when grazin', he strayed on de track;
> Dey chased him three days before he got back.
>
> Mollie McCarthy in California was foaled,
> A fit match for Ten Broeck, so it was told.
> Mollie was a sorrel, lean and thin;
> Built like a rabbit, she split thru de wind.

She'd kick up her heels and lay back her ears,
De fastest thing seen in 39 years.
So from ocean to ocean, de news it did spread.
Dat Mollie could beat Ten Broeck, at least by a head.

Go down to de stable, Tell old Tusslin' John
To clean off old Ten Broeck and walk him around.
Old Mastah bet hundreds, Old Missus bet pounds,
Dat Ten Broeck beat Mollie half-way around.

Den Mollie she snorted, Mollie she flew.
Mollie made Ten Broeck throw off his front shoe.
Jedge Walker, Jedge Walker, Jedge Walker, my son –
Pull on yo' left line and let Ten Broeck run.

Oh, round on de front track Mollie done well;
Round on de back track she landed in hell.
California did weep, California did groan;
How I would love to see Mollie come home.

Forty-niners were sure dat Mollie had won,
Dey pulled out deir bottles and each cocked his gun.
De ladies did laugh and so did de gents
To see Ten Broeck pass thu de cracks in de fence.

Oh, whar is little Mollie, can anyone tell?
Mollie got lost in de Louisville canal.
When de numbers were hung, Old Ten Broeck had won,
So deir joy was drunk in juleps and rum.

Even twenty-seven years later, the unfortunate Ten Broeck–Mollie McCarthy match race remained the stuff of lore. On May 24, 1905, in a brief article about a newsman turned politician and his efforts to obtain a legislative seat, the *Springfield Sun* noted that "Harry McCarty, of the *Jessamine Journal*, was nominated for the Legislature last week. His majority indicates that he is very much faster than Mollie, who ran against Ten Broeck."

Retired to stud, Ten Broeck met with the same fate as many a great horse; he sired some good runners, but failed to reproduce himself and was therefore regarded as something of a disappointment. He is credited with a total of just eighty named foals, of which thirteen won stakes races. The best of these were Bersam, winner of the 1885 Travers Stakes; Demuth, the 1890 Long Branch Handicap winner; and Drake Carter, winner of the 1883 United States Hotel Stakes and 1884 Monmouth Handicap. Ten Broeck also sired the winners of two Tennessee Derbies when that race still held some prestige, an American St. Leger Stakes, a Kentucky Oaks, and an Alabama Stakes.

An output of eighty foals in Ten Broeck's ten years at stud sounds absurdly small, and this was explained in *Spirit of the Times*' obituary for the champion, the sporting newspaper noting sarcastically that the cause of Ten Broeck's death "could scarcely be from over service, as Mr. Harper has never allowed him to serve over the usual quota of mares."

Having utilized the occasion of Ten Broeck's death to aim a backhanded editorial blow at his owner, *Spirit*, whose masthead declared it "The American Gentleman's Newspaper," next fired a second, most ungentlemanly round at the grieving Frank Harper regarding his handling of Ten Broeck during the champion's racing career:

> *Mr. Harper was rather an indulgent trainer, and did not send the horse to the post quite as fit as he should be to meet great horses. Had he been in the hands of such masters of the trainer's art as Walden, Thompson or Huggins, it would be difficult so [sic] determine what might have been accomplished.*

Ten Broeck's death at age fifteen on June 28, 1887, earned headlines in newspapers as distant as *The New North-West*, published in Deer Lodge, Montana, and the *Middlebury (Vermont) Register*. The *New York Times*'s obituary described the champion's passing as a "national loss to the running turf," and a few weeks later, in a gesture that might normally have been reserved for a departed head of state, the *Times* reported on Ten Broeck's funeral. Already, it seems, Frank Harper was deep in thought over a suitable monument to his recently deceased titan of the turf:

Mourning for Ten Broeck.

Mr. Gus Straus, of this city, has received a letter from Mr. Frank B. Harper, the owner of the famous Ten Broeck, who died the other day. . . . [I]n it he gives an account of the funeral of this celebrated horse, and tells how he was buried and where. He says: "All are sad over the death of Ten Broeck. It was so unexpected to us. We laid him to rest in a nice coffin and buried him in front of his stable door. His grave is still decorated with flowers.

We are going to erect a monument over his last resting place and inclose [sic] it with a fence. The stables are all draped in mourning, as is also the front gate." Thus is one of the greatest race horses the world ever produced put away after his races are all run and for him the bell has tapped for the last time. This short letter of Mr. Harper shows how much the true Kentuckian thinks of that noble and faithful animal— the horse.

The National Museum of Racing, ignoring *Spirit of the Times*'s sometimes scathing reviews of Ten Broeck and his owner and recognizing his victories against the stopwatch and his overwhelming reputation during the post–Civil War era, inducted the Nantura champion into its Hall of Fame in 1982.

Tom Ochiltree

Tom Ochiltree never competed again following the Great Sweepstakes. Perhaps the big five-year-old suffered an undisclosed injury in his loss to Parole and Ten Broeck; more likely, owner George Lorillard and trainer Wyndham Walden concluded that the stallion would never get his rematch with Ten Broeck, the only important horse of the era he had never defeated, and that the best option was now to send him to the breeding shed. With Tom Ochiltree's record of twenty-one wins in thirty-three lifetime starts, his $43,555 in career earnings, and his towering reputation, excellent breeding, and powerful frame, there was every reason to expect that he would be an outstanding success at stud.

Unfortunately, this did not work out in practice. The son of Lexington had a long retirement, but "his progeny failed to earn unusual distinction on the turf." The records indicate that he sired only five winners of recognized stakes races: Anecdote, which in 1900 won the Fashion Stakes; Cynosure, winner of the 1889 Brooklyn Derby; Major Domo, hero of the 1892 Brookdale and Parkway Handicaps; Sluggard, winner of the 1888 Sapphire Stakes; and 1884 Juvenile winner Triton.

The last-place finisher in the historic Pimlico race met his end on December 29, 1897, just days short of what would have been his twenty-sixth birthday. By this time, the erstwhile "Big Tom" was known around the barn as "Old Tom." Alone among the equine participants in the Great Sweepstakes, Tom Ochiltree has yet to be inducted into the National Museum of Racing and Hall of Fame, this despite his unquestioned standing as one of his era's top thoroughbreds. Fourteen decades after his death, his chances for enshrinement in the Saratoga Springs museum seem infinitesimal.

Three Other Horses of Note

Mollie McCarthy (or McCarty)

The California mare that gave her all against Ten Broeck produced only three foals after her retirement from racing. The first, an 1880 filly named Fallen Leaf, was good enough to have been known as "The California Wonder," winning "races between one and four miles in the east and in the Golden State," including Latonia Park's Gidelia Stakes and the Illinois Oaks at the Chicago Driving Park. Mollie's second foal, a pony-sized colt named Brandy-Wine, was of little ability; her third and final offspring, poignantly named Mollie McCarty's Last, had a moderately successful career, winning the Society Stakes at two, the Hunter Handicap at three, and the Turf Handicap at four. She won two minor races as a six-year-old.

Mollie McCarthy succumbed to an infestation of bots, the parasitic larvae of the gadfly, which attack the digestive systems of large grazing animals. She was but ten years of age at her end.

Iroquois

Following his Epsom Derby and St. Leger triumphs, the son of Leamington was in preparation for a triumphant four-year-old campaign when he burst a blood vessel in training. This cost the colt the entire season, and when he did return to the races it was as a somewhat fragile five-year-old that could no longer be trained for long distances.

Returned to the United States so that the American public could view the famous horse (and to allow his famous owner one final burst of the Epsom Derby winner's reflected glory), Iroquois received some hasty preparation and was sent on what would today be labeled a farewell tour. He did not win any of his races, but did finish third in both the Pimlico and Monmouth Stakes. After Iroquois ran poorly to future Hall of Famer Miss Woodford in his final start, Lorillard decided to retire his champion. A year later, Fred Archer, visiting New York, said, "They shouldn't have raced him here. He was in no condition when he left England to race over a mile."

Initially sent to stud at Rancocas, Iroquois went under the hammer with the farm's other stock when Lorillard broke up his stable in 1886, bringing a winning bid of $20,000 from General W. H. Jackson of Tennessee's Belle Meade Stud. Iroquois was sent to Tennessee at once to commence stud duty, and when General Jackson was later forced to sell Belle Meade, he paid $34,000 to keep the stallion.

Iroquois was a great success at stud, leading all American stallions in 1892 when his offspring earned $183,026 and won 145 races, and the following year he placed third on the list. His son Gotham won the 1894 Tremont Stakes, and two daughters, Geisha and Indian Fairy, took consecutive renewals of the Gazelle Handicap; Indian Fairy also won the Matron. His son Tammany earned $113,290 at a time when six-digit career earnings were anything but commonplace, and another son, Senator Grady, won Monmouth's 1893 Sapling Stakes, defeating future Hall of Famer Henry of Navarre.

Iroquois died in 1899 at the age of twenty-one, and was "buried in an unknown location on the original Belle Meade Mansion grounds." At the time his death was announced, General Jackson stated his intention to have the stallion's hooves removed and made into cups, finely mounted. This was done, and the ensconced hooves remain on public display at Belle Meade.

Playfellow

The brother to the immortal Man o' War, subject of a court battle that may have produced more in legal fees than he ever earned on the track, was retired to stud in 1924. While Playfellow came nowhere near to re-creating the brilliance of his illustrious relation, he did sire 106 registered runners, of which 29 won.

James F. Johnson, who had purchased Playfellow as a yearling for approximately $2,000 and nearly succeeded in selling him for fifty times this amount, was embittered by his unsuccessful effort to enforce the sale of the colt to Rancocas. The names given his next crop of foals—Poor Sport and Caveat Emptor are but two examples—suggest his disgust and dissatisfaction with Harry Sinclair, Sam Hildreth, and the entire Playfellow ordeal.

Man o' War, foaled a year ahead of Playfellow, also outlasted his sibling. Playfellow's death at age twenty-five was announced in May of 1943. Man o' War, attended until nearly the end of his life by a personal groom, Will Harbutt, would continue welcoming visitors to his stall at Kentucky's Faraway Farm for another four years, finally surrendering to extreme old age in 1947 as a nationally revered thirty-year-old.

THE OWNERS

John Harper and Longfellow

John Harper, who had first turned the Nantura Stock Farm toward thoroughbred breeding, was long valued for his honesty, for his insistence that his racehorses run to win. As the *Kentucky Livestock Record* stated it: "If his horse was the best, the orange colors would be sure to come under the string first. He indulged in no bargain, no intrigue," insisting that his horses compete every time at their highest level, or, in his quaint phrase, "from eend to eend." A lifelong bachelor, Harper devoted himself primarily to his horses, less as objects of value than as beloved playthings that gave him pleasure when they defeated the thoroughbreds of other owners.

It was after a long career of quiet devotion to Nantura's horses that Harper suddenly achieved national fame with the extraordinary Longfellow. The odd pair—the shabbily dressed owner and his big, elegant thoroughbred—made national headlines. "The papers were full of Harper and Longfellow, for it is only once in a generation that such a quaint and striking pair rivets the public eye."

But despite moments of racetrack adulation and the respect of those who valued his integrity and shared his love for fast horses, Harper's was a tragic life. His last surviving brother and sister had been brutally murdered, casting a "deep shadow upon the declining years of Uncle John"; his brother Adam had been shot by horse thieves raiding his farm during the Civil War. Many felt that the grievous injury to Longfellow was the beginning of the long decline to death for the Harper family patriarch.

Longfellow survived until 1893, living to the ripe equine age of twenty-four, and it seems particularly fitting that Frank Harper erected over the first of the Nantura superstars a monument every bit as magnificent as that which already covered the grave of Ten Broeck. The words on Longfellow's tombstone read as follows:

LONGFELLOW
THE KING OF THE TURF
BROWN HORSE
FOALED MAY 10, 1867
DIED
NOVEMBER 5, 1893
17 STARTS 14 TIMES FIRST
KING OF RACERS
AND
KING OF STALLIONS

Which, although it may not be poetry, at least makes an effort to go beyond the cold facts and hard figures displayed on Ten Broeck's marker. One suspects "Uncle John" would have approved.

Frank Harper

Frank Harper had inherited a fortune from his mother even before agreeing to help his aging uncle with the physically and emotionally challenging task of running Nantura. He apparently moved to his uncle's farm not for the money, but because he shared his aging uncle's love of fast horses.

History does not record the undemonstrative Harper's response to the critical articles—primarily in *Spirit of the Times*—disparaging his beloved Ten Broeck and, in equal measure, his own training philosophy, but the uncomplimentary comments regarding his horse and his methods must surely have stung the old horseman.

Harper never rediscovered the formula that had brought the farm Longfellow and Ten Broeck, but he remained a respected member of the Kentucky thoroughbred establishment. He treated his horses with a deep, abiding love, as reflected both in the poetic lines that begin this chapter, and in the monuments he erected over their final resting places. He honored Nantura's best in death as he had exalted them in life.

By the early 1890s, with Nantura's two finest products buried within sight of his own back door and the public now following other racing idols, Harper appeared to tire of the racing and breeding industry, and as age began to take its toll he gradually gave up the life of the breeder. The owner of Ten Broeck, who would be eulogized as "one of the most interesting characters in the thoroughbred breeding world of America," lived for more than twenty-seven years following the shocking defeat of his great thoroughbred, passing away on April 4, 1905, at the age of eighty-one.

For Frank Harper, who had lost his vision to cataracts five years before and had been left paralyzed and without speech by a stroke, the end was probably a relief. As the *Louisville Courier-Journal* noted in its obituary for the old hardboot, "his death at any time within the past six months would not have been surprising." A local newspaper, the *Richman (Kentucky) Climax*, described Harper's funeral as "the occasion of one of the greatest turnouts of prominent horsemen ever seen here."

Like that of fellow owner Pierre Lorillard, Harper's will provoked controversy. The value of Nantura was estimated to be "at least $150,000," not in Lorillard's league but nonetheless a substantial sum of money in the America of 1905. Harper left the farm to the son of his niece, a separate six-hundred-acre spread to his brother, bequests to various relatives, a political contribution to Senator Joseph Clay Stiles Blackburn, and $2,500 to his cook, Susan Stafford, who had attained near legendary status for the feasts she had prepared at Nantura.

Harper left nothing, however, to either of his two surviving sisters, and they challenged his will on their own behalf, as well as for "10 nieces and nephews of the dead turfman not remembered in his will." By June 30, members of the Harper family, among them the children of Harper's brother Adam, who had been among the suspects in the 1871 murders of Uncle Jake and Miss Betsy, had filed papers contesting Harper's bequests. Clearly, Harper had never completely dismissed from his mind the belief that Adam might have played a role in the grisly murders.

In the end, a compromise was achieved, and approximately $35,000, about one-fifth of the Harper estate, was awarded to the various litigants. And with that sad conclusion, the saga of the man who had once raced what was, to that point in time, arguably the greatest racehorse ever seen in America, was closed.

George Lorillard

Despite the defeat of his redoubtable Tom Ochiltree in the Great Sweepstakes, "Master George" continued as one of the most successful and popular sportsmen in America. Always striving to escape the vast shadow of older brother Pierre, George brought his own competitive spirit and "a liberal outlay of money" to the task of overcoming Pierre's racers on the turf.

By 1880, the *New York Times* was able to note that George's "Westbrook Stable still has some first-class stock in training, and . . . in Grenada Mr. George Lorillard may boast of owning the champion 3-year-old in the Eastern States, if not in the country." Grenada had already won for George his third consecutive Preakness, following Duke of Magenta and Harold; Saunterer and Vanguard would win the race in 1881 and 1882. At this point, the younger Lorillard could have been crowned by acclamation as "the most popular turfman in the country."

But all was not well with George Lorillard, who was increasingly ill and in intensifying pain with his lifelong rheumatic condition. In 1882, the younger Lorillard brother could no longer manage the operation of a racing and breeding business, and was compelled to turn over control of his stable to his trainer, R. Wyndham Walden.

From that point, George's health spiraled rapidly downward. By 1884, just two painful years later, the younger Lorillard brother was forced to retire altogether from racing:

> *His reason for selling is his health, which has been poor for many years. He has suffered from hip disease, which compelled him to use a heavy cane or crutch. . . . The place and the horses are offered for $200,000, which Pierre Lorillard says is less than they cost. . . . Mr. Lorillard decided in 1882 to reduce his stable, which had been the largest in the country, except that of his brother Pierre. . . . Mr. Lorillard is now President of the Monmouth Racing Association.*

One can easily imagine such a person, an avid and successful sportsman left a cripple in the prime of life, becoming bitter, but George Lorillard was not of this nature. Quoting from *Spirit of the Times*:

> *Men who suffer from the slow ravages of disease are usually broken in spirit and temper, but throughout his painful illness Mr. Lorillard never lost that bright, cheery good nature and good fellowship that endeared him to all who knew him . . . and during a race meeting it was a familiar sight to see him holding a levee from his coach, while trainers, bookmakers, and men of the humblest positions in life crowded up to shake his hand and inquire after his health. Had he chosen the path of politics, there is no doubt he would have attained the highest distinctions within the gift of the people.*

Advised to seek a gentler climate, the younger Lorillard brother traveled to Europe, settling in for a long winter in Nice, which one can only hope provided some relief. But the end was approaching with ever-increasing speed, like his racer, Tom Ochiltree, with an adversary to catch.

George Lorillard died on February 3, 1886, in Nice, days before what would have been his forty-third birthday. His passing was mourned both in the racing world and in society in general. The *New York Times* noted that "he was a very generous man, and spent from $30,000 to $40,000 a year in assisting embarrassed friends"; the *Turf, Field and Farm* reported that "the turf loses one of its brightest ornaments and the community a good citizen"; the *Kentucky Live Stock Record* declared that "no face or colors will be more missed from the turf." *Spirit of the Times* opined that "no event of the kind that has happened in years could have been the cause of more general regret, nor can we record the death of a turfman or sportsman who has ever enjoyed an equal degree of popularity."

Following a funeral attended by family, friends, and much of the racing community, George Lorillard was laid to rest in the family vault in Brooklyn's Greenwood Cemetery. His will provided $5,000 to a former employee, with the remainder going to his widow and her two daughters from an earlier marriage. Lorillard's lands and property were estimated to be worth $2 million.

Within a year, those lands and properties were selling briskly. On November 16, 1887, Lorillard's executors "expressed themselves satisfied" at realizing more than the $197,000 estimated valuation of ten pieces of property deemed "not up to the average in desirability." On August 19 of the following year, Mrs. Lorillard's runners in training and yearlings were sold at Monmouth Park amid what was reported to be "spirited" bidding, bringing prices "far beyond anticipation."

In February of 1889, almost exactly six years after her husband's death, the former Mrs. George L. Lorillard married the Count Casa de Agreda in Cornwell, England. It was her third marriage, and the count, who had visited America the previous summer, was a familiar figure at the races. It was reported that the count was "considerably younger" than his new bride.

Lily Livingston

Following her sale of Rancocas to Harry Sinclair, the woman who had once been known as Mrs. Allien moved with her husband George to Cobourg, Ontario, Canada. Her most memorable runner there was the mare Sotemia, which twice won the Ontario Jockey Club Cup, and on October 7, 1912, raced four miles at Churchill Downs in 7 minutes, 10⅘ seconds, a record for the distance that remains on the books more than a century later. Given the unlikelihood that the sport will return to four-mile heat racing, Sotemia's mark, and Mrs. Livingston's place in history as the owner of an American record holder, will remain on the books in perpetuity.

In her later years, Lily Livingston reduced her presence in the sport substantially, moving to Virginia and maintaining a few broodmares, a few racers. She overcame the final vestiges of public opprobrium from her involvement with Pierre Lorillard, and was treated with great kindness in the press. As one publication noted regarding her relationship with the people of her community:

> *She finds her enjoyment in playing Lady Bountiful to the poor of the village and surrounding country-side. There is no question about her popularity in the many humble homes where her advent has brought relief from sickness and other forms of distress.*

Her husband George passed away in 1931 at the age of seventy, but Mrs. Livingston, whose final days were spent in a Virginia nursing home, lived for more than fourteen additional years. She breathed her last in November of 1945 at the age of eighty-five.

Harry Sinclair

The Ladana affair having permanently blighted any desire Sinclair might have harbored to resume his racing activities, the oilman returned to the business that had brought him both wealth and scandal. He earned several more fortunes before retiring as president of Sinclair Oil and Gas in 1949 to become chairman of the board, a position he held for five more years.

Sinclair lasted to age eighty before passing away in Pasadena, California, a fabulously wealthy man and one whose eventful life had left him a great many memories, most of them fond, some less so. One obituary described him as "among the most colorful and controversial figures in the recent history of American business." He was laid to rest in the Calvary Cemetery in East Los Angeles, California.

William Helis

Having purchased Rancocas from Sinclair, "The Golden Greek" might have led the historic establishment to new days of glory, but his time at the head of Pierre Lorillard's former showplace proved all too brief.

His success at the helm of what had once been known as Rancocas was dazzling. He catapulted from 123rd on the list of leading earners in 1948 to twelfth among the nation's leaders in both 1952 and 1953.

Annual Leading Breeder: Money Won

Year	Earnings	Rank
1948	$76,502	123rd
1949	$147,122	51st
1950	$290,039	21st
1951	$365,634	16th
1952	$488,937	12th
1953	$519,081	12th

But William Helis, who passed away in July, 1950 following surgery for a respiratory ailment, did not live to see his farm's peak successes. Honored for his philanthropy, particularly his devotion to war relief activities in his native Greece, Helis was recognized by the racing community as the savior of the Fair Grounds Racetrack in New Orleans, which he and a partner had rescued from bankruptcy, and of Tanforan in San Francisco, which he had purchased in 1947. As his final illness progressed, the Helis racing and breeding empires became the responsibility of his son, William George Jr., who continued his father's successes for years to come.

THE TRAINERS

R. Wyndham Walden

"Wyndham" Walden was a forty-two-year-old at the peak of his game when his trainee, Tom Ochiltree, finished third in the Great Sweepstakes. By this time, Walden, who had relocated his family from New York to Maryland several years earlier "to get the horses away from the dreadful Long Island mosquitoes," had already trained Tom Ochiltree to a Preakness victory, and he would train six more winners of Pimlico's classic race, including five in succession (all owned by George Lorillard) between 1878 and 1882.

Over thirteen decades later, no other trainer has approached Walden's record of seven Preakness training victories; his record of five consecutive training wins in any Triple Crown race is matched only by Woodford "Woody" Stevens, whose trainees won the Belmont Stakes every year between 1982 and 1986. Walden's final Preakness winner, a colt named Refund, was ridden by Fred Littlefield, who three years thence would marry Walden's daughter, Minnie.

But Walden's success as a trainer went well beyond his propensity for Preakness victories. It is estimated that from 1872 through 1898, horses conditioned by Walden won more than a thousand races, earned more than $1.4 million, a huge sum in those days of limited racing and minuscule purses. He trained four Belmont Stakes winners. He served as a director of the Maryland Jockey Club. Following George Lorillard's death in 1886, Walden spent several years breeding and racing his own stock, then joined the great stable of the Morris family, for whom he trained until his death in 1905.

Walden's final stakes victory, on April 25, 1905, was a wild one, as the filly Santa Catalina was awarded first place in the Excelsior Handicap at New York's Jamaica Racetrack following the disqualification of first-place finisher Preen for causing a chain-reaction accident that led to two riders being thrown under the hooves of the field. In a horrific scene, the two fallen riders "remained stretched out motionless before the horrified crowd of racegoers until stable hands from the infield picked the boys up and removed them to the jockeys' room."

One of the fallen jockeys, Joe Kelly, escaped with bumps and bruises, and was back riding two days later, taking the day's feature race at Jamaica. The other, Grover Cleveland Fuller, was not nearly so fortunate, suffering a deep gash, "extending from six inches above the knee to four inches beneath the kneepan." Fuller's wound escalated to a bone infection, and when blood poisoning set in his condition was declared critical. Four surgeries were necessary to save the leg, and Fuller remained in the hospital through mid-August. He visited the races, walking with a limp, in May of 1906, and declared that he hoped to begin riding again soon, "though," as one publication informed its readers, "he has taken on weight fast."

In the meantime, "[T]he hospital where Fuller was taken after the accident sent in such an amazingly big bill to the Jockey Club that the latter organization has held it up until it learns whether or not a mistake has been made."The *New York Tribune*, shaking its head editorially at the remarkable ability of jockeys to survive ghastly racetrack falls, declared, "That it did not terminate in a tragedy is one of the miracles which are always happening in racing."There is definitely something to be said for jockeys' sheer athleticism.

Walden was not present for the racetrack carnage, having been ill for several weeks with a respiratory infection, and three days later, at age sixty-one, he died at his home, Maryland's Bowling Brook Farm. The following day, his entrants at Baltimore racetracks were ordered scratched, and the jockeys scheduled to ride for him cancelled all of their mounts in tribute. At the Jamaica track, flags were lowered to half-staff. Wyndham Walden was named to the Thoroughbred Racing Hall of Fame in 1970.

William Brown

Brown, the man who trained Parole to victory over Ten Broeck and Tom Ochiltree, was fifty-two years of age on the date of the Great Sweepstakes. With Pierre Lorillard seeking to improve his racing stable in England, it was only natural that the master of Rancocas should dispatch his top trainer there to oversee the process.

On October 19, 1878, a Lorillard contingent sailed from New York to England: Parole, the talented but temperamental Uncas, and six yearlings. On November 9, a second ship followed, this one transporting the three-year-old Duke of Magenta, William Brown, and Lorillard jockeys Hughes, Fisher, and Barrett. Duke of Magenta would be shipped home a year later, having never raced in England, but Parole and Brown would find their greatest glory on the British turf during the season of 1880. Iroquois was among the stable's two-year-olds on that side of the Atlantic, and had Brown merely remained the trainer the following season, the glory of an English Derby victory might have been his.

But controversy interceded. Brown was brought home from England and his employment with Lorillard terminated following the 1880 season, to be replaced by Jacob Pincus; Englishman Anthony Taylor was hired on as Lorillard's chief American-based conditioner.

Why, many wondered, would Lorillard have replaced his successful trainer? Racing historian Walter S. Vosburgh claimed, "As Mr. Brown was unwilling to remain in England, Mr. Lorillard sent Jacob Pincus to Newmarket and engaged Anthony Taylor to train the horses racing at home," but this seemed an odd, back-of-the-hand manner for Lorillard to have treated the man who conditioned Parole to his historic victory over the great Ten Broeck, who had served "six years of a faithful and a brilliant engagement covering two hemispheres."

The *Turf Field and Farm*, memorializing Brown following his death, insisted that the conditioner had wanted nothing more than to remain in England for the 1881 season, and blamed his sacking on unnamed third parties: "That year [1880] Brown brought out Iroquois when two years old, winning four races out of twelve, and predicted his Derby victory, an event he was ambitious to train him for, but the unexpected happened by Mr. Lorillard recalling him to America, through the instrumentality of tale-bearing busybodies (it is ever thus), and it was a hasty act and an error."

It was not until fifteen years later, in its obituary for Jacob Pincus, that the *Thoroughbred Record*, citing statements made by Brown's widow, suggested the reason for the trainer's unexpected sacking. The *Record* reported that Brown had "claimed when in England and here, Iroquois was pulled [purposely restrained from winning] in some of his races [as a two-year-old]." Lorillard would not have tolerated even the suggestion of a race-fixing scandal originating in his stable, from the mouth of his own trainer. Perhaps this explains Brown's dismissal.

Brown never recovered from the loss of his position at Rancocas. It "came as an electric shock, a dart, mentally deep, that pierced his confiding heart. [U]nhealed it oozed, dripping bitterness unforgiven, and finally enshrouded in his unperishable tomb."

Brown retired to his farm in Monmouth County, New Jersey, and began breeding horses, but for Parole's former trainer the end was shockingly near. Contracting an incurable illness, he lingered briefly, then passed away on July 5, 1881, little more than a month after Iroquois's epic victory at Epsom.

Buried at Holmdel Cemetery in New Jersey, Brown received a belated if no less heartfelt compliment from former employer Pierre Lorillard, as the master of Rancocas reminisced in 1885 about the best of his horses, riders, and trainers. "I would rather have back old man Brown drunk," said Lorillard, "than the rest of my trainers put together sober."

Jacob Pincus

Pincus, who inherited the role of trainer for Iroquois when William Brown was summoned back from England, was in the right place at the right time when Pierre Lorillard's colt won the Epsom Derby in 1881.

The British press had initially criticized Pincus's training methods, which featured two-mile gallops, declaring that the Rancocas conditioner was "galloping his horses to death," but many saw the light after Iroquois defeated their best three-year-olds. One proclaimed, "Hats off to America! Lorillard, Iroquois, Pincus, Archer, I salute ye."

Pincus would remain in Britain for another year as Lorillard's head trainer, but there were no more like Iroquois in the Rancocas pipeline, and following the 1882 season the trainer returned to America with the Derby winner in tow.

Pincus eventually moved on, training for various owners and serving as starter at Jerome Park. In retirement, he became a popular fixture at racetracks, yearling auctions, even horse shows, until his death at age eighty (or, according to one source, eighty-five) in 1918. He was inducted into the National Museum of Racing and Hall of Fame in 1988, a mere 107 years after demonstrating with an Epsom Derby victory that America could compete with any nation in the world of thoroughbred racing.

Matthew Byrnes

Apprenticed to Pincus when the former August Belmont employee signed on to train for William Astor, Byrnes was promoted to first assistant trainer when Pincus moved next to Rancocas. In 1881, when Pincus was dispatched to England to condition Lorillard's overseas contingent, the tobacco magnate briefly hired Englishman Anthony Taylor to train his American-based stable, but when Taylor's "convivial habits"—he was too familiar with the bottle—"precluded a long tenure to his engagements," Byrnes was "offered the post by Mr. Lorillard on no less than three occasions—something like Caesar being offered the crown." Byrnes at first declined, uncertain that he was prepared for the responsibility, but finally accepted the job.

Byrnes's confidence must surely have soared when, shortly after assuming command of Lorillard's American contingent, his trainees won four races in one day at Jerome Park, and the presence of the eternal Parole, which would win twelve races in 1881 and fifteen more over the next two years, ensured that he would suffer no confidence-shattering losing streaks. Byrnes cemented his position in Lorillard's affections by begging the tobacco magnate to keep the filly Hiawasse, whom Taylor had recommended be sold. Hiawasse won practically every important race for her age and gender.

Byrnes was also the hero of an aborted effort to "nobble" Pizarro, one of Lorillard's top runners of the post-Parole era, at Monmouth Park. Awakened by a noise from the stable, Byrnes grabbed a pistol and sprinted to the scene, where he startled a man at the barn door. The trainer fired over the man's head, but the would-be fixer, who had already picked the lock, escaped in the darkness. Given a few more moments, the mysterious man would doubtless have done harm to Pizarro.

Byrnes remained with Lorillard for five years, or until the tobacco magnate temporarily lost interest in the sport and sold his stock. He then followed many of the former Lorillard horses to the stable of the Dwyer brothers, whose racing operations rivaled those of Rancocas's quantity and quality. The peripatetic Byrnes was later hired by James Ben Ali Haggin, sending postward future Hall of Famers Salvator and Firenze, who between them won 63 of 101 starts, with 32 additional second- and third-place finishes.

Rare indeed is the trainer fortunate enough to get his hands on even a single Hall of Fame thoroughbred; Byrnes managed to have two in his barn simultaneously, this after having handled another in Parole—all by the time he was thirty-five years old. In his later years, Byrnes described Firenze as the best filly or mare he ever trained, and Salvator as the best horse he ever saw. And Byrnes saw Man o' War.

With so impressive a resume, Byrnes had little trouble finding work when Haggin decided to devote his full attention to breeding. Joining the Bitter Root Stable of copper magnate Marcus Daly, Byrnes sent to the track a steady succession of stakes horses, and following Daly's death in 1900 purchased a farm not far from Monmouth Park and raced his own stock. When the Hart-Agnew Act shut down racing in New York, Byrnes sold the farm and worked as a bloodstock adviser and shipping agent for owners seeking financially greener climes, primarily in Argentina.

Eighty-year-old "Matt" Byrnes was a revered grand old man of the turf when he succumbed to pneumonia in New Jersey in 1933. He was inducted into racing's Hall of Fame in 2011 through the historic review process, which reconsiders the merits of those whose exploits occurred during racing's nearly forgotten past.

Harry Colston

Unlike the horses, owners, riders, and other trainers involved in the Great Sweepstakes, the life path of Harry Colston, the African-American trainer of Ten Broeck, appears to vanish into history shortly after his participation in the race.

Following Ten Broeck's defeat, Colston continued training for Frank Harper until the autumn of 1879, when the two became embroiled in a dispute dating back to the Ten Broeck–Mollie McCarthy match race of a year earlier. It was Colston's contention that the aging horseman had promised to give him Irish King, one of the stable's promising colts, if Colston could train Ten Broeck into condition to defeat the mare. Ten Broeck was victorious in the race, and Colston believed he was now the owner of Irish King.

However, in the $5,000 Great Stallion Stakes, contested at Louisville on September 25, 1879, and providing to the winner a trophy valued at $1,500, Harper entered two colts, Jils Johnson and Irish King, in his own name. He later claimed to have had a tacit understanding with Colston to split the purse, although Colston insisted that he had rejected this arrangement prior to the race.

The result of the Great Stallion Stakes was not satisfactory to Harper. Irish King raced without incident and won, equaling the American record for the distance with a 3:05¼ clocking, but Jils Johnson was bumped in the final furlong by another runner, costing him his chance for victory. According to *Spirit of the Times*,

> *[Harper] collected the amount of the stakes, $5,155, and received the plate, of which $4,855 and the plate, belonged to the winner. It was a great deal of money—Mr. Harper . . . went off and got to thinking about it, and he concluded that he could not give it up. He conceived that Colston had conspired to defraud him, and charged that he had caused Jils Johnson to be pulled, that Irish King might win.*

Colston protested to his employer, demanding the purse, the trophy, and the horse, and was summarily fired by Harper, who directed him to take Irish King and leave. When Harper still refused to surrender the purse and the trophy, Colston filed suit.

The African-American trainer received a surprising level of public support for his legal action. *Spirit of the Times* described Harper's refusal to make good on his offer to Colston as "a turf scandal of more than ordinary magnitude," proclaiming, "[t]he ways of the courts are devious at times, but from the facts, and a common sense idea of justice between man and man, we think that in the race between him and Mr. Harper, Colston has the pole." In due time, the court showed more interest in the elements of the verbal agreement between Harper and Colston than in Harper's protestations regarding an allegedly rigged race, or even in the racial differences between the claimants. Harper was ordered to pay Colston the purse money, transmit to him the plate, and withdraw his claims on the horse.

All of which left Colston with a legal victory but without an employer. And at this point, as the trainer begins his fade into oblivion, it becomes necessary to follow the career of his horse, Irish King, to retain even a glimpse of the former Nantura Stable conditioner.

Irish King's first start following his enforced change of ownership occurred at Baltimore on October 21, two-mile heats for a purse of $700. Irish King won for a jockey named Costello; the owner was listed as "H. Colston." Following this performance, Colston was offered $3,000 for the colt, but not surprisingly, given Irish King's potential and the effort Colston had undertaken to gain ownership, he rejected the offer. Instead, Colston traveled with the colt to Washington, DC, for the 1½-mile Potomac Sweepstakes. Facing stronger competition in his final start of 1879, Irish King earned the runner-up share of the purse.

Irish King's 1880 campaign began in Nashville, in a $250 race with Harper's erstwhile jockey, William Walker, in the irons, as he would be for all of Irish King's 1880 starts. This was primarily a conditioning spin for the colt, but Irish King finished a creditable third. His following start was a losing effort in a match race, but Irish King rebounded to win his next outing, at 1½ miles for a $300 purse.

Now the Irish King contingent shipped back to Kentucky, where their charge ran fourth in the 2¼-mile Louisville Cup, then won a $1,000 event at four miles. Colston, Walker, and Irish King next headed to Cincinnati, where on June 2 they won a $500 purse. With Irish King now at the top of his game, Colston determined that his next start should be in Chicago's Garden City Cup. Irish King, again stepping up in class, could manage only a third-place finish in the 2¼-mile race.

But somewhere between Cincinnati and Chicago, something had changed for Colston and Irish King. In each of the colt's nine outings since Colston's court victory, the official record had listed "H. Colston" as Irish King's owner. For the Garden City Cup, the owner was "H. Colston & Co."

Irish King's next start occurred a month and a half later, on August 9 at New York's Saratoga Race Track. Irish King, Walker in the saddle, was sent postward in a 1⅝-mile event for a purse of $500, but there was a new owner, L. W. Jerome, and Colston's name was nowhere in the official record. Perhaps this was Leonard Jerome, the man for whom Jerome Park was named, but if so, how had he come to acquire the colt? Irish King ran poorly that day and earned nary a dime for his new owner, and, indeed, would not win in any of his three remaining 1880 starts. Irish King would begin the following year as the property of L. W. Jerome, but would change owners again at midyear, moving to the stable of a G. B. Bryson.

The "H. Colston & Co." designation in the official record of the Chicago race marks the last time Colston's name appears in a race chart, or, as best the author can determine, in print anywhere. Irish King, the colt he had acquired as part of a disagreement so bitter that it cost him his job and his relationship with Frank Harper, continues to race for others, though not particularly well, but Colston seemingly drops off the face of the earth.

It is an odd ending—if, indeed, it is the ending—to the career of one of the key figures in one of the most important thoroughbred races ever conducted in the United States, and, more important, a man who was among the first to demonstrate that an African-American man could receive fair treatment in a dispute with a white defendant in the court-rooms of a former slave state.

Sam Hildreth

The unquestioned genius behind the success of Rancocas Stable during the Harry Sinclair era, Hildreth won three Belmont Stakes in just under ten years with Rancocas. Victories by Grey Lag in 1921, Zev in 1923, and Mad Play in 1924 brought his total wins in the classic to seven.

Having already led the nation's owners in money won on three separate occasions and pushed Rancocas to the top of the listing three more times, having led all trainers in earnings five times on his own and four more times with Sinclair's horses, Hildreth added yet another title to his resume in 1927, leading the nation's conditioners with seventy-two races won.

But time was growing short for the Rancocas mastermind. In September 1929, after reluctantly agreeing to curtail his training activities, the sixty-three-year-old underwent surgery for an abdominal condition that had been worsening for over a year. He never rallied, and died on September 24. Racetracks flew their flags at half-staff in his memory, and Harry Sinclair was interviewed in his prison cell. "News of his death comes as a grievous shock to me," said the oilman. "He was one of the best friends I ever had, one of the most loyal. As a trainer he had no equal anywhere."

It seems likely that at the time of his death, Hildreth's legion of train-ees had earned more money on the track than those of any other trainer in the history of the sport. He was inducted into the National Museum of Racing and Hall of Fame in 1955, a member of the initial class of internees.

Hildreth's was one of four deaths of prominent racing men to occur within a few months. Just weeks earlier, Hall of Fame trainer James Rowe had passed away, and on October 20, the racing world lost Marshall (Mars) Cassidy, for decades the official starter for the New York tracks. And belying the commonplace saying that deaths in industries occur in groups of three, on November 3, John E. Madden, master of Kentucky's legendary Hamburg Place breeding farm, became the fourth giant of the sport to breathe his last.

If there was a challenger for the title "America's Greatest Trainer" among Hildreth's contemporaries it would have been Rowe, whose Hall of Famers included Hindoo, Luke Blackburn, Miss Woodford, Peter Pan, Colin, Commando, Maskette, Regret, Sysonby, and Whisk Broom II. Rowe trained more champions (thirty-four) than any other conditioner, and holds the record for most training wins in the Belmont Stakes (eight). His training career covered a third of a century, from 1876, when, like so many of the trainers discussed in this volume, his increasing weight ended his riding career, through his death in 1929.

Unlike Hildreth, who rode quarter horses over rough sagebrush courses in the Midwest, Rowe had ridden some of the era's greatest thoroughbreds at racing's showplace tracks. He rode two Belmont Stakes winners, and brought home a collection of trophies from other major races. It had been Rowe in the saddle when Harry Bassett defeated John Harper's beloved Longfellow in that great runner's disastrous final start.

Despite his quarter-century of prominence on the New York tracks, Mars Cassidy is probably best remembered for a day he spent in bed.

The date was August 13, 1919, and Man o' War, just two years of age but already on the verge of legendary status, was entered in Saratoga's Sanford Memorial Stakes. For one of the rare times during his long tenure as the Jockey Club's official starter, Cassidy, who ten years later would be described as "remarkable for his vitality, and wonderful physique," was at home, recuperating from illness.

Cassidy's replacement on the starter's platform, a placing judge named C. H. Pettingill, "did very badly all day, getting only two really good starts on a program of seven events." One of the worst occurred in the Sanford Memorial, which was described in the official *Daily Racing Form* chart with the words, "Start, poor and slow."

One that got a particularly poor start was Man o' War, which left the barrier sixth in the seven-horse field and then, unaccustomed to racing behind horses, gathered himself for a furlong or two before beginning a feverish pursuit of the front-running Golden Broom and Upset. When he found himself blocked in midstretch, Man o' War, carrying fifteen pounds more than Upset, altered course and powered around the logjam, but fell a half-length short of his aptly named opponent.

Twenty feet beyond the wire, Man o' War had passed his final rival, but thoroughbred racing does not offer contests of six furlongs plus twenty feet. It is the stuff of legend that, had Cassidy been at his accustomed post and Pettingill been in his judge's stand, the Sanford would have been another Man o' War victory. At Man o' War's retirement the following year, the Sanford Memorial would be the only race the colt ever lost.

John E. Madden was, with Harry Payne Whitney, one of the two greatest thoroughbred breeders of his era. Madden bred five Kentucky Derby winners (Old Rosebud in 1914, Triple Crown winner Sir Barton in 1918, Paul Jones in 1920, Zev in 1923, and Flying Ebony in 1925); won a Preakness with Sir Barton, and bred five winners of the Belmont Stakes (Joe Madden in 1909, The Finn in 1915, Sir Barton, Grey Lag in 1921, and Zev in 1923). He owned and trained 1898 Derby winner Plaudit.

From 1917 through 1928, Madden-bred runners led the nation annually in number of races won, and in many of those years he also topped the list of leading money-earning breeders, alternating with Whitney atop the ranking. Ironically, it was Madden who began his strongest rival in the thoroughbred business, encountering two of the wealthy Whitney brothers at the racetrack and suggesting to them, "Why don't you get into this business?" As encouragement, he gave the two brothers one of his horses; they could pay him a fair price if the horse performed well; if not, there would be no charge.

At the time of his passing, "the Wizard of the Turf," who in his younger days had served as a sparring partner for bareknuckle heavyweight champion John L. Sullivan, was a millionaire many times over, having amassed a fortune from his Wall Street investments to supplement the bonanza he'd accumulated selling Hamburg Place's well-bred thoroughbreds.

THE JOCKEYS

William Walker

The rider of Ten Broeck in his losing effort against Parole, Walker pushed the Nantura superhorse to victory against Mollie McCarthy with what was described at the time as a "cyclonic charge" but was later recognized, given Mollie's near breakdown after 2½ miles, as something closer to a breezy gallop. Following the race, Walker had earned the plaudits of even the laconic Frank Harper, who exclaimed to the assorted men of the press, "That boy is the best in the country."

As his career gradually wound down, Walker began investing in Louisville real estate and applying his agile mind to a detailed study of thoroughbred pedigrees. Here was a rare instance—then as now—of an athlete retiring with both money in his pockets and a basis for future employment.

Walker began his post-retirement years as a trainer, but it was his nearly encyclopedic knowledge of equine bloodlines that would render the former rider invaluable to John Madden and other leading breeders of the era. Soon, the racing world began observing a curious but recurring tableau: the wealthy, white master of Hamburg Place conferring deferentially with a tiny black man, the descendant of slaves from a backwater Kentucky farm, as he considered the purchase of a yearling or the planned mating of a broodmare to an exotically bred stallion. But while Madden was elected to the Thoroughbred Racing Hall of Fame in 1983, William Walker, on whose knowledge and advice Madden doted, has yet to be inducted.

Walker died September 20, 1933, at seventy-two or perhaps seventy-three. For years before his passing, he had been "privileged to enter any tack room in the Midwest, regardless of whether men of affluence and high social standing or racing commissioners were present, and invariably was permitted to join in any and all debates which might be in progress."

And then, for some sixty-three years, racing forgot William Walker. In 1943, the *Thoroughbred Record* published a long history of the accomplishments of African-American jockeys, recalling the achievements of many long-passed riders, but somehow the name of the jockey who had accompanied Ten Broeck on his record-setting runs, whose skills had been essential to the out-of-condition Nantura star's victory over Mollie McCarthy, who had won the Kentucky Derby aboard Baden-Baden and had served as John Madden's breeding consultant, is nowhere to be found.

Walker's grave in a Louisville cemetary remained unmarked, his riding feats left to the dust of history, until 1996, when Churchill Downs commissioned a headstone, with an epitaph outlining Walker's career highlights, erected over the pioneering jockey's final resting place. It was a generous, if belated, gesture of remembrance for one of the great jockeys of yesteryear.

George Barbee

Suspended for the 1878 season, George Barbee returned to racing on October 9, 1879, winning a $400 purse race in his return to the track. He had remained in condition, continuing to scale 110 pounds, but the suspension had cost him both financially and in the public's awareness. When Barbee returned to the saddle his prodigious physical skills remained, but his client list had shrunken.

Following his reinstatement, Barbee rode for Pierre Lorillard in 1880 and 1881, returning to his native England to pilot Iroquois and some of the tobacco magnate's other outstanding runners. He lost the Great Metropolitan Stakes when he misjudged the finish line aboard a runner fittingly named Mistake. Returning to America, he experienced success aboard many a Rancocas horse.

By 1884, however, fewer mounts were coming the twenty-five-year-old Barbee's way, and he retired from the riding profession. While racing records of the period are decidedly murky and incomplete, the Thoroughbred Racing Museum and Hall of Fame credits the Englishman with 136 victories in "approximately 490" races. If these numbers are even remotely correct, and the museum's statistics are among the most cautious to be found, his winning percentage of 27.8 percent would place him among racing's all-time elite jockeys.

Following his retirement, Barbee undertook a training career, creating enough notice that in 1884, the *New York Times* reported that the stable of James A. Kelly was "under the tuition of George Barbee, the able jockey," who was "developing the best quality of a trainer, and the horses under his care are in good condition."

Perhaps the new career wasn't right for Barbee, however, for he later returned to the saddle, winning 42 races in 232 starts in New York and New Jersey during 1890 and 1891, competing against such all-time great jockeys as Isaac Murphy, Edward "Snapper" Garrison, and another whip specialist of renown, the powerful Fred Taral. Close finishes involving Taral and Barbee must have been violent affairs, the two slashing their way down the stretch, whips flailing, each doing everything in his considerable power to bludgeon his mount past the other's.

Barbee's name had fallen out of the news until a curious incident in 1903, when it was reported that "[a] controversy between H.E. Rowell, the Western trainer, and George Barbee, the old-time jockey, in the paddock at Sheepshead Bay [Racetrack] yesterday over a business transaction reached the point where interference by the police was necessary, and Barbee, on Rowell's complaint, was ordered off the grounds." Late in his life, Barbee lost his left leg to cancer.

In the years preceding his death in 1941, Barbee was, aside from the rare radio interview or newspaper nostalgia piece, almost forgotten by the sport. This remained the case until the early 1990s, when a great-grandson, Army Sergeant Dale Kerlin, became curious about his ancestor's life and was surprised to learn that his relative had been one of the greatest jockeys of a bygone era, but had never been honored by racing's Hall of Fame. Sergeant Kerlin went about remedying the oversight.

Kerlin's quest to learn ever more about his distinguished relative was a difficult one, made more so because decades earlier a fire at Pimlico Racetrack had destroyed much of the documentation from Barbee's racing days. But Kerlin persevered, involving the press in publicizing Barbee's accomplishments, and slowly, more than half a century after the jockey's passing, his campaign reawakened the sport to his ancestor's achievements. Kerlin's tenacity was rewarded in 1996 when the Hall of Fame's Historic Review Committee selected Barbee for induction. Today, the jockey's plaque resides not far from those of Duke of Magenta and Parole, two of the many great thoroughbreds Barbee rode during the days when he was one of racing's leading reinsmen.

William Barrett

For Parole's rider on that exciting day at Pimlico, victory in one of history's greatest races led rapidly to a cruel and ultimately fatal downward turn. Barrett's sad fate is detailed in Appendix B, "'Wasting' Away: Racing's Rules and the Death of William Barrett."

Barrett continued riding for Pierre Lorillard through 1879, but by 1880 normal growth had pushed his weight beyond the feathery levels demanded in racing's early days. Trainer William Brown, who had seen many riding careers end when otherwise capable jockeys gained too much weight, gave Barrett what mounts he could, including a ride or two aboard Parole. But for Barrett, time was growing short.

Appendix A

Tijuana Speed:
The Fall of Ten Broeck's Final Record

*Worthman took the lead at once and won all the way, but his lead
appeared in jeopardy at two miles, then came away when called on,
but was a tired horse at the end and probably would have been beaten
in another sixteenth.*

—From the official *Daily Racing Form* chart for the
fifth race at Tijuana, February 22, 1925

One mark of a truly great thoroughbred's records is that they
remain on the books for extended periods of time. In considering this
standard, one can recall Swaps's 1⅝-mile record of 2:38⅕, set on July 25,
1956, and unthreatened for nearly six decades; Secretariat's Triple
Crown–clinching Belmont Stakes, accomplished with 1½ miles in 2:24
that remains unchallenged after more than forty years; Dr. Fager's 1:32⅕
for the mile, still on the books after forty-five years; and Spectacular Bid's
1¼ miles in 1:57⅘, still the best time for America's classic distance after a
third of a century. Kelso's American standard for 2 miles, 3:19⅕, accomplished a half-century ago, seems likely to endure forever, given the reduc-
tion in distance of the Jockey Club Gold Cup, the last American 2-mile
stakes race of any consequence, to 1½ miles in 1976.

Ten Broeck's records had longevity. His 1⅝-mile record, set over the
Lexington Association course on September 9, 1875, was on the books
for nearly seven years; his 3-mile record, set on September 23, 1876, at
Churchill Downs, lasted nearly six. Ten Broeck's record for the mile, a
1:39⅘ clocking on May 23, 1877, remained on the books for over thirteen years, and his much-celebrated 4-mile record—a 7:15¾ recorded on
September 27, 1876—remained the standard for more than twenty years,

falling to Lucretia Borgia's 7:11 on May 20, 1897. Ten Broeck's record for 2 miles, a 3:27½ clocking in Louisville on May 29, 1877, lasted nearly twenty-one years before Judge Denny's 3:26½ on February 12, 1898, sent it into eclipse.

Ten Broeck's final record remained untouched for more than forty-eight years, and it was beginning to appear that his 4:58½ for 2⅝ miles, set at Lexington on September 16, 1876, might remain eternally the standard for the distance. On February 25, 1925, however, at the Tijuana, Mexico, racetrack, a steed named Worthman ran the distance in 4:51⅖, slicing seven seconds from Ten Broeck's seemingly insurmountable time and erasing the post–Civil War superstar's name forever from racing's record book.

But wait. Looking back at the racing records of the 1920s, one quickly notices an oddity. Between January 11 and March 8, 1925, records tumbled like dice in Tijuana. They fell in a way that had never been observed in the previous history of the sport, and has never been seen since.

Date	**Distance**	**Record Setter**	**Time**	**Approx. Margin Over Prior Record**
January 11, 1925	1⅞ mi.	Jolly Cephas	3:16⅘	⅘ sec.
February 8, 1925	2⅜ mi.	Wiki Jack	4:15	N/A[1]
February 22, 1925	2⅝ mi.	Worthman	4:51⅗	7 sec.
March 1, 1925	2¾ mi.	Just Right	4:50⅗	8 sec.
March 8, 1925	2⅞ mi.	Bosh	5:23	N/A[1]

[1] No previous record listed for the distance.

We noted previously that Ten Broeck's records had once led to speculation regarding "slow watches and India rubber tracks." Now, here at Tijuana, was the real deal: a track so absurdly fast that nondescript thoroughbreds such as Worthman, Jolly Cephas, and Just Right could shave multiple seconds from hallowed American records.

Were these runners deserving of a spot among racing's elite thoroughbreds? All five could boast long careers, too slow, perhaps, to fall prey to the injuries that so often compromise the raceworthiness of more capable thoroughbreds. Jolly Cephas won for the first time over the half-mile track at Youngstown, Ohio, as a superannuated six-year-old, and possessed the tenacity to compete through age twelve. Worthman raced 263 times, and also earned purse money as a twelve-year-old. But mere longevity does not necessarily confer greatness. The lifetime records of the five Tijuana record-setters form a *res ipsa loquitur* case for their mediocrity:

Horse	Starts	1st	2nd	3rd	Unplaced	Lifetime Earnings
Jolly Cephas	156	27	18	16	95	$15,075
Wiki Jack	74	13	8	18	34	$11,940
Worthman	263	52	37	29	140	$40,985
Just Right	54	13	7	8	23	$6,470
Bosh	116	20	14	15	66	$21,112

Lest the reader assume that Worthman's career earnings of $40,985 might suggest excellence during the pre-inflation days of the Roaring Twenties, the following chart is provided, displaying the records for the leading earners of the decade—and bear in mind that the "Earnings" column reflects single-year, rather than career earnings:

Year	Leading Earner	Starts	1st	2nd	3rd	Earnings
1920	Man o' War	11	11	0	0	$166,140
1921	Morvich	11	11	0	0	$115,234
1922	Pillory	7	4	1	1	$95,654
1923	Zev	14	12	1	0	$272,008
1924	Sarazen	12	8	1	1	$95,640

Year	Leading Earner	Starts	1st	2nd	3rd	Earnings
1925	Pompey	10	7	2	0	$121,630
1926	Crusader	15	9	4	0	$166,033
1927	Anita Peabody	7	6	0	1	$111,905
1928	High Strung	6	5	0	0	$153,590
1929	Blue Larkspur	6	4	1	0	$153,450
1930	Gallant Fox	10	9	1	0	$308,275

One can only conclude that while the Tijuana contingent had had its brief moments of glory, all fell woefully short of the greatness displayed by the runners whose places among America's record holders they had usurped.

It is therefore appropriate that the *Daily Racing Form*, in its magnificent annual compendium of racing news, facts, and statistics, the *American Racing Manual*, no longer recognizes as records any of the marks established by the Tijuana runners during that supercharged two-month stretch.

One, Jolly Cephas's standard for 1⅞ miles, is now owned by Asserche, who at Laurel Racetrack on March 20, 1994, covered the distance in 3:11⅖, more than 5 seconds faster than the time posted at Tijuana.

Bosh's 2⅞ miles in 5:23 remained on the books until 2001, when it was replaced in the *Manual* by the 5:08⅕ recorded by Call Louis at Delaware Park on August 24, 1986. Curiously, Bosh's name was not removed at that time from the listing; instead, the distance of his race was unaccountably revised to 2¹⁵⁄₁₆ miles, and for that one year, both he and Call Louis were recognized as record holders. Bosh's name dropped out of the record book the following year, followed by Call Louis's in 2003. The 2013 edition of the *Manual* lists no American record holder for either distance.

The 2¾-mile record established by Just Right at 4:50⅗ fell in 1940, when Shot Put ran the distance in 4:48⅗, two seconds faster than the previous standard, at Washington Park. Shot Put's time, recognized as both the American and the world's record for the distance, remained the official standard until the 2001 *Manual*, when Fourth Flight, which in

1973 had posted a 5:35⅖ clocking, was credited with the record. Fourth Flight's clocking, despite being some 44⅘ seconds slower than Shot Put's, remains, for reasons never explained, the recognized American standard for the distance.

A similar situation exists with regard to Wiki Jack's 4:15 for 2⅜ miles, which remained on the books until 1979, when Pamroy ran a 4:10⅗ on turf at England's Goodwood Race Course. There was no listed dirt record for 2⅜ miles from that point until 2001, when the standard was credited to Naughty Nipper, which had run the distance in 4:34⅕ at the Lincoln State Fair in Nebraska. Naughty Nipper's time, 19⅕ seconds slower than Wiki Jack's, nevertheless remains the listed American record for the distance.

Then there's that final record of Ten Broeck's.

The 2⅝-mile standard that Worthman usurped from the Kentucky crack was hijacked from the Nantura star's conqueror in the 2001 edition of the *American Racing Manual*, which recognized Amber Dare as the new record holder. Already the holder of two long-distance races over the track at Finger Lakes, Amber Dare had raced 2⅝ miles at the Canandaigua, New York, venue in 5:12⅖ on November 11, 1973. Amber Dare was not then credited as an American record holder, nor should he have been, given that his best time for the distance was 21 seconds slower than Worthman's. It was nearly 14 seconds slower even than Ten Broeck's 4:58½, set in 1876.

For twenty-seven years after Amber Dare's 2⅝-mile jaunt, the *American Racing Manual* gave the gelding's effort the appropriate attention, listing his time among the Finger Lakes records, where it seemed likely to remain for a very long time indeed. Throughout those years, the *Manual* continued to credit Worthman with history's fastest 2⅝ miles. In 2001, however, Amber Dare's time abruptly joined the listing of American records, and Worthman was dropped from the list, his name likely never to be seen again. Until now.

Frank Harper, Ten Broeck's cantankerous owner, had always claimed that time records were broken not because horses improved dramatically from generation to generation, but because racing conditions improved, and times improved with them. In Tijuana, in 1925, Harper's assertion was demonstrated, as his champion's final record fell to a slow horse competing over a lightning fast Tijuana racetrack. But what even Harper underestimated was how adroitly history can be manipulated, how official records can be declared valid for decades, only to be supplanted, without explanation, by slower times.

Were he somehow returned to life in the twenty-first century, Harper would undoubtedly be startled to observe that his champion's final remaining record had been replaced by a slower clocking posted ninety-seven years after his champion's record posting. Never prone to verbosity, but never lacking an opinion about the sport and the animals that formed his *raison d'être*, the Kentuckian would almost certainly voice a succinct response. One doubts that his reaction would be one of amusement.

Appendix B

"Wasting" Away: Racing's Rules and the Death of William Barrett

If ever the Jockey Clubs want an argument in favor of increasing the weights, the case of Barrett is a good one for them.
—The *New York Sportsman*, January 13, 1883

William Barrett, who rode Parole to his epic victory in the Great Sweepstakes of October 24, 1877, died in his home, of a form of self-inflicted starvation leading to a fatal pneumonia, less than six years after his triumph.

The weights carried by jockeys during the 1880s, as they are today, were determined based upon variants of the weight-for-age scale invented by Admiral Henry John Rous during his service as steward of the English Jockey Club during the 1850s. Rous's invention of the weight-for-age scale had two aims: to encourage wagering, by requiring more accomplished runners to lug more weight than less capable horses, and, more important, to reduce the stress on delicate equine legs by limiting the weights the horses were required to carry. The weight scales of the 1880s demanded exceptionally light jockey weights, especially in races for younger horses.

Rous spent many hours considering how his weight scales might minimize a race's impact on the physiology of young horses, but seems to have spent few sleepless nights considering his invention's effect on the jockeys who would be striving to make the weights his system demanded. Throughout this volume, we have read the stories of horsemen—Walden, Pincus, Byrnes, Hildreth, Rowe—who began their racing careers as riders, then were forced into other aspects of the sport when they literally grew out of their riding careers. But these were merely the handful of jockeys-turned-trainers who happened to have a connection to the Great Sweepstakes of 1877. One can be certain that researching more deeply into this subject would turn up hundreds, perhaps thousands, of similar stories.

In 1877, William Barrett had been not merely one of the nation's top jockeys; he was *the* top jockey, as confirmed by the listing of the year's leading riders:

Top 10 Winning Jockeys of 1877

Jockey	Wins
Barrett	36
Barbee	29
Evans	24
Murphy	20
Hughes	15
Kelso	14
Walker	13
Allen	13
Sayers	10
Sparling	10

Just three years after Parole's triumph over Ten Broeck, however, Barrett was well along the path to becoming yet another victim of the era's weight scale. At this point in his career, Barrett was approaching the peak of his physical strength, and could call upon several years of experience in the saddle. But now, smaller, lighter, younger jockeys were receiving the riding opportunities that had previously been Barrett's.

There was but one alternative left if Barrett wished to continue race riding, and that was to undergo "wasting"—losing weight, on a daily basis, through such drastic measures as extreme dieting, heavy exercise, denial of liquids, sweating, and induced vomiting. In an earlier era, masters insistent upon the lightest possible weights for the slaves who rode their horses would order the riders buried to their necks for hours in horse manure, to sweat away precious ounces in the warm, if unsanitary and decidedly unpleasant effluvium. Thankfully, this was one indignity to which Barrett was not subjected.

The official race charts of the 1870s do not approach the data provided in modern-era *Daily Racing Form* charts, but for most races *Krik's Guide*, *Goodwin's*, and the other official record keepers of thirteen decades ago did indicate basic facts for each race: the purse money distributed to the winner and runner-up, the race's distance, the names of the horses (for those that had been given names), the owners, the jockeys, the runners' finishing positions, and the weights carried.

This information enables us to observe the unbearable burden inflicted upon the riders of the late 1800s by the era's scales of weights. Reprinted below are the official charts of two races contested in Kentucky during the 1877 racing season: one from the Lexington Association meeting, the other from Churchill Downs, which in 1877 hosted the third running of the race that would one day be known throughout the world as "The Run for the Roses." William Walker won that 1877 Kentucky Derby aboard Baden-Baden. His weight assignment for the race was 100 pounds.

There are two factors particularly worth noting in these races: first, the impossibly low weights at which the jockeys were required to ride; and second, the small amounts of purse money for which these athletes first starved themselves, and then placed their lives in jeopardy in competition. And it should, of course, be borne in mind that the jockeys were not competing for the totality of the purse money. Far from it, in fact. Most of the money would be awarded to the owners of the winning and runner-up thoroughbreds:

Fifth Day of the Annual Fall Meeting of the Louisville Jockey Club, October 5, 1877

Purse $350 for all ages, with selling allowances, mile and a quarter, $350.

Horse	Age	Selling Allowance	Weight Carried	Jockey	Finish
Salyer's Charles Gorham	3 yrs.	$750	82 lbs.	Ringo	1
Williams' Springbranch	3 yrs.	$1,000	87 lbs.	Allen	2

Horse	Age	Selling Allowance	Weight Carried	Jockey	Finish
Megibben's Malmistic	4 yrs.	$750	100 lbs.	Kelso	3
Jennings & Co.'s Oily Gammon	3 yrs.	$1,000	90 lbs.	Doty	0
Grinstead's Mohur	3 yrs.	$750	82 lbs.	Douglas	0

Time 2:11¼
Gorham the favorite. Won by 2 lengths.

Kentucky Association Meeting at Lexington, May 14, 1877

Fourth Renewal of the Sweepstakes for two-year-old fillies; half a mile; 15 subs.; $850, $50.

Horse	Weight Carried	Jockey	Finish
Williams' (McKee's) Waterwitch	87 lbs.	Murphy	1
Grinstead's Queechy	87 lbs.	Douglas	2
Megibben's Ch. f, by Asteroid-Jennie H.	87 lbs.	Gross	3
Smoot & Co's Grapple	87 lbs.	Shelton	0
Pennistan's Cordelia	87 lbs.	Buckner	0
Wilson's Minuet	87 lbs.	Butler	0
Buford's Nettie Hopkins	87 lbs.	James	0
Grinstead's Bobadilla	87 lbs.	Green	0
Keene Richards' Ch. f, by War Dance, dam by Wagner	87 lbs.	Ringo	0
McGrath's Florence Payne	87 lbs.	Williams	0
Reardon's Enchantress	87 lbs.	Adams	0

Time, 52¼ s.
Grinstead's pair the favorites. Won by a good length, after an indifferent start.

The first of the races was won by a three-year-old named Charles Gorham, which was assigned to carry eighty-two pounds. That is not a typographical error; it is *eighty-two* pounds, which would have included the rider's saddle, boots, and silks. It is well known that people were smaller and lighter in the past, but how much excess weight would even the tiniest of men have been forced to shed, to ride at that weight?

The winning jockey, a man named Ringo, having tortured off enough weight to scale eighty-two pounds, would have earned $350 for owner Salyer. Ringo's share might have been $35.

The second race, a contest among two-year-old fillies won by Water-witch, called for eleven adult male human beings to scale eighty-seven pounds, which again would have included silks, boots, and saddle. The reward to winning rider Isaac Murphy, one of history's great African-American jockeys, might have been 10 percent of the $850 winner's purse, or $85; a rider of Murphy's repute might have wangled a few extra dollars. Second money was $50, of which the runner-up jockey, a man named Douglas, would have received perhaps 10 percent: five dollars for starving himself sufficiently to scale eighty-seven pounds, and then risking his life piloting an inexperienced two-year-old filly in a pack of ten other nervous two-year-olds.

And this was a half-mile race, for which the weight scale permitted relatively moderate weights. How much would jockeys have been permitted to weigh in a race for two-year-olds entered to run a longer distance? If the race had been a mile event contested in May, the weight standard would have been seventy pounds:

	2-year-olds					
Distances	May	June	July	Aug.	Sept.	Oct. & Nov.
½ Mile	80	82	85	88	91	95
¾ Mile	75	77	80	83	86	90
1 Mile	70	72	74	76	78	80

The racing press was well aware of the negative impact caused when older, more experienced, but heavier jockeys were displaced by younger and lighter riders with less experience and, perhaps as a result, less awareness of the need for caution on the race course; it was a theme that would continue to resound for decades. In 1892, for example, a *New York Sun* article noted "a lamentable lack of talent in the saddle, the weights being so low that many of the better riders cannot follow their vocation," and decrying "the spectacle of eight or ten horses ridden by ninety-pound midgets who turn their mount's head loose at the crucial time, pick up the whip, and go careening over the stretches endangering their own, and the lives of their fellows. It is dangerous."

Barrett was eighteen at the time of the Great Sweepstakes and rode at these weights for as long as his growing body would permit. According to *Krik's Guide*, Barrett raced 114 times in 1877, and in 53 of those races he performed at fewer than 100 pounds. He rode once at 87 pounds, three more times at 88. By 1880, however, the 21-year-old veteran of the saddle was able to ride just 28 times, at an average weight of over 115 pounds. Recognizing at that point that he could no longer maintain even the semblance of a riding career, he retired and visited his native Ireland. He married. And he returned to Oceanport, New Jersey, where he opened a training stable. But by this time, wasting had irreversibly compromised Barrett's health. The results would be lethal.

Barrett had perhaps the most unfortunate of timing. The fields of microbiology, diagnostics, immunology, and nutrition would one day save countless millions from illness, and both cure and prevent diseases that in the 1880s would send vast swaths of humanity to early graves. But in 1883, fields of science that were yet in their infancy could not preserve the life of one desperately ill twenty-four-year-old man.

What medical interventions might have been available for Barrett, as pneumonia gradually destroyed his ability to fill his lungs with precious oxygen? Bleeding, thankfully, was no longer commonplace as a pneumonia treatment; even in 1841, a medical text had cautioned those utilizing this technique that it might prove more deadly than the disease: "dread to carry it too far, lest the patient may never recover from the collapse." Another researcher noted that through 1838, of seventy-eight test pneumonia cases treated by bleeding, twenty-eight had proven fatal. In an understatement of near epic proportions, this author observed that "the facts relative to the fatal cases . . . seem still further to limit the utility of bloodletting."

Other pneumonia cures had also been found wanting, among them the administration of antimonials, compounds intended to induce vomiting as a means of reducing the body's store of noxious fluids, and the application of tesicatories, agents that caused blistering of the skin. As late as 1892, Sir William Ostler, a distinguished Canadian physician who had been among the founders of Johns Hopkins University, would write of pneumonia: "It is a self-limited disease, and has its course uninfluenced in any way by medicine." There is a reason Barrett died in his home rather than in a hospital; in 1883, hospitals simply had no effective means of battling profound pneumonia.

As 1882 began, a series of severe colds ravaged Barrett's respiratory system, and a doctor suggested that a vacation in the warmth of Florida might be necessary to improve his outlook. Dutifully, or perhaps by this time desperately, Barrett traveled south. The doctor's advice, however, backfired catastrophically. On Thanksgiving Day, 1882, Barrett was caught outdoors in a storm, and his most recent cold escalated to pleurisy, then to pneumonia. Barrett returned to New Jersey to await the inevitable.

He spent his final days in the company of friends, making every effort to shield his young wife from the certainty of his fate. "Courageous to the last," Barrett succumbed on January 6, 1883, at the age of twenty-four. Among those in attendance at his funeral was George Barbee, one of the jockeys Barrett had defeated in the Great Sweepstakes.

The *New York Sportsman* noted in Barrett's obituary that "the widow has no means, and a movement is on foot to subscribe a sum sufficient to place her beyond the reach of want for some time at least. It is a deserving case, and *The Sportsman* will undertake to forward any sum sent to us for the purpose." It is not known how much was collected by *The Sportsman* for Mrs. Barrett, or what might have become of Barrett's widow following her husband's tragic early death.

Appendix C

Where Did They Get Their Names?

Marse Henry Watterson, publisher of the Louisville Courier-Journal *and a pallbearer at [Richard] Ten Broeck's funeral in 1892, said Ten Broeck was "the most intrepid gambler who ever backed a horse, bucked a tiger, or bluffed on a pair of deuces."*
— Kent Hollingsworth, *The Great Ones*

Ten Broeck

The Kentucky crack was named for Richard Ten Broeck, the racing man and raconteur who had imported Ten Broeck's sire, Phaeton, from England to stand at stud in America. Richard Ten Broeck's alleged exploits range from resigning from West Point to fight a duel, to living as a professional gambler aboard the riverboats plying the Mississippi, to racing the mighty stallion Lexington during his career on the turf, to selling Lexington for an unheard-of price, to creating—and then winning—the richest race of the era.

Any of these would be of interest; combine them—and these are only a handful of the tales surrounding Richard Ten Broeck's life—and they become the stuff of legend.

Born in 1811 into a privileged family in Albany, New York, Richard Ten Broeck first made known his proclivity for controversy by resigning—or being expelled, depending on the source—from West Point during his first year at the military academy. The reason for his abrupt departure was his belief that he had been insulted by one of his instructors, and had challenged the other man to a duel. Here, the story accelerates in wildly different directions: One version has him leaving the school after assaulting the instructor; another—one that was never denied by

Ten Broeck—holds that the duel ended with the teacher's death, and that Ten Broeck fled south to avoid prosecution.

Whatever the truth, Ten Broeck's abrupt departure from West Point severed his relationship with his family, and the young man seems to have spent much of the next ten years living by his wits as a riverboat gambler. Certainly, he looked the part. Portraits of Richard Ten Broeck depict an intense, bearded, humorless face with icy blue eyes "that could make Bat Masterson throw in his hand without drawing a card."

It was around 1840 that Ten Broeck moved on to New Orleans, at the time among the most populous cities in the growing United States, and became involved in horse racing. By 1847, he had become manager of two of the Crescent City's more successful racetracks, the Mobile and Metarie courses, and by 1851 he had purchased Metarie, which would become famous for its opulent, high-end approach to the sport. As Ten Broeck improved Metarie's image, a steady stream of top thoroughbreds followed the money flowing down the Mississippi and into the track's purse structure.

Attending the Lexington Association races in May of 1853, Ten Broeck chanced to see a colt named Darley lose the first heat of the Citizens' Stakes, then storm back to win the second. Impressed, Ten Broeck inquired as to the colt's selling price, and had soon negotiated a deal: $2,500 now, $2,500 additional if the colt won the Great State Post Stakes, a race that Ten Broeck was promoting at Metarie. Ten Broeck formed a syndicate with several associates, which, to his chagrin, took effect only after Darley had won the final heat, and a few days later *Spirit of the Times* announced his purchase, adding that henceforth, the animal would be known as "Lexington."

The Great State Post Stakes, scheduled for April 3, 1854, was intended to be the richest race ever, requiring a $5,000 buy-in, with a limit of one entrant per state. The rich buy-in guaranteed outsized publicity for the race; the limitation on starters by state ensured a small field but a substantial attendance. Only four horses were entered, but they were very good horses.

Lining up for the first heat were: future Hall of Famer Lexington, representing Kentucky and Ten Broeck's syndicate; future Hall of Famer

Lecomte, representing Mississippi and Ten Broeck's bitter rival, General Thomas Jefferson Wells; Highlander, representing Alabama; and Arrow, representing Louisiana. Adding a touch of dignity to the festivities was the presence of former President Millard Fillmore, who had been drafted by Ten Broeck as an official judge.

Lexington won both heats easily, with the previously undefeated Lecomte a disappointing second; Arrow and Highlander struggled to reach the distance marker. Given Ten Broeck's reputation, it is a near certainty that his gambling winnings for the day vastly exceeded his share of the purse money.

A week later, in the $2,000 Jockey Club Purse, Lecomte reversed the outcome, defeating Lexington in consecutive four-mile heats, clicking off the first in seven minutes and twenty-six seconds, six full seconds faster than the record established by the filly Fashion twelve years earlier. Some believe that Lexington's oncoming blindness may have contributed to his defeat; that he may have hesitated when he could hear his rival's footsteps but could not see him clearly. Ten Broeck immediately began pursuing Wells and Lecomte, challenging Lecomte to a rematch with articles planted in *Spirit of the Times*.

Ten Broeck's single-minded pursuit of his adversary included an attempt to break Lecomte's newly established record. Lexington was trained to a peak of fitness, the local and national press received saturation-level reports on the five-year-old's progress, and on April 2, 1855, at a packed-to-the-roofbeams Metarie course, Lexington took to the track with two pacemakers, Arrow and Joe Blackburn.

A running start, and Lexington almost immediately left Joe Blackburn in the dust, powering alongside and then clear of Arrow while posting lightning-fast miles (for the time) of 1:47¼, 1:52¼, 1:51½. A final circuit of the track in 1:48¾, and Lexington had run four miles in 7:19¾, some 6¼ seconds faster than Lecomte's time. A local newspaper would describe Lexington's all-out stampede around the course as "[t]he most brilliant event in the sporting annals of the American turf."

Wells's attention was now thoroughly engaged, and two weeks later, on April 14, 1855, Lexington and Lecomte went postward together again. Once again the confrontation attracted a large and enthusiastic crowd, but Lecomte, recovering from a recent attack of equine colic, was not up to a peak performance, and Lexington outran him easily in the first four-mile heat. When Lecomte was too ill to return to the track, Lexington was declared the winner.

This would be Lexington's final race. He had always had one bad eye, damaged when he raided the farm's food supplies, and now the other failed. He would conclude his career with just one flaw on an otherwise perfect record—six victories and the possibly excusable loss to Lecomte.

Ten Broeck now announced that he would be leaving for England in 1857, and made an offer for Lecomte. Wells, perhaps knowing more about Lecomte's health than he was telling the detested Ten Broeck, negotiated a deal that included Lecomte's three-year-old half-sister, Prioress. As Ten Broeck prepared to unleash his new purchases on the British, Wells took over his former showplace, Metarie Race Course.

It wasn't long after Ten Broeck's arrival in England that he happened upon a fellow American, R. A. Alexander, who was seeking to purchase well-bred breeding stock for his Woodburn Stud Farm. The two men struck up a deal, and for $15,000 Alexander purchased Ten Broeck's blind stallion, which had been servicing mares at John Harper's Nantura Stud, just down the road from Woodburn.

It was a deal that would benefit both men. For Ten Broeck, it brought the largest sum of money ever paid for an American-bred thoroughbred, on either side of the Atlantic. For Alexander, it would mean decades of success as a breeder. Lexington would top the American sire list sixteen times, fourteen in succession, drawing ever-greater stud fees to Alexander's farm. At his death, "the blind hero of Woodburn" was unquestionably the greatest stallion in the nation's history.

Questioned regarding his decision to pay so high a price for an unproven stallion, Alexander vowed that one day he would sell a Lexington foal for more than the purchase price. This he did, selling the young Norfolk—to Theodore Winters, who would one day race Mollie McCarthy against Ten Broeck's namesake thoroughbred—for $15,001.

Lecomte would prove hugely disappointing to Ten Broeck, and in 1857 the horse suffered a relapse of his colic and died. Prioress, however, was a revelation, winning the 1857 Cesarewitch Handicap, with Ten

Broeck reportedly cashing a £10 wager at 100-to-1 odds. It was a near thing, though; Prioress was one of the three runners in a much-debated triple dead heat, then won the runoff to take home the trophy and clinch Ten Broeck's wager.

Richard Ten Broeck won his fair share of races as the years progressed, but never found the horse that would send him to the pinnacle of the British turf. For a time he managed the stable of James R. Keene when that intrepid horseman tried his hand at English racing. He would occasionally purchase promising breeding stock for a customer's farm.

Eventually, the aging Ten Broeck returned to America, where he grew more irascible as the years progressed. Despite whatever family he might still have found in New York, despite his roots in Kentucky, despite his history in New Orleans, he chose to live near San Francisco, in the suburb of San Mateo. And one day in 1892, after Ten Broeck had reached his eighty-first year, the following appeared in the local news:

Richard Ten Broeck Dead

San Mateo, Aug. 1—Richard Ten Broeck, the old horseman, was found dead in bed at his home, "The Hermitage," near here, at 11 o'clock this morning. He was alone at the time and had been for some time, as he experienced great difficulty in keeping help on account of his extremely nervous and irritable temperament, which of late years had grown on him to such an extent as to lead his friends to believe that he was bordering on insanity.

Ten Broeck's body was returned to Louisville, where the fabled riverboat gambler and horse trader, who had dispatched to America the equine father of a racing megastar, was quietly laid to his final rest under the peaceful skies of old Kentucky.

Tom Ochiltree

Having given birth to Thomas Peck Ochiltree in Alabama on October 26, 1839, young Thomas's parents quickly corrected their oversight, traveling the following year with their son to Texas, where his father would serve many years as a judge. If anyone was ever intended to be a Texan, it was assuredly Tom Ochiltree, who would spend much of his life closely connected with—if not always residing in—the Lone Star State.

Ochiltree was a man whose life would have innumerable twists and turns. He was a fourteen-year-old enlistee in the Texas Rangers, an Indian fighter and Civil War soldier, a member of the Texas state legislature and a shipping company agent, a newspaper correspondent and editor, and a US congressman. He was a twenty-year-old Texas delegate to the Democratic Convention in Baltimore that in 1860 nominated John C. Breckenridge for a presidential run against the Republican nominee, Abraham Lincoln.

Ochiltree was anything but a man of quiet modesty. The story was often told—primarily by Ochiltree himself in his stump speeches—of the time his father delegated the eighteen-year-old, who had just earned his law license, to add his name to the shingle advertising the family law firm. Ochiltree went about the task at once, commissioning a sign with huge lettering that could be seen from near and far: T.P. Ochiltree and Father, Counselors and Attorneys at Law. Somehow, considering the larger-than-life persona that Ochiltree would cultivate throughout his life, one wonders whether this story was merely apocryphal.

During the Civil War, Ochiltree had fought on the side of the Confederacy in the Armies of Northern Virginia, New Mexico, Louisiana, and Arkansas, describing himself years later (with perhaps no more than the usual dose of Ochiltreean exaggeration) as "chuck full of martial ardor," ready "cheerfully to kill ten Yankees before breakfast and many hundreds more after a hearty meal." Promoted to the rank of brevet colonel, Ochiltree was captured by Union troops during the final days of the conflict while working as a volunteer aide on the staff of General Henry Hopkins Sibley.

Imprisoned on Johnson's Island in Lake Erie at war's end, Ochiltree recognized that, as one among many Confederate prisoners awaiting emancipation, he could conceivably spend a substantial amount of time in the unproductive role of prisoner before the inevitable mass release. Seeking to accelerate the process, he launched letters to President Andrew Johnson and Confederate General Benjamin F. Butler, who had served as a fellow delegate to the 1860 Democratic Convention.

The missive dispatched by Ochiltree to the president of the United States is instructive, conveying his willingness to accept terms similar to those that might be offered to the supreme military leader of the Confederacy. "Mr. President Johnson," his letter begins, "when you get ready to let me leave your island, please let me know, and I will accept the same terms as General Lee." Perhaps Johnson appreciated the audacity of his approach, and Ochiltree was granted an early release. And shortly thereafter, the erstwhile Confederate officer found opportunity—in the North as a writer for the *New York News*.

But the field of journalism, as was the case for so many positions undertaken by the restless Ochiltree during those early post-war years, proved unfulfilling for the Texan. Returning to the Lone Star State in late 1865, a restless Ochiltree tried various occupations without finding one that he deemed satisfactory.

Finally, and significantly both for Ochiltree's financial well-being and his legend, the former colonel found work as a merchants' representative in Europe, tasked with promoting a shipping line between Liverpool and Galveston. It was an enterprise that ultimately failed, due not to any shortcoming on Ochiltree's part, but because the project lacked investors. In the process, however, Ochiltree determined that it would be worthwhile to increase the immigration to Texas of Europeans who might improve the state's economy. To this end, he developed and presented a series of lectures throughout Europe, regaling his listeners with the glories of the Lone Star State.

Returning next to the United States, Ochiltree announced his candidacy for Congress, eventually bowing out of the race. Again, he took on a series of positions—lobbyist for Louisiana railroads, bond salesman, immigration agent. In 1873, Ochiltree was appointed US Marshal in Eastern Texas, a post he held until late in 1874, when his vocal opposition to the ruling Republican Party led to his removal. First, however, Ochiltree unleashed a torrent of speechifying that the *Washington Herald* declared comparable to the finest rhetoric of Daniel Webster. Ochiltree loved to tell a story of those times regarding himself, President Grant, and an outraged citizen who questioned his work on behalf of Texas. Displaying a sheaf of newspaper clippings to the president, the citizen had complained that Ochiltree seemed to spend an inordinate amount of his time at racetracks—Long Branch, Saratoga, Jerome Park. How could Ochiltree expect to serve the needs of Texans, the citizen asked, while spending so much time at East Coast racing emporiums?

Ochiltree had a ready answer: "Oh, that's easily explained, Mr. President," he replied. "I'm not the Tom Ochiltree those fellows are talking about. He is a race horse that John Chamberlain named after me."

Now Grant understood. "That explains, then," was the president's reply, "why all those articles were headed 'Ochiltree wins.'"

In 1875, the colonel resumed the role of lobbyist, living in Washington, meeting with Presidents Grant and Hayes on issues related to Texas, and dining in the East's finest restaurants. When he deemed it necessary, he would make the occasional foray to Paris, London, and other European capitals, where he arranged meetings with those who might help his cause and sampled the sumptuous cuisine of the great cities of Europe. As historian Claude H. Hall understated, "Tom enjoyed a good life."

Having lost a close race for sheriff of Galveston County, Ochiltree relocated next to Washington, in 1882 becoming the first native Texan elected to the US Congress. He represented an enormous and obviously gerrymandered district that "embraced 37,000 miles, contained twenty-seven counties, and stretched from Galveston on the gulf to Eagle Pass on the Rio Grande."

Ochiltree's road to his seat in the House of Representatives was, to put it mildly, a circuitous one, and the *New York Times* found the erstwhile colonel's election worthy of closer scrutiny. "This result," the *Times* noted, "is certainly peculiar . . . While personal considerations must doubtless have been at work to some extent in accomplishing this result, it would be far from correct to place the outcome to the fact of the one candidate's popularity or the other candidate's unpopularity. There was far more than this in the matter. . . . [Ochiltree] has been credited with being the special candidate of certain Galveston interests."

The *Times*, however, chose to withhold any further commentary on Ochiltree's election, preferring merely to reprint the final paragraph of an article that had appeared in the *Galveston News*, which seemed to be holding its editorial nose at the election result, hoping fervently for the best, and seeking to maintain cordial relations with the newly elected representative (whom they nonetheless demoted from colonel to major):

> *That Major Ochiltree will make a useful working member of Congress is not to be doubted. He is a man of very clear perceptions, quick in the mastery of details, and not lacking in executive faculty. . . . While he is a Republican in principle, his record in the past is a guarantee of conservative action that may be calculated upon as coming into play in all that pertains to the material welfare of the district.*

Which might best be translated to: "We may not care for his politics, but we think he'll make us some money."

And almost immediately, Ochiltree was back in Europe, where he

> *discussed politics with Lord Randolph Churchill, the son-in-law of his friend Leonard Jerome of New York, and dined with the Marquis of Salisbury, soon to become Prime Minister. Then he was off to France for a stay at the American minister's chateau, talks with Clemenceau and Victor Hugo, and visits to the theatre. As time permitted, he even wrote dramatic reviews comparing the histrionic abilities of American and European actors, always managing to keep his name before Texas and the public.*

As a sitting congressman, Ochiltree would be expected at some point to return to Washington, DC, and, his European sojourn at a regrettable end, he alighted in the capital, where he "began to tell stories that delighted the House and made him a welcome addition to every gathering." A big, wide, bluff man with flaming red hair, piercing eyes, and a drooping walrus mustache, Ochiltree had by this time added a nickname, "The Red-Headed Ranger from Texas," that would remain with him for the rest of his life. It was claimed that "by a series of good stories and amusing reminiscences he frequently secured the passage of a measure he desired passed when simple logic would have failed." Some in Congress were said to consider "The Prince of Good Fellows" to be "funnier than the minstrels."

His primary aim as representative for Galveston was to achieve funding sufficient to deepen the city's harbor, and at this he was notably unsuccessful. After much effort on one occasion, a congressional committee reported a bill allocating $250,000 for Ochiltree's project, which the congressman promptly rejected as "a pittance." It would, in fact, not be until 1890 that Congress would finally designate sufficient funding to complete the Galveston Harbor project, by which time Ochiltree had long since moved on to other interests.

Colonel Ochiltree, a Republican serving an almost solidly Democratic state, was not regarded by all in the most positive light. The *Louisville Courier-Journal* saw fit to cite a question raised by an unnamed "old-fashioned senator": "What did they ever name a horse Tom Ochiltree for? Was he fleet of foot?" The *Courier-Journal* went about explaining:

> *Did you never hear the expression, 'He can lie as fast as a horse can run?' Well, that was Tom Ochiltree's great forte, and hence the belief that no horse named after him can ever be beaten.*

This opinion, though certainly not universal, was echoed in the epitaph that his Democratic rivals proposed for him prior to an 1884 election in which he eventually chose not to participate:

> Here LIES Tom Ochiltree—
> All he ever did!

Ochiltree would, thankfully, elicit kinder memorials when finally he breathed his last. Indeed, while it was certainly common for those of other parties and political stances to disagree with Ochiltree regarding the issues of the day, it seemed almost impossible that anyone might actually dislike the Red-Headed Ranger. Commentaries about the congressman seem to dwell almost universally upon his charm, his nearly infinite collection of stories, his ability to turn difficult political situations to his own advantage with a display of self-deprecating humor.

One associate portrayed him as a "charming man of the world. He has met everybody worth meeting, has seen everything worth seeing and comes about as near knowing everything worth knowing as any man I ever heard of. . . . When he chooses to be so he is simply irresistible. One may have just heard . . . something to his discredit, but two or three minutes of his charming talk is sufficient to sweep all disagreeable impressions of him to the four winds." As one journalist described him:

> *he was as gay and breezy at the Waldorf-Astoria as he was at a German spa or a Paris café, as much an attraction in the House of Representatives as in the stateroom of an Atlantic steamer. . . . He had chatted with Clemenceau about Civil War strategy, feuded with Bismarck, argued with Napoleon III, talked politics with Gladstone and Disraeli, and to the dismay of the American minister, had even sung "John Brown's Body" to a shocked Queen Victoria. He greeted the Prince of Wales with a slap on his back and a cheery, 'Wales, let us take a drink.' A hit play, 'Colonel Tom,' based on his life, appeared on Broadway.*

Ochiltree is known to have made more than sixty trips to Europe between 1865 and 1902, living lavishly and burnishing his reputation as a bon vivant. He grew wealthy, trading on dozens of highly placed, powerful friends past and present, who included the likes of Jefferson Davis and Ulysses S. Grant, Rutherford B. Hayes and Chester A. Arthur, Civil War generals from both sides and captains of all branches of industry. His access to scarce and valuable information was said to be second to none.

In 1894, when the short story writer O. Henry (William Sydney Porter) was penning the satirical semi-editorial "A Snapshot at the President," his plot line required a familiar name for his readers to associate with the slow-grinding, pork-barrel-rich politics of the first Grover Cleveland administration. He chose Ochiltree to serve as his stereotypical political hack. Thus, the world was given the lines:

> *"You Texans have a great representative in Senator Mills," he said. "I think the greatest two speeches I ever heard were his address before the Senate advocating the removal of the tariff on salt and increasing it on chloride of sodium.*

"Tom Ochiltree is also from our State," I said.

But high living, which in Ochiltree's case included liberal doses of rich food and fine wine, must eventually have its cost, and by 1896, the colonel's health was in decline. He suffered bouts of pneumonia, made pilgrimages to spas in the United States, and voyaged to France, England, and Germany to seek out the advice of the best-known doctors. A form of personal tragedy overtook the colonel in 1899, when fire ravaged the Windsor Hotel in New York City, which housed much of his library and art treasures, and his correspondence of several decades. Ochiltree's losses were extensive, and the cost to history may have been huge. Surely, a read through the colonel's correspondence would have proven a fascinating experience.

Upon his return to the United States following a final British sojourn to seek ever more desperately needed medical assistance, it was necessary to place him on a stretcher before debarking the ship. In a last-ditch effort to improve his flagging health, Colonel Ochiltree traveled to Hot Springs, Virginia, for a therapeutic stay in a warmer climate, but it was too little, too late. He died at the age of sixty-three, his body borne to Arlington National Cemetery in a casket bearing an inscription that may well have been penned by the colonel himself:

Col. Thomas P. Ochiltree
Died Nov. 25, 1902
One of the Best

As one journalist had written in 1884, Tom Ochiltree seemed to have been intended to serve Texas, given that his "vastness . . . expansiveness . . . longitude and latitude, as it were . . . [seemed] particularly fitting to represent that great state."

There is much in Colonel Ochiltree's life that can be regarded as controversial: his days serving the rebel cause; his abrupt and apparently financially motivated embrace of the victorious Union's agenda; his use in Congress of entertaining stories and personal charm where the logic of his proposals might have been lacking, etc. (there are, indeed, likely a great many etceteras). It appears to be the consensus, however, among those who had the good fortune to encounter him during his eventful life, that the Red-Headed Ranger from Texas crammed a great deal of living into those sixty-three years.

PAROLE

The winner of the Great Sweepstakes was named after a tobacco brand manufactured by his owner's Lorillard Tobacco Company.

Appendix D

Congress Adjourns

Excerpt from the *Congressional Record*, Tuesday, October 23, 1877

In Senate.

Papers Withdrawn and Referred

On motion of Mr. SAULSBURY, it was

Ordered, *That the petitions and papers relating to a claim of William Bowes against the District of Columbia be taken from the files and referred to the Committee on the District of Columbia.*

On motion of Mr. ANTHONY, it was

Ordered, *That the petition and papers of the heirs of Asbury Dickins be taken from the files and referred to the Committee on Claims.*

On motion of Mr. INGALLS, it was

Ordered, *That George A. Schreiner have permission to withdraw his papers from the files of the Senate.*

On motion of Mr. PLUMB, it was

Ordered, *That the papers in the case of Amos B. Ferguson be taken from the files and referred to the Committee on Military Affairs.*

Adjournment to Thursday

Mr. BECK. If there be no further communications from the President, I move that when the Senate adjourn to-day it be to meet on Thursday next. Our committees can go to work in the mean time.

The motion was agreed to; there being on a division—ayes 34, noes 12.

Excerpt from the *Congressional Record*, Wednesday, October 24, 1877

House of Representatives.

Mr. *MILLS took the floor.*

Mr. *WOOD. If the gentleman from Texas will yield to me, I will now move the House adjourn.*

Mr. *MILLS. I will yield the floor with the understanding that I shall be entitled to it to-morrow morning when this subject is resumed.*

The SPEAKER. The gentleman will be entitled to the floor after the reading of the Journal.

Mr. *PRIDEMORE. I ask the gentleman from New York to withdraw the motion to adjourn for a few minutes.*

Mr. *REAGAN. I also desire to move for the withdrawal of certain papers.*

Mr. *WOOD. I must decline to yield.*

And then (at three o'clock and twenty-five minutes p.m.) the House adjourned.

Excerpt from the *Journal of the House of Representatives of the United States*, October 24, 1877

By Mr. Wood: The petition of Mrs. Annie M. Dudley, late widow of William H. Voorhies, alias William J. Brown, late of Company F, One hundred and fifty-ninth Regiment New York Volunteers, to have the charge of desertion removed from the record of her late husband; to the Committee on Military Affairs, when appointed.

Also, the petition of Henry Theysohn, late corporal Company H, Fifty-sixth regiment New York Volunteers, for his pension to date from the day he received his injury; to the Committee on Invalid Pensions, when appointed.

Also, the petition of Henry Weldon, for compensation for stores burned by the United States Army; to the Committee on War-Claims, when appointed.

Also, the petition of Samuel P. Todd, for compensation for losses while a purser in the United States Navy; to the Committee of Claims, when appointed.

The Speaker stated the regular order of business to be the consideration of the resolution submitted by Mr. John T. Harris as a substitute for the motion of Mr. Hale, that James B. Belford be sworn in as a Representative from the State of Colorado, pending when the House last adjourned.

After debate,
On motion of Mr. Wood, at 3 o'clock and 25 minutes p.m., the House adjourned.

ACKNOWLEDGMENTS

We are like dwarfs on the shoulders of giants, so that we can see more than they, and things at a greater distance, not by virtue of any sharpness of sight on our part, or any physical distinction, but because we are carried high and raised up by their giant size.
—BERNARD OF CHARTRES, 1159

IT ALL BEGINS WITH MY WIFE, THE INIMITABLE, UNSURPASSABLE, IMPOSsibly wonderful Fran Wintroub, or Dr. Fran, as she is known to her many patients, some of whom have been known to refer to me as Mr. Dr. Fran. During the course of writing this book, the author has depended upon Fran to serve as wife, editor, chef, mother confessor, psychoanalyst, critic, and travel agent, and she has earned rave reviews in every role.

Fran has truly been my jill of all trades, master of everything. One area in which she has particularly shone is that of researcher. On our research sojourns to Washington, DC, Kentucky, and elsewhere Fran has labored patiently by my side, leafing through 140-year-old newspapers, seeking out the historical information without which a book such as this cannot happen. It is thanks in no small measure to Fran that I was able to enumerate the story of the Lorillards, the Harpers, their racetrack rivalry, and 1877's Great Sweepstakes.

And so, there is no other place to begin these acknowledgments than with Fran, no other words to begin them with, except to thank her for helping me to write this book, and thereby fulfill a dream of over thirty years. And if I could add just one more comment, it would be this: Fran, you are the greatest love of my life. You have been from the day we met, and you will be forever.

There have been many others who have overwhelmed me with their kindness during the course of my researches, and at the head of this list is Vivian Montoya, librarian at the California Thoroughbred Breeders' Association Library. The racing gods thankfully chose to locate the CTBA

Library across the street from Santa Anita Racetrack, about twenty minutes from my home, and to place Vivian at its helm. Vivian's assistance has been a key factor not merely in the creation of this book, but in practically every magazine article I have published for more than fifteen years. It would not be in the least an exaggeration to state that without Vivian and the CTBA Library, I might not have a writing career.

And so, thank you, Vivian, thank you CTBA, for helping me to be a writer.

I also owe the deepest of thanks to Cathy Schenck, the marvel who runs the Keeneland Library, which must surely be the world's most beautiful library dedicated exclusively to the Sport of Kings.

Fran and I twice traveled to Keeneland, under the deluded impression that two Kentucky visits would be sufficient to accomplish the research requirements for this book, and it was Cathy Schenck who pointed us to the perfect sources in the library's vast array of publications from the 1870s. These included, among others, the *Kentucky Live Stock Journal*, the *New York Sportsman*, the *Turf, Field and Farm* and *Spirit of the Times*, whose reporters' sharply honed opinions helped to bring the Great Sweepstakes' panoply of fascinating characters alive for me.

And as I neared the completion of this book and realized that there were areas still to be addressed, it was Cathy, in response to a "Please help me!" e-mail, who fired off to me a six-inch-thick collection of 140-year-old articles that went to the heart of every issue. Without the assistance I received from Cathy Schenck and the Keeneland Library, the document now in your hands would be approximately the depth of a pamphlet. Cathy, I am forever in your debt.

And while we're on the topic of libraries, much of the information in the section on the Harper murders became available because the beautiful Lexington Public Library had both an excellent collection of Kentucky newspapers on microfilm from the 1870s, and a kind group of patient staffers willing to spend time helping me find articles that fit my needs. Thank you to everyone at Lexington's wonderful library. You have a marvelous facility, made even more so by an impossibly helpful group of employees.

I would also like to thank Megan Rosenbloom and Nicole Rich of the University of Southern California's Norris Library, who allowed me to access the library's rare medical tomes of yesteryear, and thereby gain an understanding of Pierre Lorillard's fatal illness and the plight facing Parole's jockey, William Barrett, as he neared his tragic end. As a graduate of your university's four-initialed cross-town rival, I still won't be rooting for your school on the gridiron or the basketball court, but thanks to your caring help, I will always feel a warmer glow when I hear the initials U.S.C.

Many, many thanks to my agent, Greg Aunapu of the Salkind Agency, the first person outside my family who believed in *The Great Sweepstakes*. Greg instantly became this neophyte's desperately needed guide through the complexities of Getting Published, my three-thousand-mile-distant guru. Greg's expertise, experience as a writer and agent, his hard work, and above all his patience were the keys to both selling this book and keeping the author's sanity more or less intact.

Thanks also to everyone at Lyons Press, particularly senior editor Keith Wallman and assistant editor Stephanie Scott, for helping make this book as good as it could possibly be. Thanks to senior production editor Meredith Dias for making the editing process as painless as possible.

It was my great good fortune to discover Frank Torcher of Endaxi Graphics when my efforts to obtain high-resolution photographs for this book became nerve-wrackingly difficult. The portrait photographers of the 1870s, whether specializing in human subjects or equines, did not concern themselves with DPI counts or other high-tech issues; they were quite content when an image acceptably resembled their human client, or was recognizable as a horse. It was Frank's technical artistry, applied to many of my 140-year-old photos and drawings, that made the images book-worthy.

Thanks to Holly Gale, law librarian and cousin by marriage, who steered me in the right direction as I tried to find information about Harry Colston's lawsuit.

I have been privileged over the past forty-two years to work with superbly talented magazine editors who have published my writing, improved it through their thorough but always kind critiques, and encouraged me to produce more. Les Woodcock of the much-lamented *Turf & Sport Digest* was the first person outside of my family to suggest that I might actually have the talent to be a writer, and while I lost touch with Les long ago, if he should chance to read this, here's a much-belated thank you for your encouragement. Thanks also to Jim Corbett, longtime editor at *American Turf Magazine*, and to the magazine's current editor, Joe Girardi (no, not *that* Joe Girardi), both of whom have allowed me considerable space to grow in the pages of their publication.

Two websites essential to the writing of this book are the *New York Times* archive and the Chronicling America site of the Library of Congress, and I would thank everyone who makes both sites possible. The *Times's* archive includes every article from the newspaper's earliest days to the present; the newspapers available in the Library of Congress site do not begin until 1836 and conclude in 1922, but given the vast range of newspapers included in the website, from dozens of states, this author is not complaining.

Anyone living in the twenty-first century and writing about thoroughbred racing is automatically indebted to my longtime Internet friend, Laura Hillenbrand, whose *Seabiscuit: An American Legend* reawakened America to the power, the beauty, and the poetry endemic to the Sport of Kings. My own introduction to the sport was Joe Palmer's book *This Was Racing*, inadvertently sent to me by a sports book club I had joined in 1958, when I was a baseball-crazy ten-year-old. I am writing this page on May 11, 2014; Laura's *Seabiscuit* therefore remains the best racing book I've read in fifty-six years as a fan. I don't expect ever to read a better one.

The author also owes a vote of thanks to Marlin Mitchell, who owns the land still known as Nantura. Fran and I spent the better part of a Sunday afternoon searching fruitlessly through Woodford County, Kentucky, for the gravesites of Longfellow and Ten Broeck, which, we discovered upon returning home to California, are on Mr. Mitchell's private property. I contacted Mr. Mitchell, who was kind enough to send me photographs of the tombstones that helped me considerably in creating the descriptions in chapter 1 and the epilogue. Thank you, sir, for your response to the request of a total stranger.

There are a great many others who deserve a share of the credit for this book. My mother- and father-in-law, Bertha and Ray Wintroub, have long encouraged my writing, and despite not being racing fans, insisted that they enjoyed my first book, *Superhorse: The Search for America's Greatest Thoroughbred*, which unfortunately never found a publisher. Thanks, Bertha and Ray, for your encouragement and support.

My aunt, Mary Stern, always encouraged my writing, and I hope she enjoys this book after so long a wait. Mike Stern, my cousin and lifelong best friend, and the person who first set me on the path to sports addiction, certainly owns a share of the responsibility for what you hold in your hands. Thanks, and much love, to my son, Sean Shrager, for his lifetime of patience with my horse-racing obsession.

There are so many others who have helped or encouraged or guided me along the path, and if I've forgotten to include you here, you know who you are, and please know how much your kindness meant to me.

And finally, I would like to mention my Uncle Red Stern, gone these many years, who made my early days as a racing fan so much fun. Uncle Red and his friends, Irv and Charlie, would carry my occasional $2 long shot bet to Santa Anita or Hollywood Park while I was a college student, returning at day's end without much money, but with long, loud, ludicrous stories of the thousand-and-one ways their horses—and mine—had managed to lose races that, in Irv's Brooklynese, "dey just had ta win." Red may not have taught me everything I know about racing, as he would occasionally proclaim when we were regaling the relatives with stories about our latest racetrack forays, but he taught me a lot—mostly about how to enjoy life. If there's a more important lesson to be learned, I'm still searching for it.

NOTES AND SOURCES

PREFACE

vii. and House Member Joseph Rainey of South Carolina: Brief biographies of these African-American political pioneers can be found in the *Biographical Directory of the United States Congress, 1774–2005.* Washington, DC, United States Government Printing Office, 2005. Extending suffrage to newly freed black men had immediate implications in Congress. By 1868, John Willis Menard of Louisiana had earned the majority of the vote in an election held to complete the unexpired term of James Mann, defeating Caleb S. Hunt and technically becoming the first African American elected to Congress. Hunt challenged the result, and both Menard and Hunt were invited to address the House of Representatives. Only Menard accepted the invitation, and his speech would prove largely a symbolic act. Menard, who was described in the *Washington Evening Star* as "a rather intelligent-looking negro, smiling all over and all the time" ("Washington News and Gossip," *Washington (DC) Evening Star*, February 27, 1869), was initially directed to the clerk's platform to address the House, a deprecating invitation that he declined, choosing instead to speak from the Republican side of the aisle. Despite holding a certificate of election signed by Governor Henry C. Warmoth, which should have been *prima facie* evidence of his election, Menard failed to gain the support of sufficient House members. He would never be seated in Congress.

vii. the first female member of Congress: Congresswomen's Biographies, Women in Congress website.

vii. with the Confederacy: Henry Steele Commager, editor, *Documents of American History, Ninth Edition.* Englewood Cliffs, NJ: Prentice-Hall, Inc., 1973, pages 374–376.

viii. could attend a horse race: *Pimlico Press Book*, 1967.

viii. perhaps upwards of 850,000: J. David Hacker, International *New York Times* website, "Opinionator: Recounting the Dead," September 20, 2011.

ix. bayonet strikes, or other human violence: CivilWarHome.com, "The Price in Blood! Casualties in the Civil War."

ix. after Lee laid down his sword: John Wesley Morris, *Ghost Towns of Oklahoma.* University of Oklahoma Press, 1977, pages 68–69.

ix. already near the breaking point: The 1876 presidential election spawned a cottage industry of books, some relatively neutral in character, others, even fourteen decades after the event, surprisingly vitriolic in tone. The reader is referred to William H. Rehnquist, *Centennial Crisis: The Disputed Election of 1876.* New York: Random House Books, 2004;

Harold Cecil Vaughn, *The Hayes-Tilden Election of 1876: A Disputed Presidential Election in the Gilded Age*. New York: Franklin Watts, Inc., 1972; and Lloyd Robinson, *The Stolen Election: Hayes vs. Tilden—1876*. New York: A Tom Doherty Associates Book, 1968, as just three among many possibilities.

ix. to delay Hayes's inauguration: Robinson, *The Stolen Election: Hayes vs. Tilden—1876*, pages 178–180.

x. to enforce the election commission's rulings: J. G. Randall and David Donald, *The Civil War and Reconstruction*. D.C. Heath and Company, 1961, page 695.

x. creating the "Compromise of 1877": Robinson, *The Stolen Election: Hayes vs. Tilden—1876*, page 202.

x. "the filthy mess of 1876": James Truslow Adams, *History of the United States Volume III, War and Reconstruction*. New York: Charles Scribner's Sons, 1933, page 256.

x. and little business done": "Sporting News," *Chicago Tribune*, October 25, 1877.

CHAPTER 1

1. The *Baltimore Sun*, October 22, 1877: "Telegraphic News from Washington: Congress and the Races," *Baltimore Sun*, October 22, 1877.

2. within easy driving range of Midway: Pamphlet, "Woodford County—Midway-Versailles, Kentucky," printed in cooperation with the Woodford County Chamber of Commerce, the Midway-Versailles-Woodford County Tourist Commission, and Kentucky Department of Travel, undated.

2. the home of their long-ago owners: Lucy Zeh, *Etched In Stone: Thoroughbred Memorials*. Lexington, KY: The Blood-Horse, Inc., 2000, pages 10–12.

2. The King of the Turf: Kent Hollingsworth, *The Great Ones*, Kent Hollingsworth, editor. Lexington, KY: The Blood-Horse, 1970, pages 174–177.

2. National Museum of Racing and Hall of Fame: Racingmuseum.org, "Thoroughbred horses: Longfellow."

3. the last rites of equines: "Mourning for Ten Broeck," *New York Times*, July 10, 1887.

3. tombstone verbiage from which to draw: Zeh, *Etched In Stone: Thoroughbred Memorials*, page 10.

3. most generous of horses": Zeh, *Etched in Stone: Thoroughbred Memorials*, page 15.

3. the tombstone reads: Jonelle Fisher, *Nantura 1795–1905*. St. Crispian Press, 2004, page 149.

4. grazed by cattle: Zeh, *Etched in Stone: Thoroughbred Memorials*, page 13.

5. cattle that might stray into their area: Byron Crawford, "Trainer Was Ahead of the Field in Paying Tribute to his Horses," *Louisville Courier-Journal*, April 14, 2000.

5, 12. any horse that ever appeared upon the American turf"; "India-rubber courses and fast timers": "Ten Broeck vs Parole," *Spirit of the Times,* November 10, 1877, page 393.

5. improved conditions, not greater horses: "Frank Harper Passes Away," *Louisville Courier-Journal,* April 5, 1905.

5. "of faultless form": "The Great Sweepstakes To-Morrow," *Turf Field and Farm,* November 2, 1877.

6. massive or gawky: "Ten Broeck: Sketched from Life at Baltimore, October 20, 1877," *Spirit of the Times,* October 27, 1877.

6. the Phoenix Hotel Stakes: The information regarding Ten Broeck's race-by-race starts is based primarily on *Krik's Guide to the Turf,* New York: H.G. Crickmore, publisher, for the years the Nantura superstar raced.

6. "Go on with him, Lewis!": Joe Palmer, *This Was Racing.* New York: A.S. Barnes and Company, Inc., 1953, page 68.

6. "two lengths well in hand": "The Turf: Fall Meeting of the Kentucky Association," *Turf, Field and Farm,* September 10, 1875, page 203.

7. of a very extraordinary time being made": "Fall Meeting of the Kentucky Association," *Turf, Field and Farm,* September 10, 1875, page 204.

7. the great colt Harry Bassett: "Fourth Day," *Kentucky Live Stock Record,* September 10, 1875, page 164.

7. the great colt Harry Bassett: "Lexington, Ky, Fall Race Meeting," *Turf, Field and Farm,* September 17, 1875, page 203.

7. by a spectacular 6¾ seconds: Untitled article regarding Ten Broeck's 1⅝-mile record, *Spirit of the Times,* September 18, 1875, page 133.

7. "Running within himself from the start"; "in a big canter"; "as he liked" by three lengths: "The Turf: The Kentucky Association: Sixth Day—Fall Meeting, 1876," *Kentucky Live Stock Record,* September 23, 1876, page 196.

8. eleven years earlier to the day, by 1¼ seconds; stopped just after going over the string": "The Turf: Louisville Jockey Club," *Kentucky Live Stock Record,* September 30, 1876, page 211.

8. in the Western country": "Summary of the Post Stakes," *Spirit of the Times,* September 30, 1876, page 202.

8, 8, 9. "on account of the wet state of the track"; "stood under the wire, and waved his hat to Walker to push ahead"; in the good old state of Kentucky": "Louisville Jockey Club Fall Meeting," *Spirit of the Times,* September 30, 1876.

8. National Museum of Racing at Saratoga": Kent Hollingsworth, *The Kentucky Thoroughbred.* Lexington, KY: The University Press of Kentucky, 2009, page 30.

8. cheer and shake hands": "The Turf: A Great Day's Sport at Saratoga: Fellowcraft Makes the Fastest Four Miles Ever Run: Lexington's Time Beaten: Reform Wins the Mile and Three Quarters," *New York Times*, August 21, 1874.

9. "The Greatest Event in the History of the Turf": "Ten Broeck's Victory: Fellowcraft's Four-Mile Record Beaten," *New York Times*, September 28, 1876.

9. among the great jockeys of the country": "Ten Broeck's 7:15¾," *Turf, Field and Farm*, October 6, 1876, page 217.

9. erupt into war: "Lexington Races: Ten Broeck Beats Fellowcraft's Four Mile Time Three and a Half Seconds," *Dallas Daily Herald*, September 28, 1876.

10. not favorable to fast time": "Spring Meeting Louisville Jockey Club," *Turf, Field and Farm*, June 1, 1877.

10. flecked with blushes like a maiden's cheek"; he tired nearing the finish: "The Louisville Jockey Club," *Kentucky Live Stock Record*, June 2, 1877, page 339.

11. pass him very slowly: "Ten Broeck's Wonderful Mile and What it Means," *Dodge City (KS) Times*, June 9, 1876.

11. just days earlier by McWhirter in 3:30½; an "immense" screaming throng; "the wonder of the age"; "When shall we look upon his like again?": "The Louisville Gathering," *Turf, Field and Farm*, June 1, 1877, pages 349–350.

11. "the grandest horse that ever pressed the turf": "Ten Broeck: The King of the Turf: His Great Race at Louisville," *Opelousas (LA) Courier*, June 23, 1877.

11. "the great conqueror": "Louisville to the Front," *Spirit of the Times*, June 2, 1877.

11. "never face a starter again": "The Late Louisville Meeting," *Kentucky Live Stock Record*, June 2, 1877, page 344; also *Turf, Field and Farm*, June 1, 1877, page 344.

11. fifteenth consecutive victory: All references to the races in this paragraph are from Fisher, *Nantura, 1795–1905*, pages 178–179.

12. ravaged during the war; the Bluegrass State had yet to fully recover: Lyman Horace Weeks, *The American Turf: An Historical Account of Racing in the United States with Biographical Sketches of Turf Celebrities*. New York: The Historical Company, 1898, pages 42–48.

12. clamoring for the champion to leave his Kentucky bastion: See, for example, the discussion of the "long cast gauntlet" in "Racing Attractions at Baltimore," *Spirit of the Times*, October 6, 1877. Also "Baltimore Fall Meeting," *Turf, Field and Farm*, October 26, 1877.

12. one of the stingiest horsemen in the country": "Frightful Fraud," *Louisiana Democrat*, July 17, 1878.

12. Will reach there to-morrow: "Ten Broeck at Baltimore," *Spirit of the Times*, October 13, 1877.

CHAPTER 2

13. worthy of his fame: "Ten Broeck, Tom Ochiltree, Parole." *Louisville Courier-Journal,* October 22, 1877.

13, 14. *Racing in America 1866–1921* by W. S. Vosburgh; he was always a monster of size": W. S. Vosburgh, *Racing in America 1866–1921.* New York: The Jockey Club, 1922, pages 100–103.

14. From the Westbrook Stable: For a full—if perhaps overly doting—description of the Westbrook Stable, see "A Princely Racing Establishment," *Turf, Field and Farm,* November 23, 1877.

14. history of the sport: The excellent racing book *A Sound of Horses,* by David Alexander (New York: The Bobbs-Merrill Company, Inc., 1966), includes a rare photograph of Lexington that clearly shows his blindness. Alexander also notes (see photo of the stallion El Tesoro on the book's following photograph page) that for reasons not stated, by 1965 the direct male line of Lexington has practically died out. The last Kentucky Derby winner to be a direct male descendant of Lexington was Manuel, who won in 1899 (Alexander, page 156).

15. issue of *Spirit of the Times*; power and endurance: *Spirit of the Times,* July 15, 1876, page 1.

15. odds of at least 20-to-1: *Watson's Racing Guide, Annual Edition, 1875–76.* New York: James Watson.

16. not yet recovered from its effects: "The Tom Ochiltree-Parole Race," *New York Times,* August 10, 1876.

16. a $700 race at two miles: *American Racing Calendar of 1876.* New York: *Turf, Field and Farm,* 1876.

17. four-year-old geldings: *Krik's Guide to the Turf, Part I, 1877–78.* New York: H. G. Crickmore, 1878.

17. was unimpressive: Amy Gregory, "An American Sportsman," *Thoroughbred Record,* February 16, 1983, page 1,090.

17, 18. East Coast two-year-old filly division; for runners of all ages: Kent Hollingsworth, *The Great Ones.* The Blood-Horse, 1970, pages 208–211.

18. 'varminty' head, light neck": W. S. Vosburgh, *Racing in America 1866–1921.* New York: The Jockey Club, 1922.

18. exclaim in admiration for him": "Excitement of the Turf," *New York Times,* October 25, 1877.

18. ribs showing through his coat: "Privateer," "The Story of Parole," *New York Sportsman,* August 18, 1883.

18. live his pace in a finish": Vosburgh, *Racing in America 1866–1921.*

CHAPTER 3

20. *Nantura 1795–1905* by Jonelle Fisher; "nine hundred and ten pounds, lawful money": Jonelle Fisher, *Nantura, 1795–1905.* St. Crispian Press, 2004, page 157.

20. family members during the 1740s: Lyman Horace Weeks, *The American Turf: An Historical Account of Racing in the United States with Biographical Sketches of Turf Celebrities.* New York: The Historical Company, 1898, page 279.

20, 21. within a few miles of the town of Midway; "not of the turfman type": William E. Railey, *History of Woodford County, Kentucky.* Frankfort, KY, 1938, reprinted Baltimore, MD: Clearfield Company, Inc., 2002, page 29.

20. the lush Kentucky Bluegrass: Maryjean Wall, "Old Glories, Old Stories," *Spur,* July/August 1985, page 34.

21. Elizabeth and Mary: Railey, *History of Woodford County, Kentucky,* page 85.

21, 23, 23. the great racehorse Longfellow; undefeated throughout the 1870 season; the longest legs of any feller I ever seen": Kent Hollingsworth, *The Great Ones.* Lexington, KY: The Blood-Horse, 1970, page 175.

21. and 13,000 as State Guards: Thomas D. Clark, *A History of Kentucky.* Ashland, KY: The Jesse Stuart Foundation, 1998, pages 319–336.

21. "I must have Kentucky.": Charles P. Roland, in *The Civil War in Kentucky,* Kent Masterson Brown, editor. Mason City, IA: Savas Publishing Company, 2000, page 23. See also page 79, in which Lowell H. Harrison quotes Lincoln: "I think to lose Kentucky is nearly the same as to lose the whole game. Kentucky gone, we cannot hold Missouri, nor, as I think, Maryland. Those all against us, and the job on our hands is too large for us. We would as well consent to a separation at once, including the surrender of the capital."

22. if necessary: Fisher, *Nantura, 1795–1905,* page 19.

22, 22, 22, 29, 30, 30. Adam fell, mortally wounded; leaning upon a stout stick"; "from eend to eend"; drinking his coffee out of a tin cup"; "worn, weary, and hermitlike"; a "sad and silent homestead": "Reminiscences of the Turf: John Harper," *Thoroughbred Record,* June 22, 1929.

22. and executed: Fisher, *Nantura, 1795–1905,* page 20.

24, 24, 25, 25. the night of September 11, 1871; news of the vicious attacks reached John; newspaper coverage of the murder; "a long rope and a short shrift": "Brutal Murder," *Lexington Observer & Reporter,* September 13, 1871.

24, 24, 25, 25, 25. he had been sleeping; weak and feeble as a child; threatened to kill him; promptly arrested the jockey"; extremely kind to their colored servants": "Brutal Murder," *Lexington Daily Press,* September 12, 1871.

24. without identifying the killer: Wall, "Old Glories, Old Stories," *Spur,* July/August 1985, page 38.

24. ran side by side: See, for example, "The Woodford Tragedy," and "Lexington Races" in *Lexington Daily Press*, September 13, 1871, and "Brutal Murder" and "The Races," in the *Lexington Observer and Reporter* of the same date.

25, 25, 25, 26, 26, 27. the killer made his escape; deal for many years"; until Friday, September 15; "Oh, I reckon not"; her consumptive condition"; "a negro man once owned by the Harpers": "The Woodford Tragedy, Further Particulars," *Lexington Daily Press*, September 14, 1871.

25. who committed the murder": "The Woodford Tragedy," *Lexington Daily Press*, September 13, 1871.

25. hauled off to the Midway jail; before Judge W. W. George: "Trial To-Day," *Lexington Daily Press*, September 15, 1871.

27. promptly dispatched Mrs. Prior to the jailhouse; baffling the best detective's sagacity": "The Harper Murder: Important Discovery," *Lexington Daily Press*, September 16, 1871.

27. except Will Prior: "The Harper Murder: Trial of the Prisoners at Versailles," *Lexington Daily Press*, September 16, 1871.

27. John Harper: "Reward of $5,000," *Lexington Daily Press*, October 9, 1871.

27. she couldn't have told anything anyhow": "The Harper Tragedy: Further Developments," *Lexington Daily Press*, September 29, 1871.

27. men and money": "The Harper Murder Case," *Lexington Observer and Reporter*, October 3, 1871.

28. expecting some relief soon": Fisher, *Nantura, 1795–1905*, page 41.

28. escaped indictment: The legal battles involving Adam and Wallace Harper are covered in both Fisher, *Nantura, 1795–1905*, pages 41–42, and Wall, "Old Glories, Old Stories," *Spur*, July/August 1985, page 40.

28. a claim for the money: Wall, "Old Glories, Old Stories," *Spur*, July/August 1985, page 40.

28. his grief-stricken uncle: "Frank B. Harper is Dead," *Thoroughbred Record*, April 8, 1905, page 220.

28. any portion of Nantura: "Makes Provision for Senator J.C.S. Blackburn," *Mt. Sterling (Ky) Advocate*, April 12, 1905, and "The Turfman's Will Contested," *Bourbon News*, June 30, 1905.

29. nearly two hundred yards ahead": "The Turf: Long Branch Races Yesterday: Over Thirty Thousand People in Attendance: Longfellow an Easy Winner," *(Woodsfield, Ohio) Spirit of Democracy*, July 9, 1872.

29. this afternoon: "Long Branch," *Nashville Union and American*, July 3, 1872.

29. more energy than necessary: "Monmouth Park," *New York Times*, July 5, 1872.

29, 30. "The Greatest Contest in American Turf History"; waved their handkerchiefs and parasols: "Saratoga: The Greatest Contest in American Turf History," *New York Times*, July 17, 1872.

30. with sorrowful looks: "Longfellow Completely Broken Down: Description of the Accident: The Horse Game to the Last," *New York Times*, July 17, 1872.

30. run he couldn't"; "Even the elements weep at thy departure": "Saratoga: Sad Condition of the Disabled Racer, Longfellow," *New York Times*, July 18, 1872.

30. It's dogon bad luck": "Longfellow Retired: What Old John Harper Said After the Race," *Petroleum Center (Pa.) Daily Record*, July 23, 1872.

30. it was blotted with tears; "ripe old age"; "alone—desolate": "Memoirs of Distinguished Kentucky Turfmen: John Harper," *Kentucky Live Stock Record*, July 23, 1875.

CHAPTER 4

32. big pots in the game: Kent Hollingsworth, *The Great Ones*, Kent Hollingsworth, editor. Lexington, KY: The Blood-Horse, 1970, page 209.

33. "Lorillard's Snuff and Tobacco": Fairfax Downey, *Lorillard and Tobacco*, P. Lorillard Company, 1951, page 20. This, like *The Lorillard Story*, printed in 1947 by the P. Lorillard Company after it went public, was a corporate house organ, which began with a section of photographs of P. Lorillard's senior management officers, none of whom, by this time, bore the name "Lorillard."

33. first to make snuff: "The Talk of the Town: American Snuff," *New Yorker*, September 22, 1934. The *New Yorker*, doubtless seeking to assist its sophisticated readers to acquire snuff in New York City, informed them that "You can find snuff in all the Harlem tobacco stores, as Negroes are big snuff users." The article also enlightens us regarding others who might partake of the product: "Women use it almost as much as men. Among men, it's popular with those who, for one reason and another, can't smoke or spit at their jobs: mechanics, college professors, judges, and a stray bishop or two."

33. l'Oreillard or l'Aureillard: Wikipedia, "Pierre Abraham Lorillard."

33, 33, 34. two essential qualities for snuff packing; a new invention: cellophane; admitted them to the firm as partners: Downey, *Lorillard and Tobacco*, page 18.

33. promotional materials: Downey, *Lorillard and Tobacco*, page 10.

33. chamomile flowers: Maxwell Fox, *The Lorillard Story*, P. Lorillard Company, 1947, page 19.

34. obscure tobacconist's apprentice": Rex Burns, *Success in America: The Yeoman Dream and the Industrial Revolution*, University of Massachusetts Press, 1976, page 59.

34. his partners in the firm: Fox, *The Lorillard Story*, page 20.

35. more prosperous than ever: P. Lorillard Company, *Lorillard and Tobacco: 200th Anniversary 1760–1960*, published by P. Lorillard Company, c. 1960, page 17. The bicentennial document, which draws heavily from the two earlier P. Lorillard Company publications, is unattributed.

35. stables for blooded horses nearby; the snuff produced at the mill: Downey, *Lorillard and Tobacco*, page 19.

36. if not damaged: Fox, *The Lorillard Story*, page 24.

36. advertising handbills: Downey, *Lorillard and Tobacco*, page 35.

37. could not swallow: P. Lorillard Company, *Lorillard and Tobacco: 200th Anniversary 1760–1960*, page 17.

37. Benjamin Disraeli: *The Oxford English Dictionary, Second Edition*, Oxford: Clarendon Press, 1989, page 785.

37. a victory over family members at the poker table; Native Americans' word for the area, "Ptuck-sepo": "Red Blood For Blue," *Time*, March 31, 1914.

38. by selling dry goods: "Millionaires," *(Stroudburg, Pa.) Jeffersonian*, May 28, 1868.

38. joint interest in the family business; from his brothers: "Pierre Lorillard Dead," *Washington (DC) Evening Star*, July 8, 1901.

38. from his brothers: "Life Ended: Pierre Lorillard Succumbs," *Louisville Courier-Journal*, July 8, 1901.

39. conspicuous consumption": Thorstein Veblen, *The Theory of the Leisure Class*. Boston: Houton Mifflin Company, 1973, pages 60–80.

39. thirty-two harrowing days at sea: "Arrival of the Yacht Vesta," *New York Times*, May 30, 1867.

40. Cornelius Vanderbilt: "Pierre Lorillard, Sr., In Critical Condition," *New York Times*, July 5, 1901.

40. strong emphasis on comfort; every convenience that comfort possibly could require"; hunting dogs and gamebirds: "Pierre Lorillard Dead," *New York Times*, July 8, 1901.

40. a $100,000 floating palace; servants' quarters, kennels, storehouses, &c.: "Houseboat Caiman Burned: Pierre Lorillard's Famous Craft Destroyed in Florida," *New York Times*, June 10, 1900.

40. use as a gambling instrument: Veblen, *The Theory of the Leisure Class*, page 104.

40, 41, 41, 41. racecourses over which they competed; known as the Dr. Conover Farm; plentiful rooms for invited guests; an elaborate swimming pool: J. H. Ransom, *Who's Who in Horsedom, Volume VIII: The 400 of the Sport of Kings*. Lexington, KY: The Ransom Publishing Company, Inc., 1956, pages 127–129.

41. a Lorillard platform: Ransom, *Who's Who in Horsedom, Volume VIII: The 400 of the Sport of Kings*, page 129.

41. on the globe: Amy Gregory, "An American Sportsman," *Thoroughbred Record*, February 16, 1983, page 1094.

42. Creedmore and Harry Hill: Churchill Downs, 124th *Kentucky Derby, Saturday, May 2, 1998 (Kentucky Derby Press Guide)*, published 1998, page 164.

42. the best horses he could import; win with horses of his own breeding: W. S. Vosburgh, *Cherry and Black, Career of Pierre Lorillard on the Turf.* Originally printed for Pierre Lorillard, Second Limited Edition, 1916, pages 55–57.

43, 43, 44. New York's Bellevue Hospital; an excellent athlete; tribesmen intent on ransom: "George Lorillard's Death," *New York Times*, February 5, 1886.

43, 43, 43, 44. "a model sportsman"; the finest shots in Europe; lost in a gale near the Bahamas; at significant risk for assassination: "Death of George L. Lorillard," *Turf, Field and Farm*, February 12, 1886, page 113.

43. April 6, 1869: "Launch of the Yacht Meteor," *New York Times*, April 7, 1869.

43, 44. ever been constructed in these waters"; include stops in numerous ports: "The Meteor: Reported Wreck of the Yacht off the Coast of Africa: All Hands Saved: Description of the Vessel," *New York Times*, December 27, 1869.

44. safe in Naples: "The Yacht Meteor," *New York Times*, January 22, 1870.

44. the *Meteor* had failed": Untitled article regarding the death of George Lorillard, *Spirit of the Times*, February 6, 1886, page 50.

45. His Westbrook Stable: "The Islip Stable," *New York Times*, March 30, 1878.

45. "no pains or expense": "A Princely Racing Establishment," *Turf, Field and Farm*, November 23, 1877.

45. history of the American turf": National Museum of Racing—Hall of Fame, "Duke of Magenta."

CHAPTER 5

46, 57. *The Great Black Jockeys*, by Edward Hotaling; may have been born at Abe Buford's nearby Bosque Bonita Farm: Edward Hotaling, *The Great Black Jockeys*. Rocklin, CA: Prima Publishing, 1999, page 232.

47. victory in the Preakness; to win the state's premier race: *Laurel and Pimlico 1996 Media Guide*, published by the Maryland Jockey Club, 1996, page 98.

47. were consecutive: *Laurel and Pimlico 1996 Media Guide*, published by the Maryland Jockey Club, 1996, page 82.

47. horseshoe-shaped tie pin: "The Great Record of R. Wyndham Walden," *Turf, Field, and Farm*, February 21, 1903, unnumbered cover page.

47. his father was a trainer: "The Great Record of R. Wyndham Walden," *Turf, Field, and Farm*, February 21, 1903, page 173.

47. the Maryland Jockey Club: Margaret Worrall, "Bowling Brook Remembered," *Maryland Horse*, March, 1987.

47. terminated his riding career: "Death of R.W. Walden," *New York Times*, April 29, 1905.

47. to keep a runner prepared: National Museum of Racing—Hall of Fame, "R.W. Walden."

47. he duly reported to his employer, Geore Lorillard; remain in the race: William H. P. Robertson, *History of Thoroughbred Racing in America*. New York: Bonanza, 1964, page 125.

48. the great Ten Broeck: Two excellent books are available on the fascinating story of African-American horsemen. The author strongly recommends Edward Hotaling's *The Great Black Jockeys*, Prima Publishing, 1999, and the more recent *Race Horse Men*, by Katherine C. Mooney, Harvard University Press, 2014.

48. "place of refuge" at Nantura: "A Tree Inhabited Seven Years," *Memphis (Tenn.) Public Ledger*, January 20, 1880.

49. a want of condition": "Breeding Farms in Kentucky. No. 3—Nantura Stock Farm," *Kentucky Live Stock Record*, January 3, 1885.

49, 49, 50, 50, 50, 50, 50, 50. agent, stable foreman, and trainer; pay you the balance; some of the better Morris horses; regardless of weather; a serious demeanor; "You were darned lucky."; is what poisoned him"; scampered home in front: J.H.M., "The Late Wm. Brown and Parole," *Turf, Field and Farm*, March 28, 1903.

50. the Morris two-year-olds: W. S. Vosburgh, *Cherry and Black, Career of Pierre Lorillard on the Turf*. Originally printed for Pierre Lorillard, Second Limited Edition, 1916, page 15.

51. went postward for the Great Sweepstakes: Vosburgh, *Cherry and Black, Career of Pierre Lorillard on the Turf*, page 25.

51. Born in Baltimore in 1833; transitioned to the ranks of trainers: National Museum of Racing—Hall of Fame, "Jacob Pincus."

51. (or perhaps it was 1838); the modern-day Belmont Stakes trophy: Eliza McGraw, "'Matchless Jew': The Belmont's Jewish Backstory," *New York Jewish Week*, June 7, 2011.

51. famous at Saratoga: Horseracing History Online—"Person Profile—Jacob Pincus."

51. $3,850 for his victory: *American Racing Manual, 1968 Edition*. New York: Triangle Publications, Inc., 1968, page 778.

51. its inevitable toll: "Death Comes to Matthew Byrnes," *Thoroughbred Record*, March 25, 1933.

52. in Norwich, England: *Famous American Jockeys*, written by "Vigilant" and published by Richard A. Saalfield for *Spirit of the Times*, New York, page 3, fixes the year of his birth as 1854, but the National Museum of Racing—Hall of Fame, in its website write-up of George Barbee states that he was born "in the early 1850s." The racing magazine the *Blood-Horse* (Judy L. Marchman, "People: Getting His Due," *Blood-Horse*, May 25, 1996, page 2,674) in 1996 reported that Barbee had "died in 1941 with his age given in various sources as anything from 88 to 93."

52. the English Triple Crown: "Famous American Jockeys: George Barbee," *Thoroughbred Record*, March 6, 1920.

52. the savage [horse] Uncas: "Vigilant," *Famous American Jockeys*, page 5.

53. Taral could mount: Robertson, *History of Thoroughbred Racing in America*, page 159.

53. the Rancocas contingent: Neil Newman, "Geo. Barbee 'Daddy of Them All,'" unknown newspaper, December 17, 1930.

54, 54, 58. with Barbee in the saddle; Longstaff, Drennon, and Barbee were expelled; *Krik's Guide to the Turf: Krik's Guide to the Turf, Part I, 1877–78.* New York: H.G. Crickmore, 1878.

54. worthy of investigation: "Turf Notes," *New York Times*, October 16, 1877.

55, 55, 56, 56. and with the Barrett family's dissolution; took him under his protection"; many riding opportunities; five wins from thirty-two starters: "The Late Wm. Barrett, Jockey," *New York Sportsman*, January 13, 1883.

55, 56. "considerable aptitude in riding and handling horses"; for which he could ride the weights: "Death of the American Jockey, Barrett," *Turf, Field and Farm*, January 12, 1883.

56. was very effective: Vosburgh, *Cherry and Black, Career of Pierre Lorillard on the Turf*, page 25.

57. into the world at Nantura: Exactly where Walker began his life is not 100 percent certain, due to the paucity of reliable birth records for slaves in that era. The *Thoroughbred Record*, in its unattributed September 23, 1933, article, "William Walker, Man Who Rode Ten Broeck, Dead," page 178, has him "born in Woodford County, at the famous Nantura Farm of John Harper," but Ben H. "Buck" Weaver in "The Passing of 'Uncle Bill'" (in *Turf and Sport Digest*, December 1933, pages 38, 39, 86) and James Robert Saunders and Monica Renae Saunders in *Black Winning Jockeys in the Kentucky Derby* (Jefferson, NC: McFarland & Co., 2003) are willing only to concede, in the Saunderses' words, that "Walker was born into slavery in 1860, on a farm in Woodford County, Kentucky."

58. from owner Dan Swigert; the entire $10,000 winner's purse: Weaver, "The Passing of 'Uncle Bill,'" *Turf and Sport Digest*, December 1933, pages 38, 39, 86.

57, 57, 58. to capture the trophy; "best behaved jockey on the track"; he won his first stakes races: Jonelle Fisher, *Nantura 1795–1905*. St. Crispian Press, 2004, page 125.

57. "as soon as he could walk.": "William Walker, Man Who Rode Ten Broeck, Dead," *Thoroughbred Record*, September 23, 1933, page 178.

58. the leading American rider": Quoted in James Robert Saunders and Monica Renae Saunders, *Black Winning Jockeys in the Kentucky Derby*, page 21.

CHAPTER 6

60, 60, 65, 65. The *Turf, Field and Farm*, October 19, 1877; Tom Ochiltree and Parole are also there; Time will tell; flitting sunshine and shadow: "Ten Broeck, Tom Ochiltree, Parole," *Turf, Field and Farm*, October 19, 1877.

60, 61, 61. will extend you a hearty welcome. J. F. Robinson; Please answer by telegraph; shall be pleased to hear from you. J. F. Robinson: "Tom Ochiltree and Ten Broeck," *New York Times*, October 18, 1876.

61. on September 27: "Ten Broeck's Victory: Fellowcraft's Four-Mile Record Beaten: Lexington's Celebrated Time Beaten by Four Seconds: The Greatest Event in the History of the Turf: The Race at Louisville Yesterday," *New York Times*, September 28, 1876.

63. a challenge from Ten Broeck: "The Racing Season of 1877," *New York Times*, March 25, 1877.

63. the sensation of the year": "Turf Notes," *New York Times*, October 5, 1877.

63. to be congratulated: "Racing Attractions at Baltimore," *Spirit of the Times*, October 6, 1877, page 259

64. without a struggle: "The Nashville Fall Meeting," *Spirit of the Times*, October 6, 1877, page 259.

64. meeting at that place": "The Baltimore Races," *New York Times*, October 10, 1877.

64. located at Pimlico": "Ten Broeck at Baltimore," *Spirit of the Times*, October 13, 1877, page 287.

65. all three of whom are entered: "Extra Race at Baltimore," *Spirit of the Times*, October 13, 1877.

65. too low in flesh": "The Maryland Jockey Club," *Kentucky Live Stock Record*, October 20, 1877, page 248.

66. speed in his exercise: "The Coming Meeting at Baltimore," *Spirit of the Times*, October 20, 1877, page 316.

66. on an American course: "The Maryland Races," *New York Times*, October 21, 1877.

66. most important that has ever happened"; they will change their minds: "The Great Sweepstakes at Pimlico," *Baltimore American and Commercial Advertiser*, October 21, 1877.

67. the requirements of the match": "The Pimlico Races," *Baltimore American and Commercial Advertiser*, October 23, 1877.

67. which was ordered: "Maryland Jockey Club Races," *Baltimore Sun*, October 23, 1877.

67, 68. "[w]eather clear and cold, track stiff and heavy"; "weather fine, track fair, not good": *Krik's Guide to the Turf, Part I, 1877–78*. New York: H.G. Crickmore, 1878, page 162.

68. during the past decade": "Now the Races Will Open," *Baltimore American and Commercial Advertiser*, October 22, 1877.

68. Ten Broeck and Ochiltree were willing to run"; Parole at $15: "The Great Sweepstakes Postponed," *New York Times*, October 23, 1877.

68. dampened by the postponement": "Ten Broeck Tumbles," *Louisville Courier-Journal*, October 25, 1877.

69. toward the "corsairs": "Maryland Jockey Club Races," *Baltimore Sun*, October 24, 1877.

69. breeze from the south-west": "Pleasures of the Turf," *New York Times*, October 24, 1877.

CHAPTER 7

70, 71, 74, 74, 75, 75, 75. *Baltimore American and Commercial Advertiser*, October 25, 1877; It surely exceeded twenty thousand; "the greatest event that has ever been seen on the American turf"; maneuvered to the outside; how a race should be won this time; That's Tom's signal for speed"; this was no walk-over for him": "The Pimlico Races: A Brilliant Day on the Turf," *Baltimore American and Commercial Advertiser*, October 25, 1877.

70, 75. could not have been desired; "the most intense excitement prevailed"; "Excitement of the Turf," *New York Times*, October 25, 1877.

71. the balconies of the club-house: "The Carrollton," "Baltimore Fall Meeting," *Turf, Field and Farm*, October 26, 1877.

73. winner by a length: *Krik's Guide to the Turf, Part I, 1877–78*. New York: H.G. Crickmore, 1878, page 163.

73, 74. the sound of a bell echoed through the Pimlico grounds; troubled sea lashed to wild commotion: "Parole's Victory," *Turf, Field and Farm*, October 26, 1877.

73, 74. the people fairly howled"; their strength gathered for a mighty spring": W. D. Burroughs, "Passing of Pimlico: When Congress Adjourned for a Horse Race," *New York Times*, April 9, 1905.

75. shouted, "Go!": "Baltimore," *Spirit of the Times*, October 27, 1877, page 339.

76. Barrett's perfectly timed ride: A drawing in the December 22 issue of *Spirit of the Times* (page 554) shows Parole taking the inside path, with Ten Broeck, identifiable primarily by the black face of Jockey William Walker, on his outside as the pair pass the judges' stand. An inside run, if the drawing is accurate, would have been a daring but dangerous maneuver by jockey William Barrett, who would have risked being pinned against the rail by Ten Broeck and Walker.

77. than from the ride: "Ten Broeck's Defeat," *Louisville Courier-Journal*, October 27, 1877.

77. suddenly become mad: "Baltimore!" *Turf, Field and Farm*, November 2, 1877.

77. $20,000 on a single bet: Terry Conway, ESPN website: "The Great Sweepstakes at Pimlico."

77. $20,000 on a single bet: In his *New York Tribune* article, "Big Betting Coups," published more than six years after Lorillard's death, Horace Temple suggested that Lorillard, through a combination of discreet information handling and his own talent as an observer of fine horseflesh, won a fortune on Pontiac, before the newly purchased colt had demonstrated its abilities to the general public. "But his new owner had seen enough of his work to have confidence in his future," wrote Temple, "so he sent him to his farm at Rancocas, near Jobstown, New Jersey, there to be quietly trained for the big event. His judgment was justified to the extent of seventy-five thousand dollars above the big stake money, and he would have won considerably more if it had not been that restrictions were placed on betting at that particular meeting." The only aspect of this story that doesn't quite ring true is that Lorillard would have allowed himself to be limited in his private wagers by racetrack rules. Temple may have correctly reported Lorillard's publicly acknowledged winnings, but not been privy to the entrepreneur's substantial side bets.

77. clean them out: "Maryland Jockey Club Races," *Baltimore Sun*, October 25, 1877.

78. the Dakota Territory: "Rattling Running," *Bismark Tri-Weekly Tribune*, October 29, 1877.

78. Wheeling, West Virginia: "Turf Notes," *Wheeling (WV) Daily Intelligencer*, October 25, 1877.

78. *Memphis Daily Appeal*: "The Great Race," *Memphis Daily Appeal*, October 25, 1877.

78. *Dallas Daily Herald*: "Parole Victor," *Dallas Daily Herald*, October 25, 1877.

78. Iola, Kansas: "Minor Notes," *Iola (KS) Reporter*, November 3, 1877.

78. *National Republican*: "Pimlico: The Great Sweepstakes of the Season Run Yesterday," *National Republican*, October 25, 1877.

78. Natchitoches Parishes": "From Everywhere: General," *People's Vindicator* (Natchitoches, LA), November 10, 1877.

79. race for the championship: W. S. Vosburgh, *Cherry and Black, Career of Pierre Lorillard on the Turf.* Originally printed for Pierre Lorillard, Second Limited Edition, 1916, page 20.

CHAPTER 8

80, 81. *The Baltimore American and Commercial Advertiser,* October 25, 1877; "poor little Parole.": "The Pimlico Races," *Baltimore American and Commercial Advertiser,* October 25, 1877.

80. the honor of the "West": "The Proposed Ten Broeck-Parole Match," *Kentucky Live Stock Record,* November 17, 1887, page 313.

80, 85, 85, 85, 86, 86, 88. Tom Ochiltree's disappointing performance; Ten Broeck's condition beat him; the remainder of the race; during the progress of the race"; "was coughing the morning of the race"; not received by Walden until after the race; but beat nothing": "The Baltimore Meeting," *Kentucky Live Stock Record,* November 3, 1877, page 280.

81. with an exclamation point: "Parole!": "Ten Broeck vs Parole," *Spirit of the Times,* November 10, 1877, page 393.

81. of a two-heat race: *Krik's Guide to the Turf, Part I, 1875–76, 1876–77, and 1877–78.* New York: H.G. Crickmore, 1876.

81. "in a canter": Jonelle Fisher, *Nantura 1795–1905.* St. Crispian Press, 2004, page 177.

81, 83, 84, 85. seconds faster than Parole's record"; keep the victory in the family; considerable comment over the result; "as well as he ever had been in his life": "Ten Broeck Tumbles," *Louisville Courier-Journal,* October 25, 1877.

83. to add $1,000: Terry Conway, ESPN website: "The Great Sweepstakes at Pimlico."

84. Ochiltree won the race for him: "Maryland Jockey Club Races," *Baltimore Sun,* October 25, 1877.

84. an off day with him": "Ten Broeck's Defeat at Baltimore," *Louisville Commercial,* October 25, 1877.

85, 87, 88. His coat shone like polished ebony"; separating them at the wire"; achieved "in a canter": "Baltimore!" *Turf, Field and Farm,* November 2, 1877.

85. they have paid dearly for it: "Excitement of the Turf," *New York Times,* October 25, 1877.

86, 87, 87, 89, 89, 89, 90. India rubber tracks"; they expected to see him beaten"; in his expressive countenance; either Saratoga or Jerome Park; matches can be made on these terms; did not want to send his horses south; all the money bet that he may wish: "Albion," Letter to the Editor, *Spirit of the Times,* November 3, 1877, page 363.

86, 87. any previous day except [Great Sweepstakes Day]"; "under a heavy pull": "The Racing at Baltimore," *New York Times,* October 27, 1877.

87. wagered on Ten Broeck: "Maryland Jockey Club Races," *Baltimore Sun*, October 26, 1877.

88. 1 to 5 against Ten Broeck: "Victory Won at the Pimlico Course Yesterday by the Kentucky Horse Ten Broeck," *Louisville Courier-Journal*, October 27, 1877.

88. "Harper in Sorrow": "Pimlico: The Great Race: Ten Broeck Not Himself: A Day of Disappointment: Harper in Sorrow," *Kentucky Gazette*, October 27, 1877.

88. work with Thoroughbreds": Katherine C. Mooney, *Race Horse Men*, Cambridge, MA, Harvard University Press, 2014, page 127.

90. at Pimlico until Tuesday: "Parole and Ten Broeck to Meet Again," *Baltimore Sun*, October 27, 1877.

CHAPTER 9

91. accept the challenge: "Editorial Notes," *Spirit of the Times*, November 10, 1877.

92. its upper-class flavor: J. H. Ransom, *Who's Who in Horsedom, Volume VIII: The 400 of the Sport of Kings*. Lexington, KY: The Ransom Publishing Company, Inc., 1956

92. of the American racing club": "The Carrollton," "Baltimore Fall Meeting," *Turf, Field and Farm*, October 26, 1877.

92. the program would be free; a "good and dry course"; St. James, and Tom Ochiltree: "Extra Day at Jerome Park," *New York Times*, October 29, 1877.

92. in the coming struggle: "The Jerome Park Races," *New York Times*, October 31, 1877.

92, 94, 94, 95, 95, 96. declared "not propitious"; 114 lbs . . . pd ft; "fearful struggle between pride and prudence"; he ever shows when at himself; and so it proved in this case; up to the time he arrived at Pimlico: "Ten Broeck vs Parole," *Spirit of the Times*, November 10, 1877, page 393.

93, 94. the other three races announced will come off; and had a "swollen ankle"; "Ten Broeck Withdrawn," *New York Times*, November 6, 1877.

95. "by a colored attendant"; 'Why don't you run him?'": "American Jockey Club: Extra Day at Jerome Park," *New York Times*, November 7, 1877.

95. "a very unpleasant situation"; "The disappointment and chagrin were great"; winning their bets in a fair race: H. Stanford, "Book Betting," *Spirit of the Times*, November 10, 1877, page 401.

96, 97, 97, 97. a few months' well-earned repose; Yours, respectfully, P. Lorillard; "Mr. Harper is compelled to accept it"; warbling the praises of Spring": "The East vs. the West," *Turf, Field and Farm*, November 16, 1877, page 312.

96, 96, 98, 98, 98, 98, 98, 98. in form for a spring campaign"; with the opening of the season; put the matter into a definite shape"; "liberal and plucky"; two weeks after their arrival"; could not divide his stable; the turf and the thoroughbred"; in transporting Ten Broeck: "East vs. West and South," *Spirit of the Times*, November 17, 1877, page 425, quoting an earlier article in the *Kentucky Live Stock Record*.

99, 99, 100. Lorillard had had a special railroad car; a factor still weighing heavily on Harper; 5 West Twenty-first Street, Tuesday evening, Nov. 21: "Ten Broeck-Parole-Tom Ochiltree," *Turf, Field and Farm*, November 23, 1877.

99. sixty thousand in attendance: Mooney, Katherine C., *Race Horse Men*. Cambridge, MA, Harvard University Press, 2014, page 20.

99. preferably the latter": Kent Hollingsworth, *The Great Ones*. Lexington, KY: The Blood-Horse, 1970, page 41.

99. by an estimated sixty yards; (Planet, a rare "binary," could do both): William H. P. Robertson, *History of Thoroughbred Racing in America*. New York: Bonanza, 1964, page 61.

100, 101. next spring between Ten Broeck and Parole?"; Mr. Harper will not come to Saratoga with Ten Broeck?: "Ten Broeck and Parole," *Turf, Field and Farm*, November 30, 1877.

102. as well as in trade: "Tom Ochiltree vs. Ten Broeck," *Spirit of the Times*, December 1, 1877, page 477.

102. yours respectfully, P. Lorillard; We should like to hear from *them*": "Mr. Lorillard Will Not Go to Kentucky," *Turf, Field and Farm*, December 7, 1877, page 361.

102. "the best matched in America": "Declination of Mr. P. Lorillard to Come to Kentucky," *Kentucky Live Stock Record*, December 15, 1877.

CHAPTER 10

104, 124, 124, 124, 124, 125, 125, 126, 126, 126, 126. *New York Times*, July 14, 1901; Bequest of Rancocas to a Woman Arouses His Family; "the most rigid and binding character"; nothing can be disposed of"; closer to $4 million; "much property in her own right"; to bring about a reconciliation; "the apple of [Lorillard's] eye"; a million dollars in upgrades; at $69,775 (nearly $2 million); who dropped out of sight years ago: "How Mr. Lorillard Divided His Estate," *New York Times*, July 14, 1901.

104. "most famous turfman of his time": "Pierre Lorillard Dead," *New York Times*, July 8, 1901.

105. bought them all: J. H. Ransom, *Who's Who in Horsedom, Volume VIII: The 400 of the Sport of Kings*. Lexington, KY: The Ransom Publishing Company, Inc., 1956, page 132.

105. countered at $7,000: W. S. Vosburgh, *Cherry and Black, Career of Pierre Lorillard on the Turf*. Originally printed for Pierre Lorillard, Second Limited Edition, 1916, pages 36–37.

105, 105, 108. which George rejected; his endeavors to get this colt from his brother"; the art of race riding horsemanship: "The Victory in the Derby," *New York Sportsman*, June 4, 1881, page 216.

105. Iroquois was a real devil": W. S. Vosburgh, *Racing in America 1866–1921*. New York: The Jockey Club, 1922, page 123.

106. winning four races: *Ruff's Guide to the Turf, 1881 Spring Edition*. London: Office of "Ruff's Guide," 1882.

106, 106, 106, 106, 108. for the following year's British classic races, others; the air sultry, and the dust stifling; to Epsom Downs from Victoria Station alone; Prince Edward of Saxe-Weimar; "Iroquois! (Pronounced 'ÎR-O-KWOY')": "Iroquois!," *Spirit of the Times*, June 4, 1881, page 462.

106. at 50-to-1 odds: "General Telegraph News: The Two Thousand Guineas Race," *New York Times*, May 5, 1881.

106, 107, 109. some lowered his odds to 11-to-2; the fortunate backers of the winner; "no chance of winning": "America Wins the Derby," *New York Times*, June 2, 1881.

107. "the wildest hilarity": Vosburgh, *Cherry and Black, Career of Pierre Lorillard on the Turf*, page 43.

107, 107, 107, 108. "splendid and exciting"; and nearly capsized him"; pressing forward on the stand side"; by three lengths if it had been required": "The Turf in England: A Great American Triumph," *Turf, Field and Farm*, June 3, 1881, page 340.

107. to make play": "The Derby next Wednesday," *New York Sportsman*, May 28, 1881, page 202.

108. activity was suspended: Amy Gregory, "An American Sportsman," *Thoroughbred Record*, February 16, 1983, page 1,092.

108, 109. a surefire means of drawing applause; but he eluded them: Vosburgh, *Cherry and Black, Career of Pierre Lorillard on the Turf*, page 44.

108, 108, 109, 109, 109, 109, 110, 110. extra editions of the evening papers"; updates on his private ticker; stopped numerous times by jubilant well-wishers; one from the Duke of Manchester; when they came in ahead"; generous 5-to-1 odds; nobody would hazard an estimate; among the trainers and stable boys: "Excitement in this City," *New York Times*, June 2, 1881.

110. "Two Millions in Bets": "America's Victory: Iroquois Wins the Derby Race," *National Republican*, June 2, 1881.

110. believing that either could beat Iroquois; that had ever faced the starter for the Derby"; Barrett was found unequal to the task: "Iroquois," *Kentucky Live Stock Record*, June 11, 1881, page 376.

110. "very wroth": "Ready for the Derby," *New York Times*, June 1, 1881.

111. some well chosen point in Central Park; for future winners of the Derby": Cited in "The Epsom Derby," *Turf, Field and Farm*, June 3, 1881, page 344.

111. carried to victory: "Iroquois," *Kentucky Live Stock Record*, June 18, 1881, page 393.

111. odds of 7-to-2: Untitled article regarding Iroquois's chances in the St. Leger, *Spirit of the Times*, September 10, 1881, page 170.

111, 112, 112, 112, 112. odds that drifted downward to 2-to-1; the splendor of his achievement this afternoon; "cloudy and cheerless"; the Lorillard cherry and black were in almost every store window; fully occupied with business on the important race": "Iroquois! America Captures the St. Leger," *Spirit of the Times*, September 17, 1881, page 192.

112. and "nobbling" Iroquois: "Iroquois and the Doncaster St. Leger," *New York Sportsman*, September 17, 1881, page 184.

112. easily by a length": "Iroquois Again a Victor," *New York Times*, September 15, 1881.

112. first to win the race: "Iroquois Wins the Doncaster St. Leger," *Kentucky Live Stock Record*, September 17, 1881, page 184.

113. and rewarding success": Ransom, *Who's Who in Horsedom, Volume VIII: The 400 of the Sport of Kings*, page 132.

113. "probably the best race-horse that was ever imported into America"; the best horse in Europe": Vosburgh, *Cherry and Black, Career of Pierre Lorillard on the Turf*, page 59.

113, 113, 114, 125. the undeveloped Tuxedo property; outside a major city had been constructed"; luxurious living in a forested setting; had been separated since the early 1890s: Tuxedo Park, NY, Official Village website, tuxedopark-ny.gov.

113, 118. most famous communities on the American social scene"; a record per-head average of $5,520: Gregory, "An American Sportsman," *Thoroughbred Record*, February 16, 1983, page 1,096.

113. sprung from the soil: The various generations of Pierre Lorillards can become confusing to researchers. An example of this is to be found in the March 31, 1914, issue of *Time* magazine, in which an article titled "Red Blood for Blue" credits Pierre Lorillard III with having constructed the facilities at Tuxedo Park. The article states that "it was Pierre Lorillard (snuff & tobacco) who foreclosed a mortgage in 1814 and began to make this wilderness into a 600,000 acre property for the Lorillards. . . . On a rainy day in September, 71 years later, Pierre Lorillard III got off a train and looked over his land. . . . Seven months from that fall day, he had built . . . 30 miles of roads, a sewage and water system, a park gatehouse 'like a frontispiece to an English novel,' 22 cottages, two blocks of stores, stables, a dam, an icehouse, clubhouse, swimming pool." But Pierre Lorillard III died on December 23, 1867, nearly eighteen years prior to the day described by *Time*. The Lorillard departing the train on that blustery day in September 1885 could only have been Pierre IV.

114. they ate out of people's hands": "Red Blood for Blue," *Time*, March 31, 1914.

114. the Astors, Iselins, Millses, Havermayers, and Vanderbilts"; most Americans have called it a tuxedo": John Steele Gordon, "The Country Club," *American Heritage*, September/October, 1990, page 78.

114. put in straitjackets long ago": Fairfax Downey, *Lorillard and Tobacco*. P. Lorillard Company, 1951, page 38.

115. with his gun and dog at his father's place"; by his slight acquaintences": "N. Griswold Lorillard," *New York Tribune*, November 5, 1888.

115. "rather serious in his manner":"Griswold Lorillard Is Dying," *New York Evening World*, October 23, 1888.

115. make friends readily: "Nathaniel G. Lorillard Dead," *New York Times*, November 5, 1888.

115. into the twentieth century: Wikipedia, "History of Tuberculosis."

115, 115, 122, 123. "as the czar rules Russia"; "but nothing came of it"; He had been severely ill for weeks; lived to see his greatest hopes realized: "Life Ended: Pierre Lorillard Succumbs," *Louisville Courier-Journal*, July 8, 1901.

115, 125, 126, 131, 131. "sustain any and all provisions of the by-laws"; as and for her absolute property; St. Mary's Church at Tuxedo; Pierre Lorillard's thoroughbred empire: "Mr. Lorillard's Will Probated in Trenton," *New York Times*, July 19, 1901.

116. over a cigarette: Maxwell Fox, *The Lorillard Story*. P. Lorillard Company, 1947, page 34.

116, 118, 122. attend to the duties of the office; Vanderbilt's breeding empire in France; had for some time been in a semi-comatose condition: "Pierre Lorillard Dead," *New York Times*, July 8, 1901.

116. rich by inheritance": "Lorillard's Record," *Minneapolis Journal*, July 5, 1901.

116. "the most 'expensive man' in New York"; a mere man of pleasure; Chevalier of the Legion of Honor: "Pierre Lorillard," *New York Times*, July 8, 1901.

116. the horses he wanted: See, for example, "Notes of the Turf: The Conflict Between Pierre Lorillard and the Dwyer Brothers," *New York Times*, October 5, 1885.

117. swathed in heavy wraps": Untitled article regarding the death of George Lorillard, *Spirit of the Times*, February 6, 1886, page 50.

117. possible to imagine: "A Princely Racing Establishment," *Turf, Field and Farm*, November 23, 1877.

117. died at age forty-two: "Death of Mr. George L. Lorillard," *Live Stock Record*, February 13, 1886.

117. hope had been abandoned": "George Lorillard Dead," *Louisville Courier-Journal*, February 5, 1886.

117. decided to give it up: "Mr. Lorillard to Retire," *New York Times*, September 3, 1893.

118. yearlings went for $23,685: William H. P. Robertson, *History of Thoroughbred Racing in America*. New York: Bonanza, 1964, page 128.

118. icily regular manner": Ransom, *Who's Who in Horsedom, Volume VIII: The 400 of the Sport of Kings*, page 134.

118, 121, 123. to purchase Lamplighter in 1891; He had suffered for over a decade; Ochre Point at Newport, Rhode Island: "Pierre Lorillard Dead," *Spirit of the Times*, July 13, 1901.

118. imported to the United States: Ransom, *Who's Who in Horsedom, Volume VIII: The 400 of the Sport of Kings*, page 135.

119. Tiffany & Company: Vosburgh, *Cherry and Black, Career of Pierre Lorillard on the Turf*, page 158.

119. operated under [their] own individual rules"; the first two volumes of the *American Stud Book*: Robertson, *History of Thoroughbred Racing in America*, pages 174 and 175.

119. founded on February 16, 1881: Ransom, *Who's Who in Horsedom, Volume VIII: The 400 of the Sport of Kings*, page 137.

120. the Jockey Club was formally chartered: The Jockey Club website, *History of the Jockey Club*.

120. the Jockey Club was formally chartered: "Trouble Ahead in Racing," *New York Tribune*, February 11, 1894.

120. the Jockey Club was formally chartered: "Jockey Club Launched," *New York Tribune*, February 14, 1894.

120. top thoroughbreds to England: Ransom, *Who's Who in Horsedom, Volume VIII: The 400 of the Sport of Kings*, page 135.

120. his horse is in winning form": "Lorillard Leaves England," *New York Times*, October 9, 1898.

120. at Epsom in June, 1901": Vosburgh, *Cherry and Black, Career of Pierre Lorillard on the Turf*, page 154.

120, 121, 122. I'll live to get in; All had been told to expect the worst; perfectly conscious and rational: "Pierre Lorillard, Sr., in Critical Condition," *New York Times*, July 5, 1901.

121. Timothy L. Woodruff: "Returning Millionaires Are Royally Welcomed," *St. Louis Republic*, July 5, 1901.

122. if they reach high levels": WebMD.com, "Uremic Syndrome."

122. cardiac arrest and death": Medscape.com, "Uremia."

122. nephritis or glomerulonephritis: Encyclopaedia Brittanica Online, "Bright Disease [*sic*]."

122. from accumulation of fluids; "prolonged in comparative comfort": StudyLight.org, 1911 Encyclopaedia Brittanica: "Bright's Disease."

122. what medications were available; with increasing frequency in the days ahead: "Pierre Lorillard Sinking," *New York Times*, July 7, 1901.

122, 124. with increasing frequency in the days ahead; from $15 to $20 million: "Pierre Lorillard Dead," *Hickman (KY) Courier*, July 12, 1901.

123. the British race course: "British Press Tributes," *New York Times*, July 8, 1901.

124, 124, 124, 126. a mere $1,797,95.23; enjoy myself for the rest of my life; small amount of the personalty he left behind him"; at $69,775 (nearly $2 million): "Metropolitan Gossip," *Thoroughbred Record*, December 21, 1901, page 294.

125. "I am not worrying"; the little east side crèche I am interested in": "Mrs. Lorillard Won't Contest," *New York Evening World*, July 13, 1901.

126, 127, 128, 128, 129, 129, 132. as and for her absolute property; wealth bestowed . . . by the millionaire; Lorillard had developd an "infatuation"; the queenly dignity of the wife; the wife's dress has no somber note"; had expressed his dislike openly on many occasions; emulate the performance of Iroquois": "Millionaire Lorillard's Widow May Contest His Will," *(St. Louis) Republic*, July 28, 1901.

127, 127, 127, 128. "the biggest publisher in New York"; president of the American Book Company; the tobacco magnate's bequest to her of Rancocas; the headline on one major daily: "Mrs. Allien Married a Woman, Friend Says," *New York Evening World*, July 27, 1901.

127. among the finest in New York: "'The Other Woman,'" *Pullman (Washington Territory) Herald*, August 24, 1901.

127, 128, 129, 129. many of the handsomest gems ever seen"; merely Lorillard's fellow passenger; not a few bachelor and middle-aged beaux"; whom Mr. Lorillard gathered around him: "Pierre Lorillard's Love," *Indianapolis Journal*, July 16, 1901.

128. in a woman's gown: "Saratoga Aghast at Mrs. Allien," *St. Paul Globe*, September 7, 1902.

128. "'You're home now, dearie'"; "beautiful woman who estranged him from his wife": "Pierre Lorillard Gave Fortune to Mrs. Allien," *New York Evening World*, July 13, 1901.

129. T. Suffern Tailer: "T. Suffern Tailer's Denial," *New York Times*, July 15, 1901.

129, 130. concerning the will of Mr. Pierre Lorillard"; her resolve not to sell is another matter: "Pierre Lorillard's Will," *New York Times*, July 17, 1901.

130. It was pure comradeship: "Mrs. Allien Makes a Public Statement," *(St. Louis) Republic*, August 8, 1901.

130. see or talk to Mrs. Allien: "Mrs. Allien at Rancocas," *New York Times*, August 7, 1901.

131. she had actually sold out to the Lorillards; so long adorned her benefactor's thoroughbreds: "To Give Up Rancocas," *Washington (DC) Times*, August 5, 1901.

131. she had actually sold out to the Lorillards: "Will Give Up Rancocas," *Indianapolis Journal*, August 5, 1901.

131. forty-two yearlings: "P. Lorillard's Estate," *New York Tribune*, December 14, 1901.

131. Mrs. Allien promptly went about selling them; as prized by the millionaire and his family: "Lorillard Horses to Go at Auction," *(NY) Evening World*, September 11, 1901.

131. by his father": "Trying Ordeal for Lorillard's Son," *Minneapolis Journal*, September 19, 1901.

132. or about $45,405: "Lorillard Horses Sold Well," *New York Times*, October 4, 1901.

132. his entrée into the area: "Mr. Whitney's Horses," *Minneapolis Journal*, November 20, 1901.

133. Mistah Pierre Lorillard had: "Mrs. Allien to Wed Clubman?," *New York Evening World*, December 11, 1902.

133. a total of $925: "P. Lorillard Buys Rancocas Yearlings," *New York Times*, June 12, 1903.

133. the man who had long been her rumored suitor, George Livingston; the comfort of her farm: "Lorillard's Heiress Weds," *San Francisco Call*, February 16, 1906.

133. the Lorillard showplace: "Burned by Oil," *Fredericksburg, Va. Free Lance*, December 15, 1908.

134, 141, 141, 142. "the social event of the season"; unsuccessful run for a State Assembly seat; dead now for thirty years; traveling, socializing, and living a good life: "Pierre Lorillard Dies in Tuxedo, 80," *New York Times*, August 7, 1940.

134. a letter of credit and other items; gone off with the valuables"; the amount reported may have been conservative: "Mrs. Lorillard's Loss Heavy," *New York Times*, May 17, 1903.

135. amateur champion of the world; a 6-0, 6-1, 6-0 shellacking of the local favorite: "Lorillard Loses to Champion Gould," *New York Times*, April 20, 1906.

135. during the month of May: "Tuxedo Golf Tournament," *New York Times*, June 16, 1907.

135. tennis club championship: "Lorillard Wins at Tuxedo," *New York Times*, December 30, 1907.

135. Washington Society Dinner: "Mrs. Lorillard a Suicide," *Berea (KY) Citizen*, April 1, 1909.

135. lady-in-waiting to Queen Victoria: Wikipedia, "Walburga, Lady Paget." Lady Paget was perhaps best known for her 1907 volume *Colloquies with an unseen friend* [*sic*—the capitalization is as preferred by Lady Paget] (Lady Paget Walburga, editor, *Colloquies with an unseen friend*. London: Philip Wellby, Publisher, 1907), a decidedly odd book that includes such chapters as "Reincarnation," "Atlantis," and "Conditions of Communications with the Invisible." Lady Paget espoused the hypothesis that the former residents of the submerged island of Atlantis continued to survive, populating cities beneath a desert. She was never able, unfortunately, to confirm this belief by bringing any back alive.

135, 135, 135, 136, 137. as having been "in fine spirits"; having removed one stocking; circlet of diamonds she had worn the previous evening; the official cause of death; before their arrival at the scene: "Find Mrs. Lorillard Dead in Bathroom," *New York Times*, March 26, 1909.

135. any one present": "Society Woman Dies by Gas," *Winchester (KY) News*, March 26, 1909.

135, 136, 136. began to prepare for her death"; the group gave up in despair; gas poisoning was the cause of death: "Gas Fumes Kill Mrs. Pierre Lorillard, Jr.," *New York Tribune*, March 26, 1909.

136, 136, 136, 136, 136, 137. "from her debutante days"; which was gradually undermined"; she would die of ennui; "taking a sedative each night to bring on the desired sleep and rest"; their contents would never be made public; "placed in the bosom of Mrs. Lorillard's grave clothes": "Grave Will Hide Tragedy Secret," *Washington (DC) Herald*, March 27, 1909; all quotations in this paragraph and the two that follow are from this source.

136. "Bury this with me—unopened": "Mrs. Lorillard's Suicide Secret Buried with Her," *Washington (DC) Times*, March 26, 1909.

137. described them as "trinkets": See, for example, "Notes Put in Coffin with Mrs. Lorillard: Written by Her and Another Some Time Ago: Trinkets Left with Them," *New York Times*, March 27, 1909.

137. most unwelcome newspaper photographer; to grab and smash the camera: "Disturbance Halts Lorillard Funeral," *New York Times*, March 28, 1909.

137. "The Vulgar Snapshot Man": "The Vulgar Snapshot Man," *New York Times*, March 29, 1909. A *New York Times* editorial regarding the repulsive, funeral-crashing predecessor to modern-day paparazzi suggested that "[h]e, and all like him, ought to be flogged."

137. the mysterious notes: "Detectives Guard Bier," *New York Tribune*, March 28, 1909.

138. but to no avail: "Louis L. Lorillard Dead," *New York Times*, October 23, 1910.

138. first-class court championship, 3-6, 7-5, 6-4: "Court Tennis at Tuxedo," *New York Times*, December 12, 1910.

138. date of the final match: "Lorillard Defeats Brokaw," *New York Times*, January 9, 1911.

138, 139. Discovered by her distraught husband; "the sudden impulse of a neurotic woman": "Mrs. B. Lorillard a Suicide by Hanging," *New York Tribune*, March 17, 1912.

138, 138, 139, 139. Mrs. Lorillard died almost instantly; thrown from a horse-drawn buggy; We had had no quarrel"; "a fit of sudden insanity": "Mrs. B. Lorillard a Hotel Suicide," *New York Times*, March 17, 1912.

139. simply "tired of it all": "Mrs. Lorillard Left a Note," *New York Times*, April 3, 1912.

139. took home a ribbon: "Matinee Races at Goshen," *New York Times*, July 14, 1912.

139. before 2,500 spectators: "Notice B. Beats Amasis," *New York Times*, July 27, 1913.

139, 140. he could not afford the cost; a "hermitage de luxe": "Lorillard in Jail for Unpaid Alimony," *New York Times*, November 8, 1914.

139. millionaire colony in Scarsdale: "Irving Lorillard in Jail," *New York Tribune*, November 8, 1914.

140. compromise the structure: "Ask City to Rebuild Lorillard Mansion," *New York Times*, April 1, 1923.

140. most splendid hemlock forest anywhere: "New York City—Historical Homes and Mansions of the Bronx," www.new-york-city.yodelout.com.

141. particularly offensive: "Mrs. Pierre Lorillard Dies in Monroe Home," *New York Times*, September 12, 1925.

141. Continental Tobacco Company: "Pierre Lorillard Dead," *New York Tribune*, July 8, 1901.

141. honeymooned in Palm Beach: "Mrs. Beard to Wed Pierre Lorillard," *New York Times*, December 30, 1930.

141. honeymooned in Palm Beach:"Mrs. Beard Weds Pierre Lorillard," *New York Times*, February 4, 1931.

141. demolished in April of 1908: "Old Hotel's Last Day," *New York Tribune*, April 5, 1908.

141. among the living: Henry R. Ilsley, "Lorillard Succeeds Maclay as President of American Horse Show," *New York Times*, January 4, 1936.

142. stage for the athletic talents of Jesse Owens; a second one-year term: "Lorillard to Retire as Horse Show Head," *New York Times*, January 3, 1937.

142. at the age of fifty-six: "Griswold Lorillard, Resident of Tuxedo," *New York Times*, September 7, 1942.

142. France and Belgium: "Nuptials Are Held of Mrs. Lorillard," *New York Times*, October 9, 1941.

CHAPTER 11

143. in the Saratoga paddock, August 13, 1931; be accepted during the meeting: "Villainous Poisoning," *Blood-Horse*, August 22, 1931.

143. Rancocas's assessed value?: "Mrs. Allien's Inheritance Tax," *New York Times*, July 22, 1901.

143. before being evicted?: "Mrs. Allien at Rancocas," *New York Times*, August 8, 1901.

144. across the Delaware River: J. H. Ransom, *Who's Who in Horsedom, Volume VIII: The 400 of the Sport of Kings*. Lexington, KY: The Ransom Publishing Company, Inc., 1956, pages 139–140.

144. of Hall of Fame caliber: National Museum of Racing—Hall of Fame, "Samuel C. Hildreth."

144, 144, 146, 146. one of the nation's largest oil fortunes; its assets would top a billion; to pilot the Rancocas horses; general manager of all operations at Rancocas: "Harry F. Sinclair," *Blood-Horse*, November 17, 1956, page 1,343.

144. posed in the winner's circle: John Kieran, "Sports of the Times," *New York Times*, September 25, 1929.

145, 148, 148, 160. topped the owner standings in 1909, 1910, and 1911; who won all ten of his starts; pushed the Calumet Stable to record earnings of $475,091; a decline from which it would never recover: *American Racing Manual, 1968 Edition*, New York: Triangle Publications, Inc., 1968.

146. this in a feeble voice from me: Samuel C. Hildreth and James R. Crowell, *The Spell of the Turf*. Philadelphia: J.P. Lippincott Company, 1926, pages 244–246.

146. his bankroll dwindle alarmingly; general manager of all operations at Rancocas: Hildreth and Crowell, *The Spell of the Turf*, page 247.

147. from cradle to saddle: "Death Claims Samuel C. Hildreth," *Thoroughbred Record*, September 28, 1929, page 195.

147. vice president of the United States: "Sam Hildreth, 63, Turf Veteran, Dies," *New York Times*, September 25, 1929.

147. wagering and swapping horses: Hildreth and Crowell, *The Spell of the Turf*, pages 28–119. These page numbers are somewhat arbitrary; open Hildreth's book to any page and one is instantly and most pleasantly transported into the lore of racing's olden days.

147. animals bred in France: Hildreth and Crowell, *The Spell of the Turf*, page 191.

147. lasted only five days: Hildreth and Crowell, *The Spell of the Turf*, pages 195–196.

147, 148. the owner died suddenly less than a week after arriving in Paris; crossed paths with another American expatriate, August Belmont: Hildreth and Crowell, *The Spell of the Turf*, page 201.

148. had been repealed: "Unostentatious Plans Are Laid to Resume Racing in New York," *Washington Herald*, March 31, 1913.

148. restore his operation to its previous prominence; shoot a few American cuss words in my direction: Hildreth and Crowell, *The Spell of the Turf*, pages 201–202.

148. the horse of the year, 1923": John Hervey, *Racing in America, 1923–1936*. New York: The Jockey Club (privately printed), 1937, pages 23–37.

148. match race at Belmont Park: "Superiority of Zev Was Never in Doubt," *New York Times*, October 21, 1923.

149. there must be some mistake": Hildreth and Crowell, *The Spell of the Turf*, page 229.

149. paying an average of $2,000 per head; Hildreth's offer had been only $100,000: "Playfellow Case Is Ready for Jury," *New York Times*, March 2, 1922.

149. several offers of $100,000: "Three Different Offers of $100,000 Refused for 3-Year-Old, Playfellow," *(New York) Evening World*, June 9, 1921.

149. offered as much as $115,000; can beat any other three-year-old in America": "Rancocas Stable Purchases Playfellow for $115,000: Sinclair Also Buys Knobbie," *New York Times*, June 18, 1921.

149. stud fees upon retirement: "Refuses $100,000 Offer for Man o' War's Full Brother," *New York Times*, June 9, 1921.

150. Second to Knobbie in Carlton Stakes": "Playfellow, Under Wraps, Runs Second to Knobbie in Carlton Stakes," *Washington Herald*, June 19, 1921.

150. drawn only three starters: "Playfellow Last in Field of Three," *New York Times*, June 21, 1921.

150. Brother of Man o' War Gives Talent Hard Jolt"; Sammy must be meshuggah": Ed Curley, "Playfellow, $115,000 Horse, Last in Fairplay [*sic*] Handicap at Aqueduct Track," *Washington Herald*, June 23, 1921.

150. $115,000 Colt in Race at Mile": W. J. MacBeth, "Playfellow Finishes Last in Field of Three in Fair Play Handicap at Aqueduct," *New York Tribune*, June 23, 1921.

150, 150, 151. "enormous weight concessions"; one of the best milers in the country"; whenever they attempted to pass him": "Playfellow's Defeat May Have Been Due to Blinkers Experiment," *New York Evening World*, June 23, 1921.

151. "an amazing lack of speed"; "bought a gold brick in Playfellow": "Hildreth Believes He Bought a Gold Brick in Playfellow," *New York Evening World*, June 28, 1921.

151. he is not sound": "Playfellow Not Sound, Says Hildreth: Requests Return of $115,000 Colt Cost," *New York Times*, June 28, 1921.

151. the Rancocas duo contacted their attorneys: "Playfellow Case May Go to Courts," *New York Times*, June 29, 1921.

151. for 14,000 pounds sterling"; "betting on the outcome has already been engaged in, with the Quincy Stable favorite": "Famous Horse Doctor Says Playfellow was 'O.K.' When Sold to Hildreth," *New York Evening World*, June 29, 1921.

151. not ever again for Rancocas: "Playfellow Not Likely to Race Again This Year: Not for Sinclair, Anyway," *New York Evening World*, June 30, 1921.

151. "cribbing" and "windsucking": "Hildreth Asks Money Back on Playfellow," *Bourbon (KY) News*, July 1, 1921.

151. emitting a grunting sound": Moira C. Reeve and Sharon Biggs, *The Original Horse Bible*. Irvine, CA: Bowtie Press, 1966, page 43.

151. more than three thousand times per day: Cynthia M. Kahn, B.A., M.A., editor, *The Merck Veterinary Manual, Ninth Edition*. Whitehouse Station, NJ: Merck & Co., 2005, page 1,305.

152. acquire the maladies: Geoffrey P. West, M.R.C.V.S., *Black's Veterinary Dictionary, Fourteenth Edition*. Totowa, NJ: Barnes & Noble Books, 1982, pages 198–199.

152. acquire the maladies: Calvin N. Kobluk, B.S.C., B.S.A., D.V.M., D.V. Sc.; Trevor R. Ames, D.V.M., M.S.; Raymond J. Geor, B.V. Sc., M.V. Sc., *The Horse: Diseases & Clinical Management*. Philadelphia: W.B. Saunders Company, 1995.

152. serve on New York juries until 1937: Holly J. McCammon, *The U.S. Women's Jury Movements and Strategic Adaptation: A More Just Verdict*. Cambridge: Cambridge University Press, 2012.

152, 153, 153. no firsthand knowledge of thoroughbred racing; dismissed the jurors before delibarations were concluded; he would refile the case: "Next Playfellow Trial in January," *New York Times*, December 20, 1921.

152. Playfellow was sound: "Sale of Playfellow Held in Good Faith by Former Owner," *New York Tribune*, December 14, 1921.

152. "merely as a precautionary measure": "Playfellow Wore 'Windsucking' Bit, Trainer Testifies," *New York Tribune*, December 15, 1921.

152. blue-blooded owners, veteran trainers: See, for example, "Wind Suckers Win Races, Says Garth at Horse Trial," *New York Evening World*, December 14, 1921.

152. the sale to Sinclair: "Playfellow Case Is on Trial Again," *New York Times*, March 1, 1922.

153. the filing would occur "right away"; the in-court odds against the Rancocas side had gone as high as 10-to-1: "Sinclair Recovers in Playfellow Suit," *New York Times*, March 3, 1922.

153, 154. which Messrs. Sinclair and Hildreth may name"; Thunderclap, or other Rancocas runners: "Playfellow May Be Raced for Charity Pending Decision," *New York Tribune*, March 22, 1922.

154. Johnson's appeal: "Appeal from Playfellow Judgment," *New York Times*, March 23, 1922.

154. no false representation to Hildreth: "Playfellow Case Up Today," *New York Times*, June 13, 1922.

154. it would reserve judgment: "$100,000 Verdict for Horse Disputed," *New York Times*, June 14, 1922.

154. appeared, at last, to be resolved: "Johnson Returns $100,000 Price Paid for Playfellow," *New York Times*, July 29, 1922.

154. neither a cribber nor a windsucker: "Playfellow Case Is to Be Revived," *New York Times*, August 12, 1922.

155. appeal was formally denied: "Johnson's Motion Denied: Court of Appeals Refuses Action in Playfellow Racing Case," *New York Times*, November 29, 1922.

155. of suspicious, "incendiary": "60 Rancocas Horses Lost in Stable Fire," *New York Times*, April 15, 1923.

155, 156. could reach the farm; sell you his wife and children": "Promising Colts Lost in Rancocas Fire," *New York Times*, April 16, 1923.

156. frenzy among attentive oilmen: John Dean, *Warren G. Harding*. New York: Times Books, Henry Holt and Company, 2004, pages 155–156.

156. impressed the observer with his importance": Robert H. Ferrell, *The Strange Deaths of President Harding*. Columbia, MO: University of Missouri Press, 1996, page 108.

156, 157. "elderly, grandfatherly"; shaped by years of calculating oil deals": Ferrell, *The Strange Deaths of President Harding*, pages 108–109.

156. during the mid-1880s: Laton McCartney, *The Teapot Dome Scandal*. New York: Random House, 2008, page 78.

157. the truth of this statement: Ferrell, *The Strange Deaths of President Harding*, page 109.

157. defrauding the US government: McCartney, *The Teapot Dome Scandal*, page 248.

157. he had been bedridden: McCartney, *The Teapot Dome Scandal*, pages 314–315.

158. (the cost of his defense had been borne by his friend Doheny): McCartney, *The Teapot Dome Scandal*, pages 311–313.

158. evidence and nothing else": McCartney, *The Teapot Dome Scandal*, page 312.

158. "Disgusting and discouraging"; "He has too much money to be convicted": McCartney, *The Teapot Dome Scandal*, page 289.

158. "Gerald the Giant-Killer": Wikipedia, "Gerald Nye."

158. American progressive ideals": Wikipedia, "George W. Norris."

158, 158, 158, 159. sentenced to 6½ months in prison; several sets of silk pajamas; fallen ill in work details; Sinclair may occasionally have partaken: McCartney, *The Teapot Dome Scandal*, pages 300–302.

159. "I wonder how Sinclair would like this!": "A Fellow Prisoner," "Sinclair Guest at Prison, Private Chef Cooked Food, Served It in Oil Man's Cell," *Pittsburgh Post-Gazette*, March 5, 1930.

160. a man of honor and integrity": "Sinclair Quits Jail; Railroaded, He Says," *New York Times*, November 21, 1929.

160. following abdominal surgery: "Sam Hildreth, 63, Turf Veteran, Dies," *New York Times*, September 25, 1929; also "Sinclair Pays Tribute," *New York Times*, September 25, 1929.

161. the odds on Happy Scot plummeted to 1-to-2: *Daily Racing Form* official chart of Burnt Hills Handicap, Saratoga, August 13, 1931.

161. a party to the skullduggery": "H.W.C.," "Horses, Horses, Horses," *Thoroughbred Record*, August 22, 1931, page 124.

162. doping horses cannot be done: "Proper Action," *Blood-Horse*, August 22, 1931.

162. Thursday next, September 3: "To Sell Rancocas Horses," *Blood-Horse*, August 29, 1931.

162. "with another strong stable": "Sale of Rancocas Horses in Training," *Thoroughbred Record*, August 29, 1931.

163. thankful to those stewards for their actions": "Sinclair's Reason," *Blood-Horse*, September 19, 1931, pages 326–327.

163. admitted that "only a dope": Joe Williams, "Only a Dope," *Blood-Horse*, December 22, 1945, page 1,387.

163. with option to buy: "Stud News: Helis Leases Rancocas," *Blood-Horse*, July 22, 1944, page 139.

163. a long and colorful career: "William Helis, 63, Succumbs," *Los Angeles Times*, July 25, 1950.

163. the Roseben and two editions of the Toboggan; for a yearling that he called Pericles: *American Racing Manual, 1944 Edition*. New York: Triangle Publications, Inc., 1944.

163. the expensive purchase earned only $5,200: *American Produce Records, 1930-1984.* Bloodstock Research Information Services, Inc., 1985, page 10,083.

164. "The Helis Stock Farm":"William G. Helis Dies in Maryland Hospital," *Thoroughbred Record,* July 29, 1950, page 32.

EPILOGUE

165. James Tandy Harris: Col. John F. Wall, *Famous Running Horses, Their Forebears and Descendants.* Washington Infantry Journal Press, 1949, page 167.

167, 168. "His Fraudulency"; the first college graduate to serve as first lady: Carter Smith, *Presidents: Every Question Answered.* New York: Hylas Publishing, 2004, pages 124–127.

167. a schoolboy longs for the coming vacation": Hans L. Trefousse, *Rutherford B. Hayes.* New York: Times Books, Henry Holt and Company, LLC, 2002, page 118.

167. a consular posting: The White House website, whitehouse.gov: "James A. Garfield."

167. so largely prevails in our country": Rutherford B. Hayes Presidential Center, *Letter from Hayes to Emile Kahn, Editor, Fair Journal of the Jewish Orphan Asylum*; see also his diary entry of September 29, 1881, in which he summarizes a letter sent that day to Frank Edgerly of Concord, New Hampshire. Hayes writes, "The most important lesson of this most pathetic tragedy . . . is the folly and wickedness of the extreme and bitter partisanship which prevails in our country."

167. "the negro question": Rutherford B. Hayes Presidential Center, *Collected Letters and Personal Diary.* "Letter to Cleveland" (presumably to President Grover Cleveland), December 17, 1884.

167. The question then is how best to educate him: Rutherford B. Hayes Presidential Center, *Collected Letters and Personal Diary.* Diary entry, December 17, 1882.

168. a feeble government": Rutherford B. Hayes Presidential Center, *Collected Letters and Personal Diary.* Diary entry, December 18, 1882.

168. the White House was often overflowing": James Truslow Adams, *History of the United States Volume III, War and Reconstruction.* New York: Charles Scribner's Sons, 1933, page 256.

169. my Lucy, is that woman: Rutherford B. Hayes Presidential Center, *Collected Letters and Personal Diary.* Diary entry, June 24–25, 1889.

169. "I know that I am going where Lucy is": Joseph Nathan Kane, *Facts About the Presidents.* New York: Permabooks, 1960, page 426.

169. These were the so-called "Cipher Dispatches": See, for example, "The Florida Cipher Telegrams," *New York Tribune,* October 8, 1878.

169. a paralytic contraction of the limbs: William H. Rehnquist, *Centennial Crisis: The Disputed Election of 1876.* New York: Random House Books, 2007, page 211.

169. "now, I fear, beyond my strength": Rehnquist, *Centennial Crisis: The Disputed Election of 1876*, page 208.

170. He loved his native land: Lloyd Robinson, *The Stolen Election: Hayes vs. Tilden—1876*. New York: A Tom Doherty Associates Book, 1968.

170. it was actually a few million short of that"; library and reading room in the City of New York: Kathie Coblentz, Rare Materials Cataloger, cited in the New York Public Library website, "Celebrating the Centennial: The Tilden Library," dated August 25, 2011.

171, 182. to win his eighth race of the season; last of the field of five: *Krik's Guide to the Turf, Part I, 1878–79*. New York: H.G. Crickmore, 1879.

171. Parole was now "past his prime"; "the Yankee mule": Kent Hollingsworth, *The Great Ones*. Lexington, KY: The Blood-Horse, 1970, page 211.

171. "no great expectations"; "but wait till they see him extended": W. S. Vosburgh, *Cherry and Black, Career of Pierre Lorillard on the Turf*. Originally printed for Pierre Lorillard, Second Limited Edition, 1916, page 30.

172. English thoroughbreds of that era: Dennis Craig, *Horse-Racing: The Breeding of Thoroughbreds and a Short History of the English Turf*. London: J.A. Allen & Co., Ltd., 1963, page 150.

172. the leaders approached "the rails": "The Turf in England: New Market Craven Meeting: Newmarket Handicap: Mr. Pierre Lorillard's Parole the Winner," *Turf, Field and Farm*, April 18, 1879.

172. "in a cluster a hundred yards off": "Sporting News from England: How Parole Won the Newmarket Handicap," *New York Times*, April 18, 1879.

172. "a bolt of lightning from an undimmed sky"; generally [unfit] him for some days": "Parole: The Triple Winner of the Newmarket, City Suburban [*sic*] and Great Metrololitan Handicaps," *Spirit of the Times*, April 26, 1879, page 267.

172. "we breed something else than weeds in America": "Parole at Newmarket," *Turf, Field and Farm*, April 25, 1879.

172. this 'effete old country'": "Augur," in *The Sporting Life*, cited in "The London Press on Parole," *Turf, Field and Farm*, May 2, 1879.

172. a match race over the Newmarket course: "Parole Challenged by the Owner of Isonomy," *New Orleans Daily Democrat*, April 24, 1879.

172. had won the previous year's Cambridgeshire Handicap; won £40,000 wagering on the Cambridgeshire: Craig, Dennis, *Horse-Racing: The Breeding of Thoroughbreds and a Short History of the English Turf*. London: J.A. Allen & Co., Ltd., 1963, page 150.

172. engagements extending into the autumn": Untitled article regarding Parole, *New York Sun*, April 25, 1879.

172. Epsom's City and Suburban Handicap: "Another Victory for Parole: Mr. Lorillard's Horse Wins the City and Suburban Handicap at Epsom," *New York Times*, April 23, 1879.

172. to the tune of £20,000: From "The Vigilant" in the British sporting tabloid *Sporting Times*, quoted in "The London Press on Parole," *Turf, Field and Farm*, May 2, 1879, page 281.

173. a reserved three-quarters of a length: "A Third Victory for Parole: He Wins the Great Metropolitan Stakes at Epsom: Mr. Lorillard's Profits," *New York Times*, April 24, 1879.

173. "a second William the Conqueror":"Parole's English Triplet," *Spirit of the Times*, April 26, 1879.

173. Primrose "a bad third": "Racing on Epsom Downs," *New York Times*, May 31, 1879.

173. upheld by the stewards' review: Vosburgh, *Cherry and Black, Career of Pierre Lorillard on the Turf*, page 38.

174. regained the lead: Hollingsworth, *The Great Ones*, page 211.

174. retired during the 1882 season: Hollingsworth, *The Great Ones*, page 147.

174. His earnings of $82,816 topped all of history's runners: William H. P. Robertson, *History of Thoroughbred Racing in America*. New York: Bonanza, 1964, pages 125–126.

174. praises of the old gelding": Vosburgh, *Cherry and Black, Career of Pierre Lorillard on the Turf*, pages 33–34.

174. taken up by the lawn, [swell] to an ovation": Vosburgh, *Cherry and Black, Career of Pierre Lorillard on the Turf*, page 132.

174. he became ill prior to the event: "The Coming Horse Show: A Large Number of Entries of Fine Quality," *New York Times*, October 18, 1885.

174. he became ill prior to the event: "The National Horse Show: A Spirited Lot of Animals in Madison-Square Garden," *New York Times*, November 4, 1885.

175. the extraordinary equine age of thirty: "Parole Died at Tuxedo Park," *Thoroughbred Record*, January 3, 1903, page 7.

175. Hall of Fame at Saratoga Springs, New York, in 1984: National Museum of Racing—Hall of Fame, "Parole."

175, 176. earned a walkover in yet another race; and by the breakdown of Aristides: *Krik's Guide to the Turf, Part I, 1877–78*. New York: H.G. Crickmore, 1878.

175, 184. Ten Broeck's storybook career; So deir joy was drunk in juleps and rum: Hollingsworth, *The Great Ones*, page 271.

175, 185, 185. considered by some to be Ten Broeck's superior; the usual quota of mares"; what might have been accomplished: Untitled article about death of Ten Broeck, *Spirit of the Times*, July 2, 1887.

176. was entered as a pacesetter: "Ten Broeck: The Gallant Horse Wins Another Hotly Contested Race: Aristides and Bill Bass Not Placed," *St. Paul Daily Globe*, May 14, 1878.

176. departure from San Francisco: "The Mollie M'Carthy-Ten Broeck Race," *New York Times*, May 14, 1878.

176. and her arrival at Omaha on May 18; the mare remained "in excellent condition": "On Her Way To Meet Ten Broeck: Arrival at Omaha of the California Mare Mollie M'Carty: She Is Reported in Excellent Condition," *New York Times*, May 19, 1878.

176. well satisfied with his form": "Ten Broeck-Mollie McCarthy," *Turf, Field and Farm*, June 21, 1878, page 392.

176. eagerness to back the mare": "Ten Broeck," *Turf, Field and Farm*, June 21, 1878.

176. never liked him better"; "never better in her life": "The Ten Broeck-Mollie M'Carthy Match," *Kentucky Live Stock Record*, June 22, 1878.

176, 177. "the grandest race ever witnessed in America"; Kentucky's honor saved from any stain": "The Ten Broeck and Mollie McCarthy Match," *Kentucky Live Stock Record*, June 29, 1878, page 408.

176. between managers and contestants: World Wide Words, worldwidewords.org, "Hippodroming."

177. anything that would smack of legerdemain": "Mollie McCarthy and Ten Broeck," *Turf, Field and Farm*, June 28, 1878, page 409.

177, 177, 181. the sun beaming down with the greatest intensity"; carriage, horseback, rail and street car; unable to have run another heat": "The Great Four Mile Match," *Kentucky Live Stock Record*, July 6, 1878, page 8.

177, 181, 181, 182. would peak at a humid ninety-two degrees; continuing to allow Colston full access to the horse; settled the fact of the dosing beyond question"; near Ten Broeck before or after the race: "An Interview with F.B. Harper: Some Inconsistencies Worth Noting," *Kentucky Live Stock Record*, August 3, 1878.

177. nondescript two-year-olds, by Goodnight: "Louisville. Ten Broeck-Mollie McCarthy Match," *Spirit of the Times*, July 13, 1878.

177, 179. that needed no further muddling; over a poorly prepared track: "The Louisville Four-Mile Heat Race," *Spirit of the Times*, July 27, 1878, page 685.

177. completed his one-mile stroll; mounted stewards, police and stable-men": "The Louisville Summer Meeting," *Turf, Field and Farm*, July 12, 1878.

178, 179, 179. "went by the string like twin bullets"; such as was heard for miles, rent the air; "The mare's broken down!": "Ten Broeck Beats M'Carthy: An Exciting Race At Louisville The Kentucky Horse The Winner," *New York Times*, July 5, 1878.

178. knocked her out of the way: Edward Hotaling, *The Great Black Jockeys*. Rocklin, CA: Prima Publishing, 1999.

178, 178, 178, 179. "The colored boy who rode Ten Broeck; would [rather] be 100 miles from Louisville"; they would not believe but that the race was thrown; he hoped to wabble through with Ten Broeck in some shape": "The Ten Broeck-Mollie McCarthy Race: The Truth at Last," *Turf, Field and Farm*, July 26, 1878, page 54.

179. And I will help to do it": Hotaling, *The Great Black Jockeys*, page 236.

179. fall dead on the track: Col. Matt J. Winn, as told to Frank G. Menke, *Down the Stretch*. New York: Smith & Durrell, 1945, page 9.

180. "a mere hand gallop": "The Great Race," *The Vernon (AL) Pioneer*, July 19, 1878.

180, 180, 180, 180, 180, 181, 182, 182. the stewards would take no action; "The Great Turf Farce"; a minimal fee for the champion's services; Harper might somehow have been intimidated into this arrangement; never owned a racehorse in his life, a speculator; the public should not be swindled"; the best horse on the American continent"; its own shame and disgrace": "The Great Turf Farce," *Spirit of the Times*, July 13, 1878, page 628.

180. Victor shorn of glory": "Ten Broeck Wins," *Pulaski (TN) Citizen*, July 11, 1878.

180. "The Great Fiasco": "The Great Fiasco," *Daily Los Angeles Herald*, July 7, 1878.

180. a "Frightful Fraud": "Frightful Fraud," *Louisiana Democrat*, July 17, 1878.

180, 182. "lease the track again for $50,000"; run her at Baltimore this Fall: "Race Reflections," *Turf, Field and Farm*, July 12, 1878, page 25.

181. to the race in winning condition: "Harper's Horses," *Memphis Daily Appeal*, October 7, 1879.

181. "He offered to bet $1,000 to $10 on it": "The Ten Broeck-Mollie McCarthy Match," *Kentucky Live Stock Record*, July 13, 1878.

182. when a horse is fit to race": "The Abuse of J.W. Conley, and the Character of Ten Broeck as a Racehorse," *Kentucky Live Stock Record*, July 27, 1878.

182. winning both of her starts for Baldwin: *Krik's Guide to the Turf, Part 1, 1879–80*. New York: H.G. Crickmore, 1880, pages 62 and 234.

183. forgotten nor violated that promise": "Frank Harper Passes Away," *Louisville Courier-Journal*, April 5, 1905.

184. who ran against Ten Broeck": No headline, *Springfield (KY) Sun*, May 24, 1905.

185. a total of just eighty named foals: pedigreequery.com: Pedigree Online Thoroughbred Database—"Ten Broeck Offspring."

185. a Kentucky Oaks and an Alabama Stakes: Clio D. Hogan, *Index to Stakes Winners, 1865-1967*. Solvang, CA: Published under sponsorship of Flag Is Up Farms, 1968.

185. Deer Lodge Montana: "Death of the Famous Ten Broeck," *New North-West* (Deer Lodge, Montana), July 8, 1887.

185. *Middlebury (Vermont) Register*: "Death of Ten Broeck," *Middlebury (VT) Register*, July 22, 1887.

185. "national loss to the running turf": "Ten Broeck Dead. One of America's Best Horses Stricken With Paralysis," *New York Times*, June 29, 1887.

186. that noble and faithful animal—the horse: "Mourning for Ten Broeck," *New York Times*, July 10, 1887.

186. into its Hall of Fame in 1982: National Museum of Racing—Hall of Fame, "Ten Broeck."

186. following the Great Sweepstakes: *Krik's Guide to the Turf, Part I, 1877–78 and 1878–79*. New York: H.G. Crickmore, 1878 and 1879.

186. the only important horse of the era he had never defeated: "Tom Ochiltree vs. Ten Broeck," *Spirit of the Times*, December 1, 1877, page 477.

186. his $43,555 in career earnings: pedigreequery.com: Pedigree Online Thoroughbred Database—"Tom Ochiltree."

186, 187. earn unusual distinction on the turf"; the erstwhile "Big Tom" was known around the barn as "Old Tom": "Death of Tom Ochiltree," *Thoroughbred Record*, January 8, 1898.

187. and 1884 Juvenile winner Triton: Hogan, *Index to Stakes Winners, 1865-1967*, page 686.

187. "The Caliornia Wonder"; in the Golden State": www.tbheritage.com: "Mollie McCarty."

187. She won two minor races as a six-year-old: Information regarding the race records of Mollie McCarthy's foals was obtained from Goodwin's *Official Annual Turf Guide* for 1884 through 1889, New York: Goodwin Bros., Publishers.

187. digestive systems of large grazing animals: Dr. D. E. Salmon, *Special Report on Diseases of the Horse*. Washington, DC: Government Printing Office, 1896.

188. burst a blood vessel in training: Vosburgh, *Cherry and Black, Career of Pierre Lorillard on the Turf*, page 51.

188. be trained for long distances: Vosburgh, *Racing in America 1866–1921*, page 122.

188. could view the famous horse: "Grand Old Iroquois," *Washington, DC Evening Star*, September 25, 1899.

188. Pimlico and Monmouth Stakes: www.pedigreequery.com: Pedigree Online Thoroughbred Database—"Iroquois Pedigree and Offspring."

188. He was in no condition when he left England to race over a mile": Vosburgh, *Racing in America 1866–1921*, pages 122–123.

188. Tennessee's Belle Meade Stud: Vosburgh, *Cherry and Black, Career of Pierre Lorillard on the Turf*, page 138.

188. he paid $34,000 to keep the stallion; Iroquois died in 1899 at the age of twenty-one: "Old Iroquois Dead," *New York Times*, September 24, 1899.

188. his offspring earned $183,026 and won 145 races: John Hervey, S. Saunders, Charles L. Stanhope, Brig.-Gen. Sir Ormonde Winter, Harry Worcester Smith, G. H. Hilliard, and James T. Wallace, *Racing & Breeding in America and the Colonies*. London: The London & Counties Press Association Ltd, 1931, page 121.

188. he placed third on the list: "Iroquois: Death of this Famous Race Horse and Sire at Belle Meade," *Spirit of the Times*, September 30, 1899, page 270.

188. future Hall of Famer Henry of Navarre: Hogan, *Index to Stakes Winners, 1865–1967*, page 602.

188. the original Belle Meade Mansion grounds": www.pedigreequery.com: Pedigree Online Thoroughbred Database—"Iroquois."

188. made into cups, finely mounted: "Death of Iroquois," *Thoroughbred Record*, September 23, 1899, page 146.

188. on public display at Belle Meade: Amanda Stravinsky in www. tnvacation.com: Tennessee Triptales, "Colorful Stories Awaken Tennessee's Past at Belle Meade Plantation." www.tnvacation.com/triptales/colorful-stories-awaken-tennessees-past-at-belle-meade-plantation.

189. was retired to stud in 1924: "Playfellow Through as Racer: Will Go to Stud Next Month," *New York Times*, August 10, 1923.

189. the brilliance of his illustrious relation: In fact, Playfellow never won another race after the two that persuaded Sam Hildreth and Harry Sinclair to make their ill-fated $100,000 offer.

189. 106 registered runners, of which 29 won: *Sires of American Stakes Horses, 1926–*. Lexington, KY: BloodStock Research and Statistical Bureau, 1975.

189. the entire Playfellow ordeal; Playfellow's death at age twenty-five was announced in May of 1943: "Man o' War's Brother," *Blood-Horse*, May 22, 1943, page 669.

189. a personal groom, Will Harbutt: Joe Palmer, *This Was Racing*. New York: A.S. Barnes and Company, Inc., 1953, pages 71–73.

189. He indulged in no bargain, no intrigue": "Memoirs of Distinguished Kentucky Turfmen: John Harper," *Kentucky Live Stock Record*, July 23, 1875.

189, 190, 190. "from eend to eend"; rivets the public eye"; the declining years of Uncle John: "Reminiscences of the Turf: John Harper," *Thoroughbred Record*, June 22, 1929.

190. King of Stallions: Jonelle Fisher, *Nantura 1795–1905*. St. Crispian Press, 2004, page 153.

191. gradually gave up the life of the breeder; would not have been surprising"; estimated to be "at least $150,000": "Frank Harper Passes Away," *Louisville Courier-Journal,* April 5, 1905.

191. greatest turnouts of prominent horsemen ever seen here": "The Harper Funeral: One of the Greatest Turnouts of Horsemen Ever Seen in Lexington," *Richmond (KY) Climax,* April 12, 1905.

192. not remembered in his will": "The Turfman's Will Contested," *Bourbon News,* June 30, 1905.

192. awarded to the various litigants: "Harper Will Case: Order Entered Approving Probate In Accordance with Compromise," *Berea (KY) Citizen,* April 13, 1905.

192. "Master George"; "a liberal outlay of money":"The Islip Stable," *New York Times,* March 30, 1878.

192. if not in the country": "American Jockey Club. Statistics of the Late Meeting: George Lorillard Still at the Head," *New York Times,* June 14, 1880.

192. "the most popular turfman in the country"; to his trainer, R. Wyndham Walden: "The Westbrook Stables: George L. Lorillard's String of Twenty-Four Racers," *New York Times,* April 6, 1882.

193. President of the Monmouth Racing Association: "George Lorillard to Retire," *New York Times,* March 10, 1884.

193. the highest distinction within the gift of the people; an equal degree of popularity": Untitled article regarding the death of George Lorillard, *Spirit of the Times,* February 6, 1886, page 50.

193. one can only hope provided some relief; spent from $30,000 to $40,000 a year in assisting embarrassed friends": "George Lorillard's Death," *New York Times,* February 5, 1886.

194. the community a good citizen: "Death of George L. Lorillard," *Turf, Field and Farm,* February 12, 1886, page 113.

194. will be more missed from the turf: "Death of Mr. George L. Lorillard," *Kentucky Live Stock Record,* February 13, 1886.

194. Brooklyn's Greenwood Cemetery: "Funeral of George L. Lorillard," *New York Times,* April 18, 1886.

194. two daughters from an earlier marriage: "George Lorillard's Will," *Louisville Courier-Journal,* February 7, 1886.

194. "not up to the average in desirability": "Real Estate Selling Well," *New York Times,* November 16, 1887.

194. prices "far beyond anticipation": "Thoroughbreds at Auction," *New York Times,* August 19, 1888.

194. "considerably younger" than his new bride: "Mrs. Lorillard's Marriage," *New York Times*, February 13, 1889.

194. remains on the books more than a century later: Paula Prather, ed., *American Racing Manual, 2013*. New York: Daily Racing Form, 2013.

195. treated with great kindness in the press; at the age of eighty-five: "Nothing Venture," "Death of Mrs. Livingston," *Blood-Horse*, November 17, 1945.

195. relief from sickness and other forms of distress: "Mrs. Allien to Wed Clubman?," *New York Evening World*, December 11, 1902.

195. Her husband George passed away in 1931 at the age of seventy: "George Livingston," *New York Times*, March 10, 1931.

195. in the recent history of American business": "Harry F. Sinclair," *Blood-Horse*, November 17, 1956, page 1,343.

196, 207. among the nation's leaders in both 1952 and 1953; alternating with Whitney atop the ranking: *American Racing Manual, 1968 Edition*. New York: Triangle Publications, Inc., 1968.

196. which he had purchased in 1947: "Helis, Oil Leader, Horseman, Is Dead," *New York Times*, July 25, 1950.

196. which he had purchased in 1947: "William Helis, 63, Succumbs," *Los Angeles Times*, July 25, 1950.

196, 197, 197. the dreadful Long Island mosquitos; would marry Walden's daughter, Minnie; those days of limited racing and minuscule purses: Margaret Worrall, "Bowling Brook Remembered," *Maryland Horse*, March, 1987.

196. between 1878 and 1882: *Laurel and Pimlico 1996 Media Guide*.

197. He served as a director of the Maryland Jockey Club: "Turfman Walden Dead," *Washington (DC) Evening Star*, April 28, 1905.

197. for whom he trained until his death in 1905: "Death of R. W. Walden," *New York Times*, April 29, 1905.

197. removed them to the jockeys' room": "Santa Catalina Won Big Race on a Foul," *New York Times*, April 26, 1905.

197. taking the day's feature race at Jamaica: *Goodwin's Official Annual Turf Guide for 1905*. New York: Goodwin Bros., Publishers, 1906.

197. four inches beneath the kneepan": "Jockey Fuller Improving," *New York Times*, August 13, 1905.

197. walking with a limp, in May of 1906; "he has taken on weight fast": "Notes of the Thoroughbreds," *New York Times*, May 18, 1906.

198. whether or not a mistake has been made": "Paddock Paragraphs," *New York Tribune*, September 14, 1905.

198. miracles which are always happening in racing": "Spill in Excelsior," *New York Tribune*, April 26, 1905.

198. Thoroughbred Racing Hall of Fame in 1970: National Museum of Racing—Hall of Fame, "R.W. Walden."

198, 199. Lorillard jockeys Hughes, Fisher, and Barrett; to train the horses racing at home": Vosburgh, *Cherry and Black, Career of Pierre Lorillard on the Turf*, page 29.

199. engagement covering two hemispheres"; some of his races [as a two-year-old]; enshrouded in his unperishable tomb: James H. McCreery, "Jacob Pincus," *Thoroughbred Record*, May 4, 1918.

199, 200. it was a hasty act and an error"; "than the rest of my trainers put together sober": J.H.M., "The Late Wm. Brown and Parole," *Turf, Field and Farm*, March 28, 1903.

200. "galloping his horses to death": Vosburgh, *Cherry and Black, Career of Pierre Lorillard on the Turf*, pages 42 and 43.

200. Lorillard, Iroquois, Pincus, Archer, I salute ye": Vosburgh, *Cherry and Black, Career of Pierre Lorillard on the Turf*, page 42.

200. in the world of thoroughbred racing; when Pincus moved next to Rancocus: National Museum of Racing—Hall of Fame, "Jacob Pincus."

200. (or, according to one source, eighty-five) in 1918: www.horseracinghistory.co.uk shows Pincus as living to 80; www. racingmuseum.org shows his birth year as 1833 and his death in 1918.

201. "precluded a long tenure to his engagements": Vosburgh, *Cherry and Black, Career of Pierre Lorillard on the Turf*, page 70.

201. like Caesar being offered the crown": Vosburgh, *Cherry and Black, Career of Pierre Lorillard on the Turf*, page 73.

201. four races in one day at Jerome Park: *Krik's Guide to the Turf, Part I, 1881-82.* New York: H.G. Crickmore, 1882, pages 286 and 287.

201. every important race for her age and gender: Vosburgh, *Cherry and Black, Career of Pierre Lorillard on the Turf*, page 74.

201. done harm to Pizarro: Vosburgh, *Cherry and Black, Career of Pierre Lorillard on the Turf*, page 76.

201, 202. the best horse he ever saw; primarily in Argentina: "Death Comes to Matthew Byrnes," *Thoroughbred Record*, March 25, 1933.

202. during racing's nearly forgotten past: National Museum of Racing—Hall of Fame, "Matthew Byrnes."

202, 203, 203, 203. rejected this arrangement prior to the race; that Irish King might win; Colston filed suit; Colston has the pole: "Editorial Notes," *Spirit of the Times*, October 11, 1879, page 252.

203. for a purse of $700: All information regarding Irish King's ownership and race performances is to be found in the various *Krik's Guides* for the years in question.

203. Colston was offered $3,000 for the colt: "Horse Talk," *Kentucky Gazette*, October 25, 1879.

204. the man for whom Jerome Park was named: Wikipedia, "Leonard Jerome."

205. As a trainer he had no equal anywhere": A renowned figure in the sporting world, Hildreth's final illness, surgery, and passing were covered extensively in both the national media and the racing press. Examples are: "Death Claims Samuel C. Hildreth," *Thoroughbred Record*, September 28, 1929, page 195; "Samuel Clay Hildreth," *Blood-Horse*, October 5, 1929, page 12; "Samuel C. Hildreth III," *New York Times*, September 23, 1929; "Trainer Hildreth Is Operated Upon," *New York Times*, September 24, 1929; "Sam Hildreth, 63, Turf Veteran, Dies," *New York Times*, September 25, 1929; "A Famous Horseman," *The New York Times*, September 25, 1929; "Sinclair Pays Tribute," *New York Times*, September 25, 1929; John Kieran, "Sports of the Times," *New York Times*, September 25, 1929; and "Hildreth Honored by Racing World," *New York Times*, September 27, 1929.

206. a member of the initial class of internees; National Museum of Racing—Hall of Fame, "Samuel C. Hildreth."

206. Sysonby, and Whisk Broom II: *Daily Racing Form, The Champions, Revised Edition, Champions from 1893–2004*. New York: Daily Racing Form LLC, 2005, pages 1–40; also National Museum of Racing—Hall of Fame, "James Rowe."

206. that great runner's disastrous final start: National Museum of Racing—Hall of Fame, "James G. Rowe Sr."

206. vitality, and wonderful physique: "Mars Cassidy," *Blood-Horse*, November 2, 1929, page 13.

207. on a program of seven events"; Man o' War had passed his final rival: "Sanford Memorial Is Won by Upset," *New York Times*, August 14, 1919.

207. "Start, poor and slow": *Daily Racing Form* official chart for Sanford Memorial Stakes, August 13, 1919.

207. Zev in 1923, and Flying Ebony in 1925: Churchill Downs, *One Hundred Twenty-Second Kentucky Derby, Saturday, May 4, 1996 (Kentucky Derby Press Guide)*, published 1996.

207. led the nation annually in number of races won; if not, there would be no charge: "J.E. Madden Dies: Was Noted Turfman," *New York Times*, November 4, 1929.

207. "the Wizard of the Turf": Hollingsworth, *The Great Ones*, page 125.

208. described at the time as a "cyclonic charge": James Robert Saunders and Monica Renae Saunders, *Black Winning Jockeys in the Kentucky Derby*. Jefferson, NC: McFarland & Co., 2003.

208. "That boy is the best in the country"; retiring with both money in his pockets; debates which might be in progress": Ben H. "Buck" Weaver, "The Passing of 'Uncle Bill,'" *Turf and Sport Digest*, December 1933, pages 38, 39, 86.

209. is nowhere to be found: "Roamer," "Negro Jockeys Rare Nowadays on Metropolitan Tracks: Many of Earlier Top Riders Were Colored Lads: Murphy One of Best," *Thoroughbred Record*, May 22, 1943, page 393.

209. the pioneering jockey's final resting place: Churchill Downs, *124th Kentucky Derby, Saturday, May 2, 1998 (Kentucky Derby Press Guide)*, published 1998.

209. winning a $400 purse race in his return to the track: *Krik's Guide to the Turf, Part I, 1878–79*. New York: H.G. Crickmore, 1879, and *Krik's Guide to the Turf, Part I, 1879–80*. New York: H.G. Crickmore, 1880.

209. when he misjudged the finish line: "Vigilant," *Famous American Jockeys*, published by Richard A. Saalfield for *Spirit of the Times*, New York, page 4.

209. 136 victories in "approximately 490" races: National Museum of Racing—Hall of Fame, "George Barbee."

210. the horses under his care are in good condition: "Turf Notes," *New York Times*, April 28, 1884.

210. winning 42 races in 232 starts; the powerful Fred Taral: Goodwin's *Official Annual Turf Guide* for 1890, New York: Goodwin Bros., Publishers, 1890, page clxxxi, and Goodwin's *Official Annual Turf Guide* for 1891, New York: Goodwin Bros., Publishers, 1891, page clxviii.

210. Barbee, on Rowell's complaint, was ordered off the grounds": "Notes from the Racetrack," *New York Times*, September 2, 1903.

210. Sergeant Kerlin went about remedying the oversight: Kent Baker, "Hall of Fame Push On for Rider of 1st Preakness Winner," *Baltimore Sun*, May 18, 1995.

210. much of the documentation from Barbee's racing days: Frederick N. Rasmussen, "Much Was Lost in the Great Pimlico Fire of 1966," *Baltimore Sun*, July 20, 2002.

211. one of racing's leading reinsmen: Judy L. Marchman, "People: Getting His Due," *Blood-Horse*, May 25, 1996.

211. William Barrett: Much of the information in this section and in Appendix B is based on two long articles published about Barrett at the time of his death: "Death of the American Jockey, Barrett," *Turf, Field and Farm*, January 12, 1883; and "The Late Wm. Barrett, Jockey," *New York Sportsman*, January 13, 1883. Other sources in these sections are cited in specific footnotes.

APPENDIX A

212. fifth race at Tijuana, February 22, 1925: *Daily Racing Form* official chart for the fifth race at Tijuana, February 22, 1925.

212. was on the books for nearly seven years: With two exceptions, the time records discussed in Appendix A have been authenticated against the appropriate edition of the *Goodman's Annual Official Turf Guide*, New York: Goodman Bros., Publishers, 1884 through 1890 editions, all of which provide tabular listings of the existing time records. The exceptions were (1) Worthman's shattering of Ten Broeck's 2⅝-mile record in 1925, for which abundant information is available in the racing press, and (2) Lida Stanhope's 1⅝-mile record, which occurred prior to the *Goodman's* guides.

The author has searched through the *Krik's Guides*, which for the most part do not provide tabular listings of time records, for the period between the establishment of Ten Broeck's 1876 record and Lida Stanhope's 1882 date with destiny, and found no three-mile races run in faster times. There were few three-mile races contested at all during this period: six in 1877, six in 1878, four in 1879, six in 1880, four in 1881, and seven in 1882.

213. forever from racing's record book: "50-Year-Old Record Broken at Tijuana," *New York Times*, February 23, 1925.

213. and has never been seen since: *The American Racing Manual for the Year 1925* and *The American Racing Manual for the Year 1926*. Ten Broeck's 2⅝-mile record of 4:58½ stood from September 16, 1876, until broken by Worthman, under 101 pounds, at Tijuana, Mexico, February 22, 1925 (4:51⅖).

213. and has never been seen since: Data for the following paragraphs are credited to *The American Racing Manual*, now published by the Daily Racing Form Press, for the years 1925, 1926, 1927, 1928, 1930, 1945, 1980, 1994, 1996, 2000 (page 851), 2001 (page 867), and 2013 (pages 744 and 909).

APPENDIX B

218, 224, 224. The *New York Sportsman*, January 13, 1883; "Courageous to the last"; any sum sent to us for the purpose: "The Late Wm. Barrett, Jockey," *New York Sportsman*, January 18, 1883, page 18.

218. steward of the English Jockey Club: Thomas Henry Bird, *Admiral Rous and the English Turf, 1795–1877*. London: Putnam, 1939.

219. listing of the year's leading riders: "Winning Jockeys of 1877," *Turf, Field and Farm*, December 7, 1877.

220. unsanitary and decidedly unpleasant effluvium: Katherine C. Mooney, *Race Horse Men*. Cambridge, MA, Harvard University Press, 2014, pages 43 and 44.

220. the winning and runner-up thoroughbreds: Both race charts from *Krik's Guide to the Turf, Part I, 1877–1878*. New York: H.G. Crickmore, Publisher, 1878.

223. It is dangerous": "The Racing Season of 1892," *New York Sun*, October 17, 1892.

223, 224. lest the patient may never recover from the collapse"; agents that caused blistering of the skin: F. Rilliet and E. Bartez, M.M., *A Treatise on the Pneumonia of Children*. Philadelphia: Carey & Hart, 1841, pages 52–64.

224. seem still further to limit the utility of bloodletting: P. C. A. Louis, M.D., *Researches on the Effects of Bloodletting in Some Inflammatory Diseases Together with Researches on Phthisis*. Boston: Hilliard, Gray & Company, 1836, pages 2–14.

224. uninfluenced in any way by medicine: Scott H. Podolsky, *Pneumonia Before Antibiotics: Therapeutic Evolution and Evaluation in Twentieth-Century America*. Baltimore: Johns Hopkins University Press, 2006, page 4.

APPENDIX C

225. Kent Hollingsworth, *The Great Ones*: Kent Hollingsworth, *The Great Ones*. The Blood-Horse, 1970, page 233.

225. the richest race of the era: David Alexander, *A Sound of Horses*. New York: The Bobbs-Merrill Company, Inc., 1966, pages 114–117.

225, 226, 226. a privileged family in Albany, New York; Ten Broeck fled south to avoid prosecution; into the track's purse structure: William H. P. Robertson, *The History of Thoroughbred Racing in America*. New York: Bonanza, 1964, pages 69–77.

226. throw in his hand without drawing a card": Robertson, *The History of Thoroughbred Racing in America*, pages 69–70.

226. among the most populous cities in the growing United States: Wikipedia, "Largest Cities in the United States by Population by Decade: 1840." The top five were: (1) New York, 312,710; (2) Baltimore, 102,313; (3) New Orleans, 102,193; (4) Philadelphia, 93,665; (5) Boston, 93,383.

226. Ten Broeck was promoting at Metarie: Hollingsworth, *The Great Ones*, page 170.

227. could not see him clearly: Alexander, *A Sound of Horses*, page 116.

227. some 6¼ seconds faster than Lecomte's time: Both Robertson's book and Hollingsworth's were immensely helpful in reconstructing Lexington's epic four-mile run.

227. [t]he most brilliant event in the sporting annals of the American turf": Quoted from *New Orleans Picayune*, April 3, 1855, in Longrigg, *The History of Horse Racing*, page 215.

228. Lexington was declared the winner: Peter Willett, *The Thoroughbred*. New York: G.P. Putnam's Sons, 1970, page 156.

228. damaged when he raided the farm's food supplies; just down the road from Woodburn; who would one day race Mollie McCarthy against Ten Broeck's namesake thoroughbred—for $15,001: Hollingsworth, *The Great Ones*, page 172.

228. Ten Broeck reportedly cashing a £10 wager at 100-to-1 odds: Hollingsworth, *The Great Ones*, page 233.

229. he was bordering on insanity: "Richard Ten Broeck Dead," *San Francisco Morning Call*, August 2, 1892.

230. He was a fourteen-year-old enlistee in the Texas Rangers: "The Late Col. Ochiltree," *Alexandria (VA) Gazette*, November 27, 1902.

230, 230, 231. nominated John C. Breckenridge for a presidential run; Northern Virginia, New Mexico, Louisiana, and Arkansas; because the project lacked investors: HistoricTexas.net, "Ochiltree, Thomas P—Col."

230, 231, 232. T.P. Ochiltree and Father, Counselors and Attorneys at Law; I will accept the same terms as General Lee"; all those articles were headed 'Ochiltree Wins'": "Incidents in the Career of 'Tom' Ochiltree": *New York Tribune*, November 30, 1902.

230. many hundreds more after a hearty meal": Claude H. Hall, "The Fabulous Tom Ochiltree: Promoter, Politician, and Raconteur," *Southwest Historical Quarterly*, January, 1968, page 347.

230. Ochiltree tried various occupations: His flurry of postwar employment is covered in a number of sources, each depicting a slightly different succession of working situations. The reader is referred to: The Handbook of Texas Online, "Ochiltree, Thomas Peck"; HistoricTexas.net, "Col. Thomas P. Ochiltree"; Infoplease, "Ochiltree, Thomas Peck (1837–1902)"; and "Col. T.P. Ochiltree Dead," *New York Times*, November 26, 1902. Suffice it to say, as does Hall in "The Fabulous Tom Ochiltree," that settling down after four years of war proved an almost impossible challenge for Ochiltree. We see much of the same today in young people returning from war.

231. regaling his listeners with the glories of the Lone Star State: Hall, "The Fabulous Tom Ochiltree: Promoter, Politician, and Raconteur," *Southwest Historical Quarterly*, January, 1968, page 355.

231. bond salesman, immigration agent: Hall, "The Fabulous Tom Ochiltree: Promoter, Politician, and Raconteur," page 358.

231. the finest rhetoric of Daniel Webster: Hall, "The Fabulous Tom Ochiltree: Promoter, Politician, and Raconteur," pages 358 and 359.

232. He is a race horse that John Chamberlain named after me: "Stories of Tom Ochiltree," *Salt Lake (UT) Herald*, December 21, 1902.

232. "Tom enjoyed a good life": Hall, "The Fabulous Tom Ochiltree: Promoter, Politician, and Raconteur," pages 359 and 360.

232, 233. Eagle Pass on the Rio Grande"; "funnier than the minstrels": "Col. Ochiltree Dead," *Washington (DC) Evening Star*, November 26, 1902.

232, 233. the special candidate of certain Galveston interests"; the material welfare of the district: "Major Tom Ochiltree's Victory," *New York Times*, November 16, 1882.

233. keep his name before Texas and the public: Hall, "The Fabulous Tom Ochiltree: Promoter, Politician, and Raconteur," page 364.

233. a welcome addition to every gathering"; simple logic would have failed": "Col. T.P. Ochiltree Dead," *New York Times*, November 26, 1902.

233. "The Prince of Good Fellows": "Colonel Ochiltree Dead," *Princeton (MN) Union*, November 27, 1902.

234. Ochiltree had long since moved on to other interests: Hall, "The Fabulous Tom Ochiltree: Promoter, Politician, and Raconteur," pages 365 and 366.

234. no horse named after him can ever be beaten: "Ten Broeck Tumbles," *Louisville Courier-Journal*, October 25, 1877.

234. Here LIES Tom Ochiltree—All he ever did!: Hall, "The Fabulous Tom Ochiltree: Promoter, Politician, and Raconteur," page 370.

235. sweep all disagreeable impressions of him to the four winds": Hall, "The Fabulous Tom Ochiltree: Promoter, Politician, and Raconteur," page 347.

235. 'Colonel Tom,' based on his life, appeared on Broadway: Hall, "The Fabulous Tom Ochiltree: Promoter, Politician, and Raconteur," page 348.

235. between 1865 and 1902: Hall, "The Fabulous Tom Ochiltree: Promoter, Politician, and Raconteur," page 371.

236. "Tom Ochiltree is also from our State," I said: O. Henry (William Sydney Porter) in Literaturecollection.com, "A Snapshot at the President."

236. the advice of the best-known doctors; and his correspondence of seven decades: Hall, "The Fabulous Tom Ochiltree: Promoter, Politician, and Raconteur," page 373.

236. before debarking the ship: Hall, "The Fabulous Tom Ochiltree: Promoter, Politician, and Raconteur," page 374.

236. in a warmer climate: Handbook of Texas Online: "Ochiltree, Thomas Peck."

236. One of the Best: "Funeral of Col. Ochiltree," *Washington (DC) Evening Star*, December 1, 1902.

236. to represent that great state: Hall, "The Fabulous Tom Ochiltree: Promoter, Politician, and Raconteur," page 376.

237. Lorillard Tobacco Company: Maxwell Fox, *The Lorillard Story*. Published as an in-house organ of the Lorillard Corporation, 1947, page 32.

APPENDIX D

238. Excerpt from *The Congressional Record*, Tuesday, October 23, 1877: *Congressional Record, October 23, 1877*. Washington, DC: Government Printing Office, 1877.

239. Excerpt from *The Congressional Record,* Wednesday, October 24, 1877: *Congressional Record, October 24, 1877.* Washington, DC: Government Printing Office, 1877.

239. Excerpt from the *Journal of the House of Representatives of the United States,* October 24, 1877: *Journal of the House of Representatives of the United States, October 24, 1877.* Washington, DC: Government Printing Office, 1877.

ACKNOWLEDGMENTS

241. Bernard of Chartres, 1159: www.iwise.com/OhFUj.

BIBLIOGRAPHY

BOOKS

Adams, James Truslow, *History of the United States Volume III, War and Reconstruction*. New York: Charles Scribner's Sons, 1933.

Alexander, David. *A Sound of Horses*. New York: The Bobbs-Merrill Company, Inc., 1966.

American Produce Records, 1930–1984, Bloodstock Research Information Services, Inc., 1985.

American Racing Calendar of 1876. New York: *Turf, Field and Farm*, 1876.

American Racing Manual, 1925 Edition. New York: Triangle Publications, 1926.

American Racing Manual, 1926 Edition. New York: Triangle Publications, 1927.

American Racing Manual, 1927 Edition. New York: Triangle Publications, 1928.

American Racing Manual, 1928 Edition. New York: Triangle Publications, 1929.

American Racing Manual, 1930 Edition. New York: Triangle Publications, 1931.

American Racing Manual, 1944 Edition. New York: Triangle Publications, Inc., 1945.

American Racing Manual, 1945 Edition. New York: Triangle Publications, 1946.

American Racing Manual, 1968 Edition. New York: Triangle Publications, 1969.

American Racing Manual, 1980 Edition. New York: Triangle Publications, 1981.

American Racing Manual, 1994 Edition. New York: Triangle Publications, 1995.

American Racing Manual, 1996 Edition. New York: Triangle Publications, 1997.

American Racing Manual, 2000 Edition. New York: Daily Racing Form Press, 2001.

American Racing Manual, 2001 Edition. New York: Daily Racing Form Press, 2002.

American Racing Manual, 2002 Edition. New York: Triangle Publications, 2003.

American Racing Manual, 2003 Edition. New York: Triangle Publications, 2004.

American Racing Manual, 2013 Edition. New York: Daily Racing Form Press, 2014.

Bird, Thomas Henry, *Admiral Rous and the English Turf, 1795–1877*. London: Putnam, 1939.

Burns, Rex, *Success in America: The Yeoman Dream and the Industrial Revolution*. University of Massachusetts Press, 1976.

Churchill Downs, *One Hundred Twenty-Second Kentucky Derby, Saturday, May 4, 1996 (Kentucky Derby Press Guide)*. Published 1996.

Churchill Downs, *124th Kentucky Derby, Saturday, May 2, 1998 (Kentucky Derby Press Guide)*. Published 1998.

Clark, Thomas D., *A History of Kentucky*. Ashland, KY: The Jesse Stuart Foundation, 1998.

Commager, Henry Steele, editor, *Documents of American History, Ninth Edition*. Englewood Cliffs, NJ: Prentice-Hall, Inc., 1973.

Congressional Record, October 23, 1877. Washington, DC: Government Printing Office, 1877.

Congressional Record, October 24, 1877. Washington, DC: Government Printing Office, 1877.

Craig, Dennis, *Horse-Racing: The Breeding of Thoroughbreds and a Short History of the English Turf.* London: J.A. Allen & Co., Ltd., 1963.

Daily Racing Form, The Champions, Revised Edition, Champions from 1893–2004. New York: Daily Racing Form LLC, 2005.

Dean, John, *Warren G. Harding.* New York: Times Books, Henry Holt and Company, 2004.

Downey, Fairfax, *Lorillard and Tobacco.* P. Lorillard Company, 1951.

Eckenrode, H. J., *Rutherford B. Hayes: Statesman of Reunion.* New York: Dodd, Mead & Company, 1930.

Ferrell, Robert H., *The Strange Deaths of President Harding.* Columbia, MO: University of Missouri Press, 1996.

Fisher, Jonelle, *Nantura 1795–1905.* St. Crispian Press, 2004.

Flick, Alexander Clarence, *Samuel Jones Tilden.* Port Washington, NY: Kennikat Press of Kansas, 1988.

Foner, Eric, *Reconstruction: America's Unfinished Revolution.* New York: Perennial Classics, 1988.

Fox, Maxwell, *The Lorillard Story.* P. Lorillard Company, 1947.

Goodwin's Official Annual Turf Guide for 1884. New York: Goodwin Bros., Publishers, 1884.

Goodwin's Official Annual Turf Guide for 1885. New York: Goodwin Bros., Publishers, 1885.

Goodwin's Official Annual Turf Guide for 1886. New York: Goodwin Bros., Publishers, 1886.

Goodwin's Official Annual Turf Guide for 1887. New York: Goodwin Bros., Publishers, 1887.

Goodwin's Official Annual Turf Guide for 1888. New York: Goodwin Bros., Publishers, 1888.

Goodwin's Official Annual Turf Guide for 1889. New York: Goodwin Bros., Publishers, 1889.

Goodwin's Official Annual Turf Guide for 1890. New York: Goodwin Bros., Publishers, 1890.

Goodwin's Official Annual Turf Guide for 1891. New York: Goodwin Bros., Publishers, 1891.

Goodwin's Official Annual Turf Guide for 1905. New York: Goodwin Bros., Publishers, 1906.

Goodwin's Official Annual Turf Guide for 1906. New York: Goodwin Bros., Publishers, 1907.

Hervey, John, *Racing in America, 1923–1936.* New York: Privately printed by the Jockey Club, 1937.

Hervey, John, S. Saunders, Charles L. Stanhope, Brig.-Gen. Sir Ormonde Winter, Harry Worcester Smith, G. H. Hilliard, and James T. Wallace, *Racing & Breeding in*

America and the Colonies. London: The London & Counties Press Association Ltd, 1931.

Hildreth, Samuel C., and James R. Crowell, *The Spell of the Turf.* Philadelphia: J.P. Lippincott Company, 1926.

Hogan, Clio D., *Index to Stakes Winners, 1865–1967.* Solvang, CA: Published under sponsorship of Flag Is Up Farms, 1968.

Hollingsworth, Kent, *The Great Ones.* Lexington, KY: The Blood-Horse, 1970.

Hollingsworth, Kent, *The Kentucky Thoroughbred.* Lexington, KY: The University Press of Kentucky, 2009.

Hoogenboom, Ari, *The Presidency of Rutherford B. Hayes.* Lawrence, KS: The University Press of Kansas, 1988.

Hotaling, Edward, *The Great Black Jockeys.* Rocklin, CA: Prima Publishing, 1999.

Johannsen, Robert W., editor, *Reconstruction: 1867–1877.* London: The Free Press, New York, 1970.

Journal of the House of Representatives of the United States, October 24, 1877. Washington, DC: Government Printing Office, 1877.

Kahn, Cynthia M., B.A., M.A., editor, *The Merck Veterinary Manual, Ninth Edition.* Whitehouse Station, NJ, 2005.

Kane, Joseph Nathan, *Facts About the Presidents.* New York: Permabooks, 1960.

Kobluk, Calvin N., B.S.C., B .S.A., D.V.M., D.V. Sc.; Trevor R. Ames, D.V.M., M.S.; Raymond J. Geor, B.V. Sc., M.V. Sc., *The Horse: Diseases & Clinical Management.* Philadelphia: W.B. Saunders Company.

Krik's Guide to the Turf, Part I, 1875–76. New York: H.G. Crickmore, 1876.

Krik's Guide to the Turf, Part I, 1876–77. New York: H.G. Crickmore, 1877.

Krik's Guide to the Turf, Part I, 1877–78. New York: H.G. Crickmore, 1878.

Krik's Guide to the Turf, Part I, 1878–79. New York: H.G. Crickmore, 1879.

Krik's Guide to the Turf, Part I, 1879–80. New York: H.G. Crickmore, 1880.

Krik's Guide to the Turf, Part I, 1880–81. New York: H.G. Crickmore, 1881.

Krik's Guide to the Turf, Part I, 1881–82. New York: H.G. Crickmore, 1882.

Krik's Guide to the Turf, Part I, 1882–83. New York: H.G. Crickmore, 1883.

Krik's Guide to the Turf, Part 1, 1883–84. New York: H.G. Crickmore, 1884.

Laurel and Pimlico 1996 Media Guide.

Longrigg, Roger, *The History of Horse Racing.* New York: Stein and Day, 1972.

Louis, P.C.A., M.D., *Researches on the Effects of Bloodletting in Some Inflammatory Diseases Together with Researches on Phthisis.* Boston: Hilliard, Gray & Company, 1836.

McCammon, Holly J., *The U.S. Women's Jury Movements and Strategic Adaptation: A More Just Verdict.* Cambridge: Cambridge University Press, 2012.

McCartney, Laton, *The Teapot Dome Scandal.* New York: Random House, 2008.

Mooney, Katherine C., *Race Horse Men.* Cambridge, MA: Harvard University Press, 2014.

Morris, John Wesley, *Ghost Towns of Oklahoma.* Norman: University of Oklahoma Press, 1977.

Oxford English Dictionary, Second Edition. Oxford: Clarendon Press, 1989.

P. Lorillard Company, *Lorillard and Tobacco: 200th Anniversary 1760–1960.* Published by P. Lorillard Company, c. 1960.

Palmer, Joe, *This Was Racing*. New York: A.S. Barnes and Company, Inc., 1953. *Pimlico Press Book*, 1967.

Podolsky, Scott H., *Pneumonia Before Antibiotics: Therapeutic Evolution and Evaluation in Twentieth-Century America*. Baltimore: Johns Hopkins University Press, 2006.

Prather, Paula, editor. *American Racing Manual, 2013*. New York: Daily Racing Form, 2013.

Railey, William E., *History of Woodford County, Kentucky*. Frankfort, KY, 1938; reprinted Baltimore, MD: Clearfield Company, Inc., 2002.

Randall, J. G., and David Donald, *The Civil War and Reconstruction*. Boston: D.C. Heath and Company, 1961.

Ransom, J. H., *Who's Who in Horsedom, Volume VIII: The 400 of the Sport of Kings*. Lexington, KY: The Ransom Publishing Company, Inc., 1956.

Reeve, Moira C., and Sharon Biggs, *The Original Horse Bible*. Irvine, CA: Bowtie Press, 1966.

Rehnquist, William H., *Centennial Crisis: The Disputed Election of 1876*. New York: Random House Books, 2004.

Rilliet, F., and Bartez, E., M.M., *A Treatise on the Pneumonia of Children*. Philadelphia: Carey & Hart, 1841.

Robertson, William H. P., *History of Thoroughbred Racing in America*. New York: Bonanza, 1964.

Robinson, Lloyd, *The Stolen Election: Hayes vs. Tilden—1876*. New York: A Tom Doherty Associates Book, 1968.

Roland, Charles P., in *The Civil War in Kentucky*, Kent Masterson Brown, editor. Mason City, IA: Savas Publishing Company, 2000.

Ruff's Guide to the Turf, 1878 Spring Edition. London: Office of "Ruff's Guide," 1878.

Ruff's Guide to the Turf, 1879 Spring Edition. London: Office of "Ruff's Guide," 1880.

Ruff's Guide to the Turf, 1880 Spring Edition. London: Office of "Ruff's Guide," 1881.

Ruff's Guide to the Turf, 1881 Spring Edition. London: Office of "Ruff's Guide," 1882.

Salmon, D. E., *Special Report on Diseases of the Horse*. Washington, DC: Government Printing Office, 1896.

Saunders, James Robert, and Monica Renae Saunders, *Black Winning Jockeys in the Kentucky Derby*. Jefferson, NC: McFarland & Co., 2003.

Sires of American Stakes Horses, 1926–. Lexington, KY: BloodStock Research and Statistical Bureau, 1975.

Smith, Carter, *Presidents: Every Question Answered*. New York: Hylas Publishing, 2004.

Tilden, Samuel Jones, *Letters and Literary Memorials of Samuel J. Tilden, Volume 1*. University of California Libraries, 1908 (online edition).

Trefousse, Hans L., *Rutherford B. Hayes*. New York: Times Books, Henry Holt and Company, LLC, 2002.

United States Government Printing Office, *Biographical Directory of the United States Congress, 1774–2005*. Washington, DC: United States Government Printing Office, 2005.

Vaughn, Harold Cecil, *The Hayes-Tilden Election of 1876: A Disputed Presidential Election in the Gilded Age*. New York: Franklin Watts, Inc., 1972.

Veblen, Thorstein, *The Theory of the Leisure Class*. Boston: Houton Mifflin Company, 1973.

"Vigilant," *Famous American Jockeys*, published by Richard A. Saalfield for *Spirit of the Times*, New York, c. 1884.

Vosburgh, W. S., *Cherry and Black, Career of Pierre Lorillard on the Turf.* Originally printed for Pierre Lorillard, Second Limited Edition, 1916.

Vosburgh, W. S., *Racing in America 1866–1921*. New York: The Jockey Club, 1922.

Walburga, Lady Paget, editor, *Colloquies with an Unseen Friend*. London: Philip Wellby, Publisher, 1907.

Wall, Col. John F., *Famous Running Horses, Their Forebears and Descendants*. Washington, DC: Infantry Journal Press, 1949.

Watson's Racing Guide, Annual Edition, 1875–76. New York: James Watson, 1876.

Weeks, Lyman Horace, *The American Turf: An Historical Account of Racing in the United States with Biographical Sketches of Turf Celebrities*. New York: The Historical Company, 1898.

West, Geoffrey P., M.R.C.V.S., *Black's Veterinary Dictionary, Fourteenth Edition*. Totowa, NJ: Barnes & Noble Books, 1982.

Willett, Peter, *The Thoroughbred*. New York: G. Putnam's Sons, 1970.

Winn, Col. Matt J., as told to Frank G. Menke, *Down the Stretch*. New York: Smith & Durrell, 1945.

Zeh, Lucy, *Etched In Stone: Thoroughbred Memorials*. Lexington, KY: The Blood-Horse, Inc., 2000.

WEBSITES

Coblentz, Kathie, Rare Materials Cataloger, cited in the New York Public Library website, "Celebrating the Centennial: The Tilden Library," dated August 25, 2011. www.nypl.org/blog/2011/08/25/my-centennial-post-tilden-library.

Conway, Terry, ESPN.com, "The Great Sweepstakes at Pimlico." http://sports.espn.go.com/sports/horse/triplecrown2010/news/story?id=5142451.

CivilWarHome.com, "The Price in Blood! Casualties in the Civil War." www.civilwarhome.com/casualties.htm.

"Congresswomen's Biographies," Women in Congress. http://history.house.gov/Exhibitions-and-Publications/WIC/Women-in-Congress.

The DaveManual website was utilized in all calculations of equivalent dollar values expressed in this book. www.davemanuel.com/inflation-calculator-php.

Encyclopaedia Brittanica Online, "Bright [*sic*] Disease." www.britannica.com/EBchecked/topic/19572/Bright-Disease.

Hacker, J. David, International *New York Times* website, "Opinionator: Recounting the Dead." http://opinionator.blogs.nytimes.com/author/j-david-hacker/?_r=0.

Handbook of Texas Online, "Ochiltree, Thomas Peck." www.tsha.utexas.edu/handbook/online/articles/OO/focl.html.

Henry, O. (William Sydney Porter), Literaturecollection.com, *A Snapshot at the President*. www.literaturecollection.com/a/o_henry/131.

HistoricTexas.net, "Ochiltree, Thomas P.–Col." www.historictexas.net/bios/2o/ochiltree-thomas-p-col.html.

Horseracing History Online, "Person Profile—Jacob Pincus." www.horseracinghistory.co.uk/hrho/action/viewDocument?id=1218.

Infoplease, "Ochiltree, Thomas Peck (1837–1902)." www.infoplease.com/biography/us/congress/ochiltree-thomas-peck.html.

Iwise, "Bernard of Chartres." www.iwise.com/OhFUj.

The Jockey Club, "History of the Jockey Club." www.jockeyclub.com/Default.asp?section=About&area=0.

Medscape.com, "Uremia." http://emedicine.medscape.com/article/245296-overview.

Menard, John Willis, "Speech Before the United States House of Representatives" (1969), BlackPast.org. www.blackpast.org/1869-john-willis-menard-speech-united-states-house-representatives.

National Museum of Racing—Hall of Fame, "Duke of Magenta." www.racingmuseum.org/hall-of-fame/duke-magenta.

National Museum of Racing—Hall of Fame, "George Barbee." www/racingmuseum.org/hall-of-fame/george-barbee.

National Museum of Racing—Hall of Fame, "Jacob Pincus." www/racingmuseum.org/hall-of-fame/jacob-pincus-0.

National Museum of Racing—Hall of Fame, "James G. Rowe Sr." www.racingmuseum.org/hall-of-fame/james-g-rowe-sr.

National Museum of Racing—Hall of Fame, "Longfellow." www.racingmuseum.org/hall-of-fame/longfellow.

National Museum of Racing—Hall of Fame, "Matthew Byrnes." www.racingmuseum.org/hall-of-fame/matthew-byrnes.

National Museum of Racing—Hall of Fame, "Parole." www.racingmuseum.org/hall-of-fame/parole.

National Museum of Racing—Hall of Fame, "R.W. Walden." www.racingmuseum.org/hall-of-fame/r-w-walden.

National Museum of Racing—Hall of Fame, "Samuel C. Hildreth." www.racingmuseum.org/hall-of-fame/samuel-c-hildreth.

National Museum of Racing—Hall of Fame, "Ten Broeck." www.racingmuseum.org/hall-of-fame/ten-broeck.

New York City, "Historical Homes and Mansions of the Bronx." www.new-york-city.yodelout.com.

Pedigree Online Thoroughbred Database, "Iroquois Pedigree and Offspring." www.pedigreequery.com/progeny/iroquois.

Pedigree Online Thoroughbred Database, "Ten Broeck Offspring." www.pedigreequery.com/progeny/ten+broeck.

Pedigree Online Thoroughbred Database, "Tom Ochiltree Offspring." www.pedigreequery.com/progeny/tom+ochiltree.

Rutherford B. Hayes Presidential Center, *Collected Letters and Personal Diary*. www.rbhayes.org/hayes/president.

Spartacus Educational, "Samuel Tilden." Spartacus-educational.com/USAtilden.htm.

Stravinsky, Amanda, Tennessee Triptals, "Colorful Stories Awaken Tennessee's Past at Belle Meade Plantation." www.tnvacation.com/triptales/colorful-stories-awaken-tennessees-past-at-belle-meade-plantation.

StudyLight.org, 1911 Encyclopaedia Brittanica: "Bright's Disease." www.studylight.org/enc/bri/view.cgi?n=5229.

Thoroughbred Heritage, "Mollie McCarty." www.tbheritage.com/Portraits/Mollie McCarty.html.

Tuxedo Park, NY, official village website. www.tuxedopark-ny.gov.

WebMD, "Uremic Syndrome." www.webmd.com/a-to-z-guides/uremic-syndrome.

The White House website, "James A. Garfield." www.whitehouse.gov/1600/presidents/jamesgarfield.

The White House website, "Lucy Ware Webb Hayes." www.whitehouse.gov/1600/first-ladies/lucyhayes.

Wikipedia, "George W. Norris." https://en.wikipedia.org/wiki/George_W._Norris.

Wikipedia, "Gerald Nye." https://en.wikipedia.org/wiki/Gerald_Nye.

Wikipedia, "Largest Cities in the United States by Population by Decade: 1840." https://en.wikipedia.org/wiki/Largest_Cities_in_the_United_States_by_Population_by_Decade.

Wikipedia, "Leonard Jerome." https://en.wikipedia.org/wiki/Leonard_Jerome.

Wikipedia, "Pierre Abraham Lorillard." https://en.wikipedia.org/wiki/Pierre_Abraham_Lorillard.

Wikipedia, "Walburga, Lady Paget." https://en.wikipedia.org/wiki/Walburga_Lady_Paget.

World Wide Words: "Hippodroming." www.worldwidewords.org/weirdwords/ww-hip1.htm.

MAGAZINE AND NEWSPAPER ARTICLES AND OTHER SOURCES

"A Fellow Prisoner," "Sinclair Guest at Prison, Private Chef Cooked Food, Served It in Oil Man's Cell," *Pittsburgh Post-Gazette*, March 5, 1930.

"Albion," Letter to the Editor, *Spirit of the Times*, November 3, 1877.

"Augur," in *The Sporting Life*, cited in "The London Press on Parole," *Turf, Field and Farm*, May 2, 1879.

Baker, Kent, "Hall of Fame Push On for Rider of 1st Preakness Winner," *Baltimore Sun*, May 18, 1995.

Burroughs, W. D., "Passing of Pimlico: When Congress Adjourned for a Horse Race," *New York Times*, April 9, 1905.

"The Carrollton," "Baltimore Fall Meeting," *Turf, Field and Farm*, October 26, 1877.

Crawford, Byron, "Trainer Was Ahead of the Field in Paying Tribute to his Horses," *Louisville Courier-Journal*, April 14, 2000.

Curley, Ed, "Playfellow, $115,000 Horse, Last in Fairplay [*sic*] Handicap at Aqueduct Track: Brother of Man O' War Gives Talent Hard Jolt," *Washington (DC) Herald*, June 23, 1921.

Gordon, John Steele, "The Country Club," *American Heritage*, September/October, 1990.

Gregory, Amy. "An American Sportsman," *Thoroughbred Record*, February 16, 1983.
"H.W.C.," "Horses, Horses, Horses," *Thoroughbred Record*, August 22, 1931.
Hall, Claude H., "The Fabulous Tom Ochiltree: Promoter, Politician, and Raconteur," *Southwest Historical Quarterly*, January 1968.
Ilsley, Henry R., "Lorillard Succeds Maclay as President of American Horse Show Association," *New York Times*, January 4, 1936.
J. H. M., "The Late Wm. Brown and Parole," *Turf, Field and Farm*, March 28, 1903.
Kieran, John, "Sports of the Times," *New York Times*, September 25, 1929.
MacBeth, W. J., "Playfellow Finishes Last in Field of Three in Fair Play Handicap at the Aqueduct," *New York Tribune*, June 23, 1921.
Marchman, Judy L., "People: Getting His Due," *Blood-Horse*, May 25, 1996.
McCreery, James H. "Jacob Pincus," *Thoroughbred Record*, May 4, 1918.
McGraw, Eliza, "'Matchless Jew': The Belmont's Jewish Backstory," *New York Jewish Week*, June 7, 2011.
Newman, Neil. "Geo. Barbee 'Daddy of Them All.'" *Blood-Horse*, December 17, 1930.
"Nothing Venture," "Death of Mrs. Livingston," *Blood-Horse*, November 17, 1945.
"Privateer," "The Story of Parole," *New York Sportsman*, August 18, 1883.
Rasmussen, Frederick N., "Much Was Lost in the Great Pimlico Fire of 1966," *Baltimore Sun*, July 20, 2002.
"Roamer," "Negro Jockeys Rare Nowadays on Metropolitan Tracks: Many of Earlier Top Riders Were Colored Lads: Murphy One of Best" *Thoroughbred Record*, May 22, 1943.
Stanford, H., "Book Betting," *Spirit of the Times*, November 17, 1877.
Temple, Horace, "Big Betting Coups," *New York Tribune*, September 29, 1907.
Wall, Maryjean, "Old Glories, Old Stories," *Spur*, July/August 1985.
Weaver, Ben H. "Buck," "The Passing of 'Uncle Bill.'" *Turf & Sport Digest*, December 1933.
Williams, Joe, "Only a Dope," *Blood-Horse*, December 22, 1945.
Worrall, Margaret, "Bowling Brook Remembered," *Maryland Horse*, March, 1987.

"Arrival of the Yacht Vesta," *New York Times*, May 30, 1867.
"Millionaires," *(Stroudburg, PA) Jeffersonian*, May 28, 1868.
"Washington News and Gossip," *Washington (DC) Evening Star*, February 27, 1869.
"General Grant and Georgia: He Does Not Want Her Members Unseated: The Case for Menard: His Speech," *Philadelphia Evening Telegraph*, February 27, 1869.
"Launch of the Yacht Meteor," *New York Times*, April 7, 1869.
"The Meteor: Reported Wreck of the Yacht off the Coast of Africa: All Hands Saved: Description of the Vessel," *New York Times*, December 27, 1869.
"The Yacht Meteor," *New York Times*, January 22, 1870.
"Brutal Murder," *Lexington Daily Press*, September 12, 1871.
"The Woodford Tragedy," *Lexington Daily Press*, September 13, 1871.
"Lexington Races," *Lexingon Daily Press*, September 13, 1871.
"Brutal Murder," *Lexington Observer & Reporter*, September 13, 1871.
"The Races," *Lexington Observer & Reporter*, September 13, 1871.

"The Woodford Tragedy, Further Particulars," *Lexington Daily Press*, September 14, 1871.

"Trial To-Day," *Lexington Daily Press*, September 15, 1871.

"The Harper Murder: Trial of the Prisoners at Versailles," *Lexington Daily Press*, September 16, 1871.

"The Harper Murder: Important Discovery," *Lexington Daily Press*, September 16, 1871.

"The Harper Tragedy: Further Developments," *Lexington Daily Press*, September 29, 1871.

"The Harper Murder Case," *Lexington Observer and Reporter*, October 3, 1871.

"Reward of $5,000," *Lexington Daily Press*, October 9, 1871.

"Long Branch," *Nashville Union and American*, July 3, 1872.

"Monmouth Park," *New York Times*, July 5, 1872.

"The Turf: Long Branch Races Yesterday: Over Thirty Thousand People in Attendance: Longfellow an Easy Winner," *(Woodsfield, OH) Spirit of Democracy*, July 9, 1872.

"Longfellow Completely Broken Down: Description of the Accident: The Horse Game to the Last," *New York Times*, July 17, 1872.

"Saratoga: The Greatest Contest in American Turf History," *New York Times*, July 17, 1872.

"Saratoga: Sad Condition of the Disabled Racer, Longfellow," *New York Times*, July 18, 1872.

"Longfellow Retired: What Old John Harper Said After the Race," *Petroleum Center (PA) Daily Record*, July 23, 1872.

"The Turf: A Great Day's Sport at Saratoga: Fellowcraft Makes the Fastest Four Miles Ever Run: Lexington's Time Beaten: Reform Wins the Mile and Three Quarters," *New York Times*, August 21, 1874.

"Memoirs of Distinguished Kentucky Turfmen: John Harper," *Kentucky Live Stock Record*, July 23, 1875.

"The Turf: Fall Meeting of the Kentucky Association," *Turf, Field and Farm*, September 10, 1875.

"Fourth Day," *Kentucky Live Stock Record*, September 10, 1875.

"Lexington, Ky, Fall Race Meeting," *Turf, Field and Farm*, September 17, 1875.

Untitled article regarding Ten Broeck's 1⅝-mile record, *Spirit of the Times*, September 18, 1875.

Spirit of the Times, July 15, 1876, page 1.

"The Tom Ochiltree-Parole Race," *New York Times*, August 10, 1876.

"The Turf: The Kentucky Association: Fifth Day: Fall Meeting, 1876," *Kentucky Live Stock Record*, September 23, 1876.

"The American Turf: Racing at Lexington, Ky.: Fourth Day," *Spirit of the Times*, September 23, 1876.

"The Turf in Kentucky: Fine Running at Louisville: Four Good Races: The Best Three-Mile Dash On Record: Ten Broeck's Great Victory," *New York Times*, September 24, 1876.

"Today's Races: Ten Broeck's Race Against Time," *New York Times*, September 27, 1876.

"Ten Broeck's Victory: Fellowcraft's Four-Mile Record Beaten: Lexington's Celebrated Time Beaten by Four Seconds: The Greatest Event in the History of the Turf: The Race at Louisville Yesterday," *New York Times*, September 28, 1876.

"Sketch of Ten Broeck," *New York Times*, September 28, 1876.

"Lexington Races: Ten Broeck Beats Fellowcraft's Four Mile Time Three and a Half Seconds," *Dallas Daily Herald*, September 28, 1876.

"The Turf: Louisville Jockey Club," *Kentucky Live Stock Record*, September 30, 1876.

Summary of the Post Stakes, *Spirit of the Times*, September 30, 1876.

"Louisville Jockey Club Fall Meeting," *Spirit of the Times*, September 30, 1876.

"Ten Broeck's 7:15¾," *Turf, Field and Farm*, October 6, 1876.

"Tom Ochiltree and Ten Broeck," *New York Times*, October 18, 1876.

"The Racing Season of 1877," *New York Times*, March 25, 1877.

"The Fastest Mile On Record: A Brilliant Days Sport at Louisville: Ten Broeck Makes the Fastest Two Miles On Record: True Blue's Record Beaten By Five Seconds: The Other Races," *New York Times*, May 30, 1877.

"Spring Meeting Louisville Jockey Club," *Turf, Field and Farm*, June 1, 1877.

"The Louisville Gathering," *Turf, Field and Farm*, June 1, 1877.

"The Louisville Jockey Club," *Kentucky Live Stock Record*, June 2, 1877.

"The Late Louisville Meeting," *Kentucky Live Stock Record*, June 2, 1877.

"Louisville to the Front," *Spirit of the Times*, June 2, 1877.

"Ten Broeck's Wonderful Mile and What it Means," *Dodge City (KS) Times*, June 9, 1877.

"Ten Broeck: The King of the Turf: His Great Race at Louisville," *Opelousas (LA) Courier*, June 23, 1877.

"Turf Notes," *New York Times*, October 5, 1877.

"Racing Attractions at Baltimore," *Spirit of the Times*, October 6, 1877.

"The Nashville Fall Meeting," *Spirit of the Times*, October 6, 1877.

"The Baltimore Races," *New York Times*, October 10, 1877.

"Harper and Longfellow," *Louisville Courier-Journal*, October 13, 1877.

"Ten Broeck at Baltimore," *Spirit of the Times*, October 13, 1877.

"Extra Race at Baltimore," *Spirit of the Times*, October 13, 1877.

"Turf Notes," *New York Times*, October 16, 1877.

"Ten Broeck, Tom Ochiltree, Parole," *Turf, Field and Farm*, October 19, 1877.

"The Maryland Jockey Club," *Kentucky Live Stock Record*, October 20, 1877.

"The Coming Meeting at Baltimore," *Spirit of the Times*, October 20, 1877.

"The Maryland Races," *New York Times*, October 21, 1877.

"The Great Sweepstakes at Pimlico," *Baltimore American and Comercial Advertiser*, October 21, 1877.

"Ten Broeck, Tom Ochiltree, Parole," *Louisville Courier-Journal*, October 22, 1877.

"Telegraphic News, Congress and the Races," *Baltimore Sun*, October 22, 1877.

"Now the Races Will Open," *Baltimore American and Commercial Advertiser*, October 22, 1877.

"Maryland Jockey Club Races," *Baltimore Sun*, October 23, 1877.

"The Pimlico Races," *Baltimore American and Commercial Advertiser*, October 23, 1877.

"The Great Sweepstakes Postponed," *New York Times*, October 23, 1877.

"Pleasures of the Turf," *New York Times*, October 24, 1877.

"Maryland Jockey Club Races," *Baltimore Sun*, October 24, 1877.

"The Pimlico Races," *Baltimore American and Commercial Advertiser*, October 25, 1877.

"Excitement of the Turf," *New York Times*, October 25, 1877.

"Sporting News," *Chicago Tribune*, October 25, 1877.

"Pimlico: The Great Sweepstakes of the Season Run Yesterday," *National Republican*, October 25, 1877.

"Maryland Jockey Club Races," *Baltimore Sun*, October 25, 1877.

"Turf Notes," *Wheeling (WV) Daily Intelligencer*, October 25, 1877.

"The Great Race," *Memphis Daily Appeal*, October 25, 1877.

"Parole Victor," *Dallas Daily Herald*, October 25, 1877.

"Ten Broeck's Defeat at Baltimore," *Louisville Commercial*, October 25, 1877.

"Defeat of Ten Broeck at Baltimore," *Louisville Commercial*, October 25, 1877.

"Ten Broeck Tumbles," *Louisville Courier-Journal*, October 25, 1877.

"The Pimlico Races: A Brilliant Day on the Turf," *The Baltimore American and Commercial Advertiser*, October 25, 1877.

"Maryland Jockey Club Races," *Baltimore Sun*, October 26, 1877.

"Baltimore Fall Meeting," *Turf, Field and Farm*, October 26, 1877.

"Parole's Victory," *Turf, Field and Farm*, October 26, 1877.

"Pimlico: The Great Race: Ten Broeck Not Himself: A Day of Disappointment: Harper in Sorrow," *Kentucky Gazette*, October 27, 1877.

"Ten Broeck's Defeat," *Louisville Courier-Journal*, October 27, 1877.

"Ten Broeck: Sketched from Life at Baltimore, October 20, 1877," *Spirit of the Times*, October 27, 1877.

"Baltimore," *Spirit of the Times*, October 27, 1877.

"The Grand Cracks at Baltimore," *Spirit of the Times*, October 27, 1877.

"Maryland Jockey Club Races," *Baltimore Sun*, October 27, 1877.

"Parole and Ten Broeck to Meet Again," *Baltimore Sun*, October 27, 1877.

"Victory Won at the Pimlico Course Yesterday by the Kentucky Horse Ten Broeck," *Louisville Courier-Journal*, October 27, 1877.

"The Racing at Baltimore," *New York Times*, October 27, 1877.

"Rattling Running," *Bismark Tri-Weekly Tribune*, October 29, 1877.

"Extra Day at Jerome Park, *New York Times*, October 29, 1877.

"The Jerome Park Races," *New York Times*, October 31, 1877.

"A Great Sweepstakes," *Louisiana Democrat*, October 31, 1877.

Untitled article, *Stark County (OH) Democrat*, November 1, 1877.

Untitled article, *Milan (TN) Exchange*, November 1, 1877.

"Maryland Jockey Club," *Turf, Field and Farm*, November 2, 1877.

"Baltimore!" *Turf, Field and Farm*, November 2, 1877.

"The Great Sweepstakes To-Morrow," *Turf, Field and Farm*, November 2, 1877.

"The Bowie Stakes," *Spirit of the Times*, November 3, 1877.

Kentucky Live Stock Record, November 3, 1877.

"The Baltimore Meeting," *Kentucky Live Stock Record*, November 3, 1877.

"Baltimore Races," *Kentucky Live Stock Record*, November 3, 1877.

"Minor Notes," *Iola (KS) Register*, November 3, 1877.

"Ten Broeck Withdrawn," *New York Times*, November 6, 1877.

"American Jockey Club: Extra Day at Jerome Park," *New York Times*, November 7, 1877.

"Ten Broeck vs Parole," *Spirit of the Times*, November 10, 1877.

"From Everywhere: General," *People's Vindicator* (Natchitoches, LA), November 10, 1877.

"Editorial Notes," *Spirit of the Times*, November 10, 1877.

"The East vs. the West," *Turf, Field and Farm*, November 16, 1877.

"The Proposed Ten Broeck-Parole Match," *Kentucky Live Stock Record*, November 17, 1887.

"East vs. West and South," *Spirit of the Times*, November 17, 1877.

"The Parole-Ten Broeck Race," *New York Times*, November 19, 1877.

"A Princely Racing Establishment," *Turf, Field and Farm*, November 23, 1877.

"Ten Broeck-Parole-Tom Ochiltree," *Turf, Field and Farm*, November 23, 1877.

"The Ten Broeck-Parole Race," *Turf, Field and Farm*, November 23, 1877.

"Parole and Ten Broeck, and Mr. Lorillard's Other Matches," *Kentucky Live Stock Record*, November 24, 1877.

"East and North vs. the South and West," *Spirit of the Times*, November 24, 1877.

"Ten Broeck and Parole," *Turf, Field and Farm*, November 30, 1877.

"Tom Ochiltree vs. Ten Broeck," *Spirit of the Times*, December 1, 1877.

"Mr. Lorillard Will Not Go to Kentucky," *Turf, Field and Farm*, December 7, 1877.

"Winning Jockeys of 1877," *The Turf, Field and Farm*, December 7, 1877.

"Declination of Mr. P. Lorillard to Come to Kentucky," *Kentucky Live Stock Record*, December 15, 1877.

Drawing of Great Sweepstakes finish, *Spirit of the Times*, December 22, 1877.

"The Islip Stable," *New York Times*, March 30, 1878.

"Ten Broeck and Mollie McCarthy," *New York Times*, April 3, 1878.

"Mollie McCarty Versus Ten Broeck," *Spirit of the Times*, April 13, 1878.

"The Mollie M'Carthy-Ten Broeck Race," *New York Times*, May 14, 1878.

"Ten Broeck: The Gallant Horse Wins Another Hotly Contested Race: Aristides and Bill Bass Not Placed," *St. Paul Daily Globe*, May 14, 1878.

"On Her Way to Meet Ten Broeck: Arrival at Omaha of the California Mare Mollie M'Carty: She Is Reported in Excellent Condition," *New York Times*, May 19, 1878.

"Ten Broeck-Mollie McCarthy," *Turf, Field and Farm*, June 21, 1878.

"Ten Broeck," *Turf, Field and Farm*, June 21, 1878.

"The Ten Broeck-Mollie M'Carthy Match," *Kentucky Live Stock Record*, June 22, 1878.

"Mollie McCarthy and Ten Broeck," *Turf, Field and Farm*, June 28, 1878.

"Four-Mile Heat Races," *Spirit of the Times*, June 29, 1878.

"The Ten Broeck and Mollie McCarthy Match," *Kentucky Live Stock Record*, June 29, 1878.

"Ten Broeck Beats M'Carthy: An Exciting Race at Louisville The Kentucky Horse The Winner," *New York Times*, July 5, 1878.

"The Ten Broeck-Mollie McCarthy Race at Louisville, Ky.: Ten Broeck the Winner," *Turf, Field and Farm*, July 5, 1878.

"The Great Four Mile Match," *Kentucky Live Stock Record*, July 6, 1878.

"The Great Fiasco," *Daily Los Angeles Herald*, July 7, 1878.

"Ten Broeck Wins," *Pulaski (TN) Citizen*, July 11, 1878.

"The Louisville Summer Meeting," *Turf, Field and Farm*, July 12, 1878.

"Race Reflections," *Turf, Field and Farm*, July 12, 1878.

"The Cause of It," *Turf, Field and Farm*, July 12, 1878.

"Louisville: Ten Broeck-Mollie McCarthy Match," *Spirit of the Times*, July 13, 1878.

"The Ten Broeck-Mollie McCarthy Match," *Kentucky Live Stock Record*, July 13, 1878.

"The Great Turf Farce," *Spirit of the Times*, July 13, 1878.

"Frightful Fraud," *Louisiana Democrat*, July 17, 1878.

"The Great Race," *Vernon (AL) Pioneer*, July 19, 1878.

"The Louisville Race: The Great Kentucky Horse in Bad Condition When He Ran," *New York Times*, July 19, 1878.

"Talk on Ten Broeck-McCarthy," *Kentucky Live Stock Record*, July 20, 1878.

"The Ten Broeck-Mollie McCarthy Race: The Truth at Last," *Turf, Field and Farm*, July 26, 1878.

"The Louisville Four-Mile Heat Race," *Spirit of the Times*, July 27, 1878.

"The Abuse of J.W. Conley, and the Character of Ten Broeck as a Racehorse," *Kentucky Live Stock Record*, July 27, 1878.

"An Interview with F.B. Harper: Some Inconsistencies Worth Noting," *Kentucky Live Stock Record*, August 3, 1878.

"The Florida Cipher Telegrams," *New York Tribune*, October 8, 1878.

"Sporting News from England. How Parole Won the Newmarket Handicap," *New York Times*, April 18, 1879.

"The Turf in England: New Market Craven Meeting: Newmarket Handicap: Mr. Pierre Lorillard's Parole the Winner," *Turf, Field and Farm*, April 18, 1879.

"Another Victory for Parole: Mr. Lorillard's Horse Wins the City and Suburban Handicap at Epsom," *New York Times*, April 23, 1879.

"A Third Victory for Parole: He Wins the Great Metropolitan Stakes at Epsom: Mr. Lorillard's Profits," *New York Times*, April 24, 1879.

"Parole Challenged by the Owner of Isonomy," *New Orleans Daily Democrat*, April 24, 1879.

Untitled article regarding Parole, *New York Sun*, April 25, 1879.

"Parole at Newmarket," *Turf, Field and Farm*, April 25, 1879.

"Parole: The Triple Winner of the Newmarket, City Suburban [*sic*] and Great Metrololitan Handicaps," *Spirit of the Times*, April 26, 1879.

"Parole's English Triplet," *Spirit of the Times*, April 26, 1879.

"The London Press on Parole," *Turf, Field and Farm*, May 2, 1879.

"Racing on Epsom Downs," *New York Times*, May 31, 1879.

"Harper's Horses," *Memphis Daily Appeal*, October 7, 1879.

"Editorial Notes," *Spirit of the Times*, October 11, 1879.

"Horse Talk," *Kentucky Gazette*, October 25, 1879.

"A Tree Inhabited Seven Years," *Memphis (TN) Public Ledger*, January 20, 1880.

"American Jockey Club: Statistics of the Late Meeting: George Lorillard Still at the Head," *New York Times*, June 14, 1880.

"General Telegraph News: The Two Thousand Guineas Race," *New York Times*, May 5, 1881.

"The Derby Next Wednesday," *New York Sportsman*, May 28, 1881.

"Ready for the Derby," *New York Times*, June 1, 1881.

"America Wins the Derby," *New York Times*, June 2, 1881.

"Excitement in the City," *New York Times*, June 2, 1881.

"America's Victory: Iroquois Wins the Derby Race," *National Republican*, June 2, 1881.

"The Epsom Derby," *Turf, Field and Farm*, June 3, 1881.

"The Turf in England: A Great American Triumph," *Turf, Field and Farm*, June 3, 1881.

"Iroquois! America Captures the Epsom Derby!" *Spirit of the Times*, June 4, 1881.

"Iroquois!" *Spirit of the Times*, June 4, 1881.

"The Victory in the Derby," *New York Sportsman*, June 4, 1881.

"The English Derby," *Kentucky Live Stock Record*, June 4, 1881.

"The America's Victory in the English Derby," *Turf, Field and Farm*, June 10, 1881.

"Iroquois," *Kentucky Live Stock Record*, June 11, 1881.

"The Derby Victory," *New York Sportsman*, June 18, 1881.

"Racing in England," *New York Sportsman*, June 18, 1881.

"Iroquois," *Kentucky Live Stock Record*, June 18, 1881.

Untitled article regarding Iroquois's chances in the St. Leger, *Spirit of the Times*, September 10, 1881.

"Iroquois Again a Victor," *New York Times*, September 15, 1881.

"Iroquois Wins the St. Leger," *Turf, Field and Farm*, September 16, 1881.

"Iroquois Wins the Doncaster St. Leger," *Kentucky Live Stock Record*, September 17, 1881.

"Iroquois! America Captures the St. Leger," *Spirit of the Times*, September 17, 1881.

"Iroquois!" *Spirit of the Times*, September 17, 1881.

"Iroquois and the Doncaster St. Leger," *New York Sportsman*, September 17, 1881.

"The Westbrook Stables: George L. Lorillard's String of Twenty-Four Racers," *New York Times*, April 6, 1882.

"Major Tom Ochiltree's Victory," *New York Times*, November 16, 1882.

"Death of the American Jockey, Barrett," *Turf, Field and Farm*, January 12, 1883.

"The Late Wm. Barrett, Jockey," *New York Sportsman*, January 13, 1883.

"George Lorillard to Retire," *New York Times*, March 10, 1884.

"Turf Notes," *New York Times*, April 28, 1884.

"Breeding Farms in Kentucky. No. 3: Nantura Stock Farm," *Kentucky Live Stock Record*, January 3, 1885.

"Notes of the Turf: The Conflict Between Pierre Lorillard and the Dwyer Brothers," *New York Times*, October 5, 1885.

"The Coming Horse Show: A Large Number of Entries of Fine Quality," *New York Times*, October 18, 1885.

"The National Horse Show: A Spirited Lot of Animals in Madison-Square Garden," *New York Times*, November 4, 1885.

"George Lorillard's Death," *New York Times*, February 5, 1886.

"George Lorillard Dead," *Louisville Courier-Journal*, February 5, 1886.

Untitled article regarding the death of George Lorillard, *Spirit of the Times*, February 6, 1886.

"George Lorillard's Will," *Louisville Courier-Journal*, February 7, 1886.

"Death of George L. Lorillard," *Turf, Field and Farm*, February 12, 1886.

"Death of Mr. George L. Lorillard," *Live Stock Record*, February 13, 1886.

"Funeral of George L. Lorillard," *New York Times*, April 18, 1886.

"Ten Broeck Dead: One of America's Best Horses Stricken With Paralysis," *New York Times*, June 29, 1887.

"Death of Ten Broeck," *Live Stock Record*, July 2, 1887.

Untitled article about death of Ten Broeck, *Spirit of the Times*, July 2, 1887.

"Death of the Famous Ten Broeck," *New North-West* (Deer Lodge, MT), July 8, 1887.

"Mourning for Ten Broeck," *New York Times*, July 10, 1887.

"Death of Ten Broeck," *Middlebury Register*, July 22, 1887.

"Real Estate Selling Well," *New York Times*, November 16, 1887.

"Thoroughbreds at Auction," *New York Times*, August 19, 1888.

"Griswold Lorillard Is Dying," *New York Evening World*, October 23, 1888.

"N. Griswold Lorillard," *New York Tribune*, November 5, 1888.

"Nathaniel G. Lorillard Dead," *New York Times*, November 5, 1888.

"Mrs. Lorillard's Marriage," *New York Times*, February 13, 1889.

"Richard Ten Broeck Dead," *San Francisco Morning Call*, August 2, 1892.

"The Racing Season of 1892," *New York Sun*, October 17, 1892.

"Tilden and Hayes: 'All a Matter of History,'" *New York Sun*, January 20, 1893.

"Mr. Lorillard to Retire," *New York Times*, September 3, 1893.

"Trouble Ahead in Racing," *New York Tribune*, February 11, 1894.

"Jockey Club Launched," *New York Tribune*, February 14, 1894.

"Death of Tom Ochiltree," *Thoroughbred Record*, January 8, 1898.

"Lorillard Leaves England," *New York Times*, October 9, 1898.

"Iroquois Dead," *Turf Field and Farm*, September 22, 1899.

"Death of Iroquois," *Thoroughbred Record*, September 23, 1899.

"Old Iroquois Dead," *New York Times*, September 24, 1899.

"Grand Old Iroquois," *Washington, DC Evening Star*, September 25, 1899.

"Iroquois: Death of the Famous Race Horse and Sire at Belle Meade," *Spirit of the Times*, September 30, 1899.

"Houseboat Caiman Burned: Pierre Lorillard's Famous Craft Destroyed in Florida," *New York Times*, June 10, 1900.

"Pierre Lorillard, Sr., in Critical Condition," *New York Times*, July 5, 1901.

"Returning Millionaires Are Royally Welcomed," *St. Louis Republic*, July 5, 1901.

"Lorillard's Record," *Minneapolis Journal*, July 5, 1901.

"Pierre Lorillard Sinking," *New York Times*, July 7, 1901.

"Life Ended: Pierre Lorillard Succumbs," *Louisville Courier-Journal*, July 8, 1901.

"Pierre Lorillard," *New York Times*, July 8, 1901.

"Pierre Lorillard Dead," *New York Times*, July 8, 1901.

"British Press Tributes," *New York Times*, July 8, 1901.

"Pierre Lorillard Dead," *New York Tribune*, July 8, 1901.

"Pierre Lorillard Dead," *Washington (DC) Evening Star*, July 8, 1901.

"Pierre Lorillard Dead," *Hickman (KY) Courier*, July 12, 1901.

"Pierre Lorillard Gave Fortune to Mrs. Allien," *New York Evening World*, July 13, 1901.

"Pierre Lorillard Dead," *Spirit of the Times*, July 13, 1901.

"Mrs. Lorillard Won't Contest," *New York Evening World*, July 13, 1901.

"How Mr. Lorillard Divided His Estate," *New York Times*, July 14, 1901.

"T. Suffern Tailer's Denial," *New York Times*, July 15, 1901.

"Pierre Lorillard's Love," *Indianapolis Journal*, July 16, 1901.

"Pierre Lorillard's Will," *New York Times*, July 17, 1901.

"Mr. Lorillard's Will Probated in Trenton," *New York Times*, July 19, 1901.

"Mrs. Allien's Inheritance Tax," *New York Times*, July 22, 1901.

"Mrs. Allien Married a Woman, Friend Says," *New York Evening World*, July 27, 1901.

"Millionaire Lorillard's Widow May Contest His Will," *(St. Louis, MO) Republic*, July 28, 1901.

"Lorillard Colors Claimed," *New York Times*, August 1, 1901.

"To Give Up Rancocas," *Washington (DC) Times*, August 5, 1901.

"Will Give Up Rancocas," *Indianapolis Journal*, August 5, 1901.

"Mrs. Allien at Rancocas," *New York Times*, August 7, 1901.

"Mrs. Allien Makes a Public Statement," *(St. Louis, MO) Republic*, August 8, 1901.

"Mrs. Allien at Rancocas," *New York Times*, August 8, 1901.

"The Other Woman," *Pullman (Washington Territory) Herald*, August 24, 1901.

"Lorillard Horses to go at Auction," *The (NY) Evening World*, September 11, 1901.

"Trying Ordeal for Lorillard's Son," *Minneapolis Journal*, September 19, 1901.

"Mr. W.K. Vanderbilt Buys Horses in Kentucky," *New York Times*, September 30, 1901.

"Lorillard Horses Sold Well," *New York Times*, October 4, 1901.

"Mr. Whitney's Horses," *Minneapolis Journal*, November 20, 1901.

P. Lorillard's Estate, *New York Tribune*, December 14, 1901.

"Metropolitan Gossip," *Thoroughbred Record*, December 21, 1901.

"Saratoga Aghast at Mrs. Allien," *St. Paul Globe*, September 7, 1902.

"Col. T.P. Ochiltree Dead," *New York Times*, November 26, 1902.

"Col. Ochiltree Dead," *Washington (DC) Evening Star*, November 26, 1902.

"The Late Col. Ochiltree," *Alexandria (VA) Gazette*, November 27, 1902.

"Colonel Ochiltree Dead," *Princeton (MN) Union*, November 27, 1902.

"Incidents in the Career of 'Tom' Ochiltree," *New York Tribune*, November 30, 1902.

"Funeral of Col. Ochiltree," *Washington (DC) Evening Star*, December 1, 1902.

"Mrs. Allien to Wed Clubman?," *New York Evening World*, December 11, 1902.

"Metropolitan Gossip," *Thoroughbred Record*, December 20, 1902.

"Stories of Tom Ochiltree," *Salt Lake (UT) Herald*, December 21, 1902.

"Parole Died at Tuxedo Park," *Thoroughbred Record*, January 3, 1903.

"The Great Record of R. Wyndham Walden," *Turf, Field, and Farm*, February 21, 1903.

"The Late Wm. Brown and Parole," *Turf, Field and Farm*, March 28, 1903.

"Mrs. Lorillard's Loss Heavy," *New York Times*, May 17, 1903.

"P. Lorillard Buys Rancocas Yearlings," *New York Times*, June 12, 1903.

"Notes from the Racetrack," *New York Times*, September 2, 1903.

"Frank Harper Passes Away," *Louisville Courier-Journal*, April 5, 1905.

"Frank B. Harper is Dead," *Thoroughbred Record*, April 8, 1905.

"Makes Provision for Senator J.C.S. Blackburn," *Mt. Sterling (KY) Advocate*, April 12, 1905.

"The Harper Funeral: One of the Greatest Turnouts of Horsemen Ever Seen in Lexington," *Richmond (KY) Climax*, April 12, 1905.

"Harper Will Case: Order Entered Approving Probate In Accordance With Compromise," *Berea (KY) Citizen*, April 13, 1905.

"Santa Catalina Won Big Race on a Foul," *New York Times*, April 26, 1905.

"Spill in Excelsior," *New York Tribune*, April 26, 1905.

"Turfman Walden Dead," *Washington (DC) Evening Star*, April 28, 1905.

"R.W. Walden, Trainer, Dead," *New York Evening World*, April 28, 1905.

"R.W. Walden Dead," *New York Tribune*, April 29, 1905.

"Death of R.W. Walden," *New York Times*, April 29, 1905.

No headline, *Springfield (KY) Sun*, May 24, 1905.

"The Turfman's Will Contested," *Bourbon (KY) News*, June 30, 1905.

"Jockey Fuller Improving," *New York Times*, August 13, 1905.

"Paddock Paragraphs," *New York Tribune*, September 14, 1905.

"Lorillard's Heiress Weds," *San Francisco Call*, February 16, 1906.

"Lorillard Loses to Champion Gould," *New York Times*, April 20, 1906.

"Notes of the Thoroughbreds," *New York Times*, May 18, 1906.

"Tuxedo Golf Tournament," *New York Times*, June 16, 1907.

"Lorillard Wins at Tuxedo," *New York Times*, December 30, 1907.

"Old Hotel's Last Day," *New York Tribune*, April 5, 1908.

"Burned by Oil," *Fredericksburg, Va. Free Lance*, December 15, 1908.

"Find Mrs. Lorillard Dead in Bathroom," *New York Times*, March 26, 1909.

"Society Woman Dies by Gas," *Winchester (KY) News*, March 26, 1909.

"Gas Fumes Kill Mrs. Pierre Lorillard, Jr.," *New York Tribune*, March 26, 1909.

"Mrs. Lorillard's Suicide Secret Buried with Her," *Washington (DC) Times*, March 26, 1909.

"Grave Will Hide Tragedy Secret," *Washington (DC) Herald*, March 27, 1909.

"Notes Put in Coffin with Mrs. Lorillard," *New York Times*, March 27, 1909.

"Disturbance Halts Lorillard Funeral," *New York Times*, March 28, 1909.

"Detectives Guard Bier," *New York Tribune*, March 28, 1909.

"The Vulgar Snapshot Man," *New York Times*, March 29, 1909.

"Mrs. Lorillard a Suicide," *Berea (KY) Citizen*, April 1, 1909.

"Court Tennis at Tuxedo," *New York Times*, December 12, 1910.

"Lorillard Defeats Brokaw," *New York Times*, January 9, 1911.

"Mrs. B. Lorillard a Suicide by Hanging," *New York Tribune*, March 17, 1912.

"Mrs. B. Lorillard a Hotel Suicide," *New York Times*, March 17, 1912.

"Unostentatious Plans Are Laid to Resume Racing in New York," *Washington Herald*, March 31, 1913.

"Mrs. Lorillard Left a Note," *New York Times*, April 3, 1912.

"Matinee Races at Goshen," *New York Times*, July 14, 1912.

"Notice B. Beats Amasis," *New York Times*, July 27, 1913.

"Red Blood for Blue," *Time*, March 31, 1914.

"Lorillard in Jail for Unpaid Alimony," *New York Times*, November 8, 1914.

"Irving Lorillard in Jail," *New York Tribune*, November 8, 1914.

"Jacob Lorillard Dead," *New York Times*, April 29, 1916.

"Sanford Memorial Is Won by Upset," *New York Times*, August 14, 1919.

"Refuses $100,000 Offer for Man o'War's Full Brother," *New York Times*, June 9, 1921.

"Three Different Offers of $100,000 Refused for 3-Year-Old, Playfellow," *(NY) Evening World*, June 9, 1921.

"Rancocas Stable Purchases Playfellow for $115,000: Sinclair Also Buys Knobbie," *New York Times*, June 18, 1921.

"Playfellow, Under Wraps, Runs Second to Knobbie in Carlton Stakes," *Washington Herald*, June 19, 1921.

"Playfellow Last in Field of Three," *New York Times*, June 21, 1921.

"Playfellow's Defeat May Have Been Due to Blinkers Experiment," *New York Evening World*, June 23, 1921.

"Playfellow Not Sound, Says Hildreth: Requests Return of $115,000 Colt Cost," *New York Times*, June 28, 1921.

"Hildreth Believes He Bought a Gold Brick in Playfellow," *New York Evening World*, June 28, 1921.

"Playfellow Case May Go to Courts," *New York Times*, June 29, 1921.

"Famous Horse Doctor Says Playfellow was 'O.K.' When Sold to Hildreth," *New York Evening World*, June 29, 1921.

"Playfellow Not Likely to Race Again This Year: Not for Sinclair, Anyway," *New York Evening World*, June 30, 1921.

"Hildreth Asks Money Back on Playfellow," *Bourbon (KY) News*, July 1, 1921.

"Wind Suckers Win Races, Says Garth at Horse Trial," *New York Evening World*, December 14, 1921.

"Sale of Playfellow Held in Good Faith by Former Owner," *New York Tribune*, December 14, 1921.

"Playfellow Wore 'Windsucking' Bit, Trainer Testifies," *New York Tribune*, December 15, 1921.

"Rumored That Jury in Playfellow Case Cannot Agree: Renders Verdict Tomorrow," *New York Times*, December 18, 1921.

"Next Playfellow Trial in January," *New York Times*, December 20, 1921.

"Playfellow Case Is on Trial Again," *New York Times*, March 1, 1922.

"Playfellow Case Is Ready for Jury," *New York Times*, March 2, 1922.

"Sinclair Recovers in Playfellow Suit," *New York Times*, March 3, 1922.

"Playfellow May Be Raced for Charity Pending Decision," *New York Tribune*, March 22, 1922.

"Appeal from Playfellow Judgment," *New York Times*, March 23, 1922.

"Playfellow Case Up Today," *New York Times*, June 13, 1922.

"$100,000 Verdict for Horse Disputed," *New York Times*, June 14, 1922.

"Johnson Returns $100,000 Price Paid for Playfellow," *New York Times*, July 29, 1922.

"Playfellow Case Is to Be Revived," *New York Times*, August 12, 1922.

"Johnson's Motion Denied: Court of Appeals Refuses Action in Playfellow Racing Case," *New York Times*, November 29, 1922.

"Ask City to Rebuild Lorillard Mansion," *New York Times*, April 1, 1923.

"60 Rancocas Horses Lost in Stable Fire," *New York Times*, April 15, 1923.

"Promising Colts Lost in Rancocas Fire," *New York Times*, April 16, 1923.

"Playfellow Through as Racer: Will Go to Stud Next Month," *New York Times*, August 10, 1923.

"Superiority of Zev Was Never in Doubt," *New York Times*, October 21, 1923.

"50-Year-Old Record Broken at Tijuana," *New York Times*, February 23, 1925.

"Mrs. Pierre Lorillard Dies in Monroe Home," *New York Times*, September 12, 1925.

"Reminiscences of the Turf: John Harper," *Thoroughbred Record*, June 22, 1929.

"Samuel C. Hildreth Ill," *New York Times*, September 23, 1929.

"Trainer Hildreth Is Operated Upon," *New York Times*, September 24, 1929

"Sam Hildreth, 63, Turf Veteran, Dies," *New York Times*, September 25, 1929.

"Sinclair Pays Tribute," *New York Times*, September 25, 1929.

"A Famous Horseman," *New York Times*, September 25, 1929.

"Hildreth Honored by Racing World," *New York Times*, September 27, 1929.

"Death Claims Samuel C. Hildreth," *Thoroughbred Record*, September 28, 1929.

"Samuel Clay Hildreth," *Blood-Horse*, October 5, 1929.

"Death of Mars Cassidy," *Thoroughbred Record*, October 26, 1929.

"Mars Cassidy," *Blood-Horse*, November 2, 1929.

"J.E. Madden Dies: Was Noted Turfman," *New York Times*, November 4, 1929.

"Sinclair Quits Jail: Railroaded, He Says," *New York Times*, November 21, 1929.

"Mrs. Beard to Wed Pierre Lorillard," *New York Times*, December 30, 1930.

"Mrs. Beard Weds Pierre Lorillard," *New York Times*, February 4, 1931.

"George Livingston," *New York Times*, March 10, 1931.

"Villainous Poisoning," *Blood-Horse*, August 22, 1931.

"Proper Action," *Blood-Horse*, August 22, 1931.

"To Sell Rancocas Horses," *Blood-Horse*, August 29, 1931.

"Sale of Rancocas Horses in Training," *Thoroughbred Record*, August 29, 1931.

"Sinclair's Reason," *Blood-Horse*, September 19, 1931.

"Death Comes to Matthew Byrnes," *Thoroughbred Record*, March 25, 1933.

"William Walker, Man Who Rode Ten Broeck, Dead," *Thoroughbred Record*, September 23, 1933.

"The Talk of the Town: American Snuff," *New Yorker*, September 22, 1934.

"Lorillard to Retire As Horse Show Head," *New York Times*, January 3, 1937.

"Pierre Lorillard Dies in Tuxedo, 80," *New York Times*, August 7, 1940.

"Nuptials Are Held of Mrs. Lorillard," *New York Times*, October 9, 1941.

"Griswold Lorillard, Resident of Tuxedo," *New York Times*, September 7, 1942.

"Man o' War's Brother," *Blood-Horse*, May 22, 1943.
"Stud News: Helis Leases Rancocas," *Blood Horse*, July 22, 1944.
"Helis, Oil Leader, Horseman, Is Dead," *New York Times*, July 25, 1950.
"William Helis, 63, Succumbs," *Los Angeles Times*, July 25, 1950.
"William G. Helis Dies in Maryland Hospital," *Thoroughbred Record*, July 29, 1950.
"Harry F. Sinclair," *Blood-Horse*, November 17, 1956.

Daily Racing Form official chart for fifth race at Tijuana, Mexico, February 22, 1925.
Daily Racing Form official chart for Burnt Hills Handicap, Saratoga, on August 13, 1931.
Daily Racing Form official chart for Sanford Memorial Stakes, August 13, 1919.
Daily Racing Form official chart for seventh race at Finger Lakes, November 17, 1973.

Pamphlet, "Woodford County—Midway-Versailles, Kentucky," printed in cooperation with the Woodford County Chamber of Commerce, the Midway-Versailles-
Woodford County Tourist Commission and Kentucky Department of Travel.

INDEX

ABOUT THE AUTHOR

Mark Shrager is a prolific turf writer, having published several hundred articles in magazines such as *Turf & Sport Digest*, *American Turf Magazine* (*ATM*), and others. His article "1,001 Surefire Ways to Lose a Horse Race" was published in the annual *Best Sports Stories* anthology. Shrager has also published two books of Breeders' Cup handicapping information. Six years of research, including stretches in Kentucky and at the Library of Congress, have led to *The Great Sweepstakes of 1877*. He lives in Altadena, California.